犬夜叉

INUYASHA™

ANI-MANGA™

Vol. 10

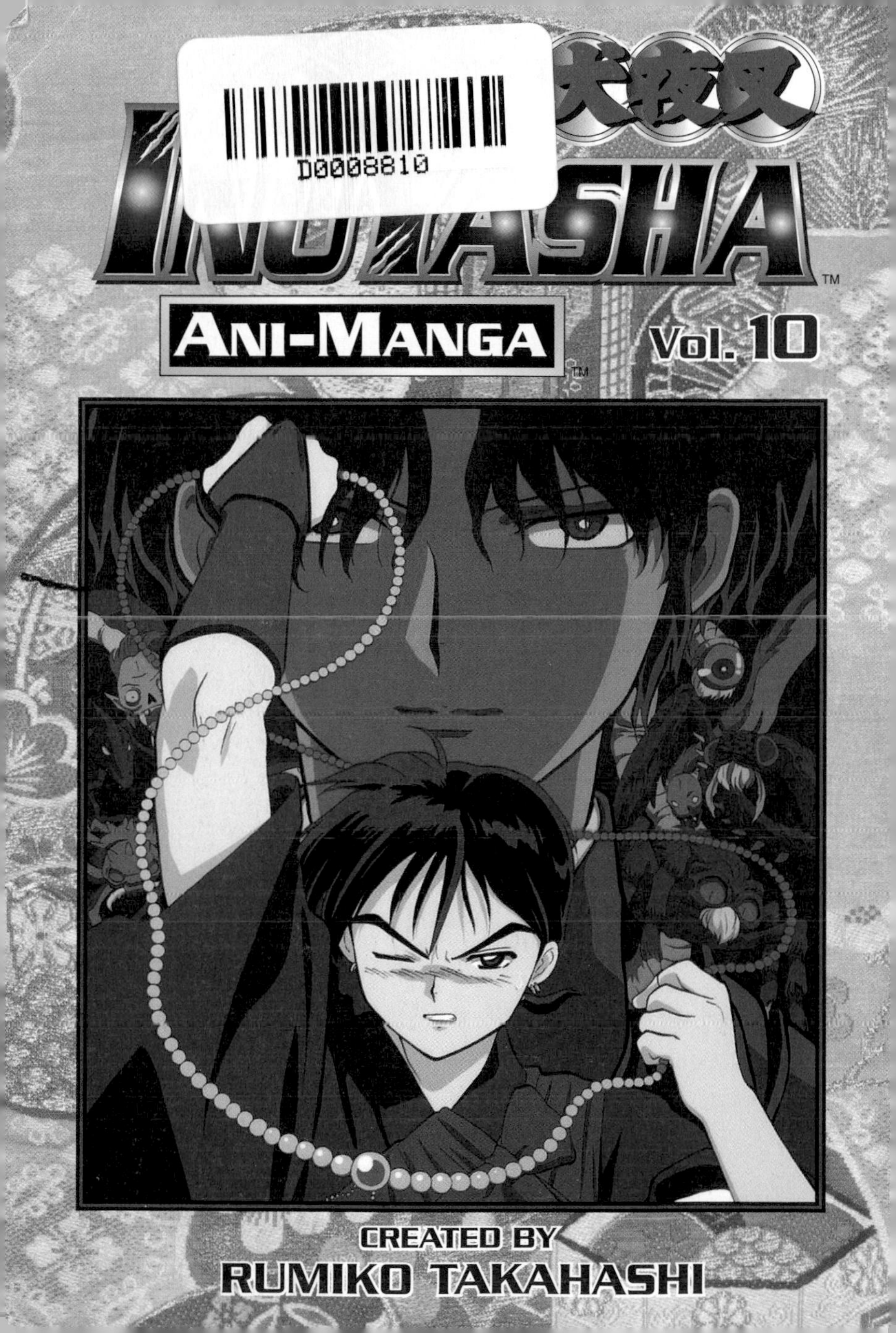

CREATED BY

RUMIKO TAKAHASHI

Inuyasha Ani-Manga™
Vol. #10

Created by
Rumiko Takahashi

Translation based on the VIZ anime TV series
Translation Assistance/Katy Bridges
Lettering/John Clark
Cover Design & Graphics/Hidemi Sahara
Editor/Frances E. Wall

Managing Editor/Annette Roman
Director of Production/Noboru Watanabe
Vice President of Publishing/Alvin Lu
Sr. Director of Acquisitions/Rika Inouye
Vice President of Sales & Marketing/Liza Coppola
Publisher/Hyoe Narita

Printed in the U.S.A.

Published by VIZ, LLC
P.O. Box 77010
San Francisco, CA 94107

10 9 8 7 6 5 4 3 2 1
First printing, July 2005

www.viz.com

store.viz.com

Story thus far

Kagome, a typical high school girl, has been transported into a mythical version of Japan's medieval past, a place filled with incredible magic and terrifying demons. Who would have guessed that the stories and legends Kagome's superstitious grandfather told her could really be true!?

It turns out that Kagome is the reincarnation of Lady Kikyo, a great warrior and the defender of the Shikon Jewel, or the Jewel of the Four Souls. In fact, the sacred jewel mysteriously emerges from Kagome's body during a battle with a horrible centipede-like monster. In her desperation to defeat the monster, Kagome frees Inuyasha, a dog-like half-demon who lusts for the power imparted by the jewel, and unwittingly releases him from the binding spell that was placed 50 years earlier by Lady Kikyo. To prevent Inuyasha from

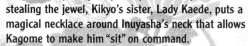

stealing the jewel, Kikyo's sister, Lady Kaede, puts a magical necklace around Inuyasha's neck that allows Kagome to make him "sit" on command.

In another skirmish for possession of the jewel, it accidentally shatters and is strewn across the land. Only Kagome has the power to find the jewel shards, and only Inuyasha has the strength to defeat the demons who now hold them, so the two unlikely partners are bound together in the quest to reclaim all the pieces of the Shikon Jewel.

Deceived by the evil Naraku into believing that Inuyasha was responsible for the annihilation of her village, Sango the demon slayer vows to get revenge. But with the help of Kagome and Miroku, Inuyasha is able to expose Naraku's lies, and they convince Sango to join them in the fight against Naraku. Though she is still recovering from devastating injuries and mourning the death of her younger brother, Sango starts traveling with Inuyasha and the others. She helps the gang learn more about the origins of the Shikon Jewel, which was born from the soul of the great priestess Midoriko, who lost her life fighting demons inside a cave near Sango's village.

INUYASHA
ANI-MANGA Vol. 10

Contents

28
Miroku Falls into a Dangerous Trap!

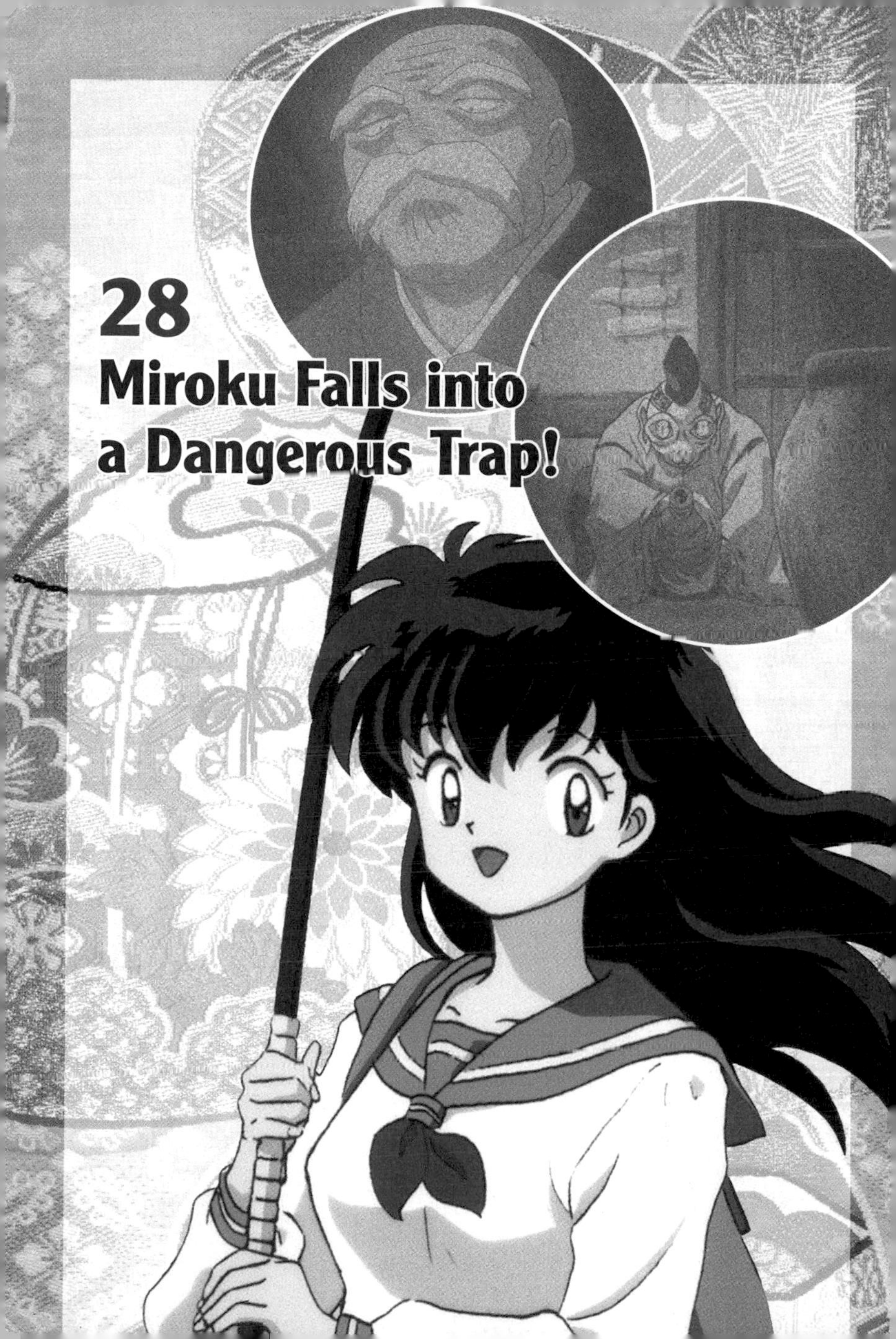

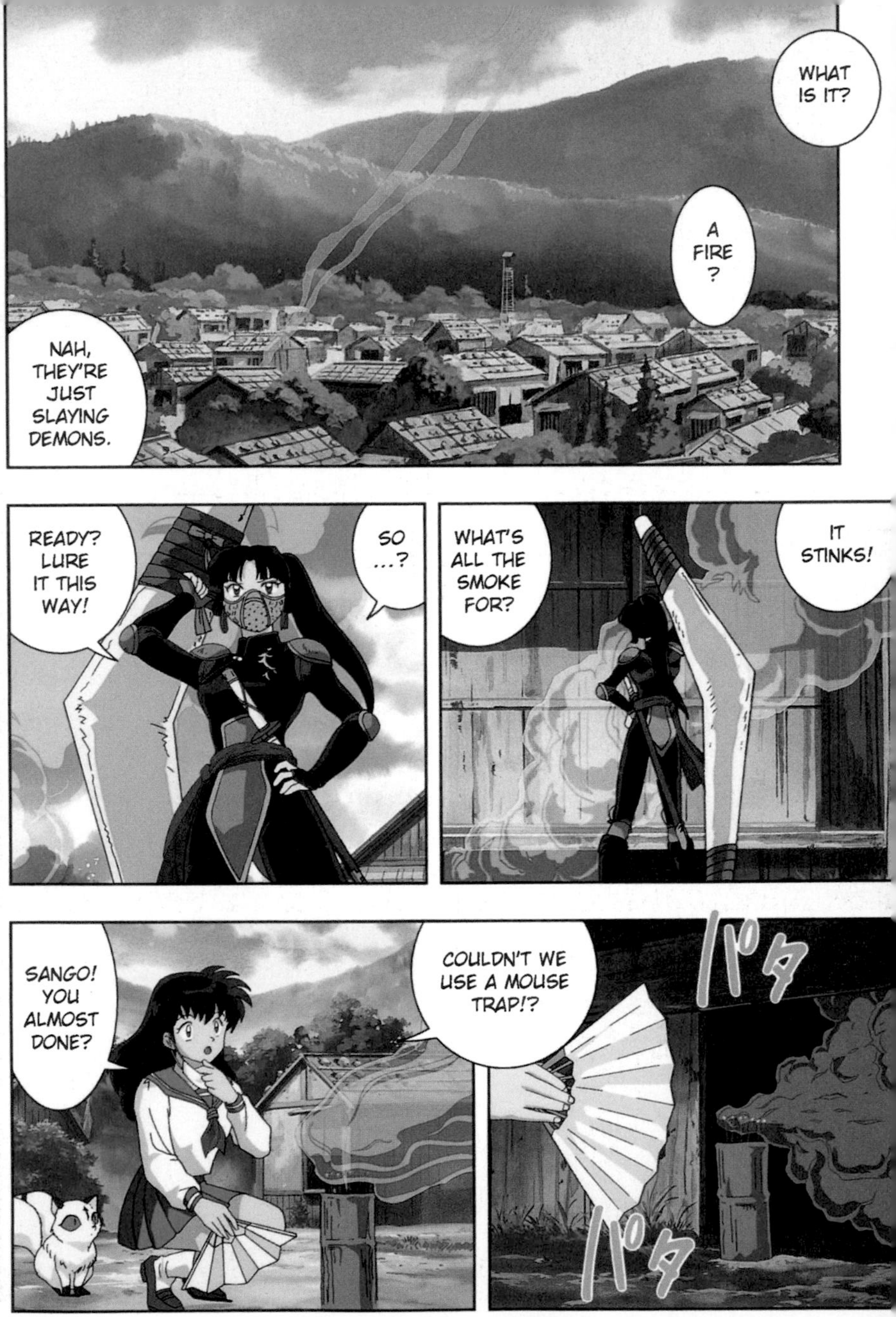
WHAT IS IT?
A FIRE ?
NAH, THEY'RE JUST SLAYING DEMONS.
IT STINKS!
WHAT'S ALL THE SMOKE FOR?
SO ...?
READY? LURE IT THIS WAY!
パタ
パタ
COULDN'T WE USE A MOUSE TRAP!?
SANGO! YOU ALMOST DONE?

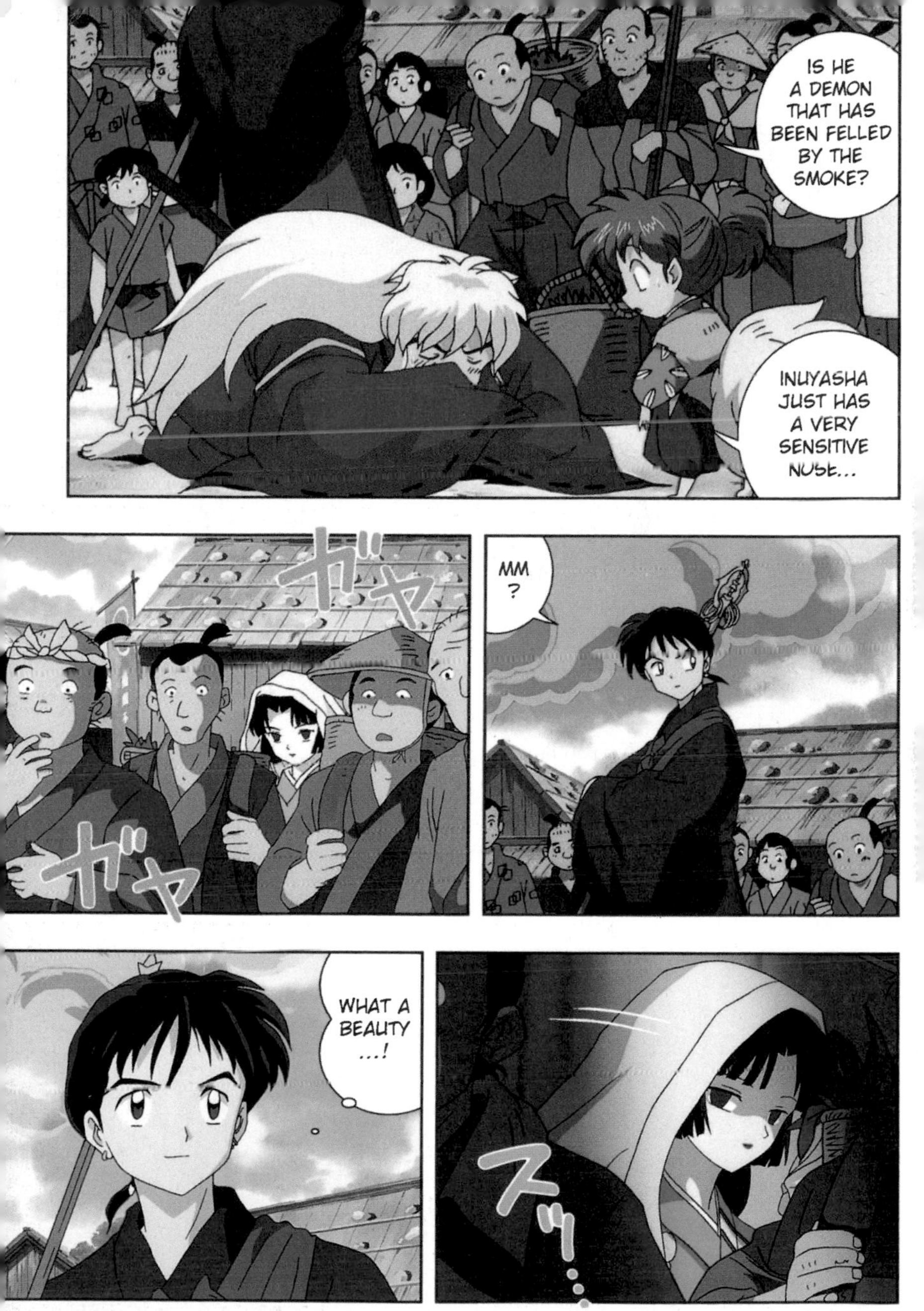

IS HE A DEMON THAT HAS BEEN FELLED BY THE SMOKE?
INUYASHA JUST HAS A VERY SENSITIVE NOSE...
MM ?
ガヤ
ガヤ
スッ…
WHAT A BEAUTY ...!

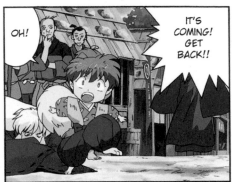

HEY, MIROKU!
WHERE ARE YOU GOING!?
IT'S COMING! GET BACK!!
OH!
ROARR!

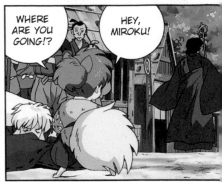

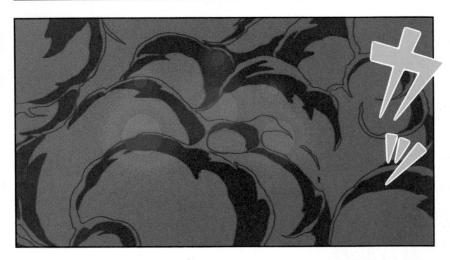

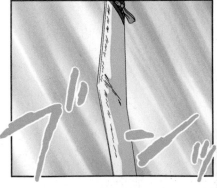

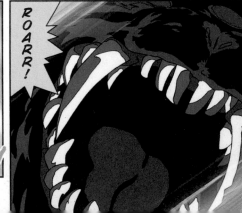

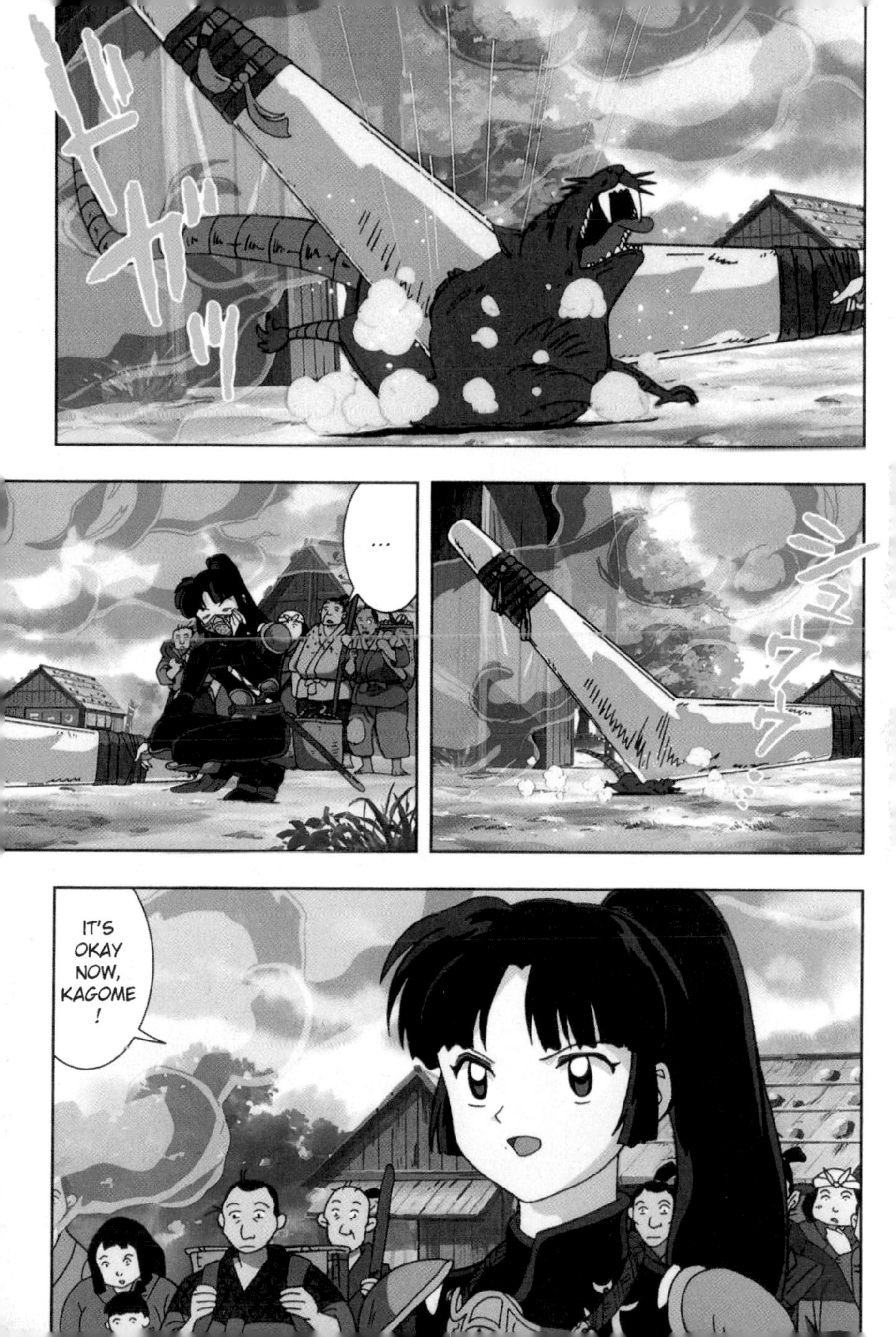
ドガッ
シュウウ…
…
IT'S OKAY NOW, KAGOME!

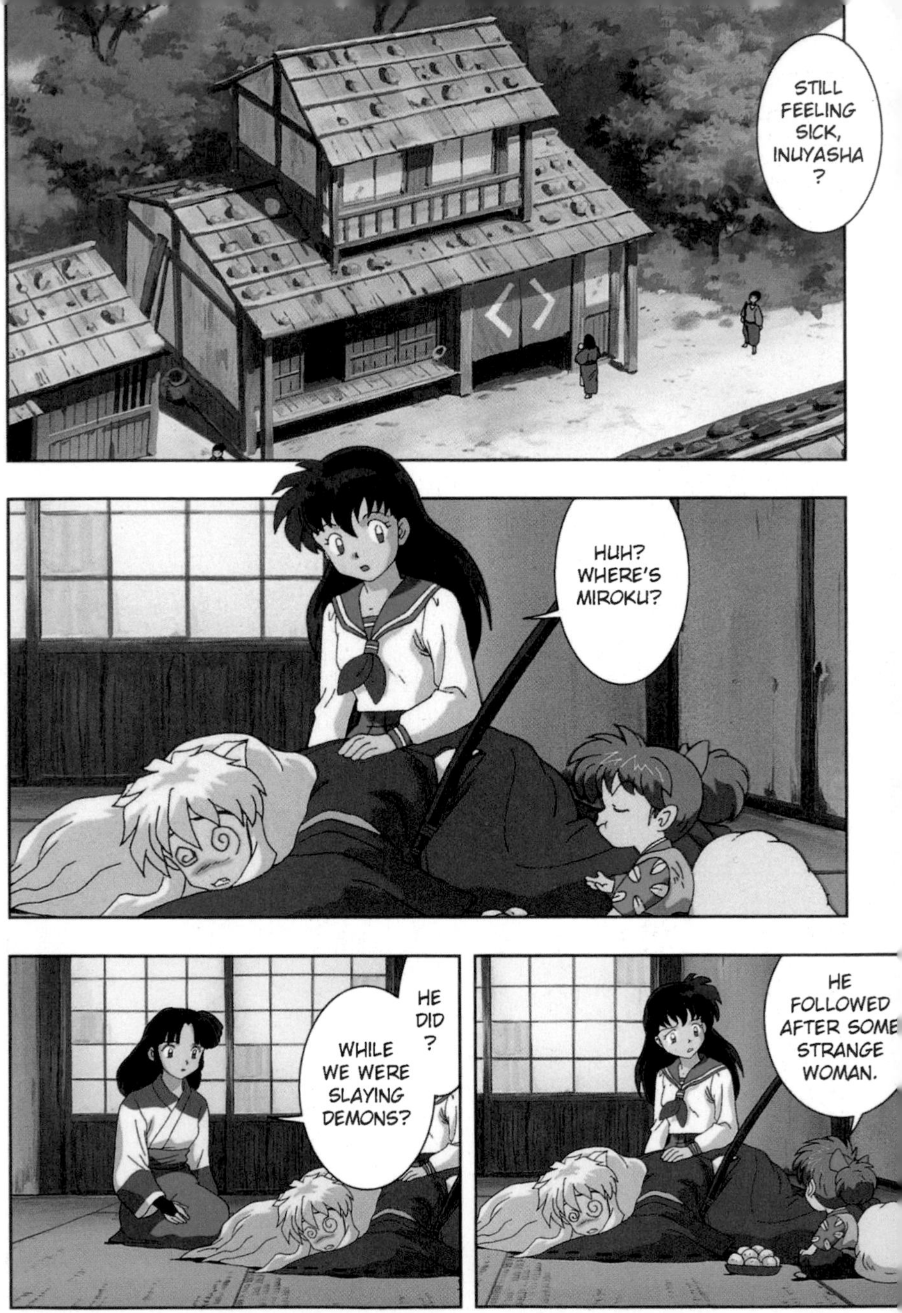
STILL FEELING SICK, INUYASHA?
HUH? WHERE'S MIROKU?
HE FOLLOWED AFTER SOME STRANGE WOMAN.
HE DID?
WHILE WE WERE SLAYING DEMONS?

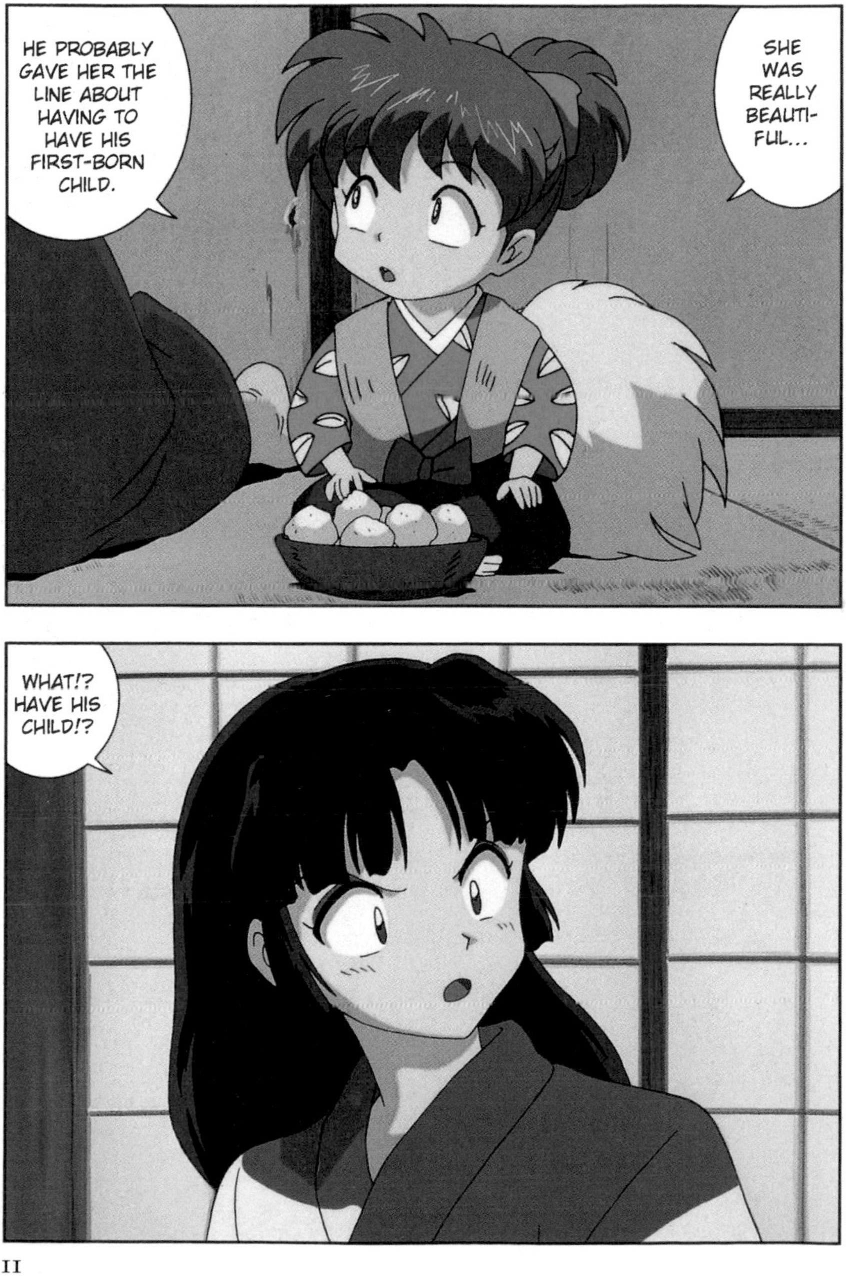
SHE WAS REALLY BEAUTI-FUL...
HE PROBABLY GAVE HER THE LINE ABOUT HAVING TO HAVE HIS FIRST-BORN CHILD.
WHAT!? HAVE HIS CHILD!?

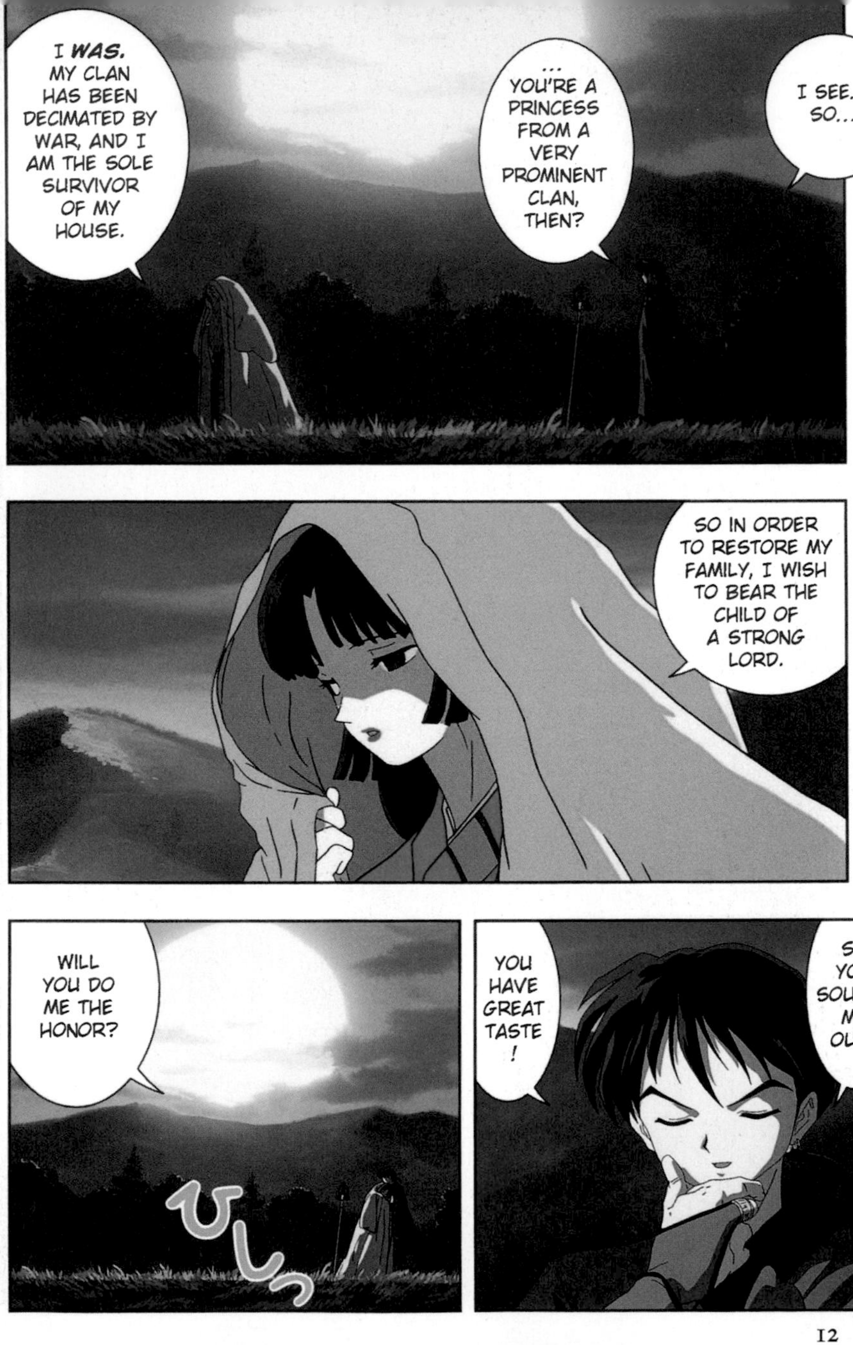
I SEE... SO...
... YOU'RE A PRINCESS FROM A VERY PROMINENT CLAN, THEN?
I **WAS.** MY CLAN HAS BEEN DECIMATED BY WAR, AND I AM THE SOLE SURVIVOR OF MY HOUSE.
SO IN ORDER TO RESTORE MY FAMILY, I WISH TO BEAR THE CHILD OF A STRONG LORD.
SO YOU SOUGHT ME OUT?
YOU HAVE GREAT TASTE!
WILL YOU DO ME THE HONOR?

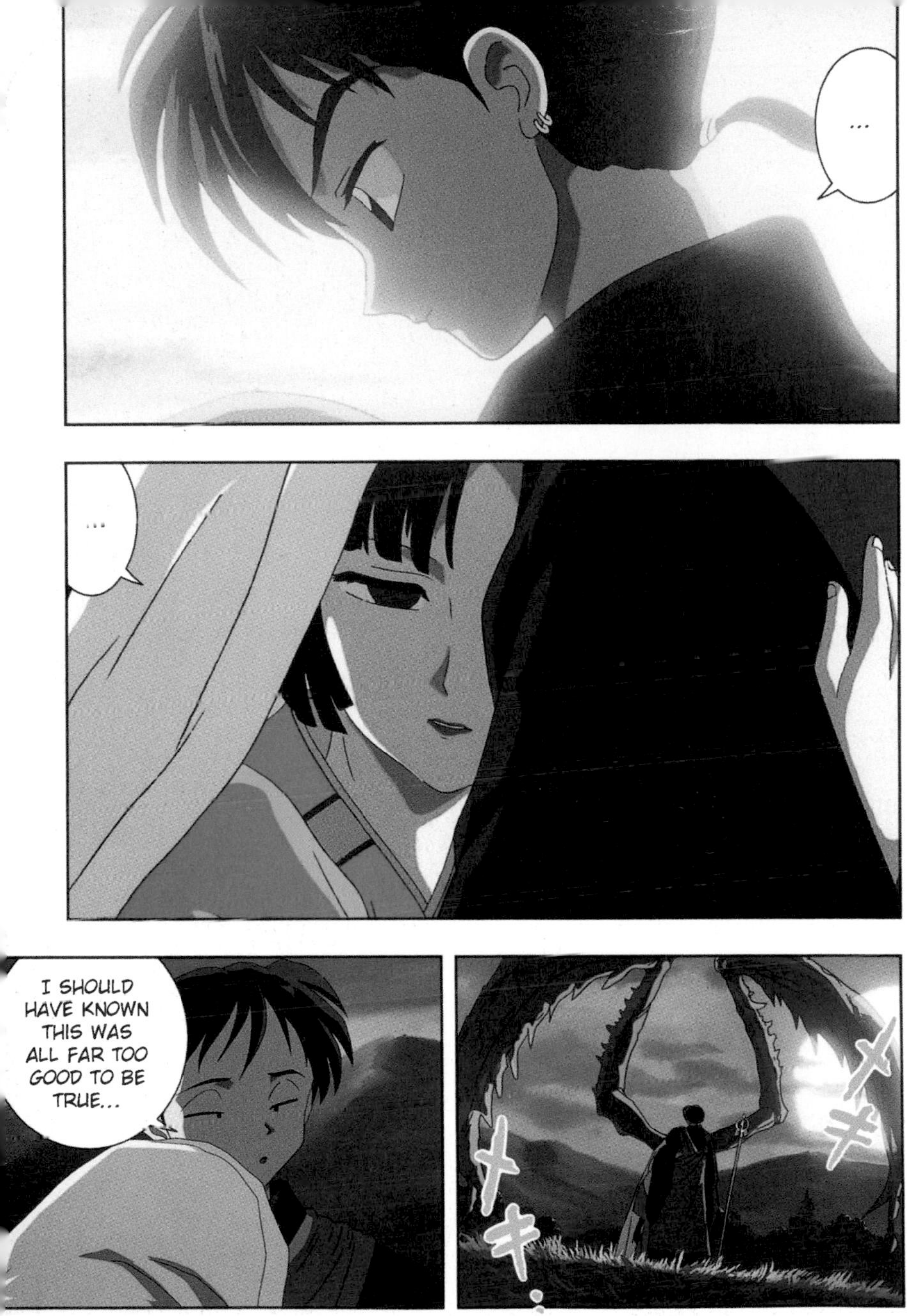
...
...
メキ
メキ...
I SHOULD HAVE KNOWN THIS WAS ALL FAR TOO GOOD TO BE TRUE...

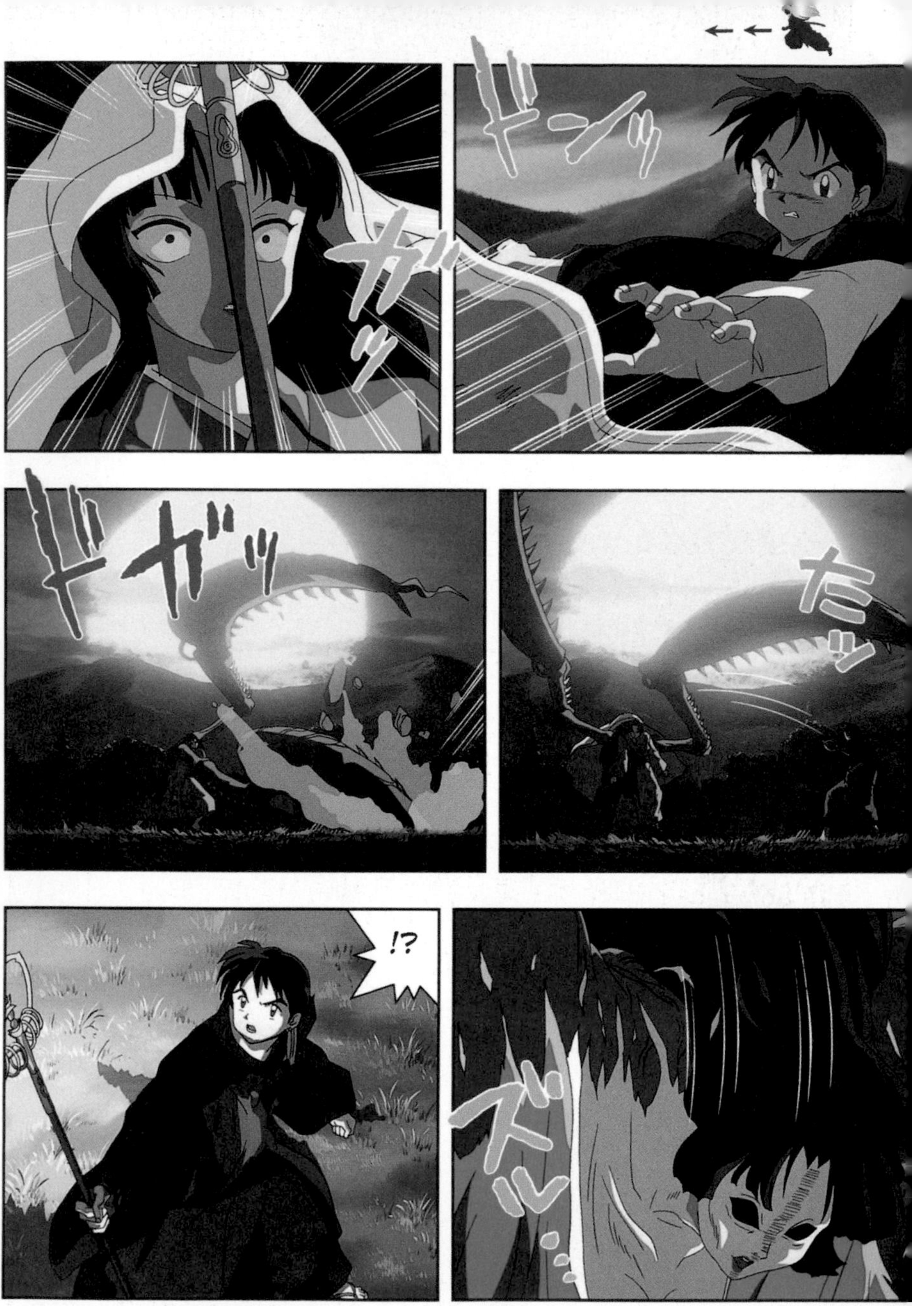
ドーンッ
ガッ
たッ
ドガッ
ズル…
!?

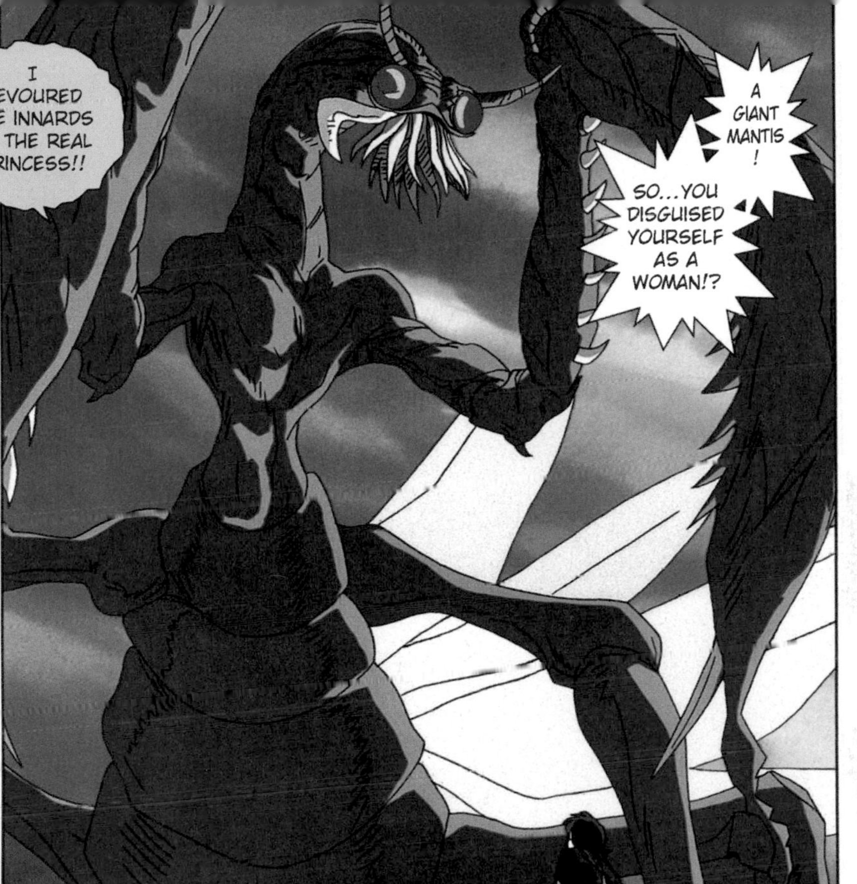
A GIANT MANTIS!
SO...YOU DISGUISED YOURSELF AS A WOMAN!?
I DEVOURED THE INNARDS OF THE REAL PRINCESS!!
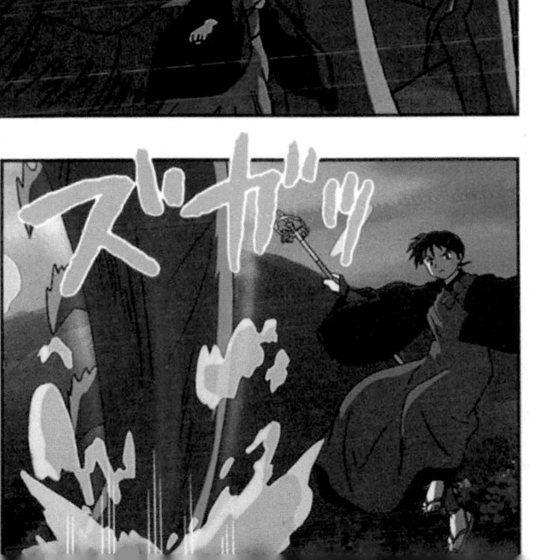
ズガッ
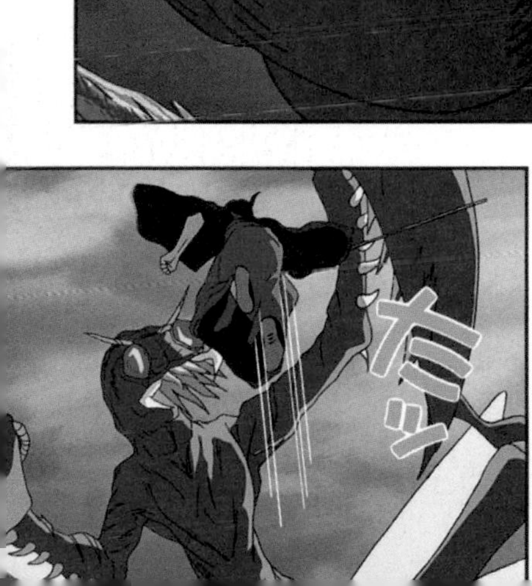
たッ

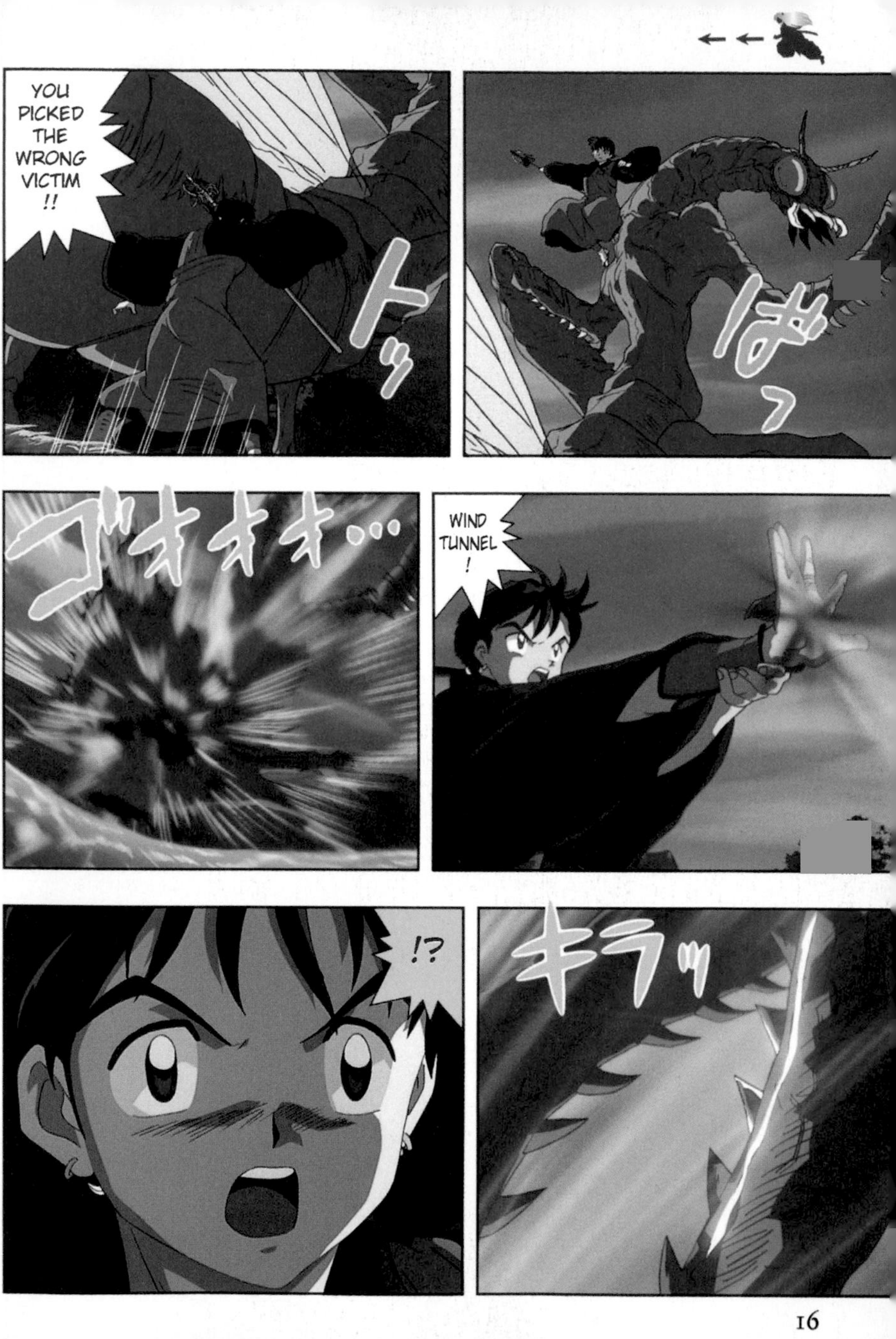
ばっ
YOU PICKED THE WRONG VICTIM !!
トッ
WIND TUNNEL !
ゴオオオ…
キラッ
!?

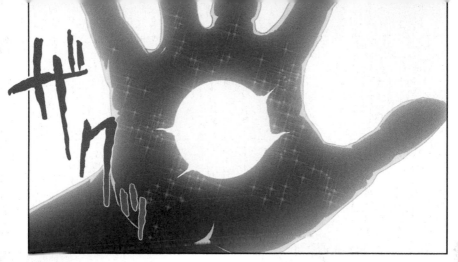

MY WIND
TUNNEL'S
INJURED
...

DAMN
!

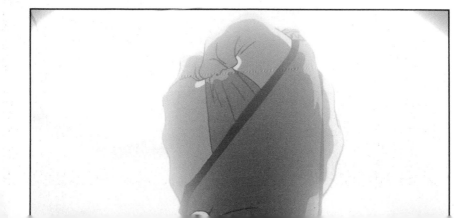

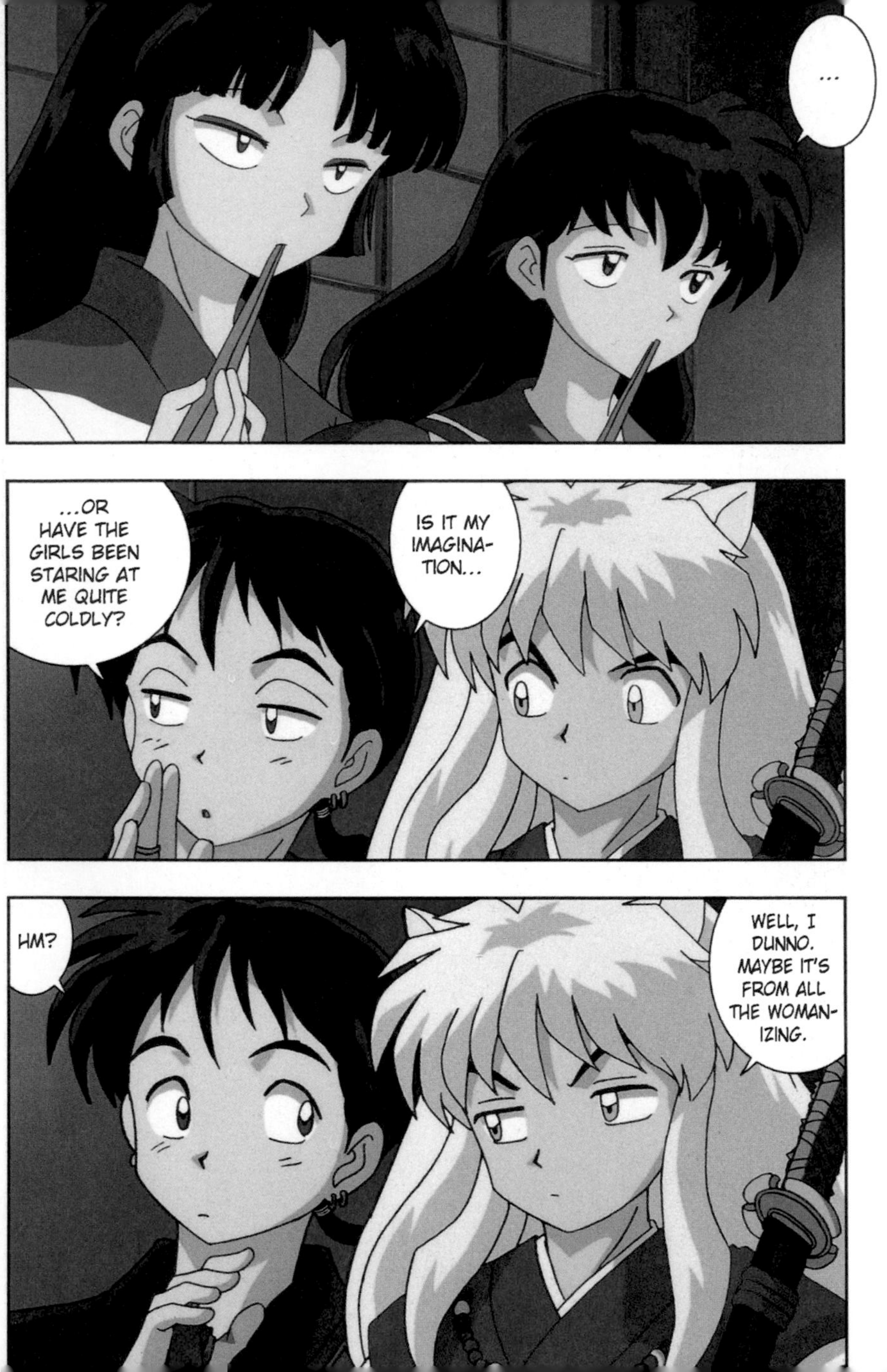
...
IS IT MY IMAGINATION...
...OR HAVE THE GIRLS BEEN STARING AT ME QUITE COLDLY?
WELL, I DUNNO. MAYBE IT'S FROM ALL THE WOMANIZING.
HM?

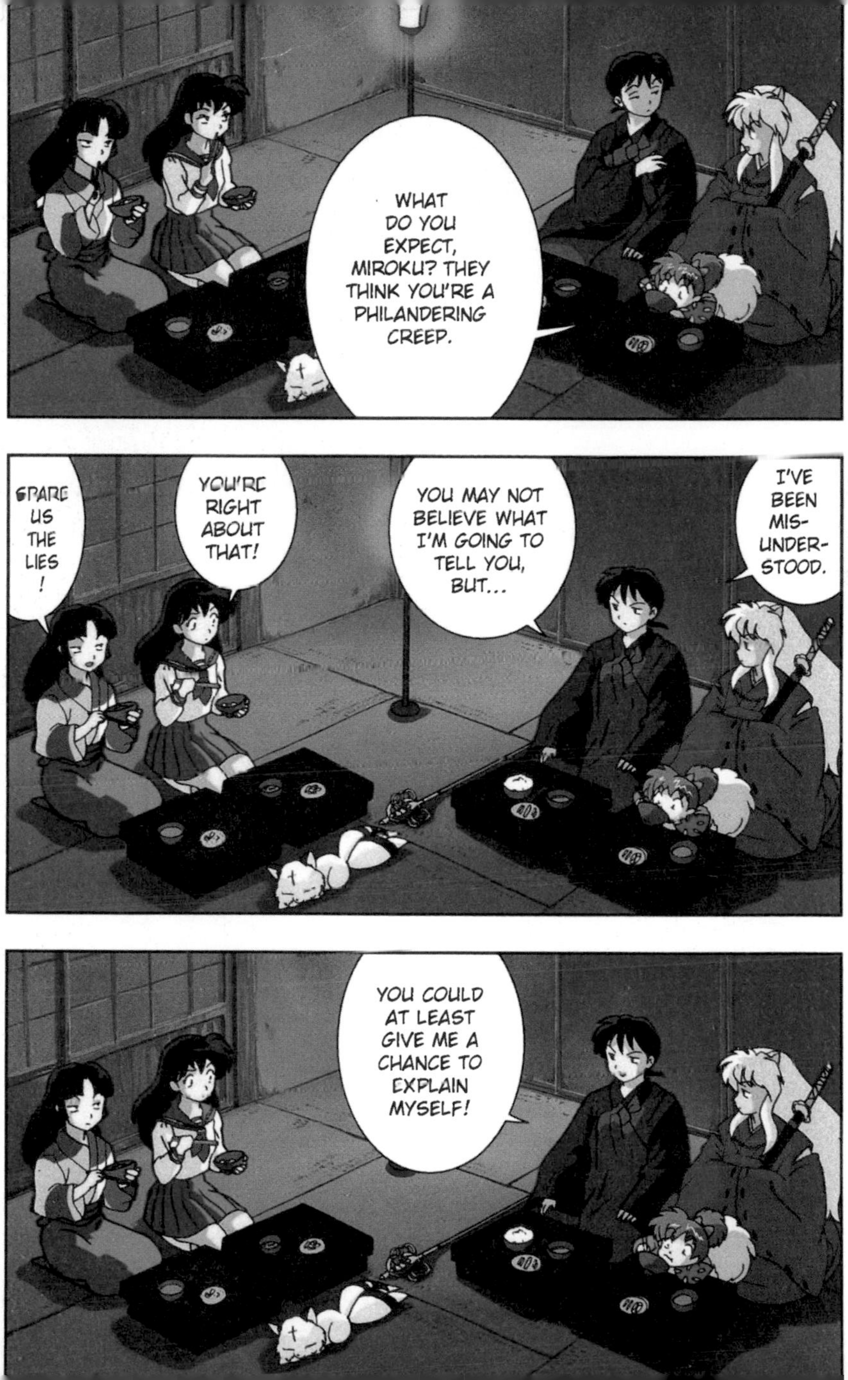
WHAT DO YOU EXPECT, MIROKU? THEY THINK YOU'RE A PHILANDERING CREEP.
I'VE BEEN MIS-UNDERSTOOD.
YOU MAY NOT BELIEVE WHAT I'M GOING TO TELL YOU, BUT...
YOU'RE RIGHT ABOUT THAT!
SPARE US THE LIES!
YOU COULD AT LEAST GIVE ME A CHANCE TO EXPLAIN MYSELF!

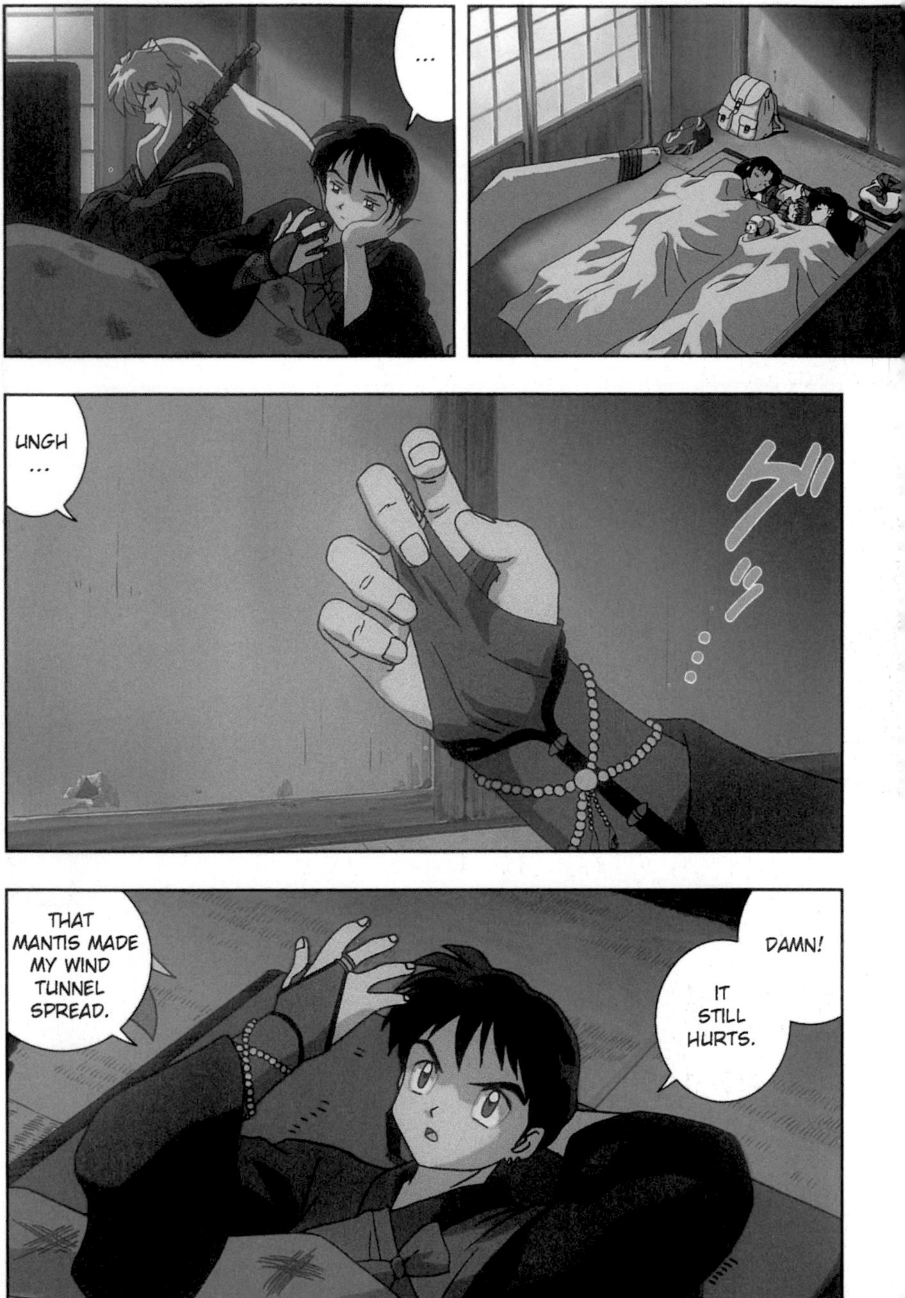
...
UNGH ...
グッ
DAMN!
IT STILL HURTS.
THAT MANTIS MADE MY WIND TUNNEL SPREAD.

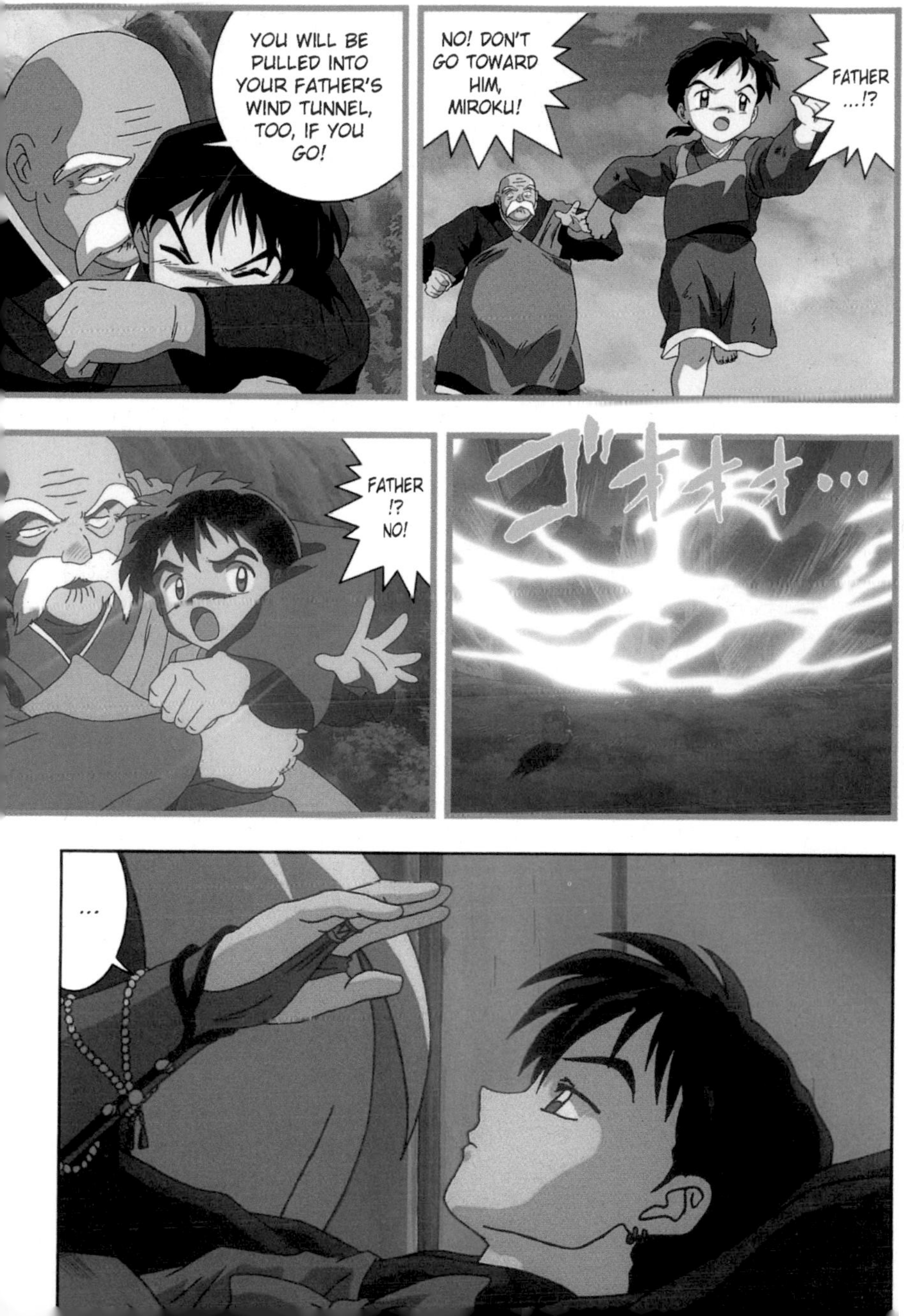
FATHER ...!?
NO! DON'T GO TOWARD HIM, MIROKU!
YOU WILL BE PULLED INTO YOUR FATHER'S WIND TUNNEL, TOO, IF YOU GO!
ゴオオオ...
FATHER !? NO!
...

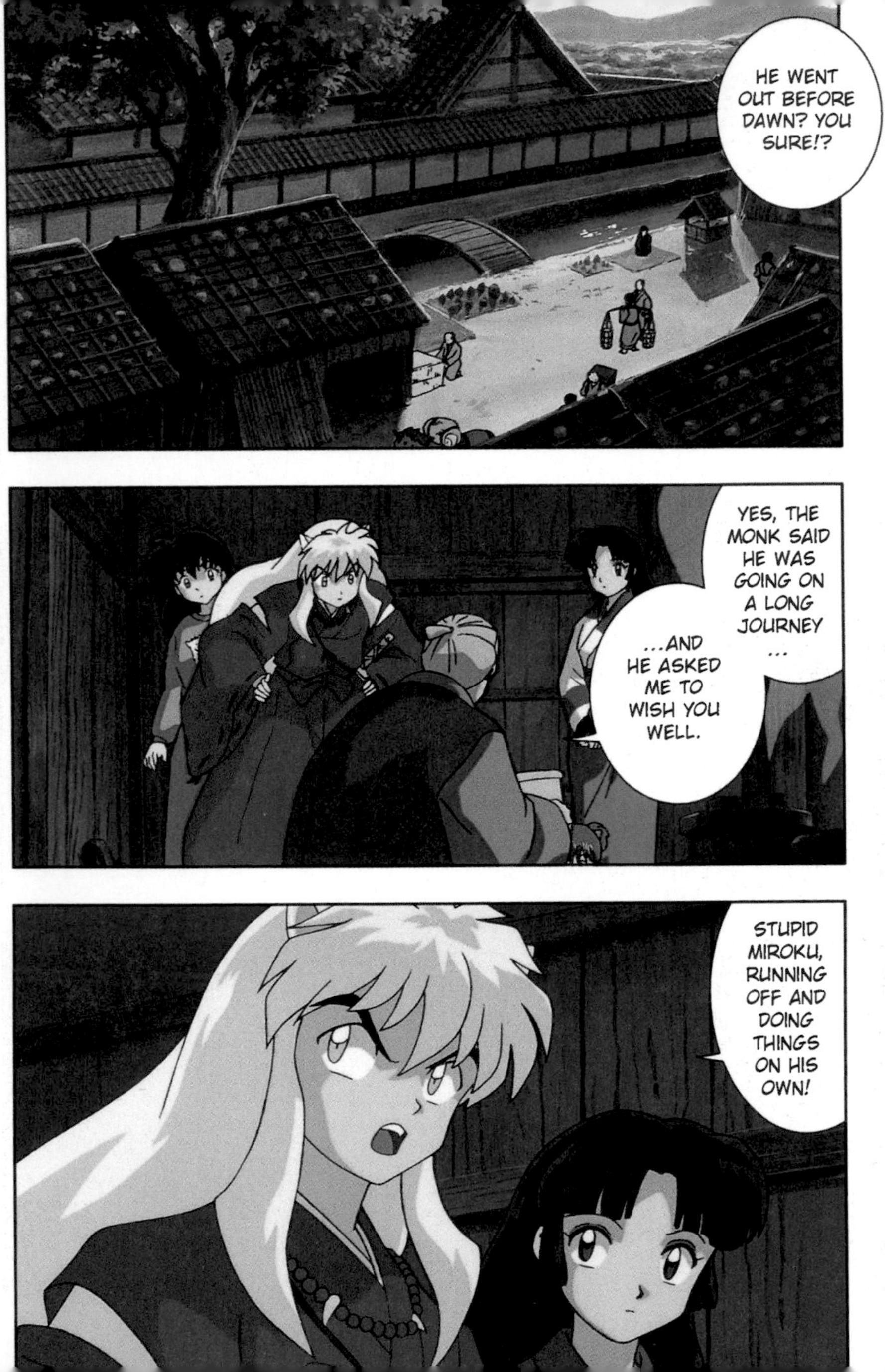
HE WENT OUT BEFORE DAWN? YOU SURE!?
YES, THE MONK SAID HE WAS GOING ON A LONG JOURNEY ...
...AND HE ASKED ME TO WISH YOU WELL.
STUPID MIROKU, RUNNING OFF AND DOING THINGS ON HIS OWN!

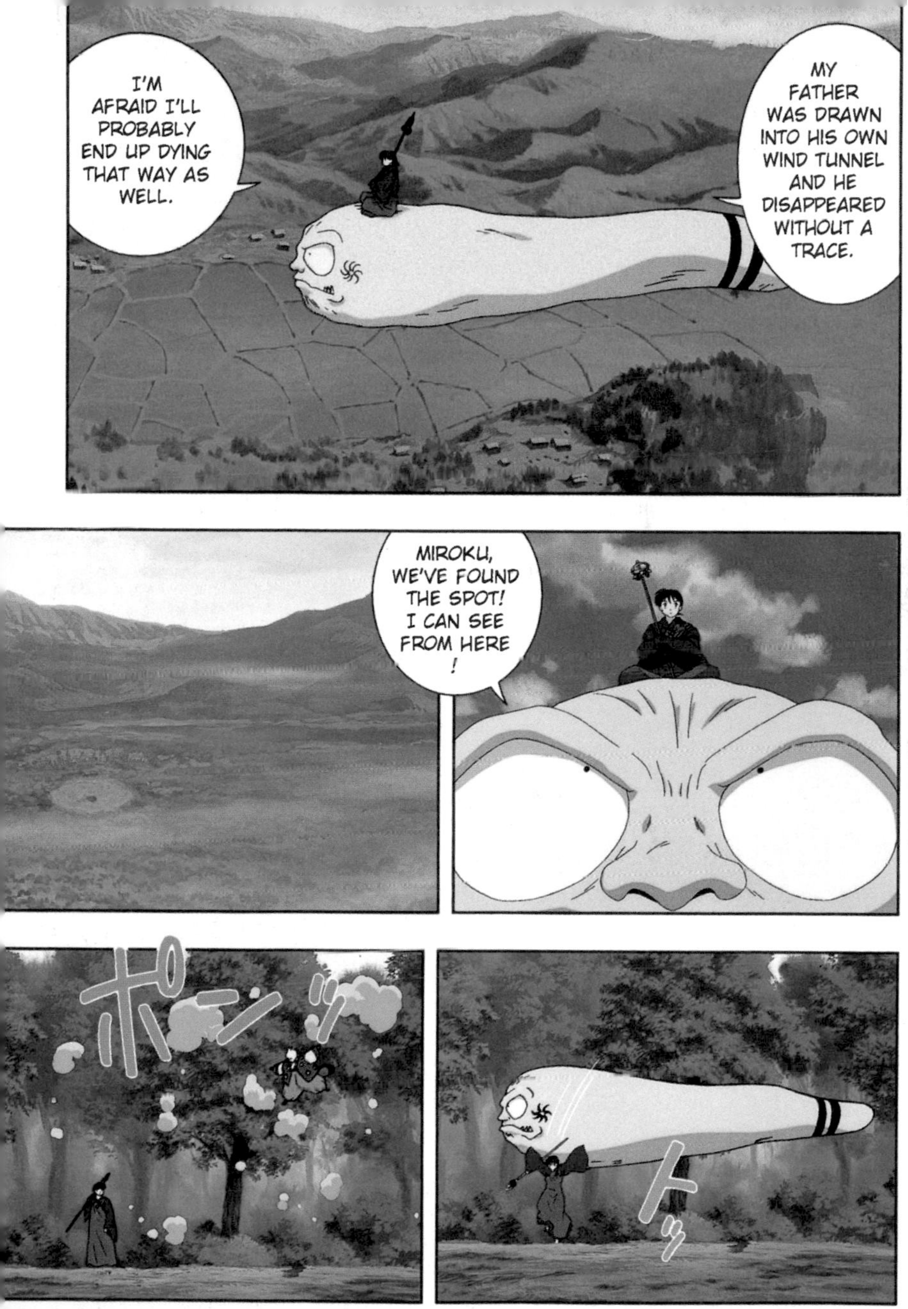
MY FATHER WAS DRAWN INTO HIS OWN WIND TUNNEL AND HE DISAPPEARED WITHOUT A TRACE.
I'M AFRAID I'LL PROBABLY END UP DYING THAT WAY AS WELL.
MIROKU, WE'VE FOUND THE SPOT! I CAN SEE FROM HERE!
トッ
ポーンッ

WHAT IS THIS GIANT HOLE?

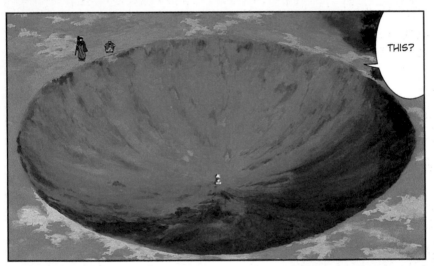

THIS?

...

THIS IS MY FATHER'S GRAVE.

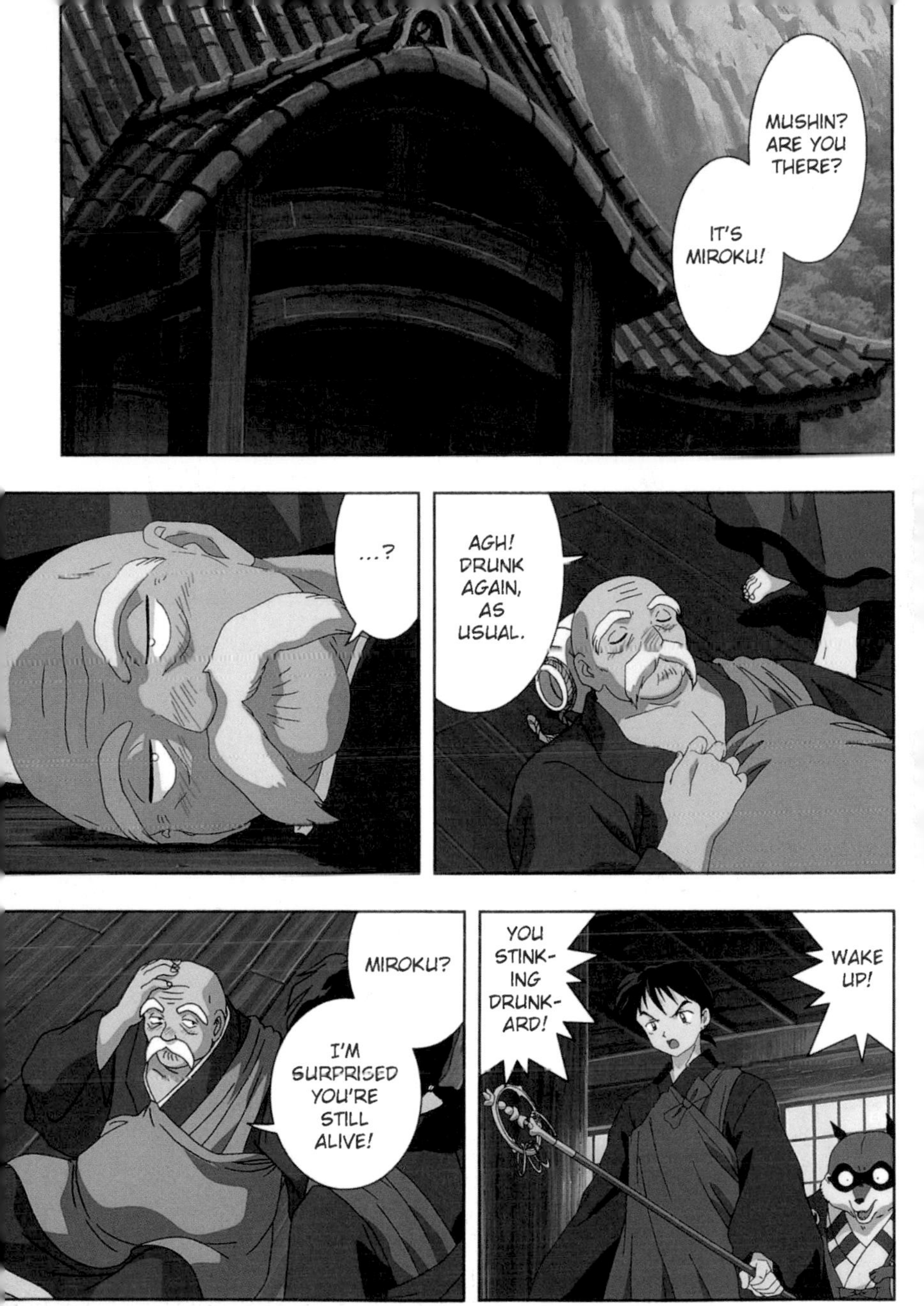

MUSHIN? ARE YOU THERE?
IT'S MIROKU!
AGH! DRUNK AGAIN, AS USUAL.
...?
WAKE UP!
YOU STINK-ING DRUNK-ARD!
MIROKU?
I'M SURPRISED YOU'RE STILL ALIVE!

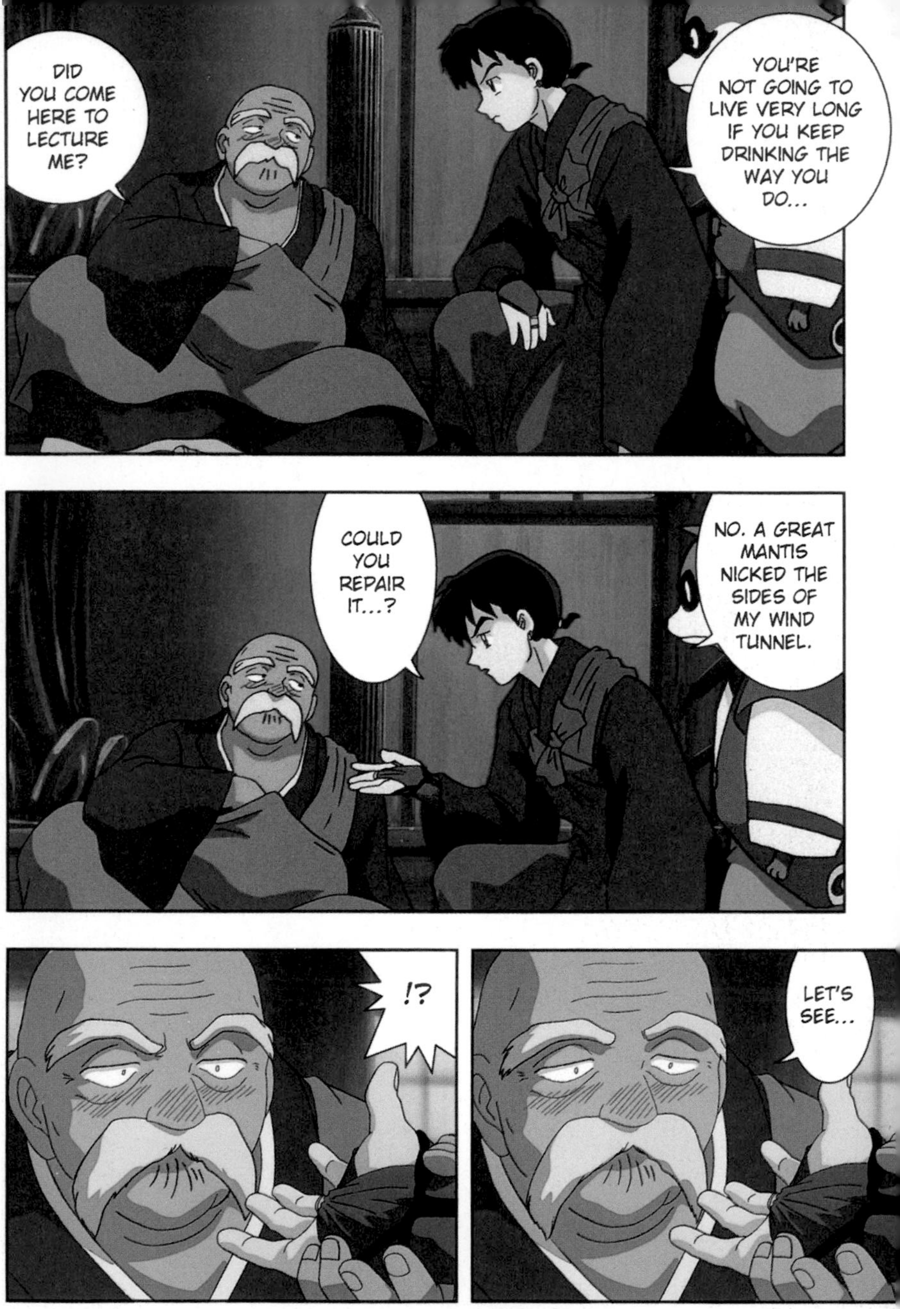
YOU'RE NOT GOING TO LIVE VERY LONG IF YOU KEEP DRINKING THE WAY YOU DO...
DID YOU COME HERE TO LECTURE ME?
NO. A GREAT MANTIS NICKED THE SIDES OF MY WIND TUNNEL.
COULD YOU REPAIR IT...?
LET'S SEE...
!?

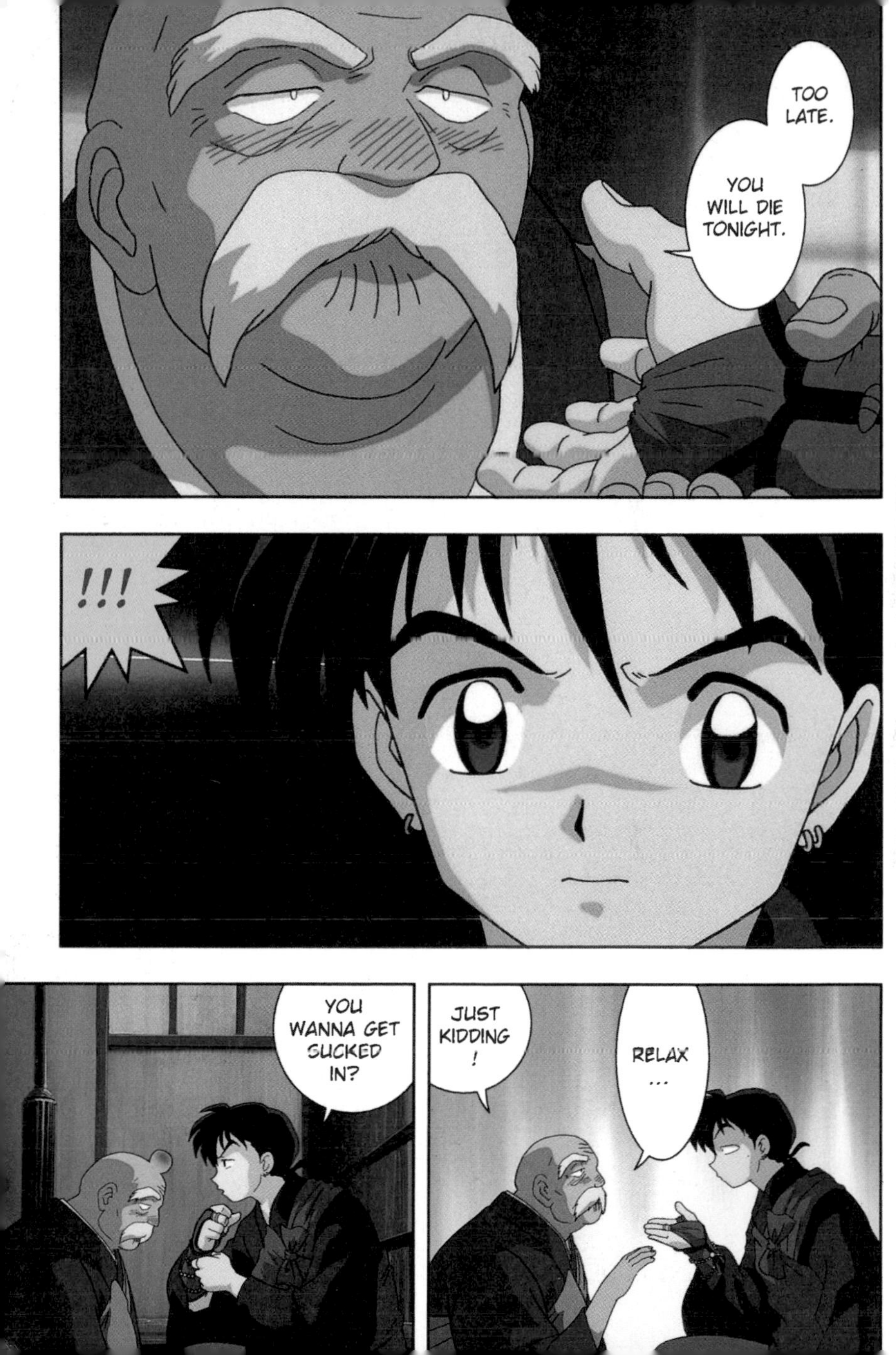
TOO LATE.
YOU WILL DIE TONIGHT.
!!!
RELAX ...
JUST KIDDING!
YOU WANNA GET SUCKED IN?

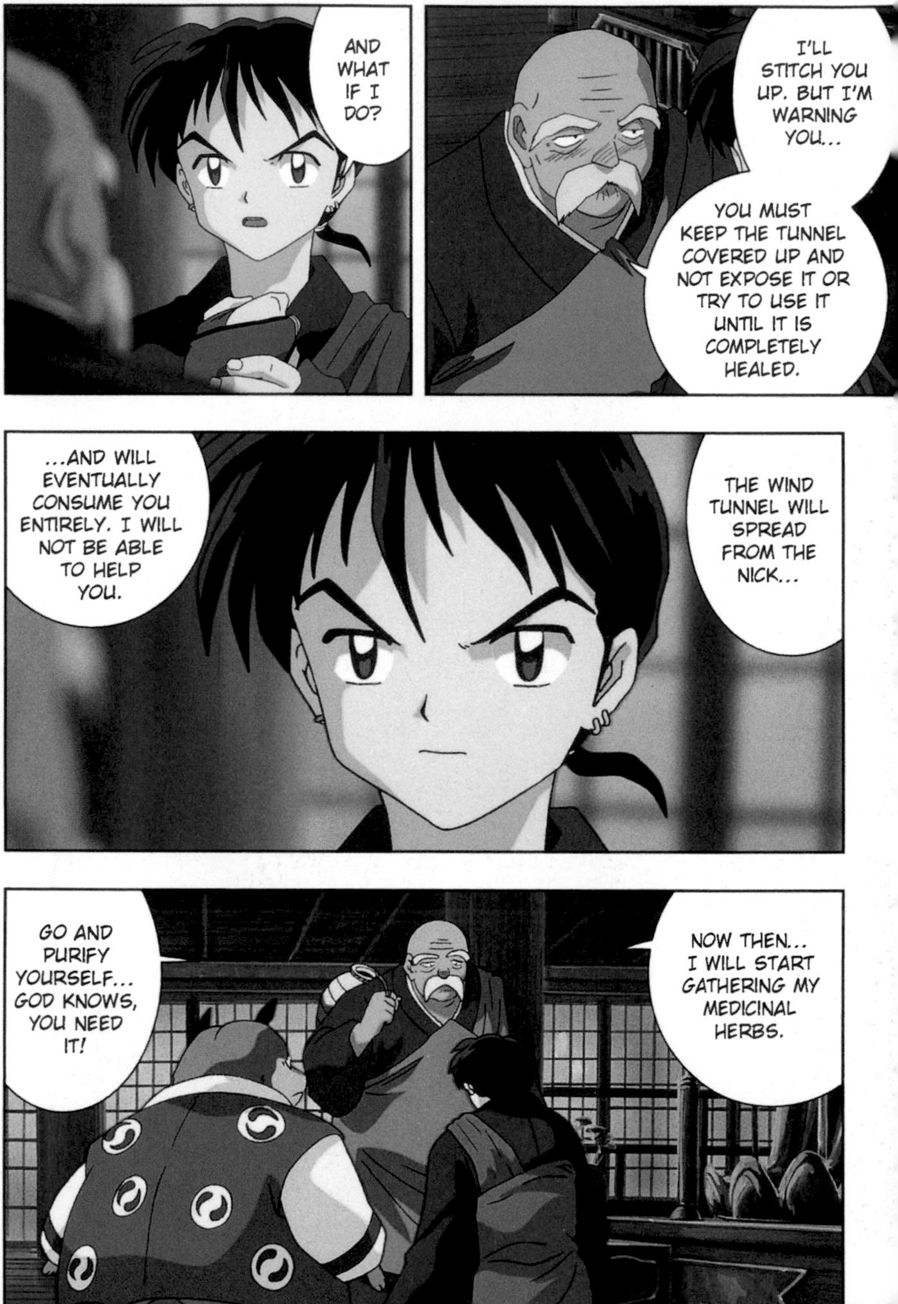
I'LL STITCH YOU UP. BUT I'M WARNING YOU...
YOU MUST KEEP THE TUNNEL COVERED UP AND NOT EXPOSE IT OR TRY TO USE IT UNTIL IT IS COMPLETELY HEALED.
AND WHAT IF I DO?
THE WIND TUNNEL WILL SPREAD FROM THE NICK...
...AND WILL EVENTUALLY CONSUME YOU ENTIRELY. I WILL NOT BE ABLE TO HELP YOU.
NOW THEN... I WILL START GATHERING MY MEDICINAL HERBS.
GO AND PURIFY YOURSELF... GOD KNOWS, YOU NEED IT!

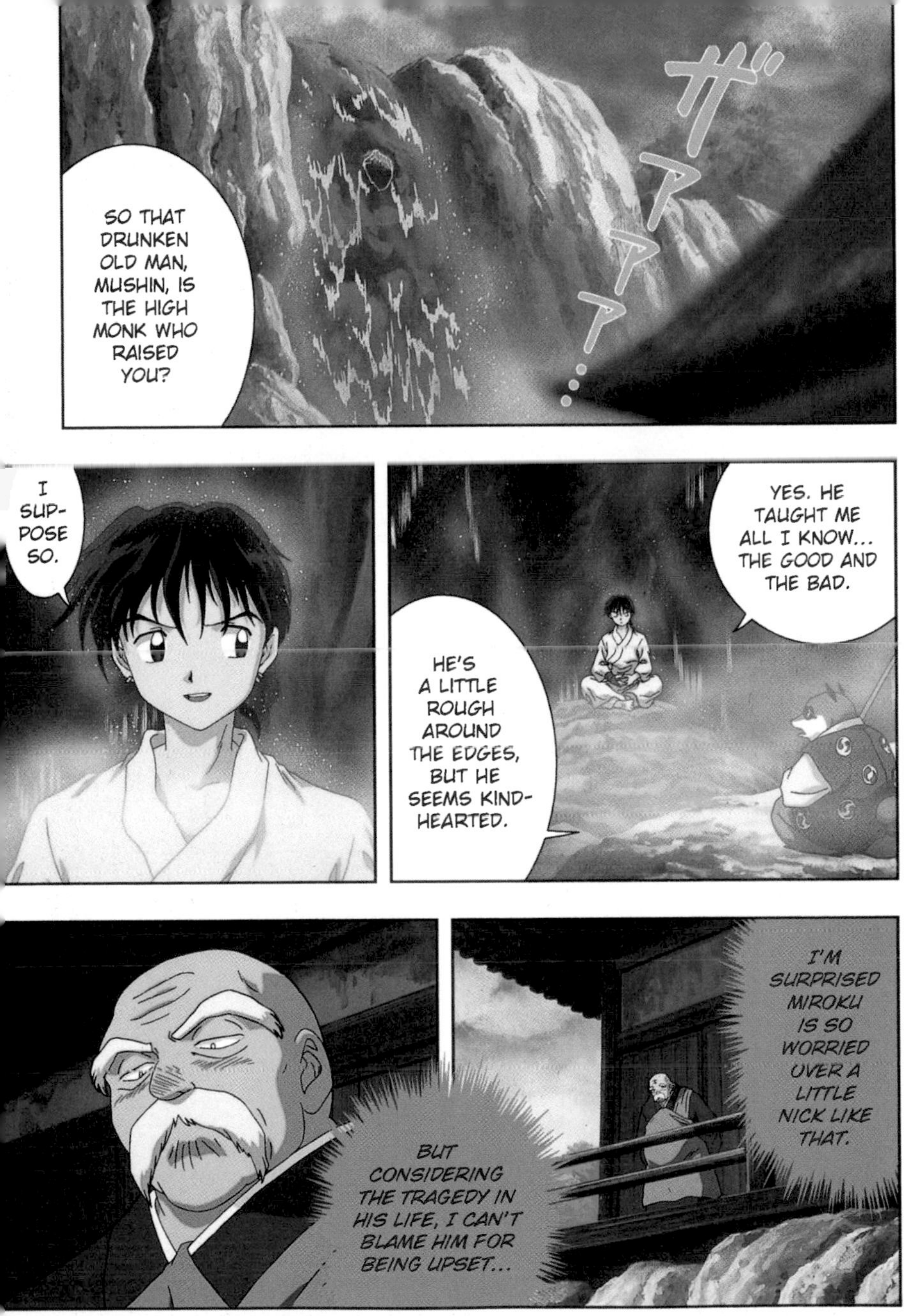
ザアアア…
SO THAT DRUNKEN OLD MAN, MUSHIN, IS THE HIGH MONK WHO RAISED YOU?
YES. HE TAUGHT ME ALL I KNOW... THE GOOD AND THE BAD.
HE'S A LITTLE ROUGH AROUND THE EDGES, BUT HE SEEMS KIND-HEARTED.
I SUP-POSE SO.
I'M SURPRISED MIROKU IS SO WORRIED OVER A LITTLE NICK LIKE THAT.
BUT CONSIDERING THE TRAGEDY IN HIS LIFE, I CAN'T BLAME HIM FOR BEING UPSET...

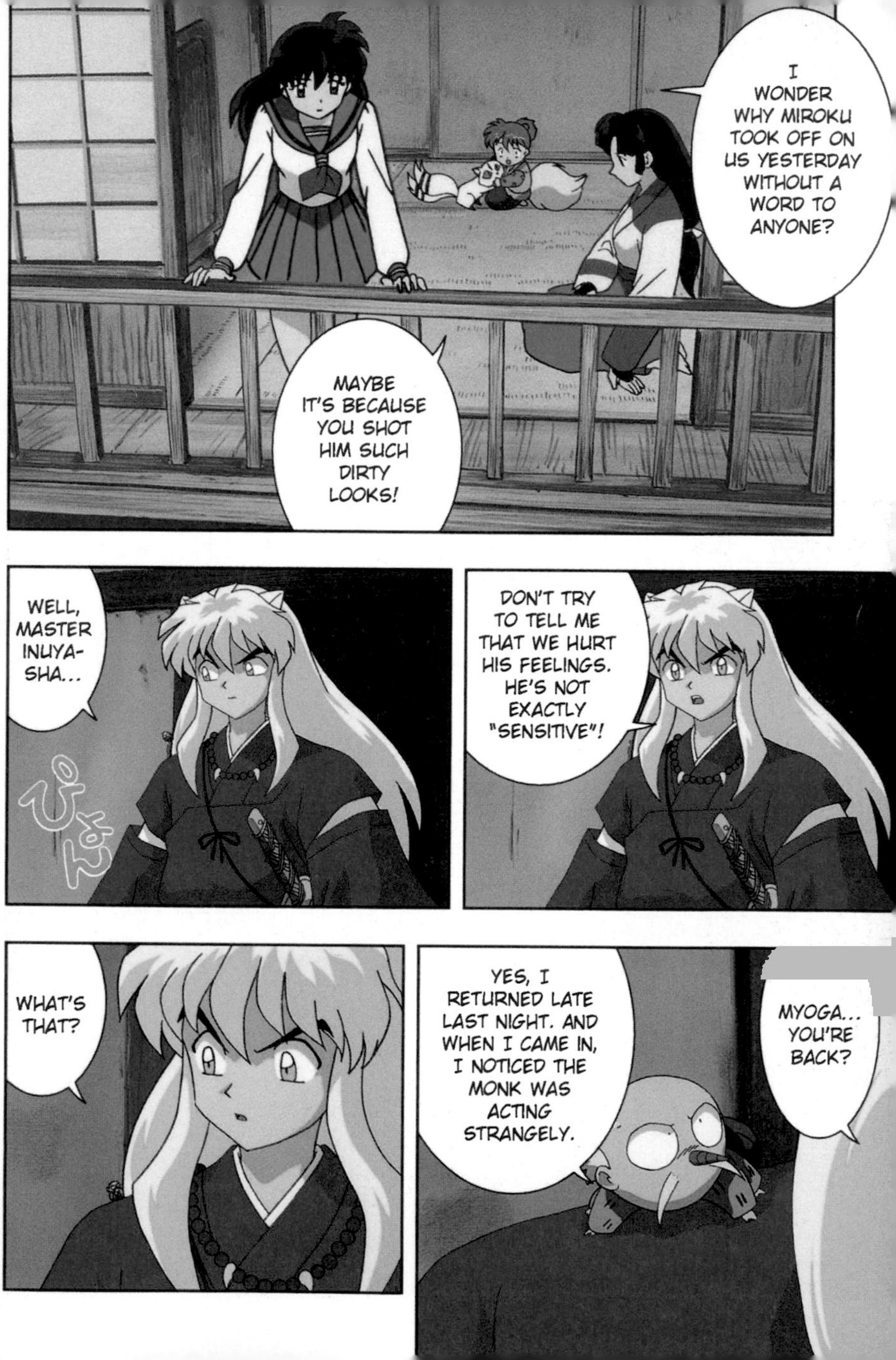
I WONDER WHY MIROKU TOOK OFF ON US YESTERDAY WITHOUT A WORD TO ANYONE?
MAYBE IT'S BECAUSE YOU SHOT HIM SUCH DIRTY LOOKS!
DON'T TRY TO TELL ME THAT WE HURT HIS FEELINGS. HE'S NOT EXACTLY "SENSITIVE"!
WELL, MASTER INUYA-SHA...
ぴょん
MYOGA... YOU'RE BACK?
YES, I RETURNED LATE LAST NIGHT. AND WHEN I CAME IN, I NOTICED THE MONK WAS ACTING STRANGELY.
WHAT'S THAT?

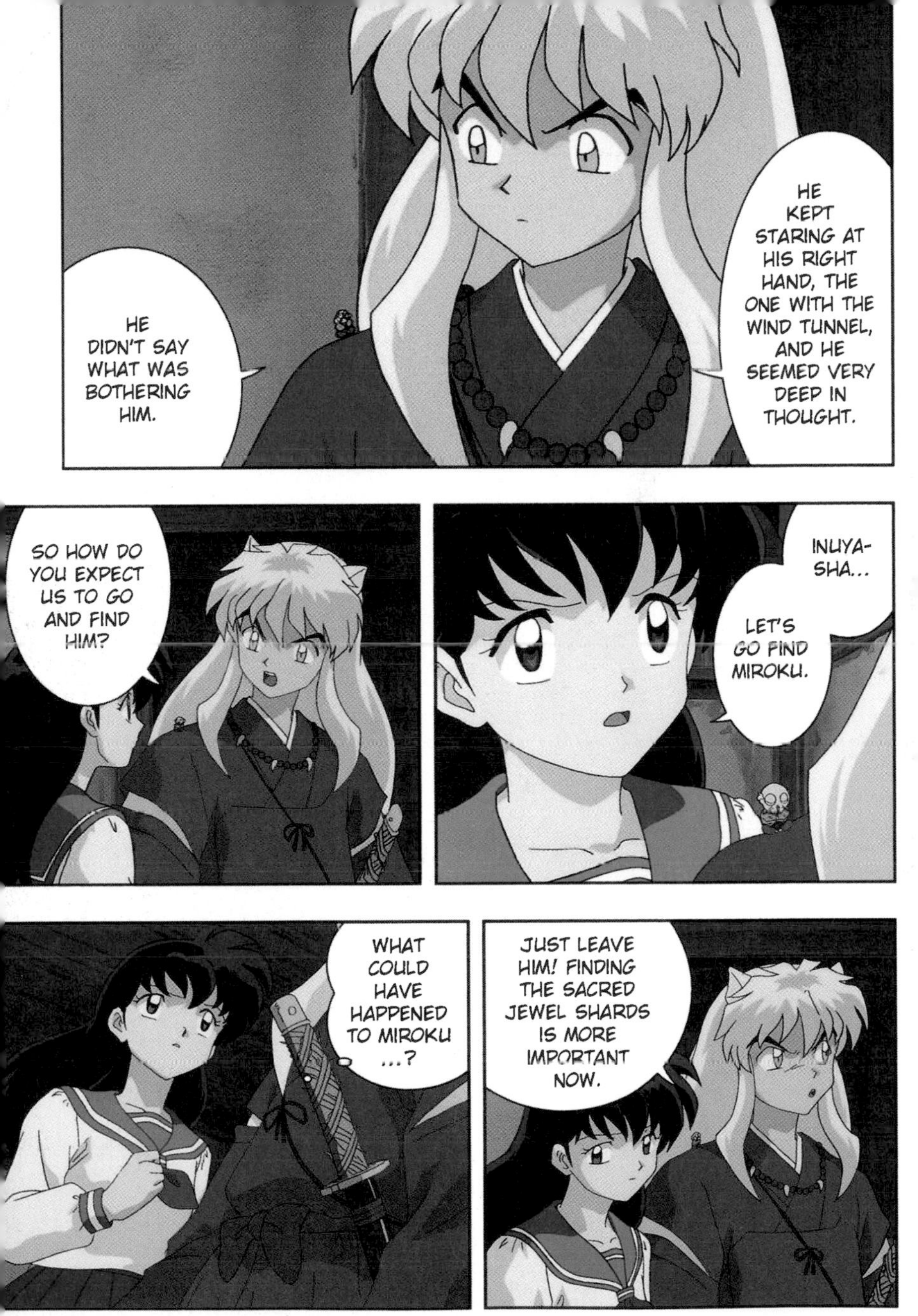
HE KEPT STARING AT HIS RIGHT HAND, THE ONE WITH THE WIND TUNNEL, AND HE SEEMED VERY DEEP IN THOUGHT.
HE DIDN'T SAY WHAT WAS BOTHERING HIM.
INUYA-SHA...
LET'S GO FIND MIROKU.
SO HOW DO YOU EXPECT US TO GO AND FIND HIM?
JUST LEAVE HIM! FINDING THE SACRED JEWEL SHARDS IS MORE IMPORTANT NOW.
WHAT COULD HAVE HAPPENED TO MIROKU ...?

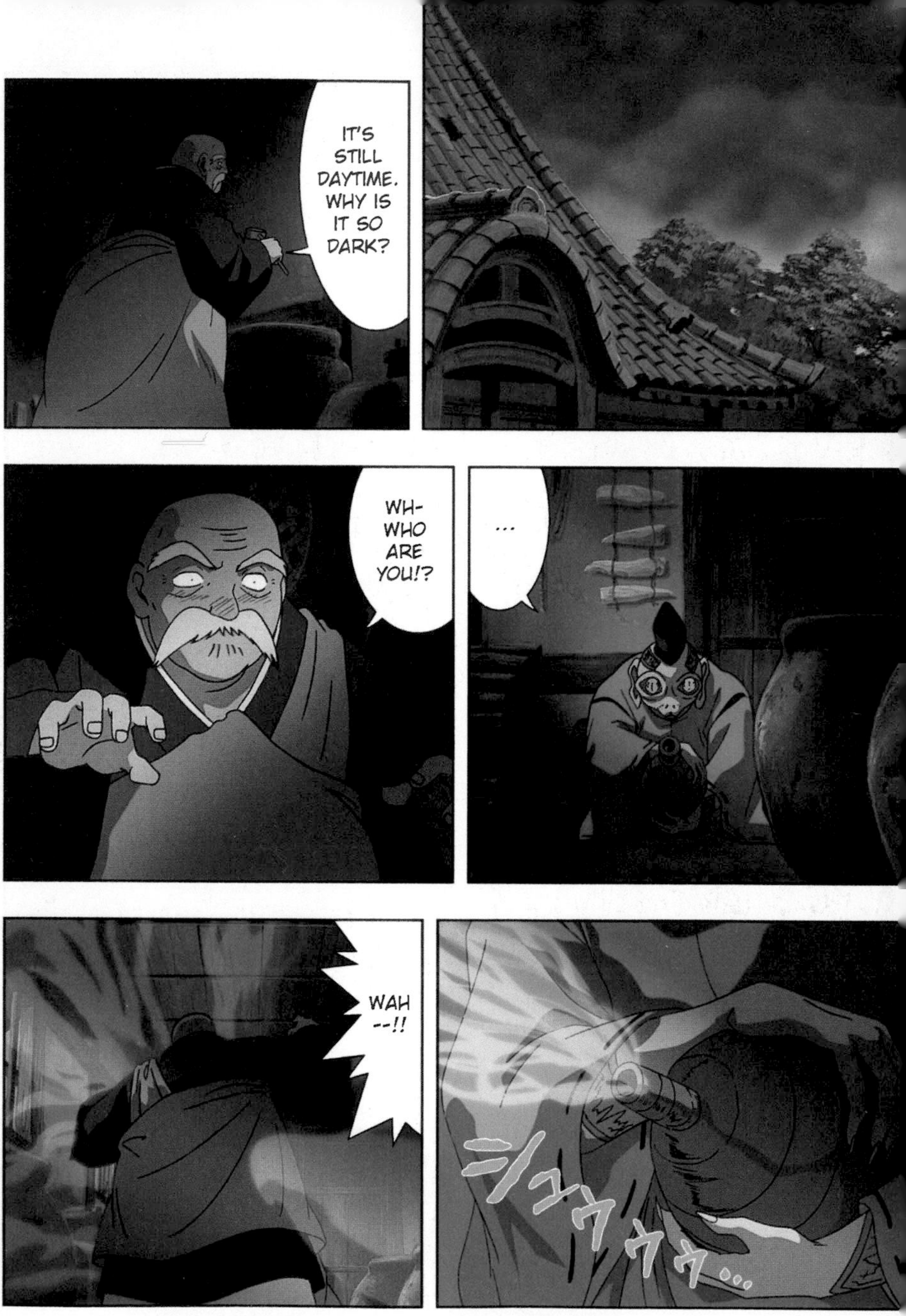
IT'S STILL DAYTIME. WHY IS IT SO DARK?
...
WH- WHO ARE YOU!?
シュウウウ...
WAH --!!

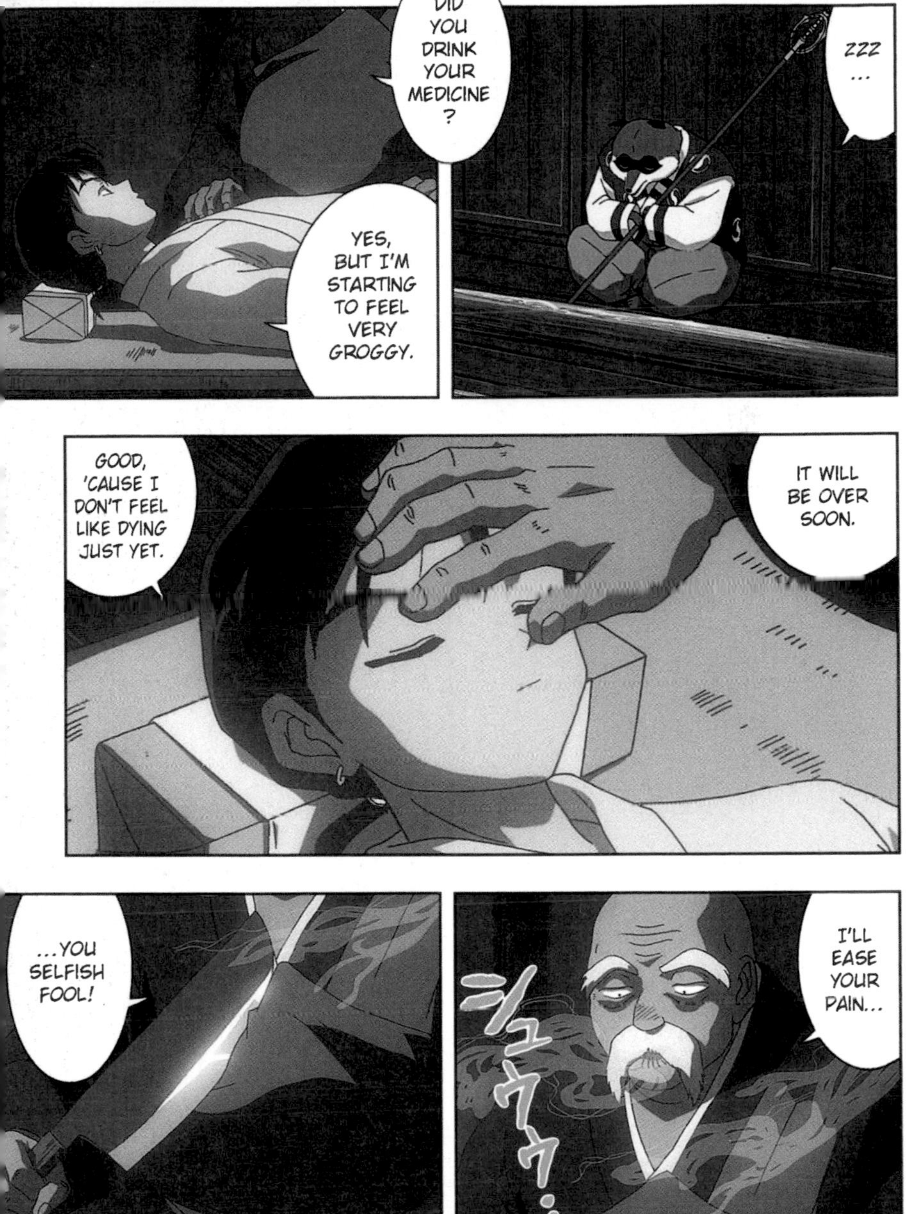
ZZZ...
DID YOU DRINK YOUR MEDICINE?
YES, BUT I'M STARTING TO FEEL VERY GROGGY.
IT WILL BE OVER SOON.
GOOD, 'CAUSE I DON'T FEEL LIKE DYING JUST YET.
I'LL EASE YOUR PAIN...
シュウウ...
...YOU SELFISH FOOL!

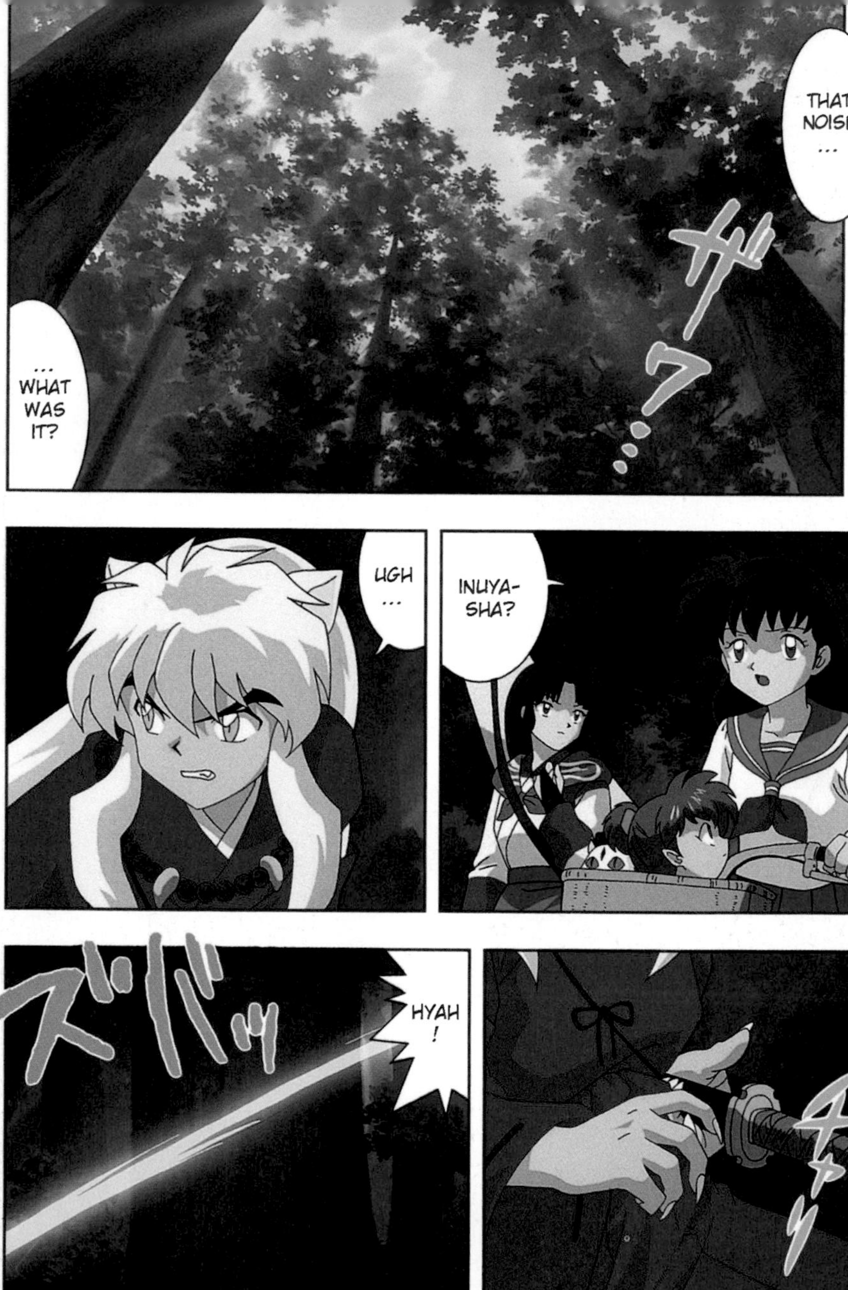
THAT NOISE ...
... WHAT WAS IT?
INUYA-SHA?
UGH ...
HYAH!

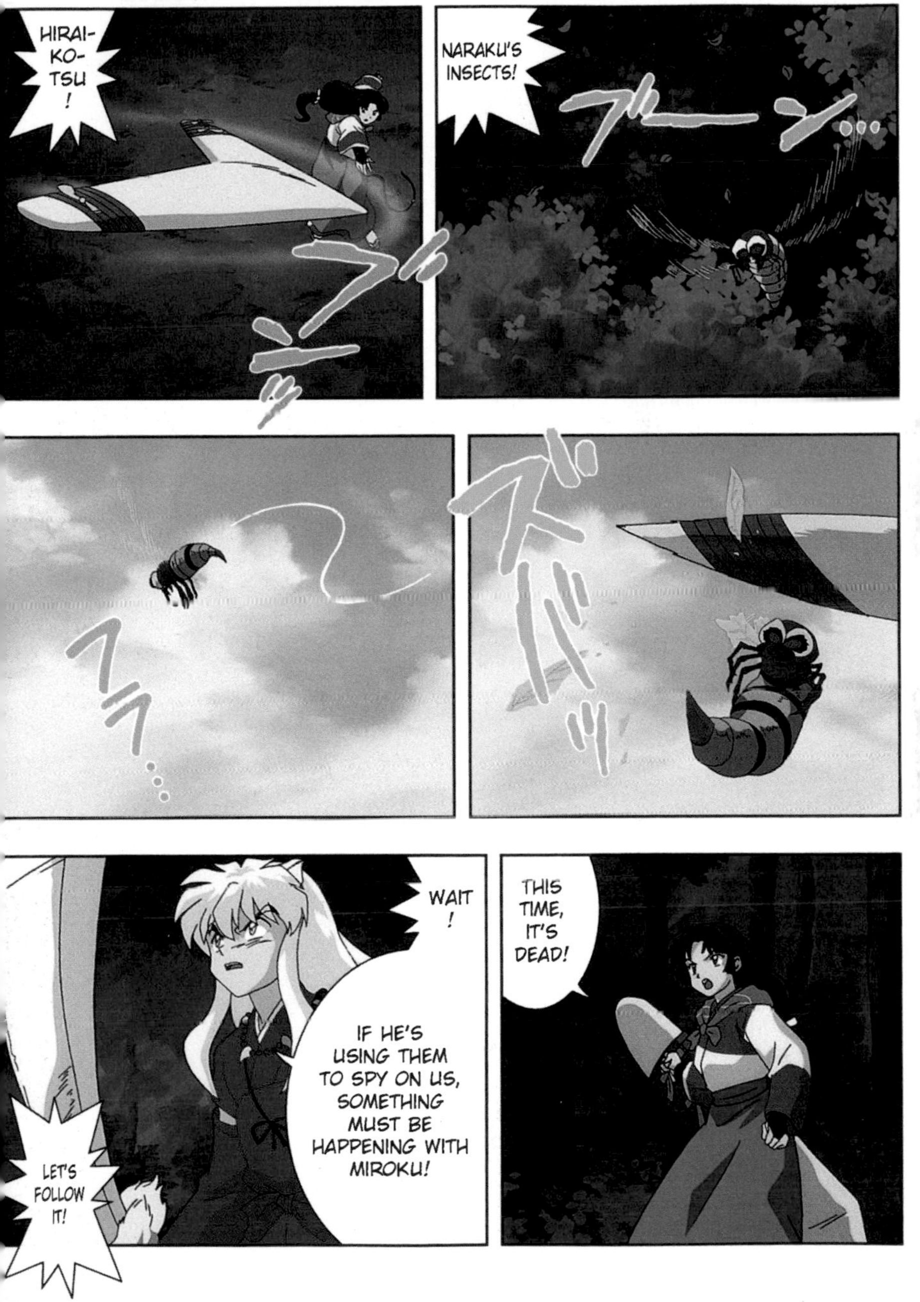
NARAKU'S INSECTS!
ブーン…
HIRAI-KO-TSU!
ブンッ
ズバッ
ヘラ…
THIS TIME, IT'S DEAD!
WAIT!
IF HE'S USING THEM TO SPY ON US, SOMETHING MUST BE HAPPENING WITH MIROKU!
LET'S FOLLOW IT!

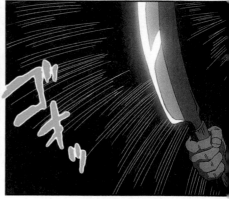

YOU'RE
NOT...

...
MUSHIN
!

ARE
YOU STILL
AWAKE?

I AM A DEMON WORM CHARMER. BUT I CAME ACROSS NARAKU AND HE PROMISED TO GIVE ME A SACRED JEWEL SHARD IF I KILLED YOU.

UNGH !!

N... NARAKU !?

REST IN PEACE !

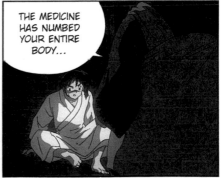

THE MEDICINE HAS NUMBED YOUR ENTIRE BODY...

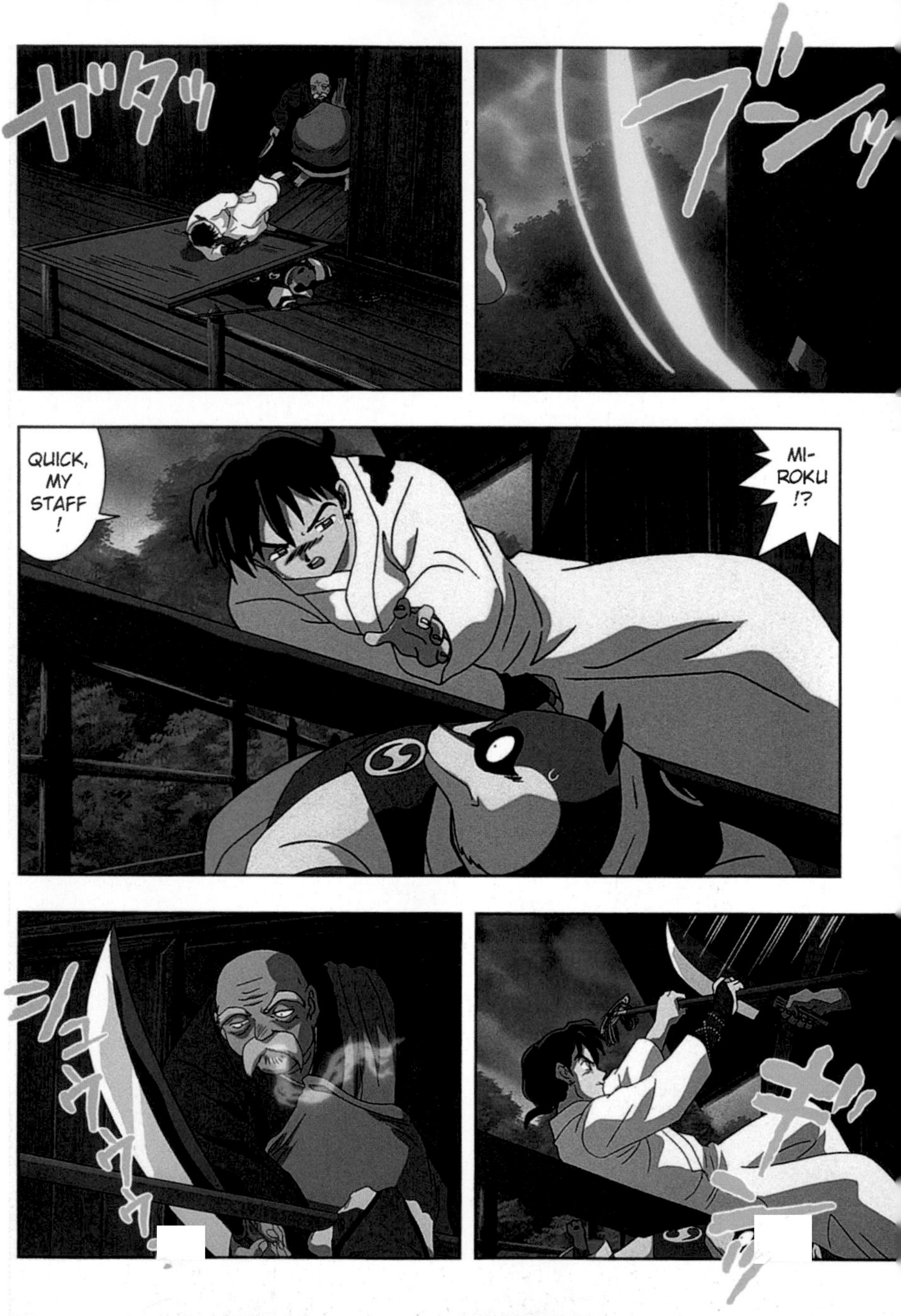
MI-ROKU !?
QUICK, MY STAFF !

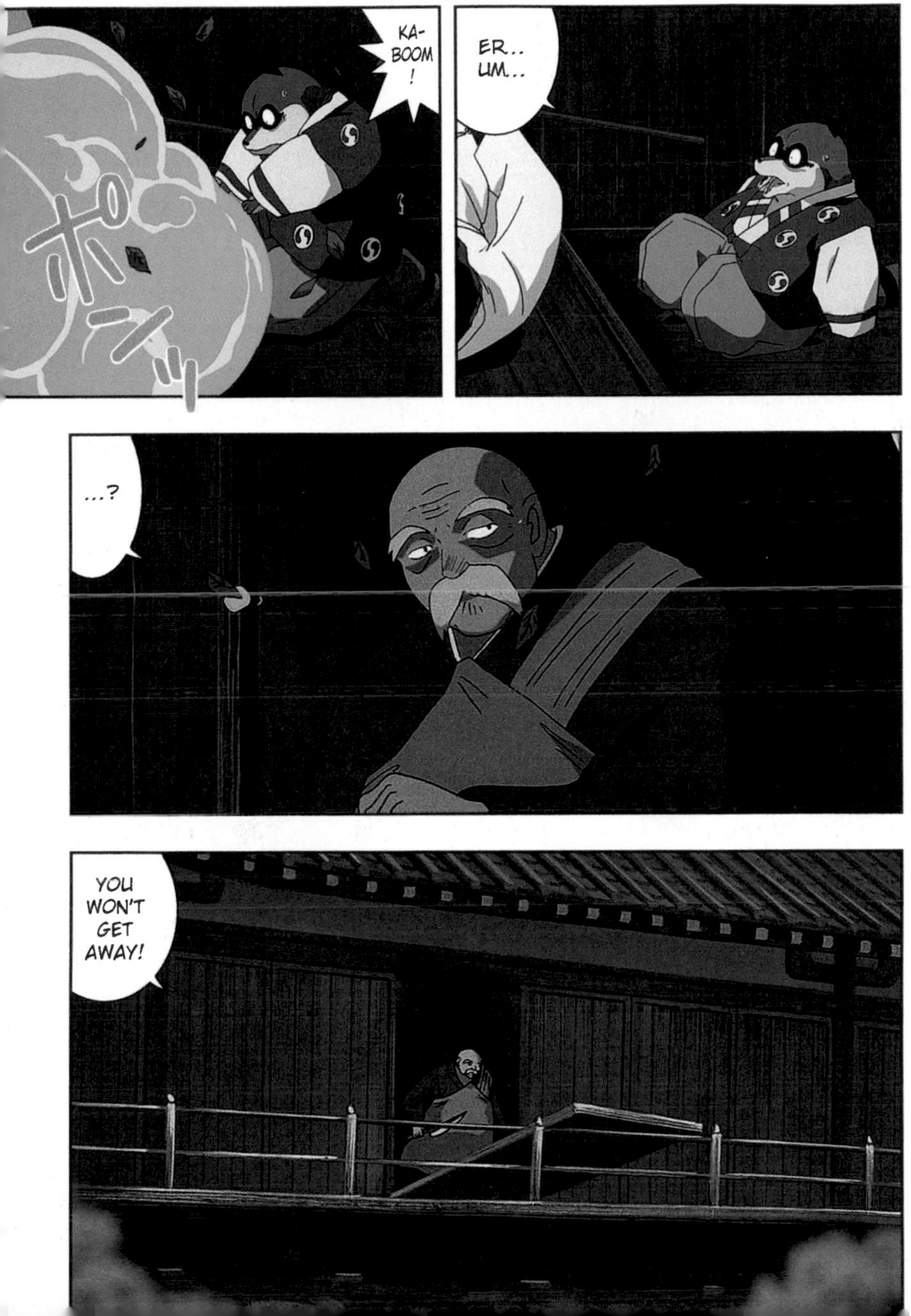
ER.. UM..
KA-BOOM!
ポンッ
...?
YOU WON'T GET AWAY!

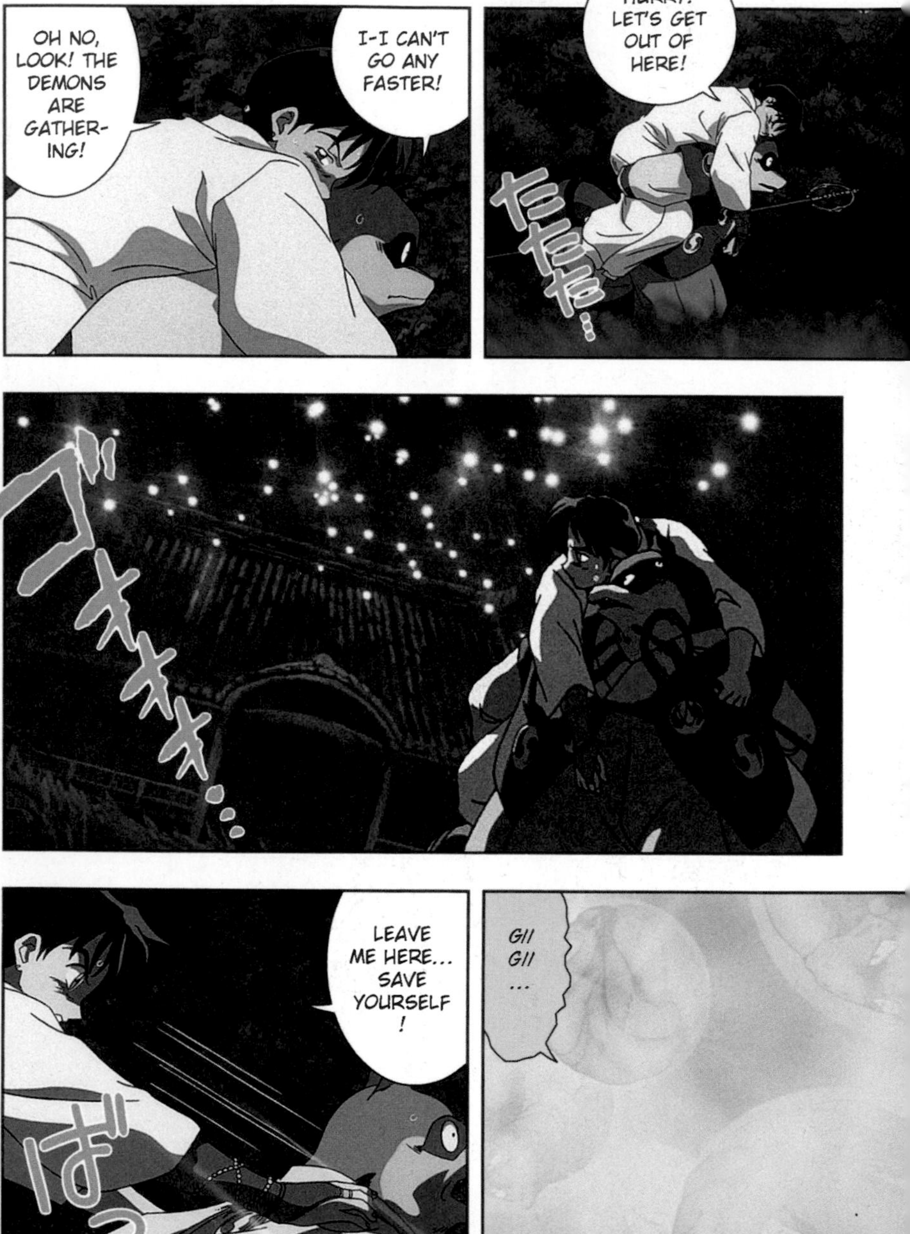
HURRY! LET'S GET OUT OF HERE!
たたた..
I-I CAN'T GO ANY FASTER!
OH NO, LOOK! THE DEMONS ARE GATHER-ING!
ゴオオオ...
GII GII ...
LEAVE ME HERE... SAVE YOURSELF!
ぱっ

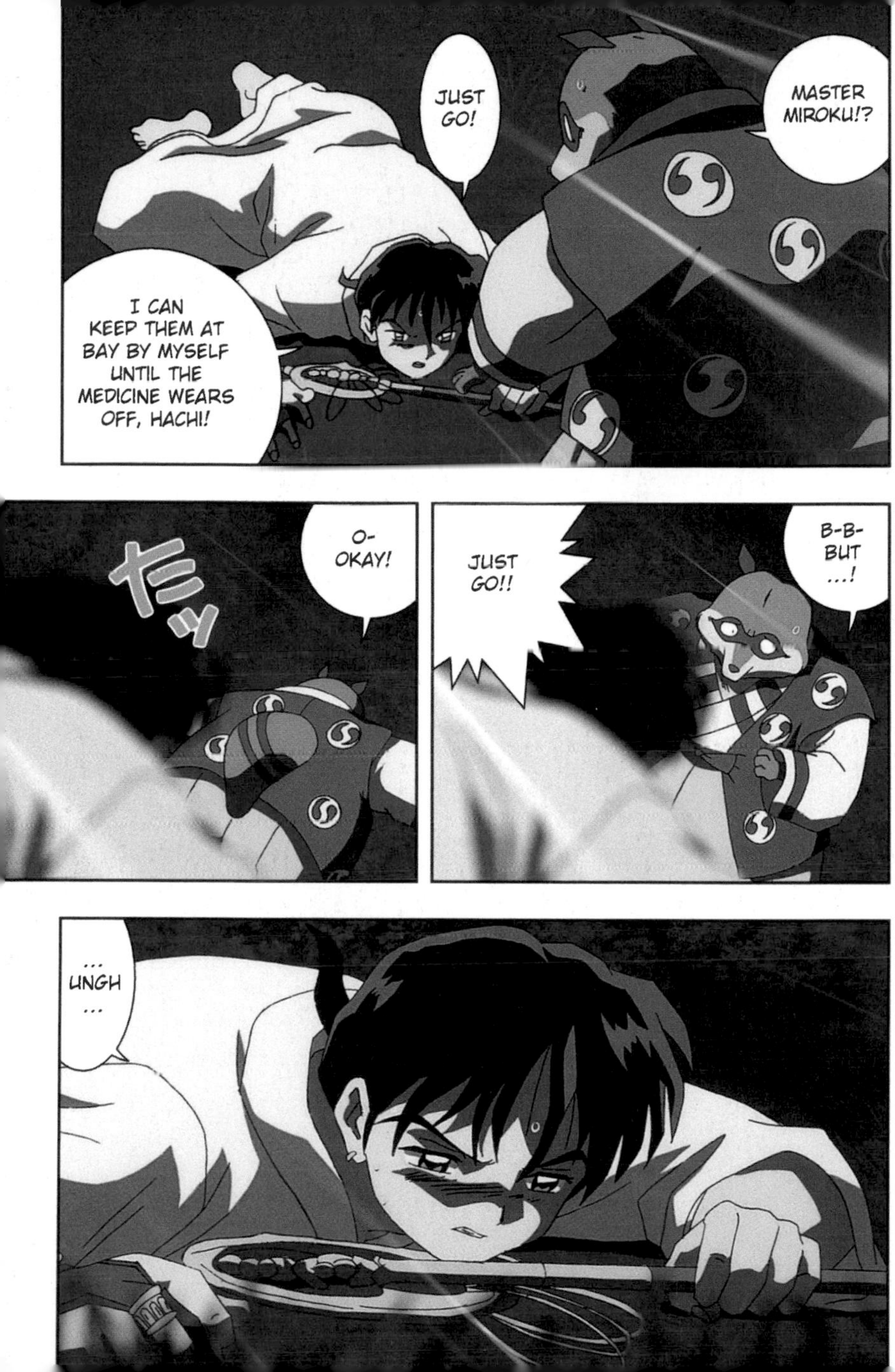
MASTER MIROKU!?
JUST GO!
I CAN KEEP THEM AT BAY BY MYSELF UNTIL THE MEDICINE WEARS OFF, HACHI!
B-B-BUT ...!
JUST GO!!
O-OKAY!
... UNGH ...

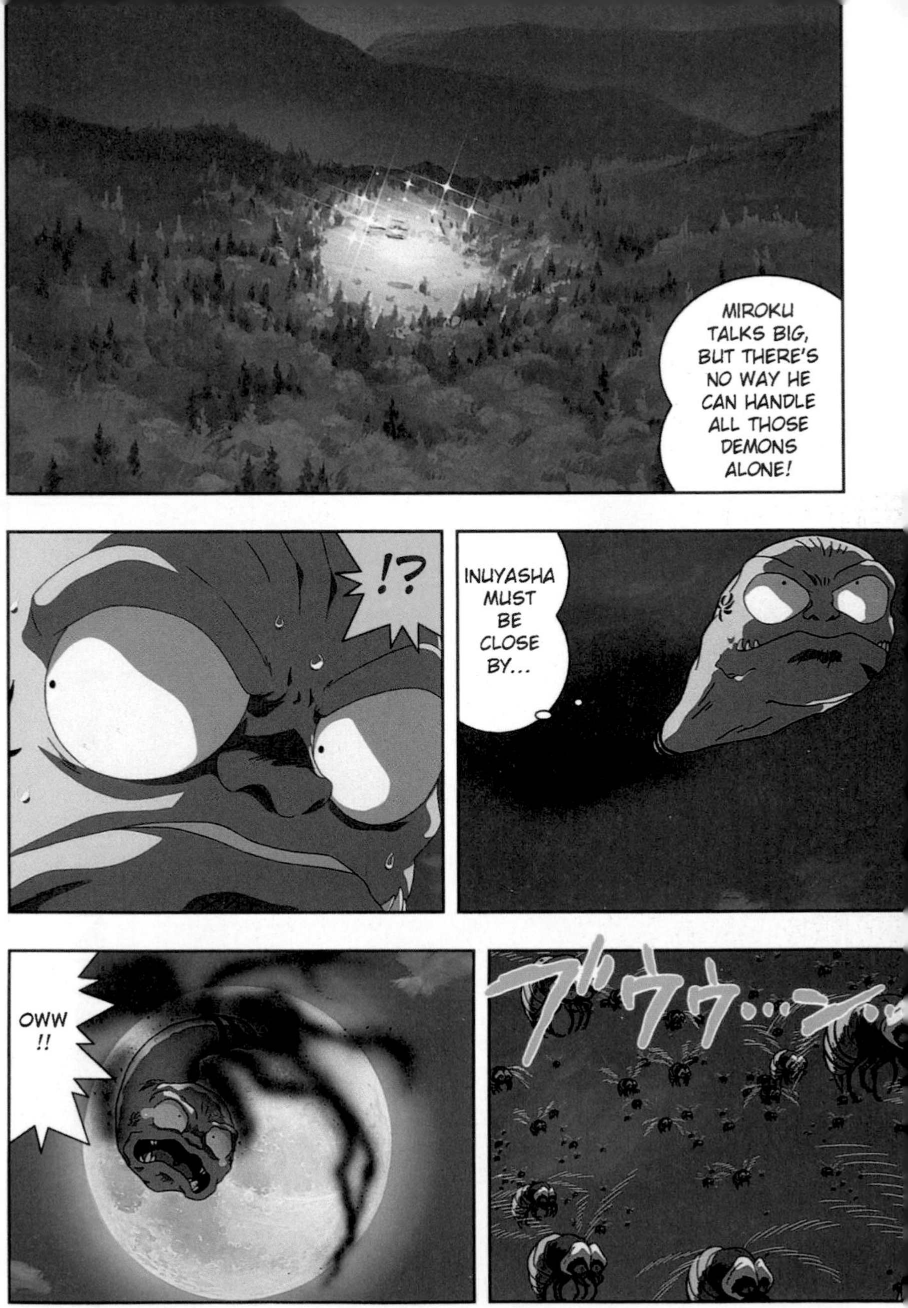
MIROKU TALKS BIG, BUT THERE'S NO WAY HE CAN HANDLE ALL THOSE DEMONS ALONE!
INUYASHA MUST BE CLOSE BY...
!?
ブウウ…ン…
OWW !!

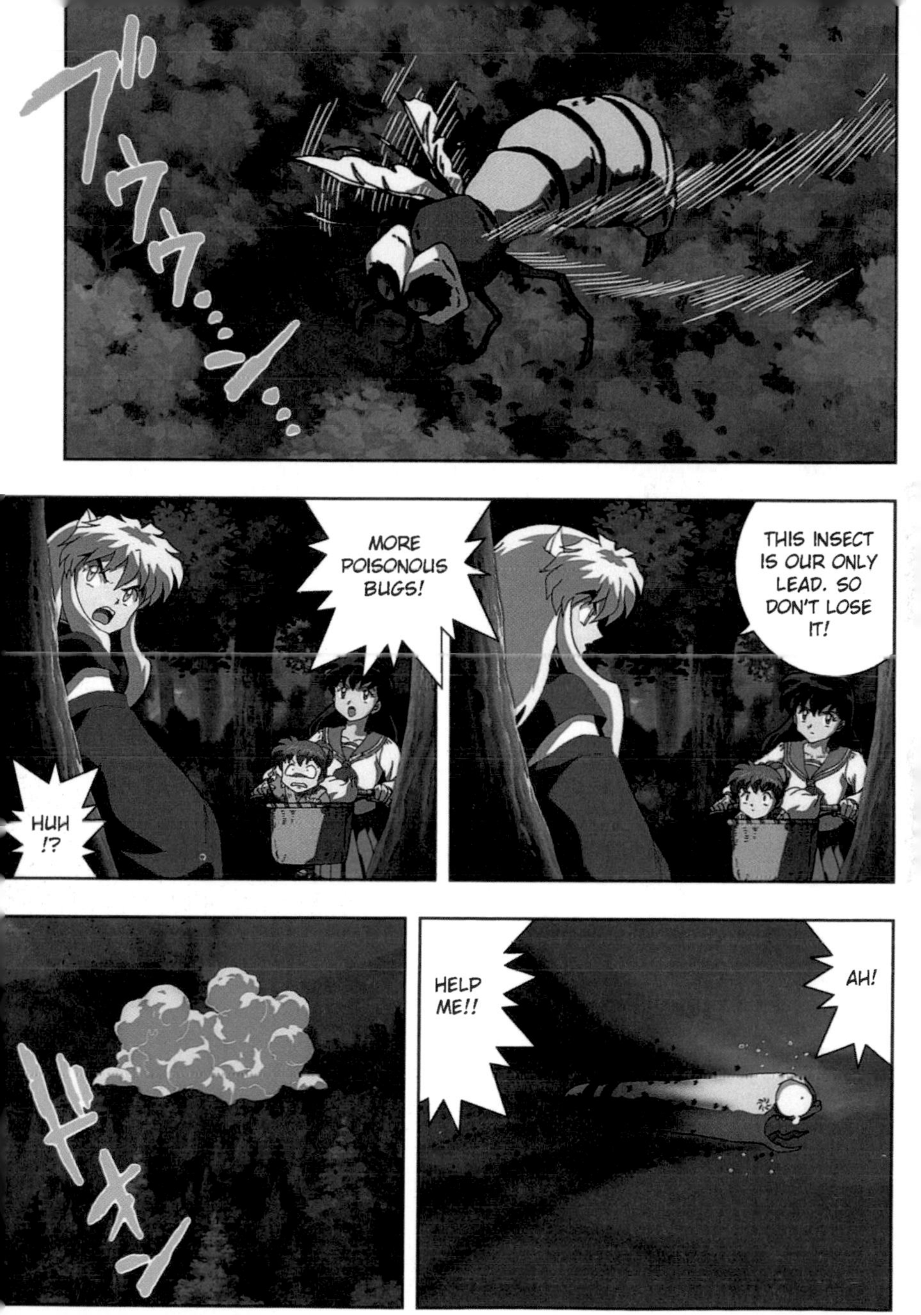
ブウウ…ン…
THIS INSECT IS OUR ONLY LEAD. SO DON'T LOSE IT!
MORE POISONOUS BUGS!
HUH !?
AH!
HELP ME!!
ドォン

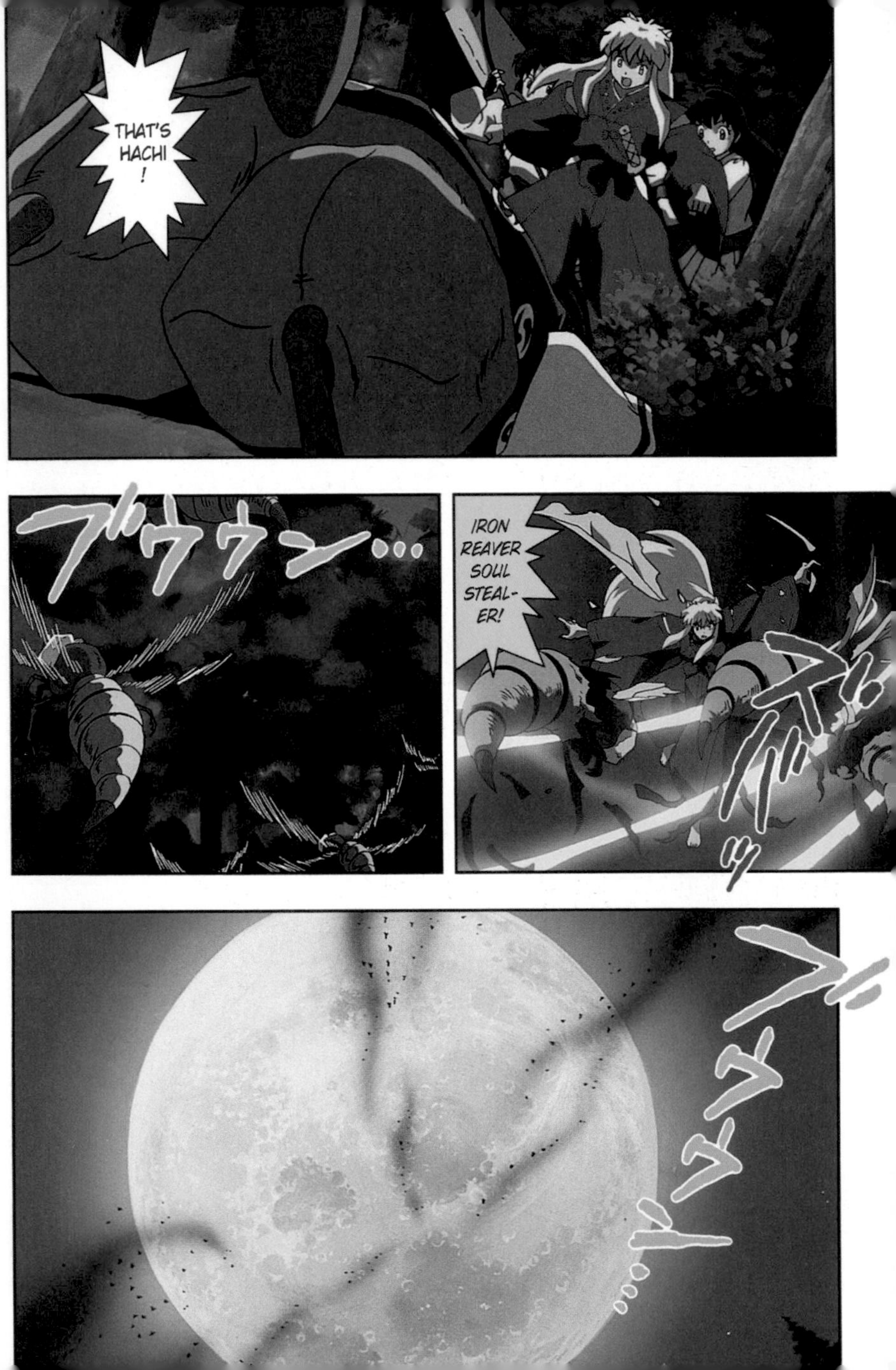
THAT'S HACHI!
IRON REAVER SOUL STEALER!
ブウウン…
ブウウン…

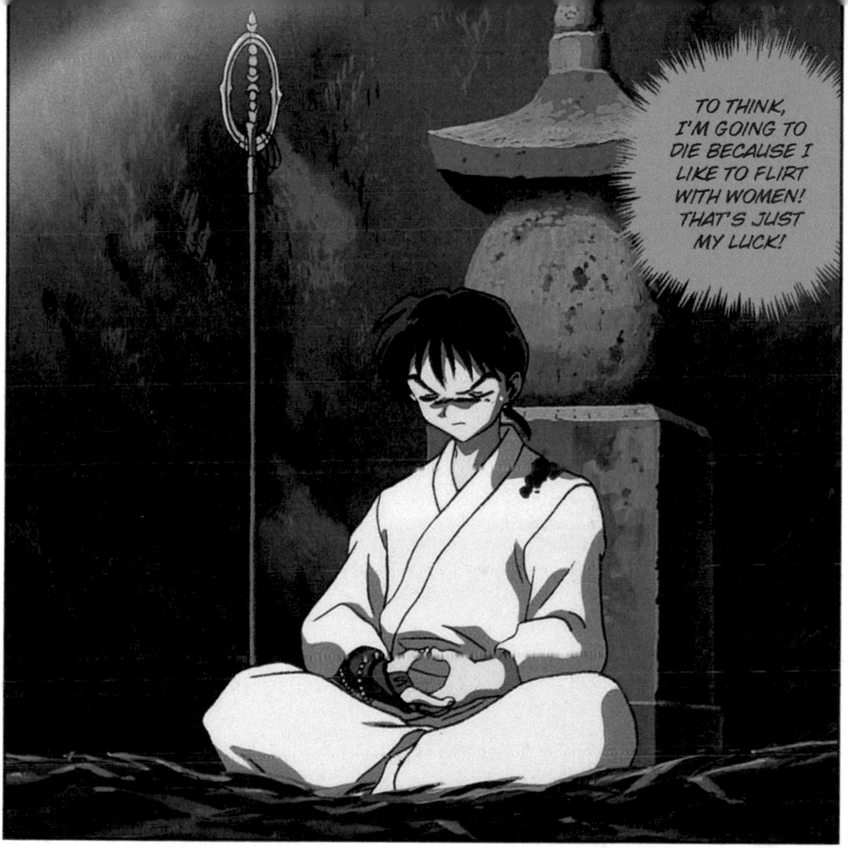
TO THINK, I'M GOING TO DIE BECAUSE I LIKE TO FLIRT WITH WOMEN! THAT'S JUST MY LUCK!

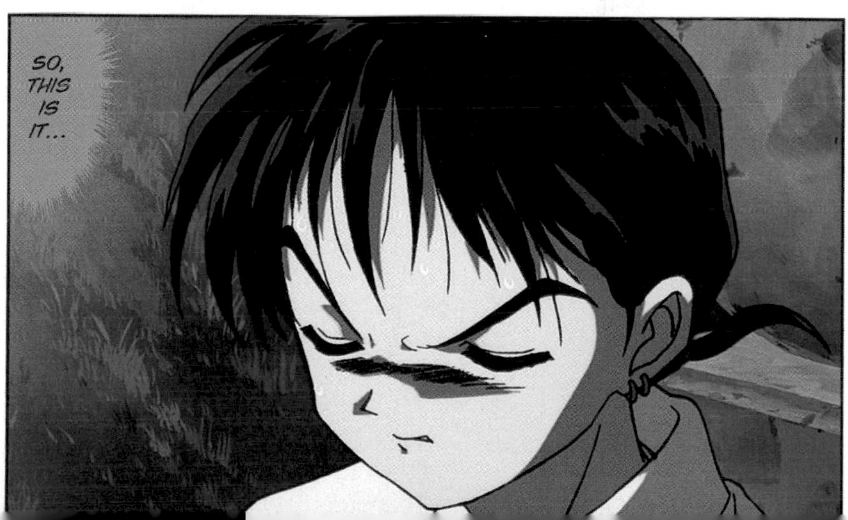
SO, THIS IS IT...

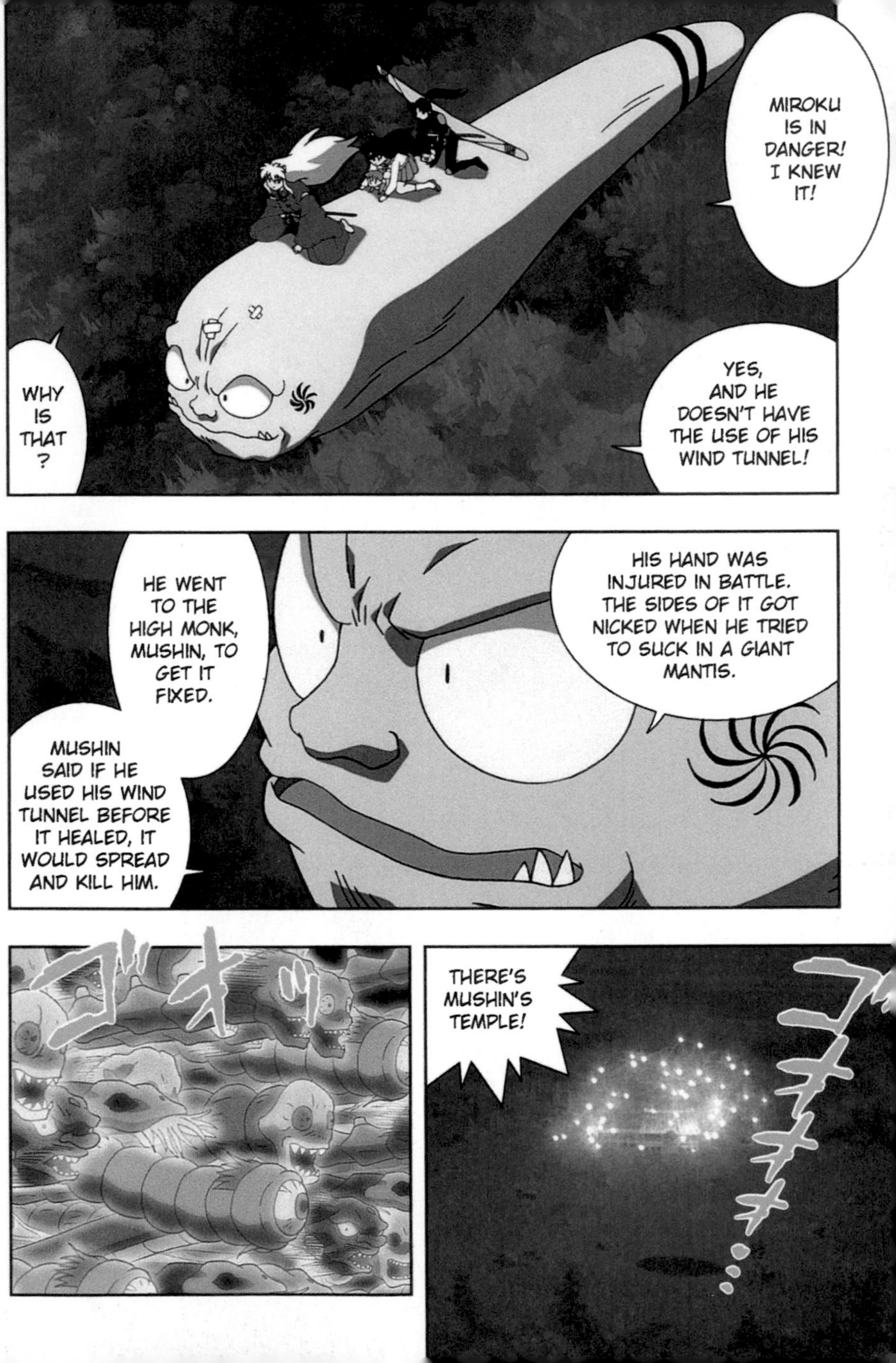
MIROKU IS IN DANGER! I KNEW IT!
YES, AND HE DOESN'T HAVE THE USE OF HIS WIND TUNNEL!
WHY IS THAT?
HIS HAND WAS INJURED IN BATTLE. THE SIDES OF IT GOT NICKED WHEN HE TRIED TO SUCK IN A GIANT MANTIS.
HE WENT TO THE HIGH MONK, MUSHIN, TO GET IT FIXED.
MUSHIN SAID IF HE USED HIS WIND TUNNEL BEFORE IT HEALED, IT WOULD SPREAD AND KILL HIM.
THERE'S MUSHIN'S TEMPLE!
ゴオッ

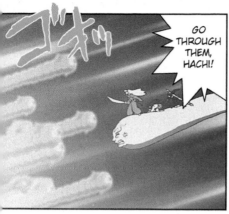

AH!
GO THROUGH THEM, HACHI!
HYAH!
YAH!
GET OUTTA THE WAY!
I AIN'T GONNA WASTE MY TIME!

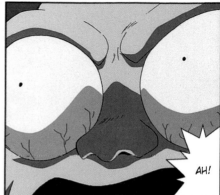

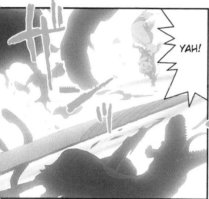

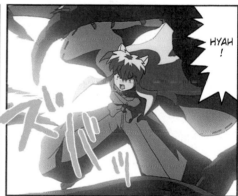

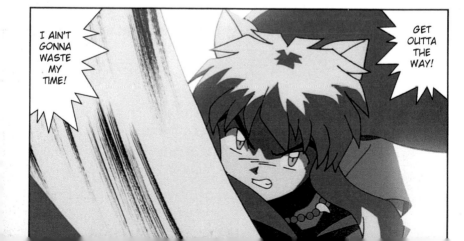

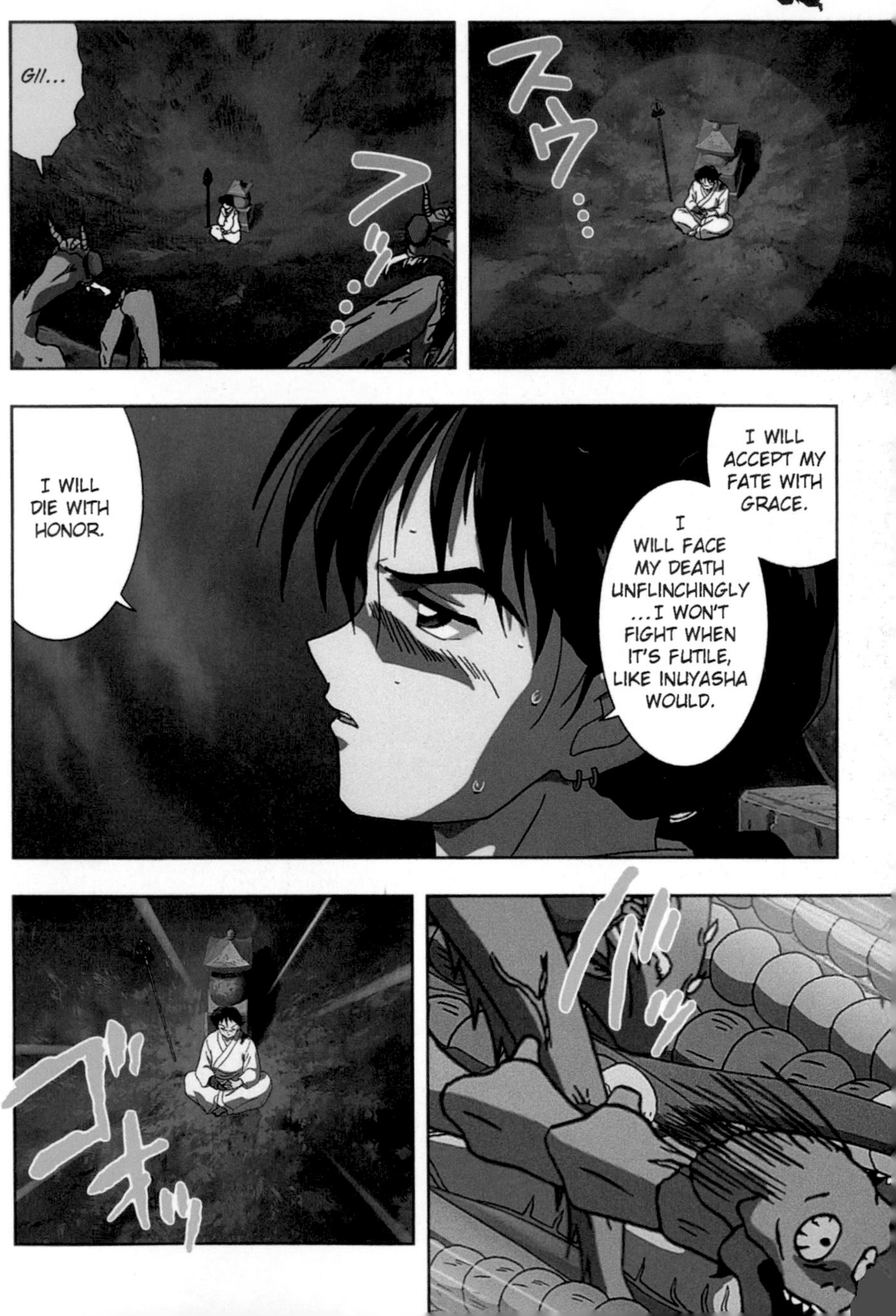

スゥ…
GII...
フッ…
I WILL ACCEPT MY FATE WITH GRACE.
I WILL FACE MY DEATH UNFLINCHINGLY ...I WON'T FIGHT WHEN IT'S FUTILE, LIKE INUYASHA WOULD.
I WILL DIE WITH HONOR.
ゴオッ

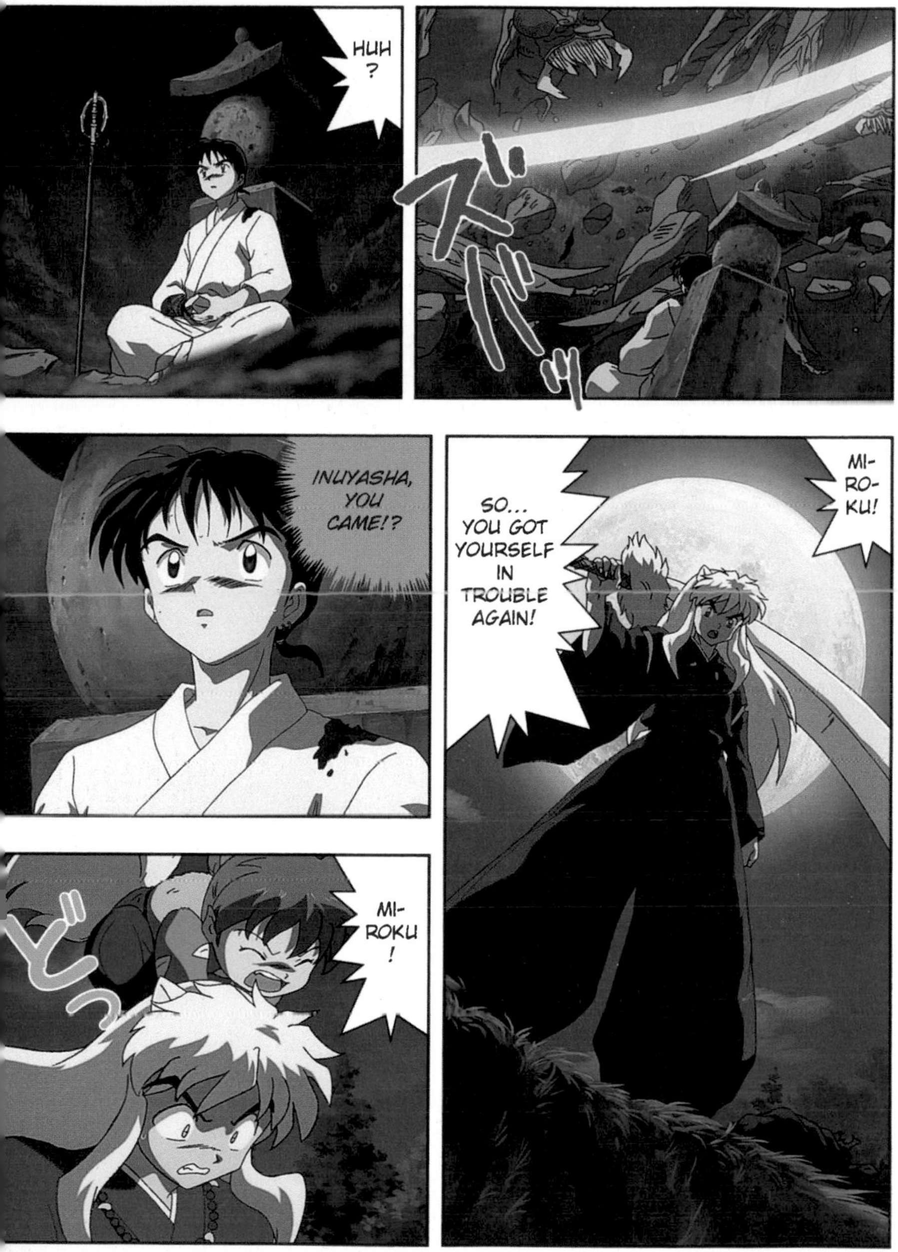
ズバッ
HUH?
MI-RO-KU!
SO... YOU GOT YOURSELF IN TROUBLE AGAIN!
INUYASHA, YOU CAME!?
MI-ROKU!
どっ

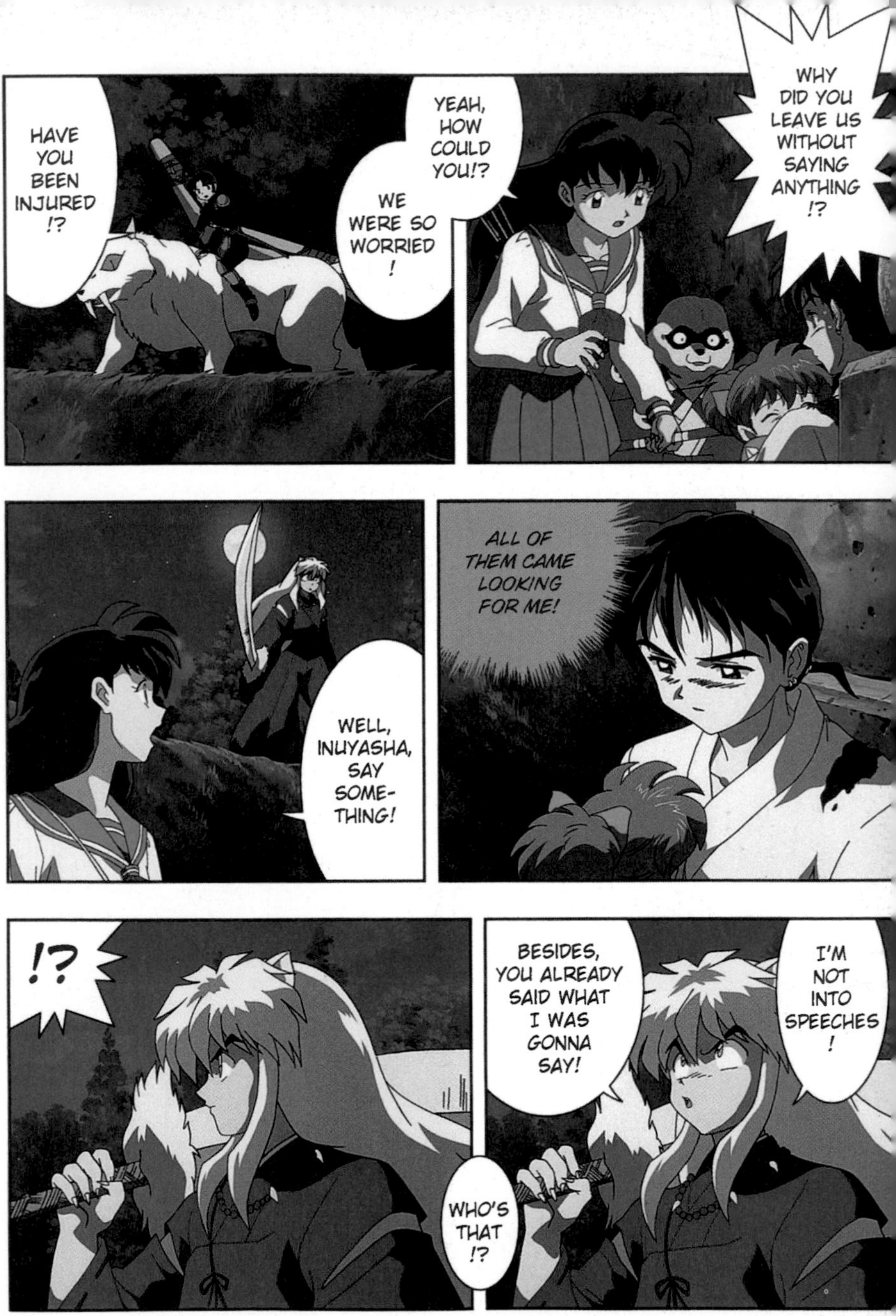
WHY DID YOU LEAVE US WITHOUT SAYING ANYTHING!?
YEAH, HOW COULD YOU!?
WE WERE SO WORRIED!
HAVE YOU BEEN INJURED!?
ALL OF THEM CAME LOOKING FOR ME!
WELL, INUYASHA, SAY SOME-THING!
I'M NOT INTO SPEECHES!
BESIDES, YOU ALREADY SAID WHAT I WAS GONNA SAY!
WHO'S THAT!?
!?

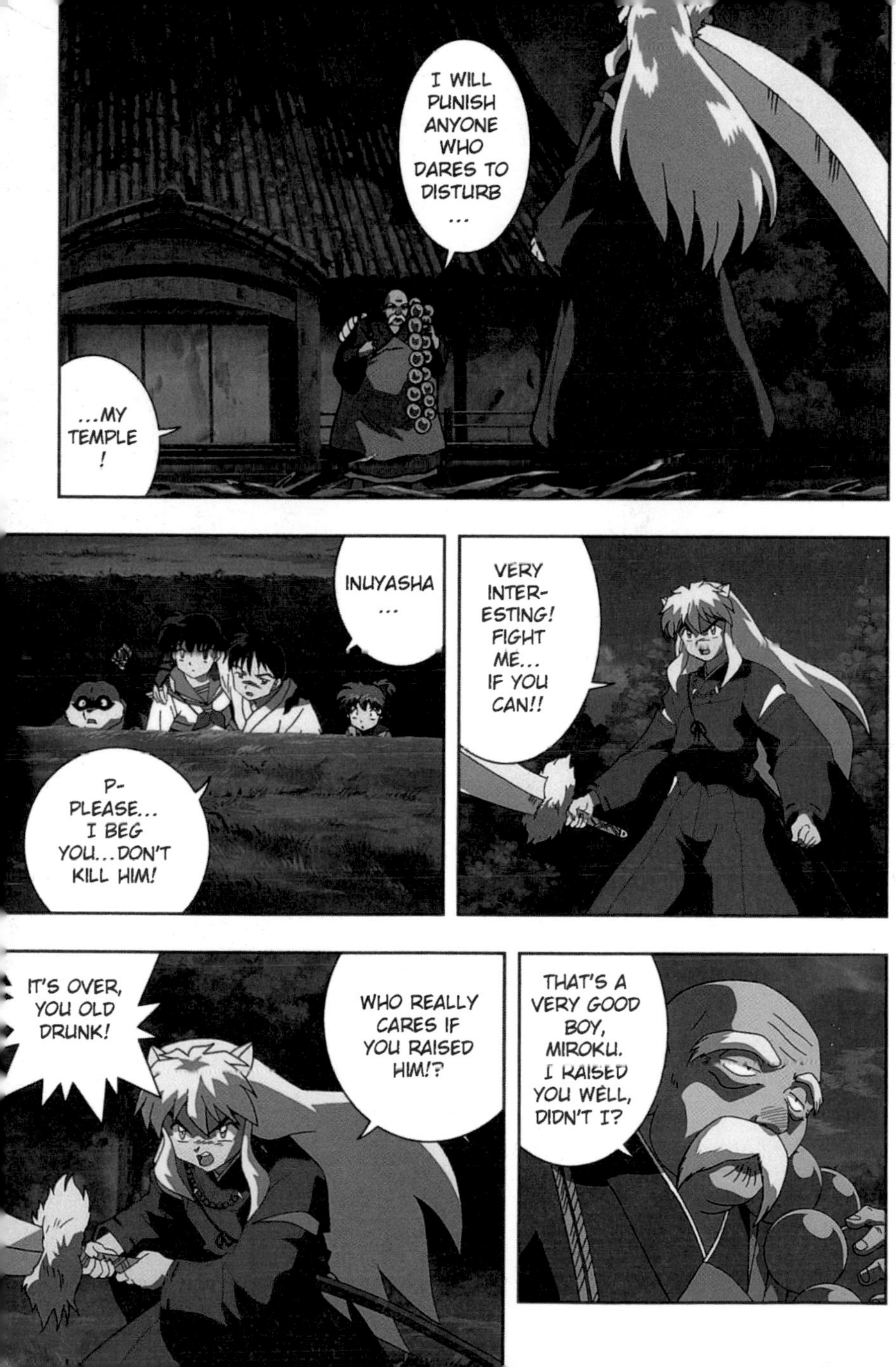
I WILL PUNISH ANYONE WHO DARES TO DISTURB ...
...MY TEMPLE!
VERY INTER-ESTING! FIGHT ME... IF YOU CAN!!
INUYASHA ...
P-PLEASE... I BEG YOU...DON'T KILL HIM!
THAT'S A VERY GOOD BOY, MIROKU. I RAISED YOU WELL, DIDN'T I?
WHO REALLY CARES IF YOU RAISED HIM!?
IT'S OVER, YOU OLD DRUNK!

!?

HMPH
!!

THE TETSUSAIGA'S BEEN TRANS-FORMED BACK!

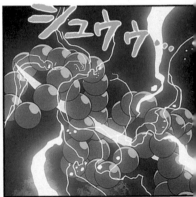

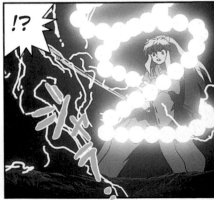

!?

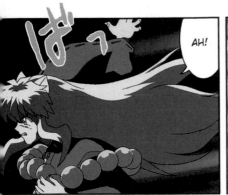

ゴオッ
ばっ
AH!
ズバッ
IRON REAVER SOUL STEALER!
MY, MY! AREN'T WE LIVELY!
カァァ…
WHAT'S GOING ON!?
バチッ

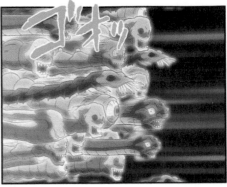

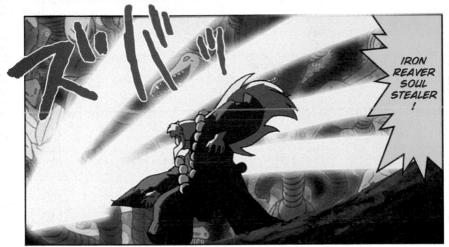

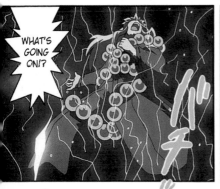

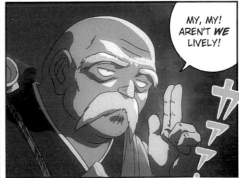

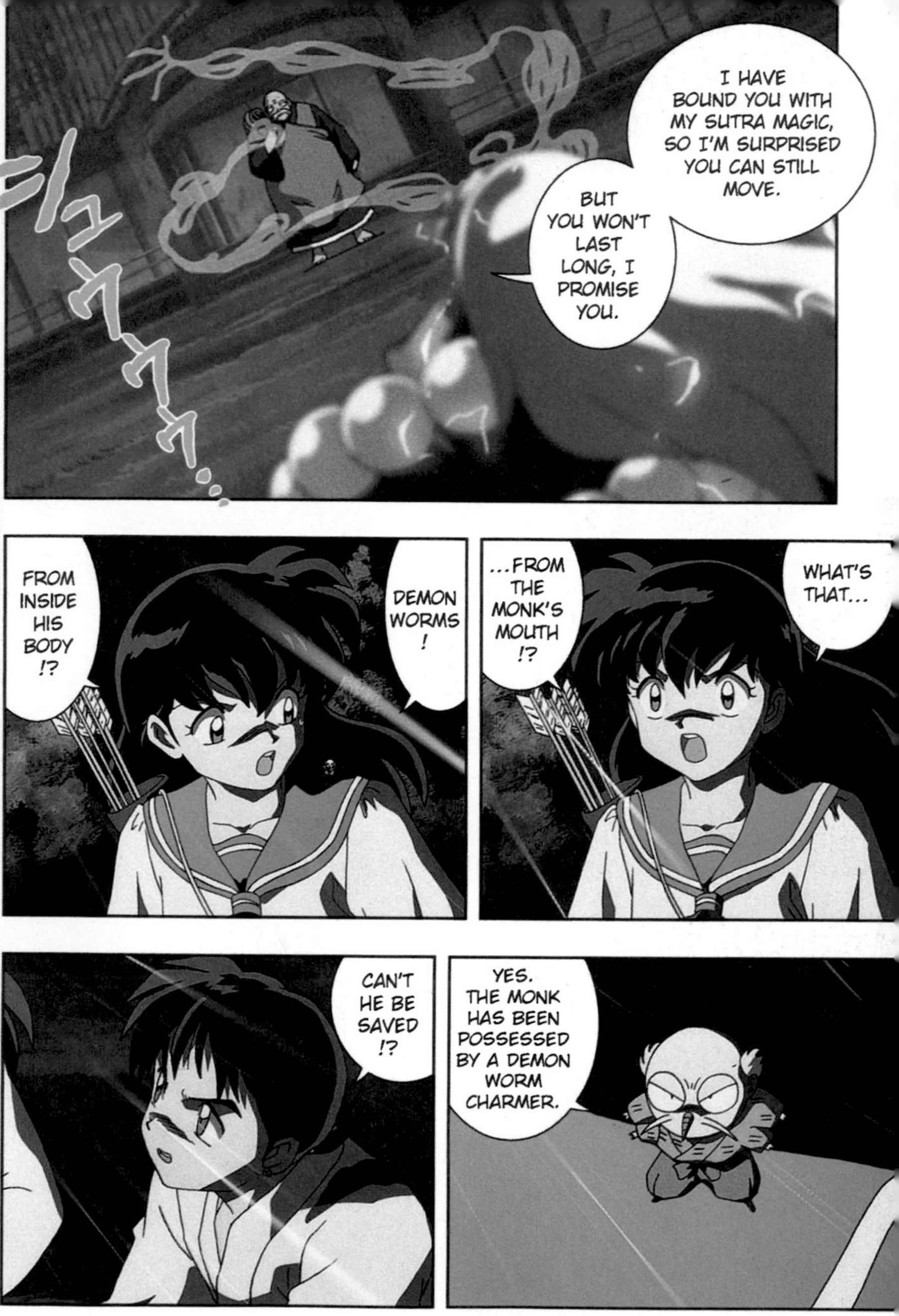
I HAVE BOUND YOU WITH MY SUTRA MAGIC, SO I'M SURPRISED YOU CAN STILL MOVE.
BUT YOU WON'T LAST LONG, I PROMISE YOU.
WHAT'S THAT...
...FROM THE MONK'S MOUTH !?
DEMON WORMS !
FROM INSIDE HIS BODY !?
YES. THE MONK HAS BEEN POSSESSED BY A DEMON WORM CHARMER.
CAN'T HE BE SAVED !?

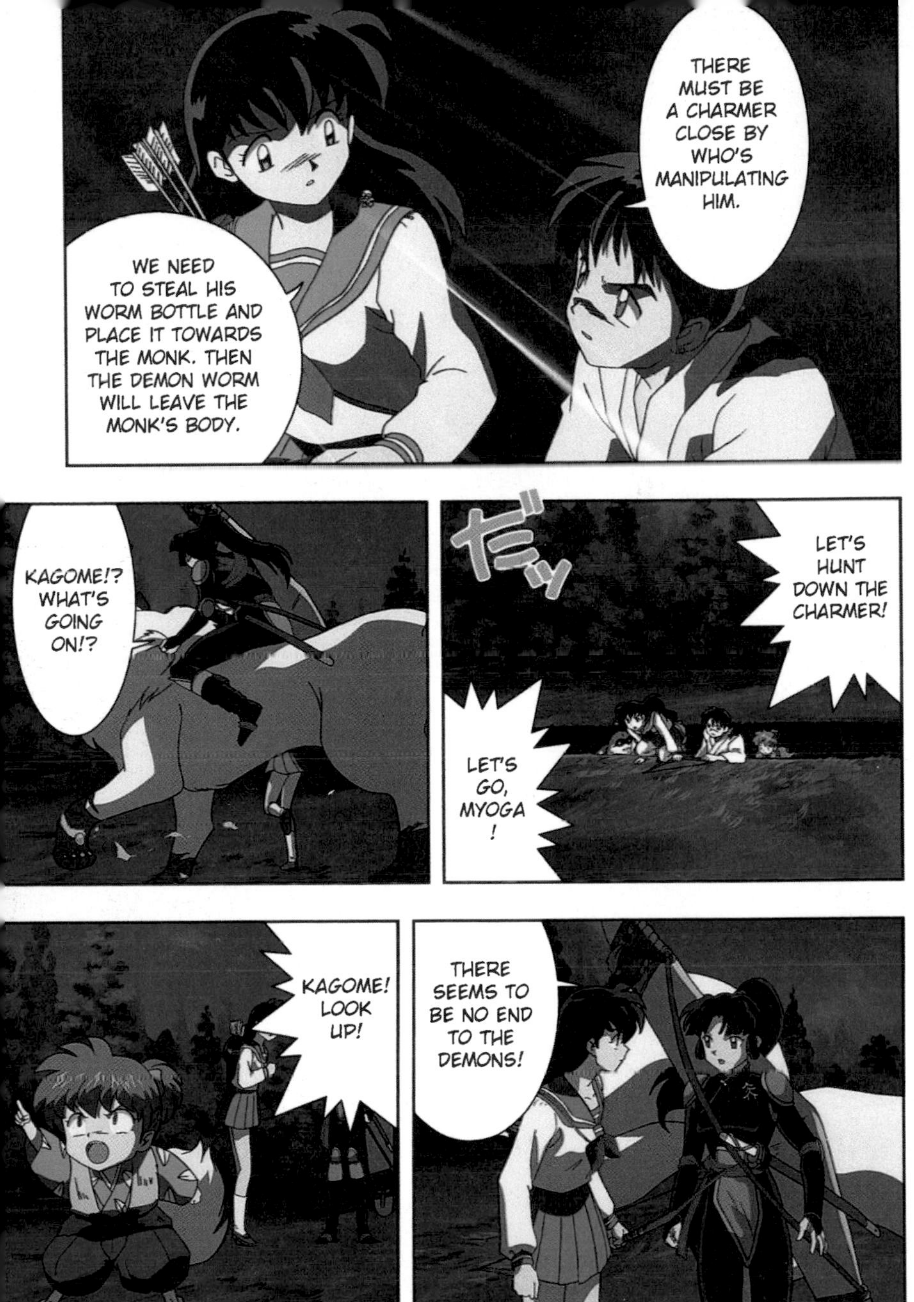
THERE MUST BE A CHARMER CLOSE BY WHO'S MANIPULATING HIM.
WE NEED TO STEAL HIS WORM BOTTLE AND PLACE IT TOWARDS THE MONK. THEN THE DEMON WORM WILL LEAVE THE MONK'S BODY.
ダッ
LET'S HUNT DOWN THE CHARMER!
LET'S GO, MYOGA!
KAGOME!? WHAT'S GOING ON!?
THERE SEEMS TO BE NO END TO THE DEMONS!
KAGOME! LOOK UP!

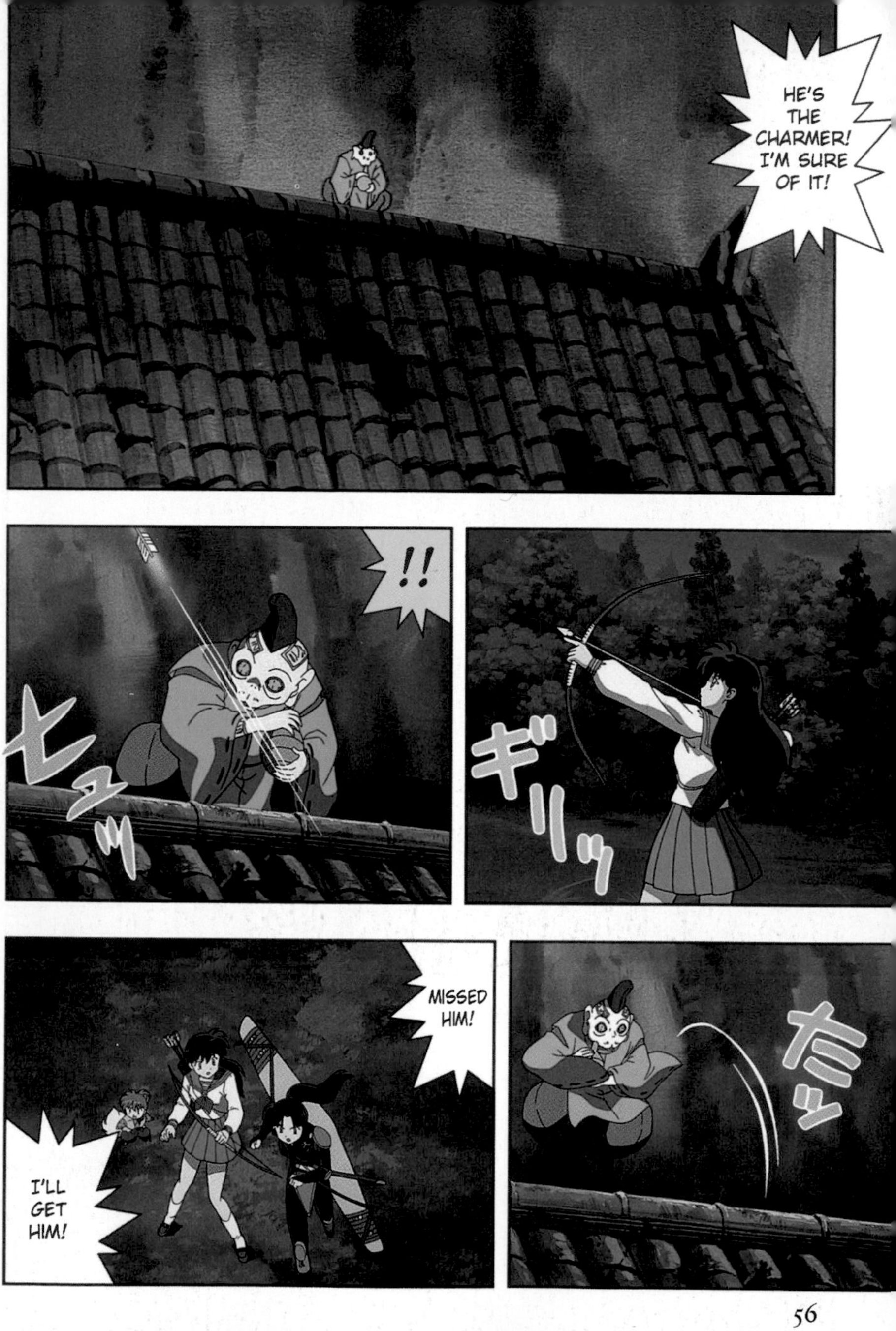
HE'S THE CHARMER! I'M SURE OF IT!
ギリッ
!!
ヒュッ
たッ
MISSED HIM!
I'LL GET HIM!

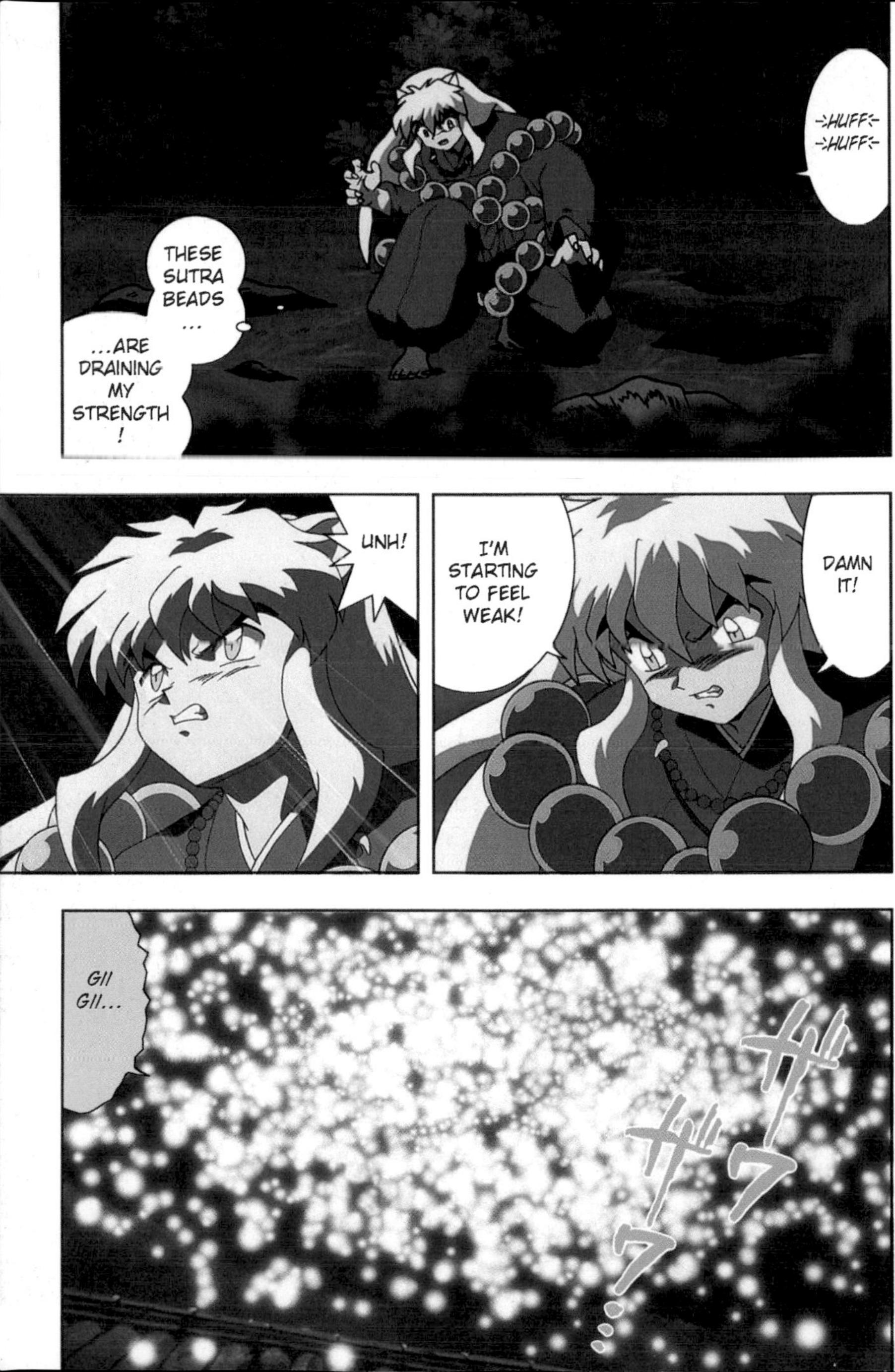

HUFF HUFF
THESE SUTRA BEADS...
...ARE DRAINING MY STRENGTH!
DAMN IT!
I'M STARTING TO FEEL WEAK!
UNH!
ザワ
ザワ
GII GII...

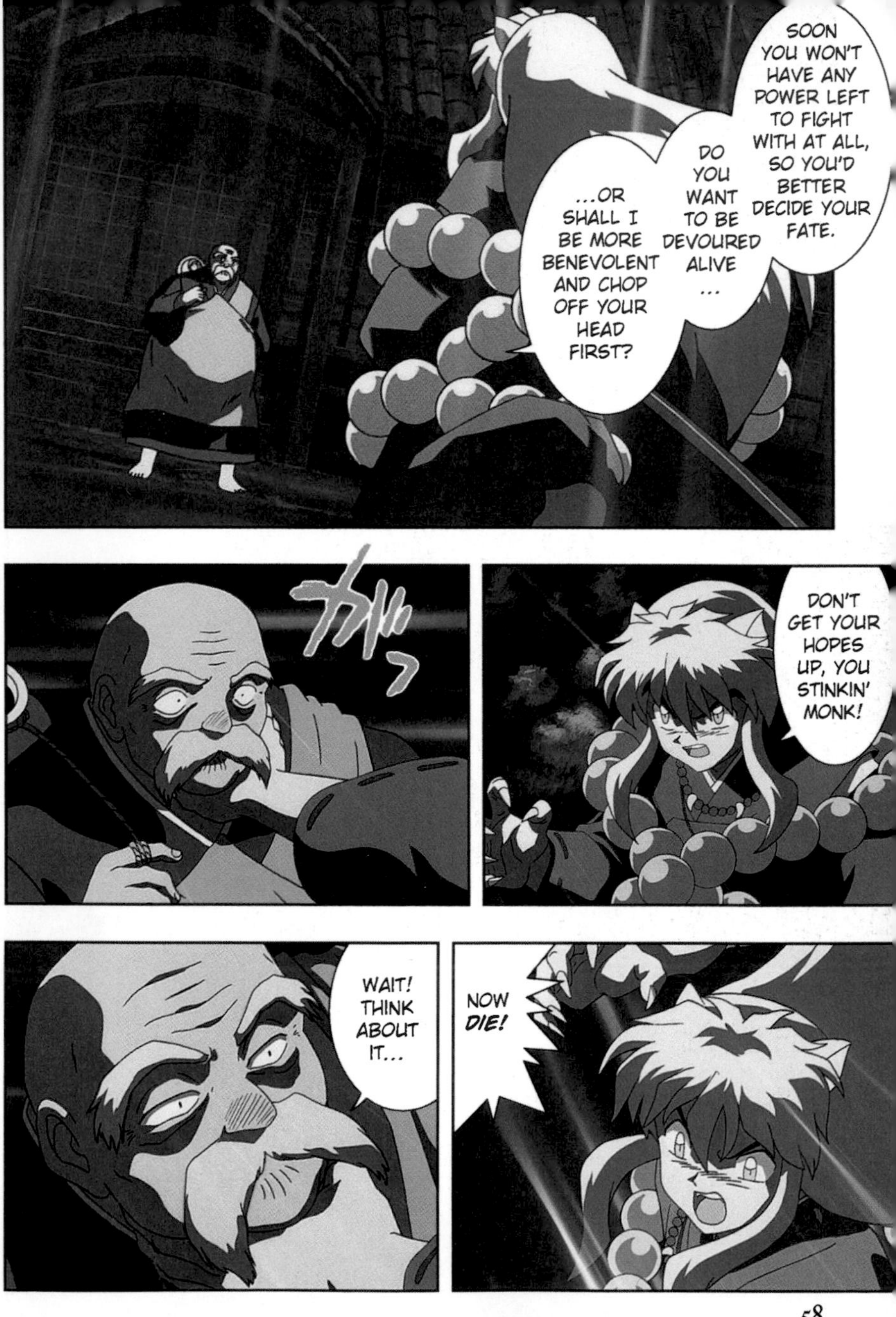
SOON YOU WON'T HAVE ANY POWER LEFT TO FIGHT WITH AT ALL, SO YOU'D BETTER DECIDE YOUR FATE.
DO YOU WANT TO BE DEVOURED ALIVE ...
...OR SHALL I BE MORE BENEVOLENT AND CHOP OFF YOUR HEAD FIRST?
DON'T GET YOUR HOPES UP, YOU STINKIN' MONK!
NOW *DIE!*
WAIT! THINK ABOUT IT...

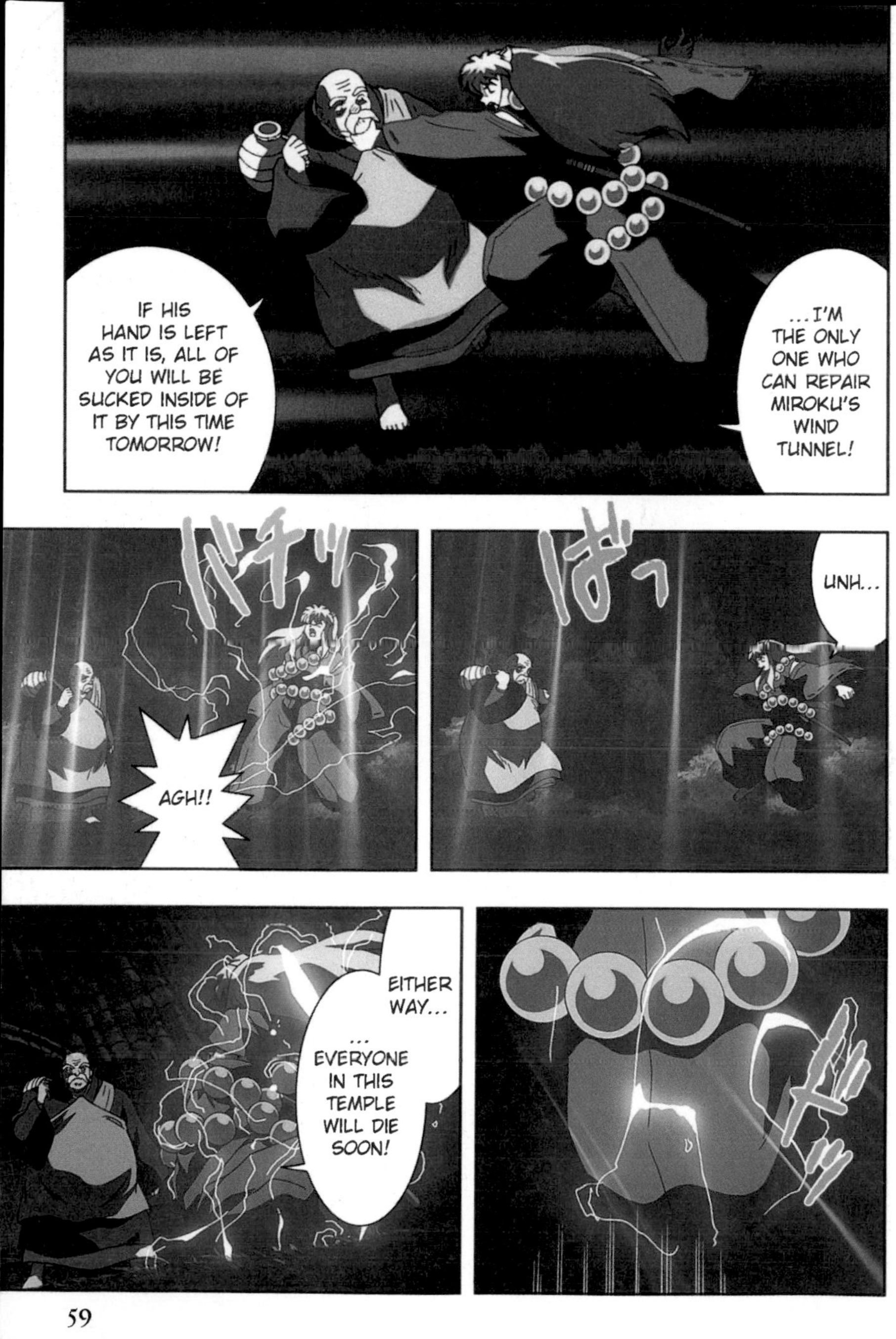
...I'M THE ONLY ONE WHO CAN REPAIR MIROKU'S WIND TUNNEL!
IF HIS HAND IS LEFT AS IT IS, ALL OF YOU WILL BE SUCKED INSIDE OF IT BY THIS TIME TOMORROW!
ぼっ
UNH...
バチッ
AGH!!
EITHER WAY...
...EVERYONE IN THIS TEMPLE WILL DIE SOON!

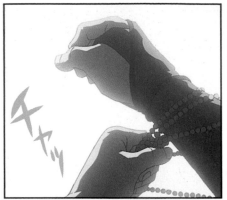

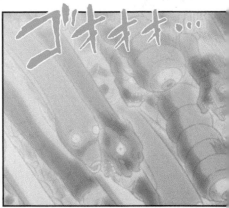

ゴオオオ…
チャッ
MASTER! THE POISON WORE OFF! YOU CAN MOVE!
EH!? THE WIND TUNNEL !?
HACHI, PREPARE YOURSELF.
WE'LL BOTH PROBABLY GET SUCKED IN THIS TIME.
ゴオオオ…
BUT IT'S BETTER THAN BEING TORN LIMB FROM LIMB AND EATEN BY A PACK OF DEMONS!

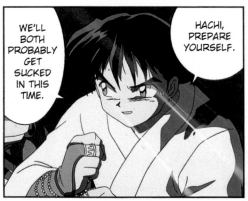

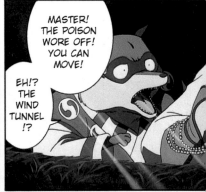

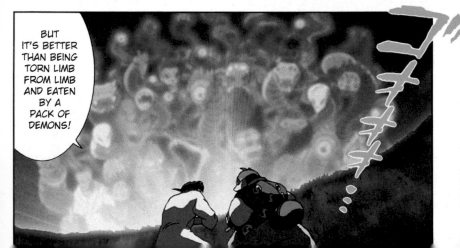

READY!?

I AGREE! I'M WITH YOU!

YES, MASTER!

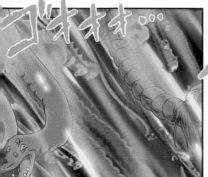

WIND TUNNEL!

HACHI, BRACE ME!

YES, SIR!

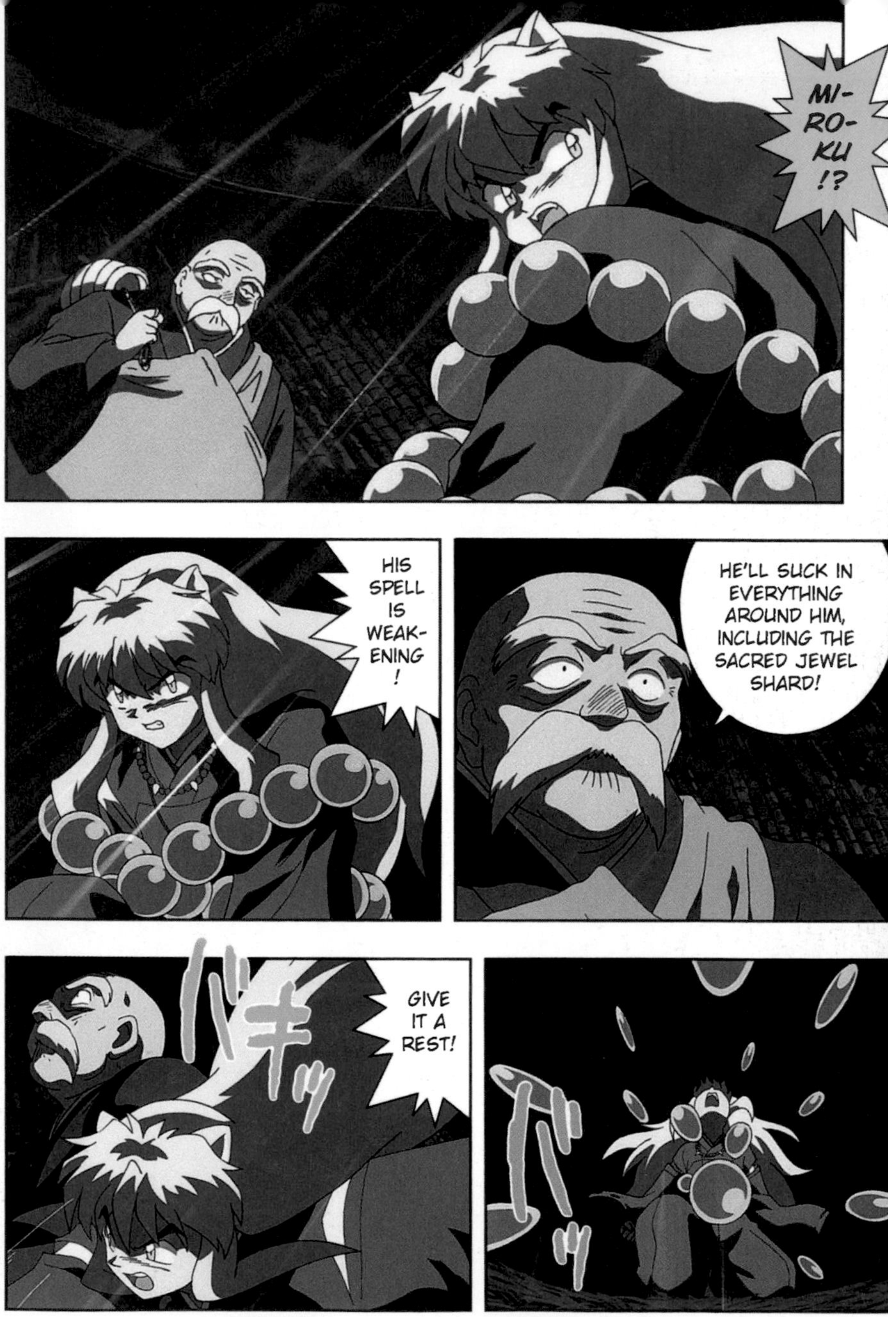
MI-RO-KU!?
HE'LL SUCK IN EVERYTHING AROUND HIM, INCLUDING THE SACRED JEWEL SHARD!
HIS SPELL IS WEAKENING!
バッ
GIVE IT A REST!
バキッ

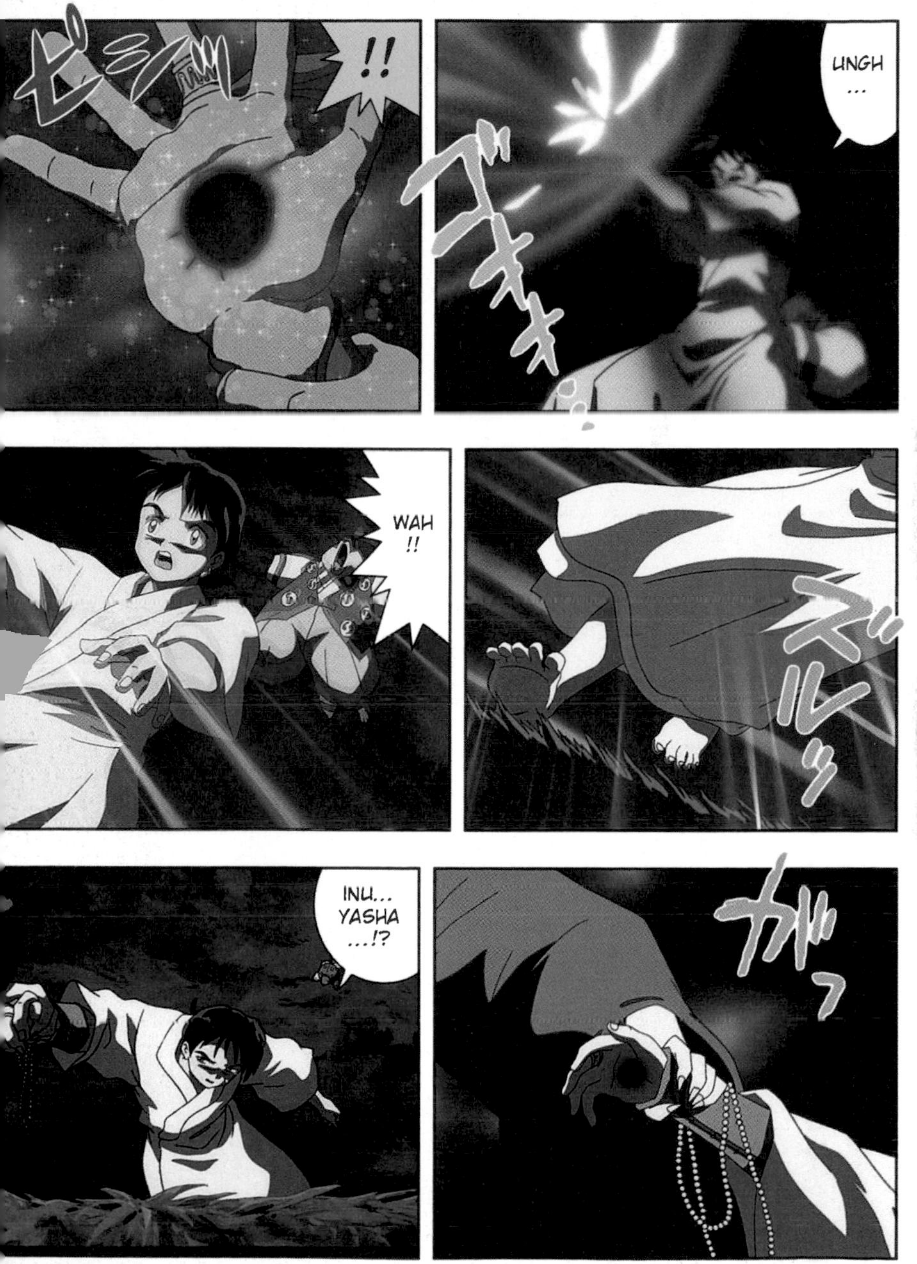
UNGH ...
!!
WAH !!
INU... YASHA ...!?

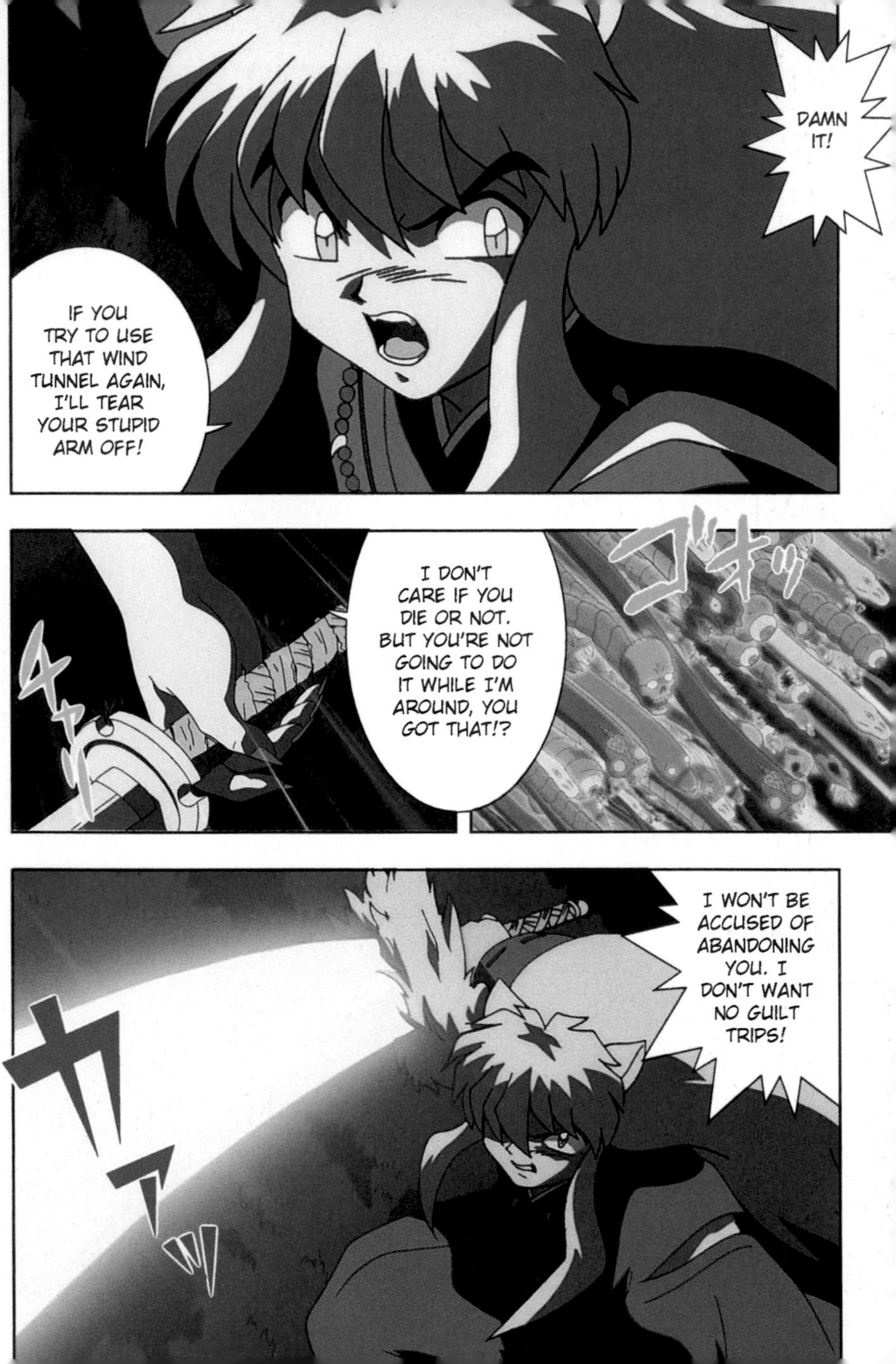
DAMN IT!
IF YOU TRY TO USE THAT WIND TUNNEL AGAIN, I'LL TEAR YOUR STUPID ARM OFF!
ゴオッ
I DON'T CARE IF YOU DIE OR NOT. BUT YOU'RE NOT GOING TO DO IT WHILE I'M AROUND, YOU GOT THAT!?
I WON'T BE ACCUSED OF ABANDONING YOU. I DON'T WANT NO GUILT TRIPS!

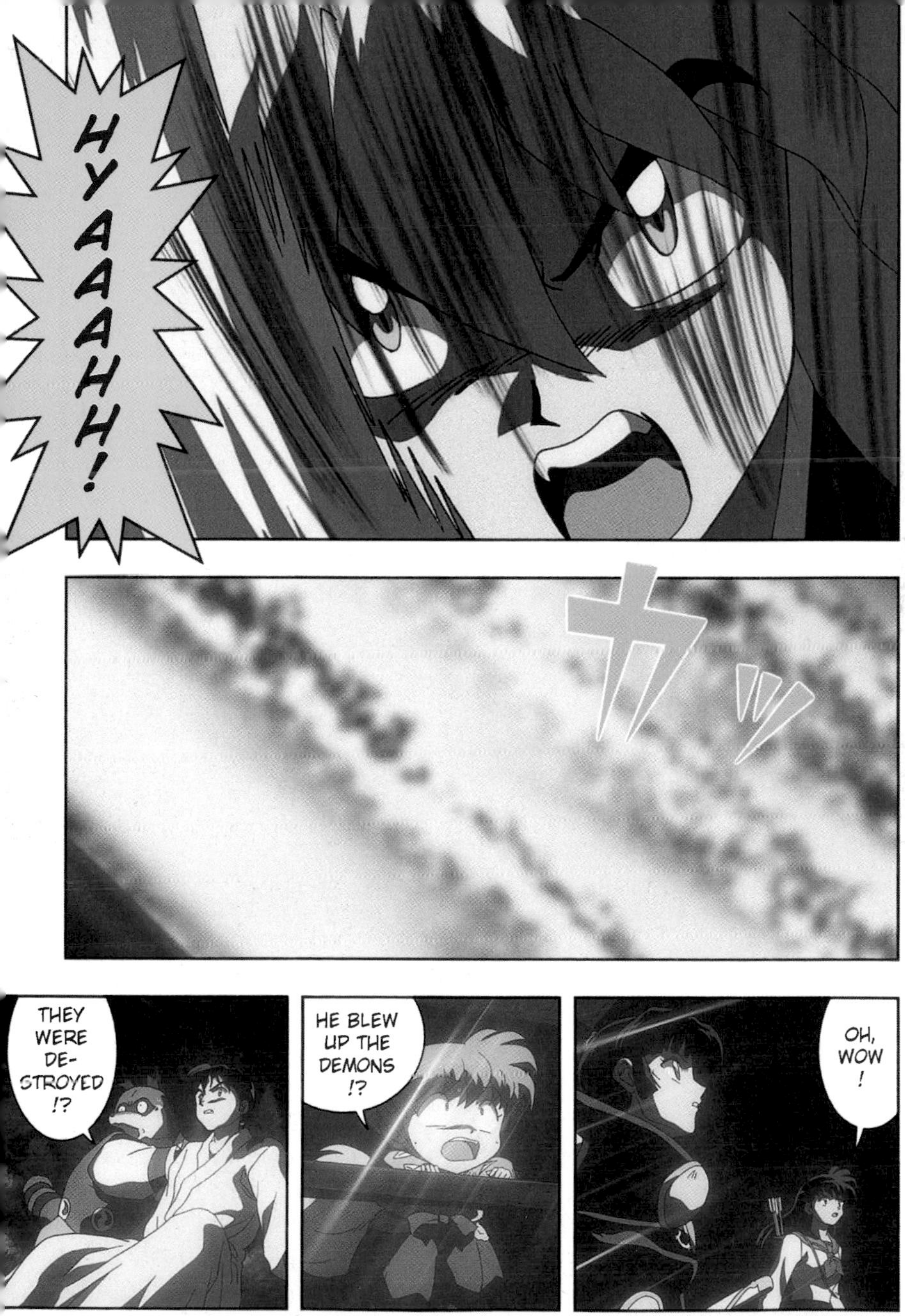
HYAAAHH!
カッ
OH, WOW!
HE BLEW UP THE DEMONS!?
THEY WERE DE-STROYED!?

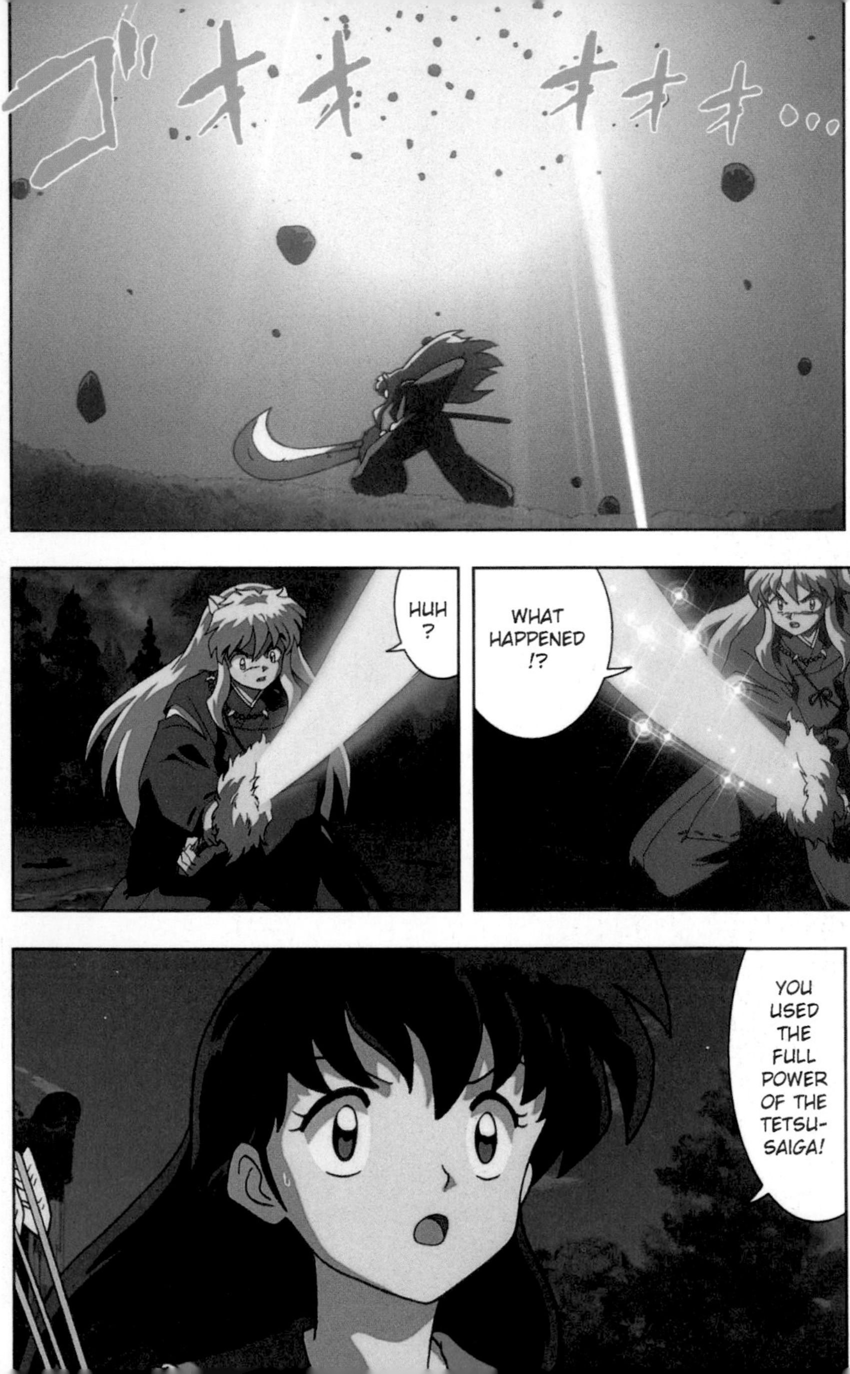
ゴオオ オオオ...
WHAT HAPPENED !?
HUH ?
YOU USED THE FULL POWER OF THE TETSU-SAIGA!

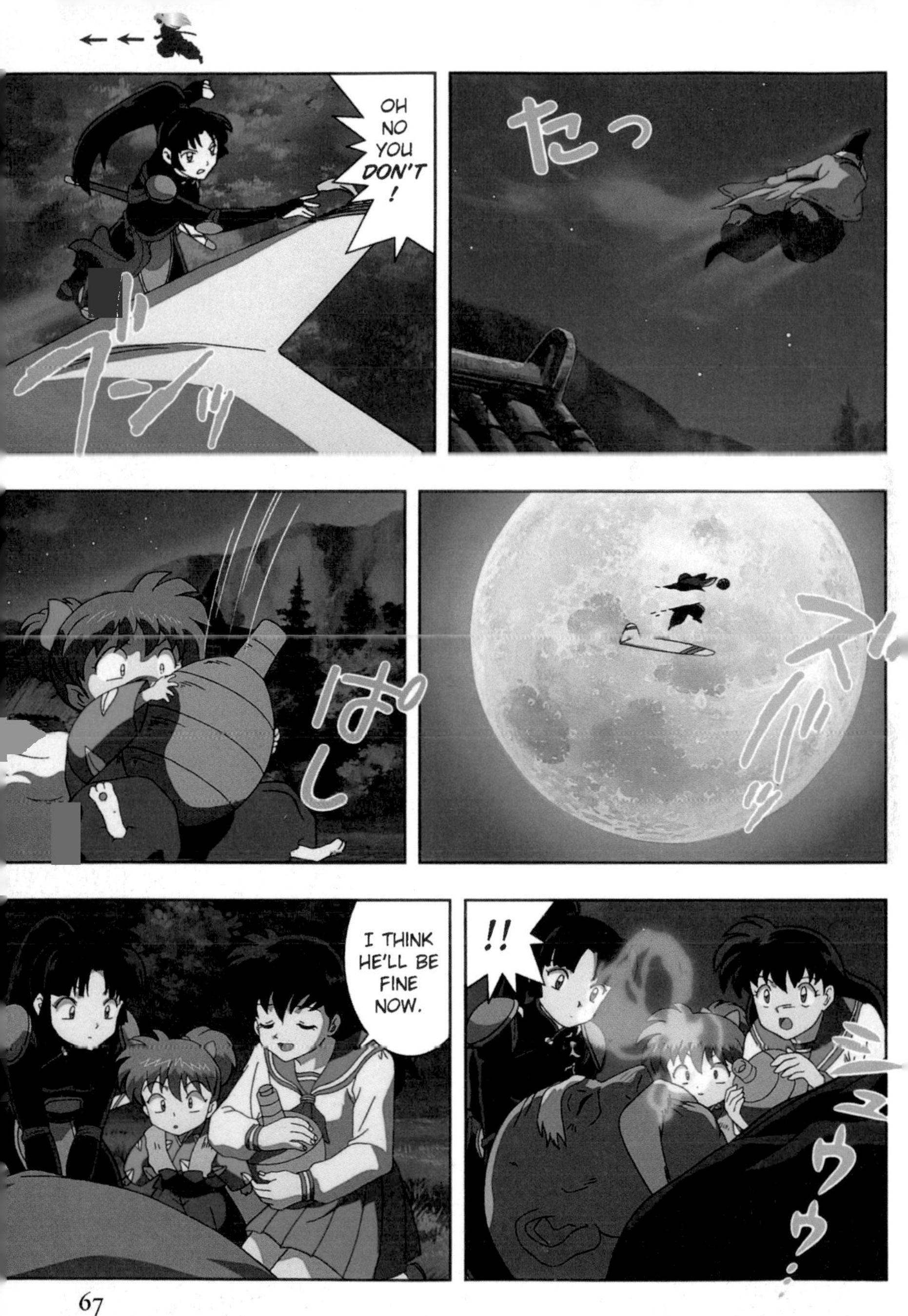
たっ
OH NO YOU DON'T!
ダンッ
ぱし
!!
I THINK HE'LL BE FINE NOW.

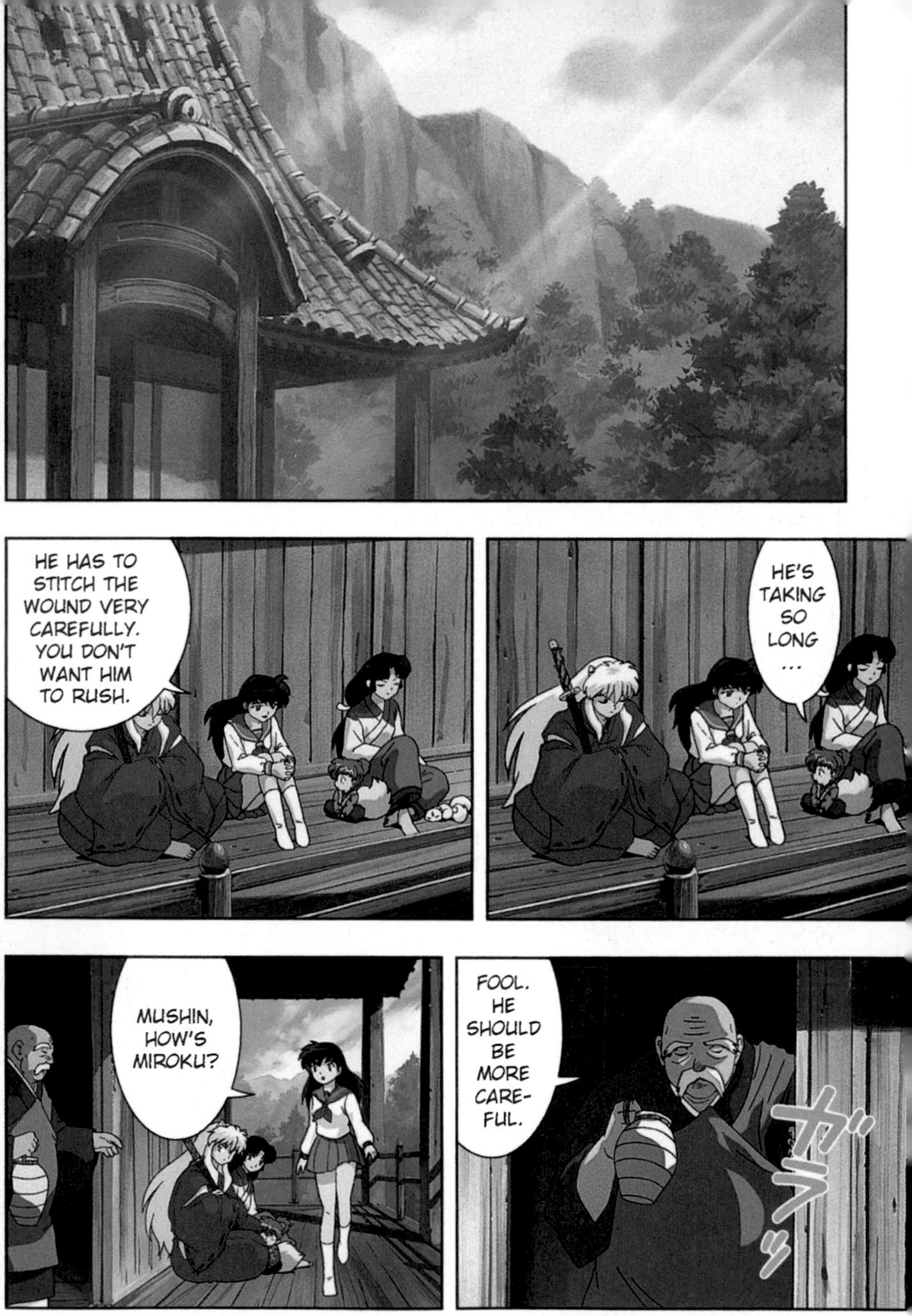
HE'S TAKING SO LONG ...
HE HAS TO STITCH THE WOUND VERY CAREFULLY. YOU DON'T WANT HIM TO RUSH.
ガラッ
FOOL. HE SHOULD BE MORE CARE-FUL.
MUSHIN, HOW'S MIROKU?

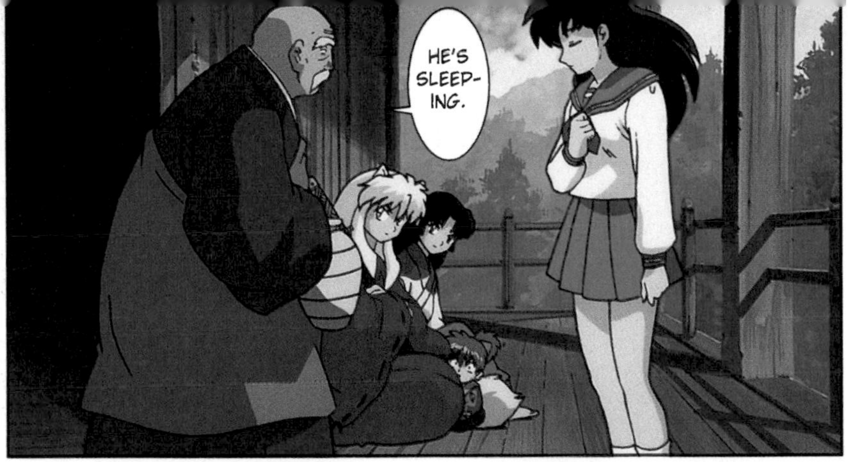
HE'S SLEEP-ING.
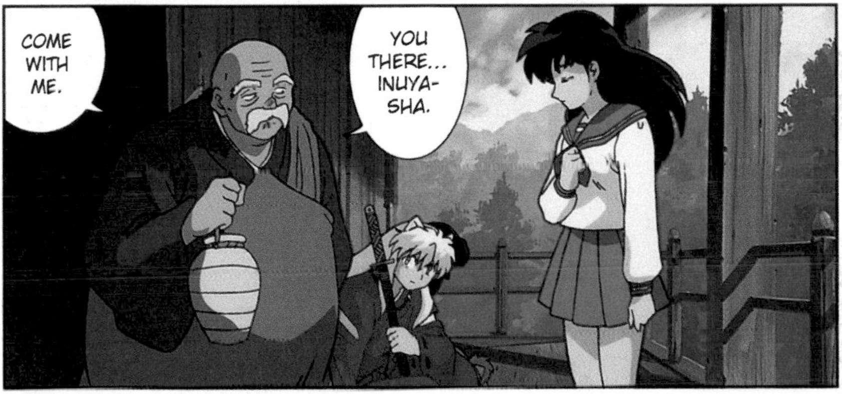
YOU THERE... INUYA-SHA.
COME WITH ME.
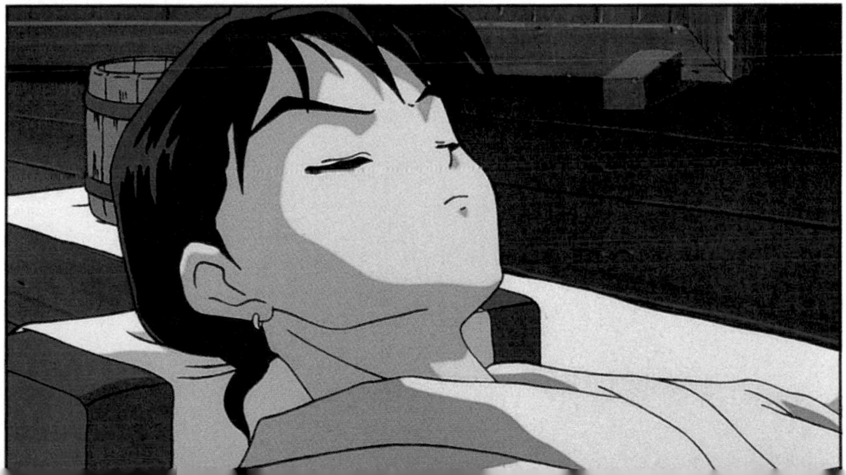

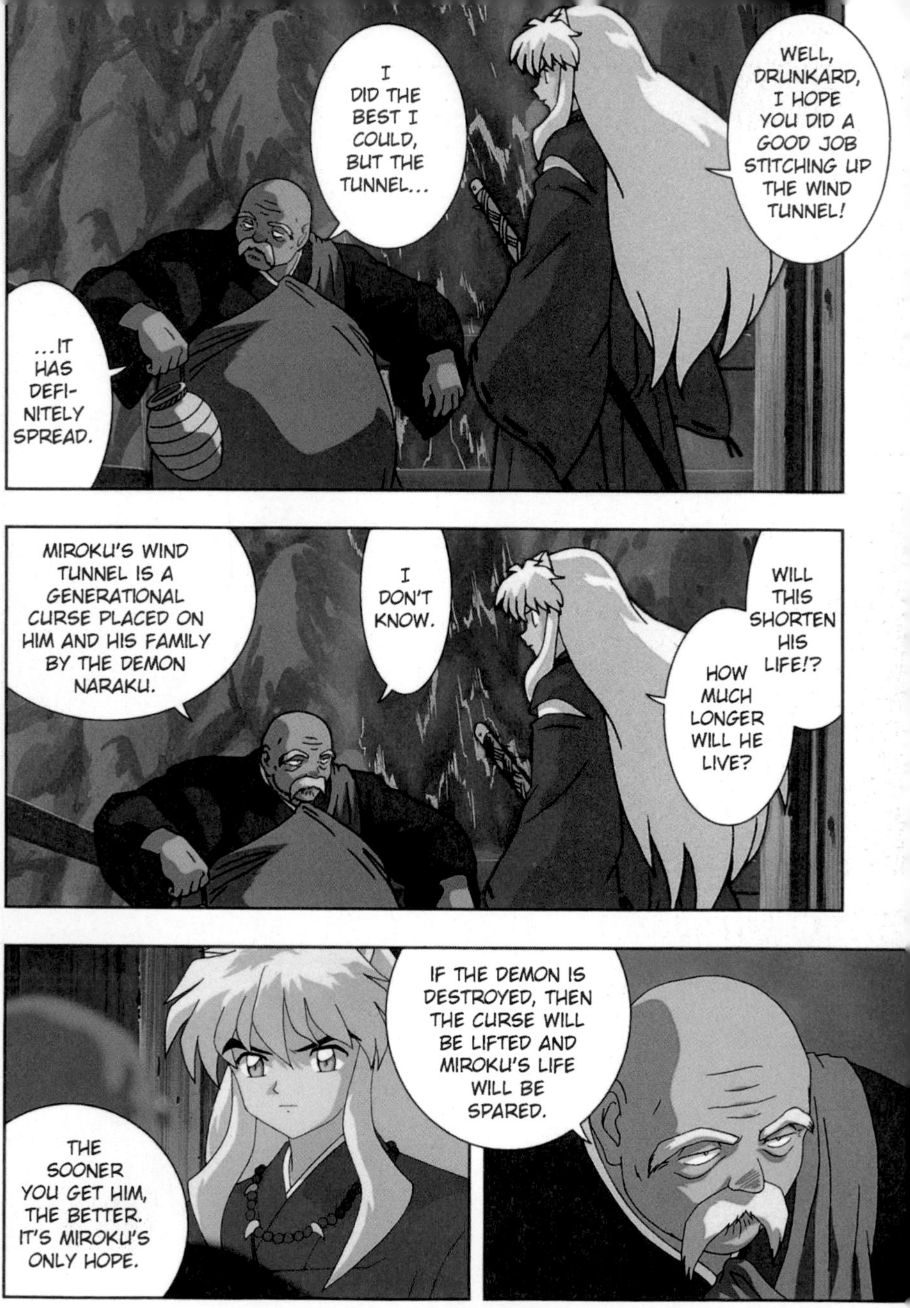
WELL, DRUNKARD, I HOPE YOU DID A GOOD JOB STITCHING UP THE WIND TUNNEL!
I DID THE BEST I COULD, BUT THE TUNNEL...
...IT HAS DEFI-NITELY SPREAD.
WILL THIS SHORTEN HIS LIFE!?
HOW MUCH LONGER WILL HE LIVE?
I DON'T KNOW.
MIROKU'S WIND TUNNEL IS A GENERATIONAL CURSE PLACED ON HIM AND HIS FAMILY BY THE DEMON NARAKU.
IF THE DEMON IS DESTROYED, THEN THE CURSE WILL BE LIFTED AND MIROKU'S LIFE WILL BE SPARED.
THE SOONER YOU GET HIM, THE BETTER. IT'S MIROKU'S ONLY HOPE.

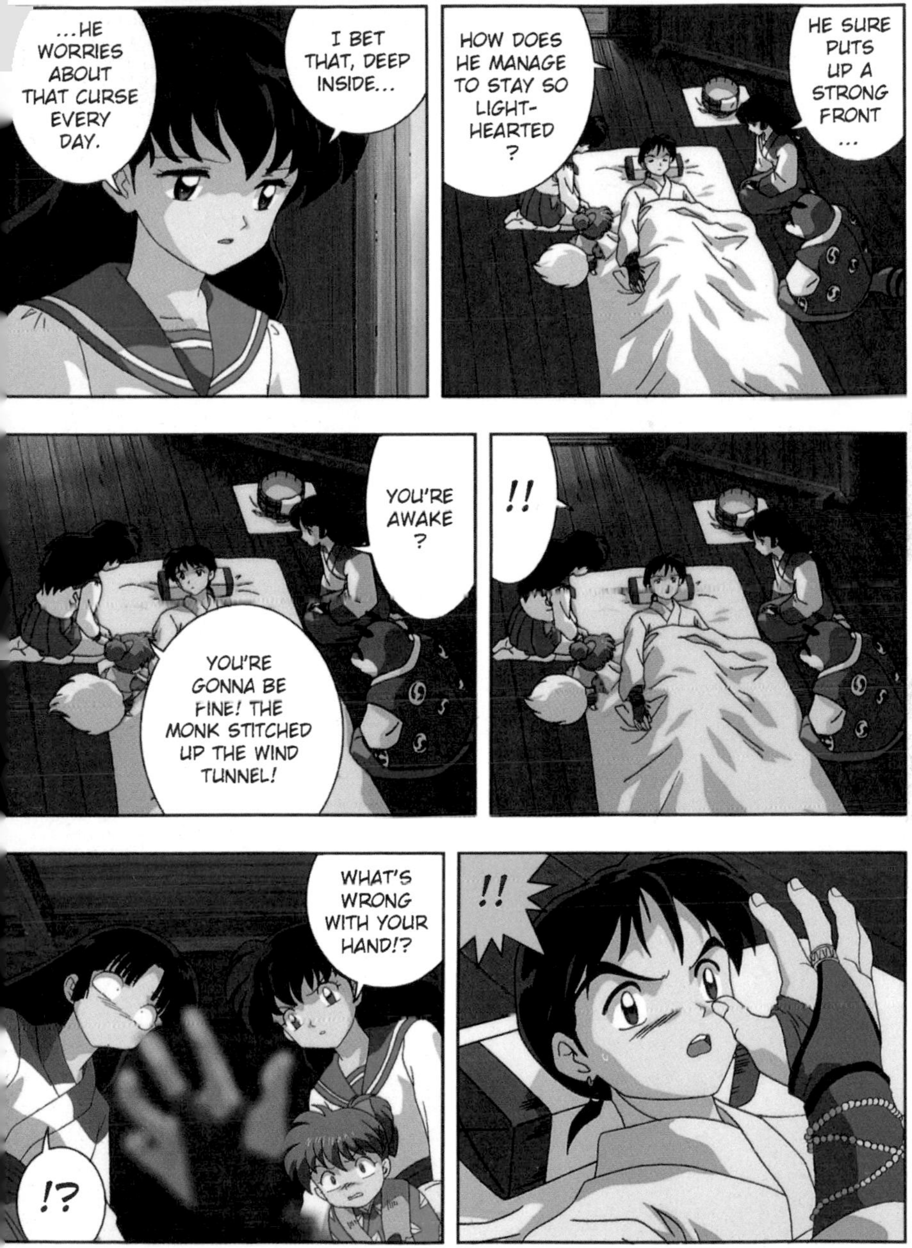
HE SURE PUTS UP A STRONG FRONT...
HOW DOES HE MANAGE TO STAY SO LIGHT-HEARTED?
I BET THAT, DEEP INSIDE...
...HE WORRIES ABOUT THAT CURSE EVERY DAY.
!!
YOU'RE AWAKE?
YOU'RE GONNA BE FINE! THE MONK STITCHED UP THE WIND TUNNEL!
!!
WHAT'S WRONG WITH YOUR HAND!?
!?

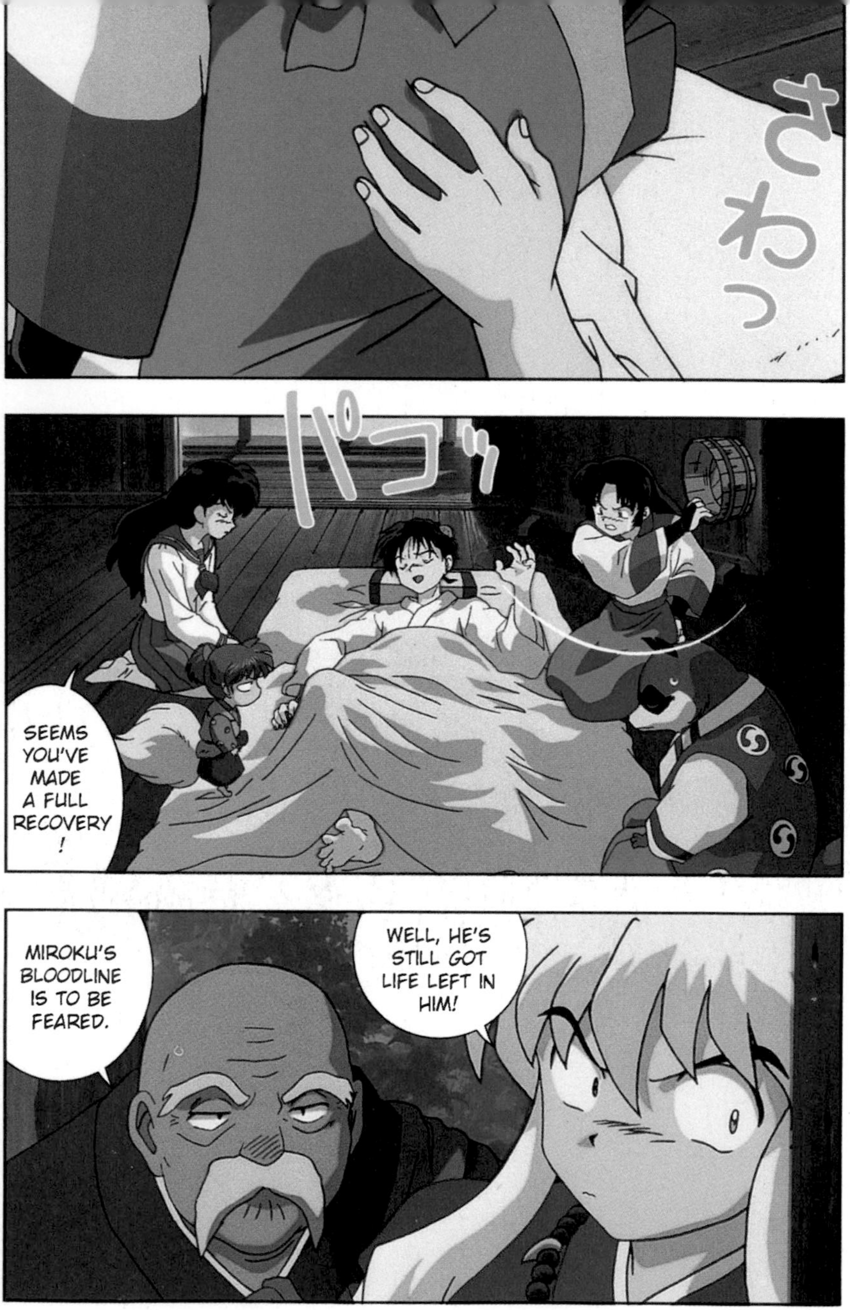
さわっ
パコッ
SEEMS YOU'VE MADE A FULL RECOVERY!
WELL, HE'S STILL GOT LIFE LEFT IN HIM!
MIROKU'S BLOODLINE IS TO BE FEARED.

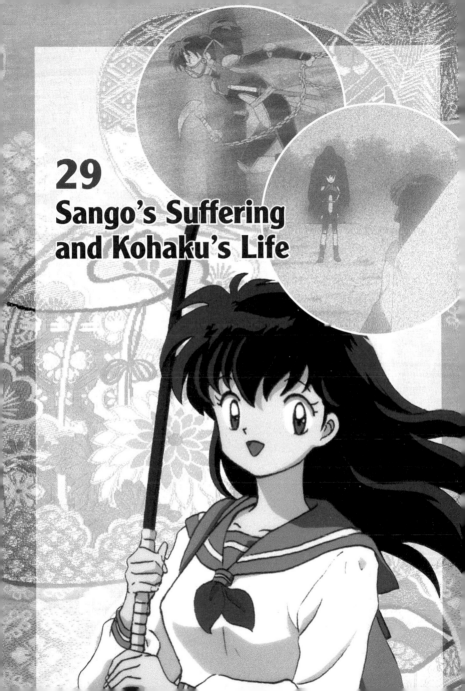

29
Sango's Suffering and Kohaku's Life

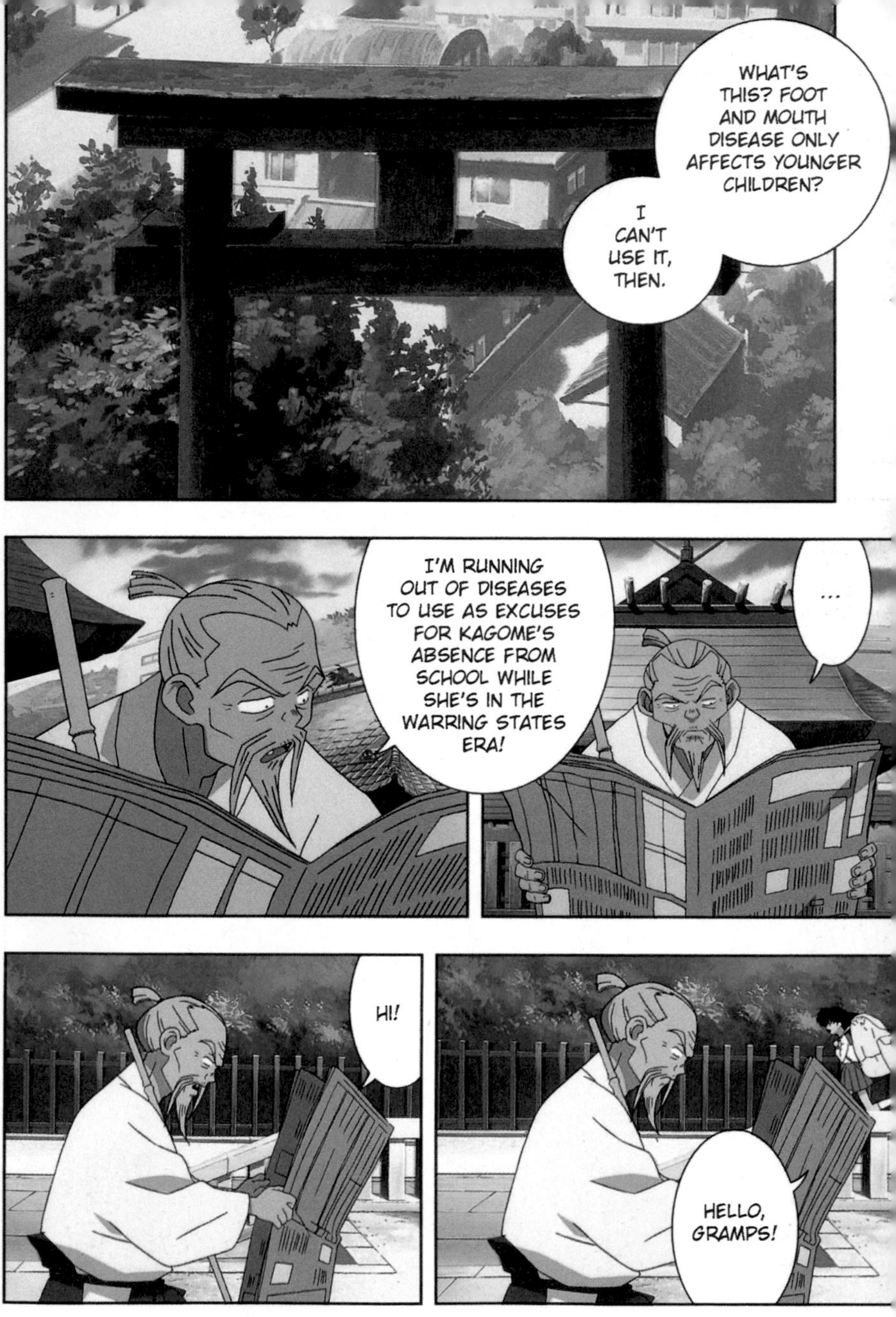
WHAT'S THIS? FOOT AND MOUTH DISEASE ONLY AFFECTS YOUNGER CHILDREN?
I CAN'T USE IT, THEN.
...
I'M RUNNING OUT OF DISEASES TO USE AS EXCUSES FOR KAGOME'S ABSENCE FROM SCHOOL WHILE SHE'S IN THE WARRING STATES ERA!
HELLO, GRAMPS!
HI!

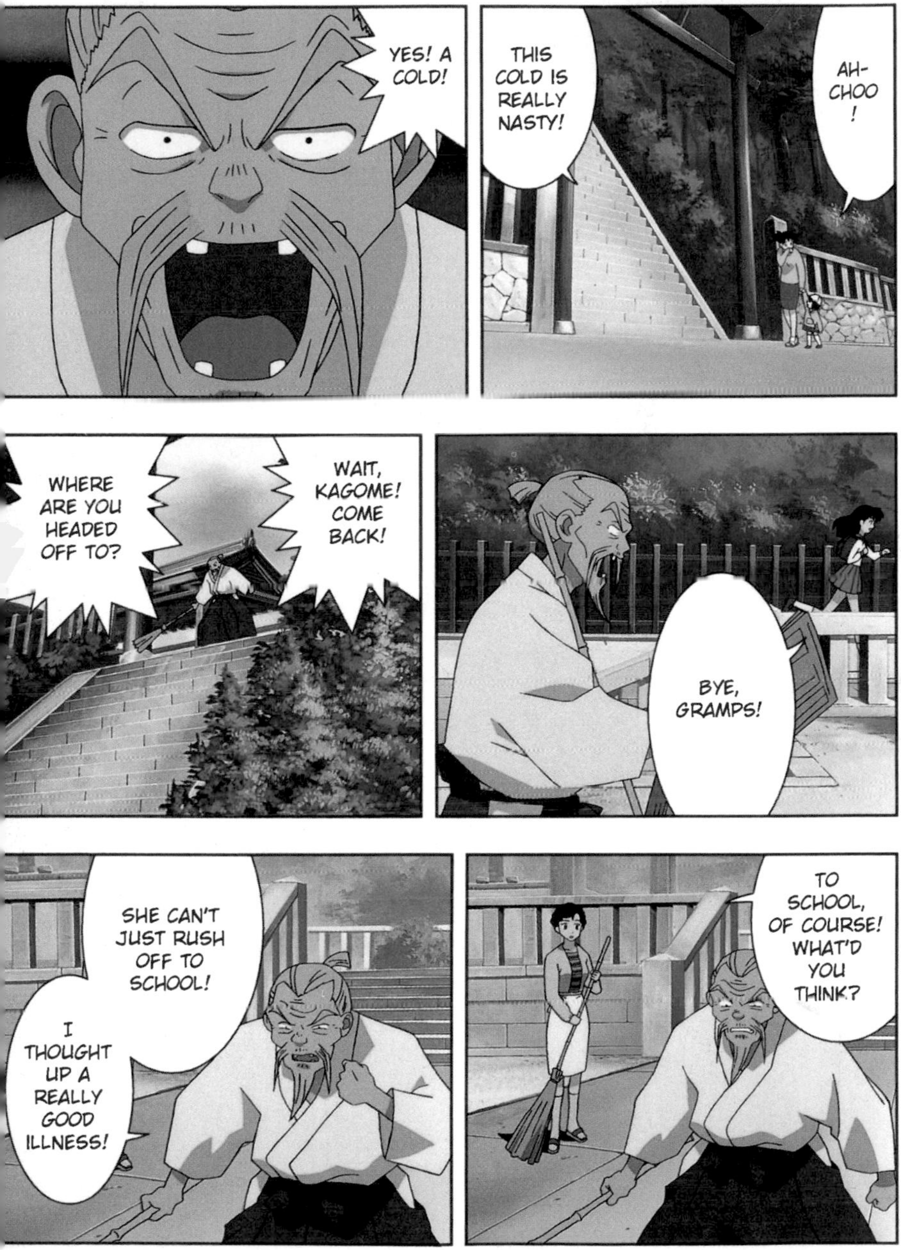
AH-CHOO!
THIS COLD IS REALLY NASTY!
YES! A COLD!
BYE, GRAMPS!
WAIT, KAGOME! COME BACK!
WHERE ARE YOU HEADED OFF TO?
TO SCHOOL, OF COURSE! WHAT'D YOU THINK?
SHE CAN'T JUST RUSH OFF TO SCHOOL!
I THOUGHT UP A REALLY GOOD ILLNESS!

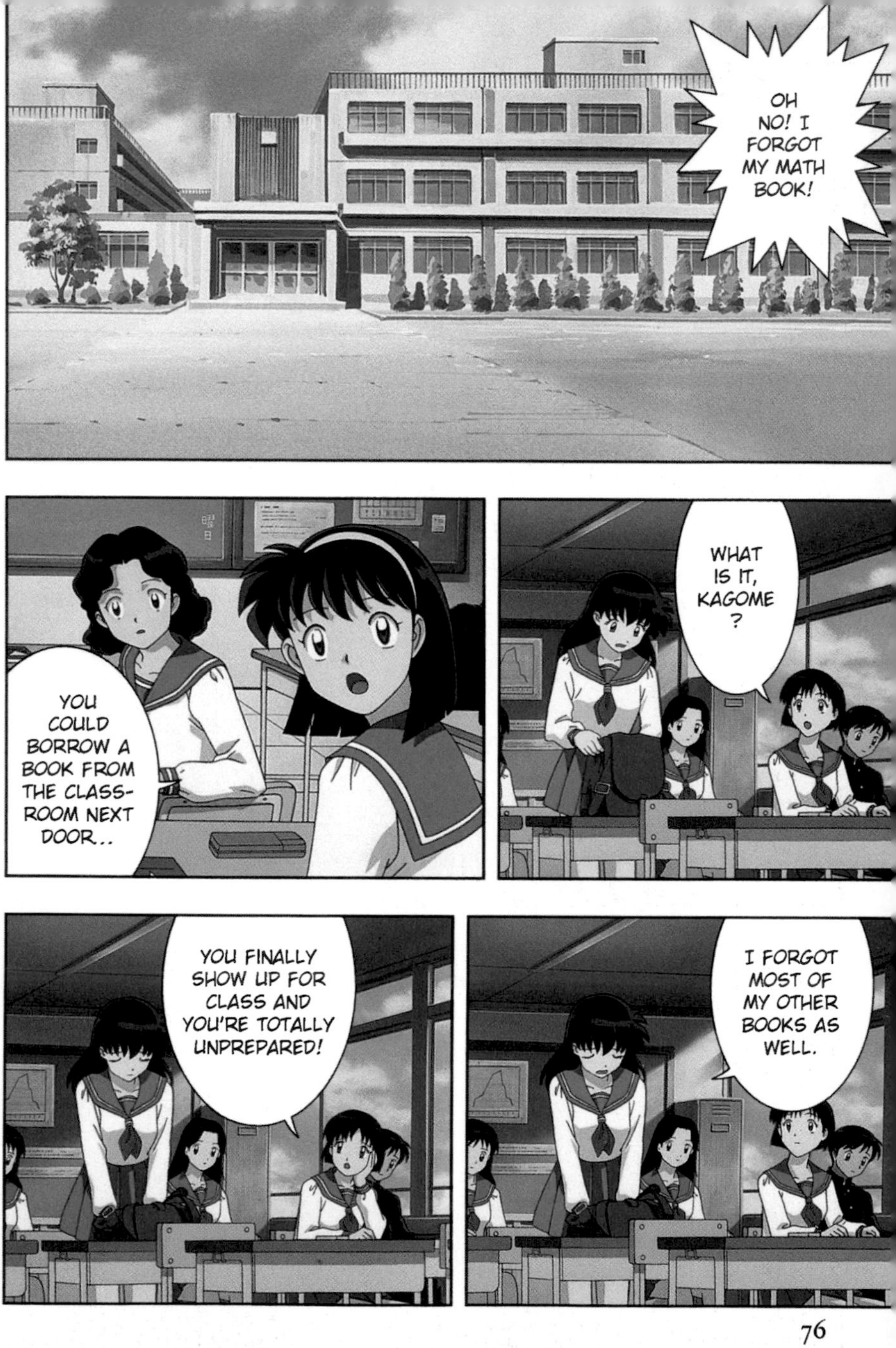

OH NO! I FORGOT MY MATH BOOK!
WHAT IS IT, KAGOME?
YOU COULD BORROW A BOOK FROM THE CLASS-ROOM NEXT DOOR...
I FORGOT MOST OF MY OTHER BOOKS AS WELL.
YOU FINALLY SHOW UP FOR CLASS AND YOU'RE TOTALLY UNPREPARED!

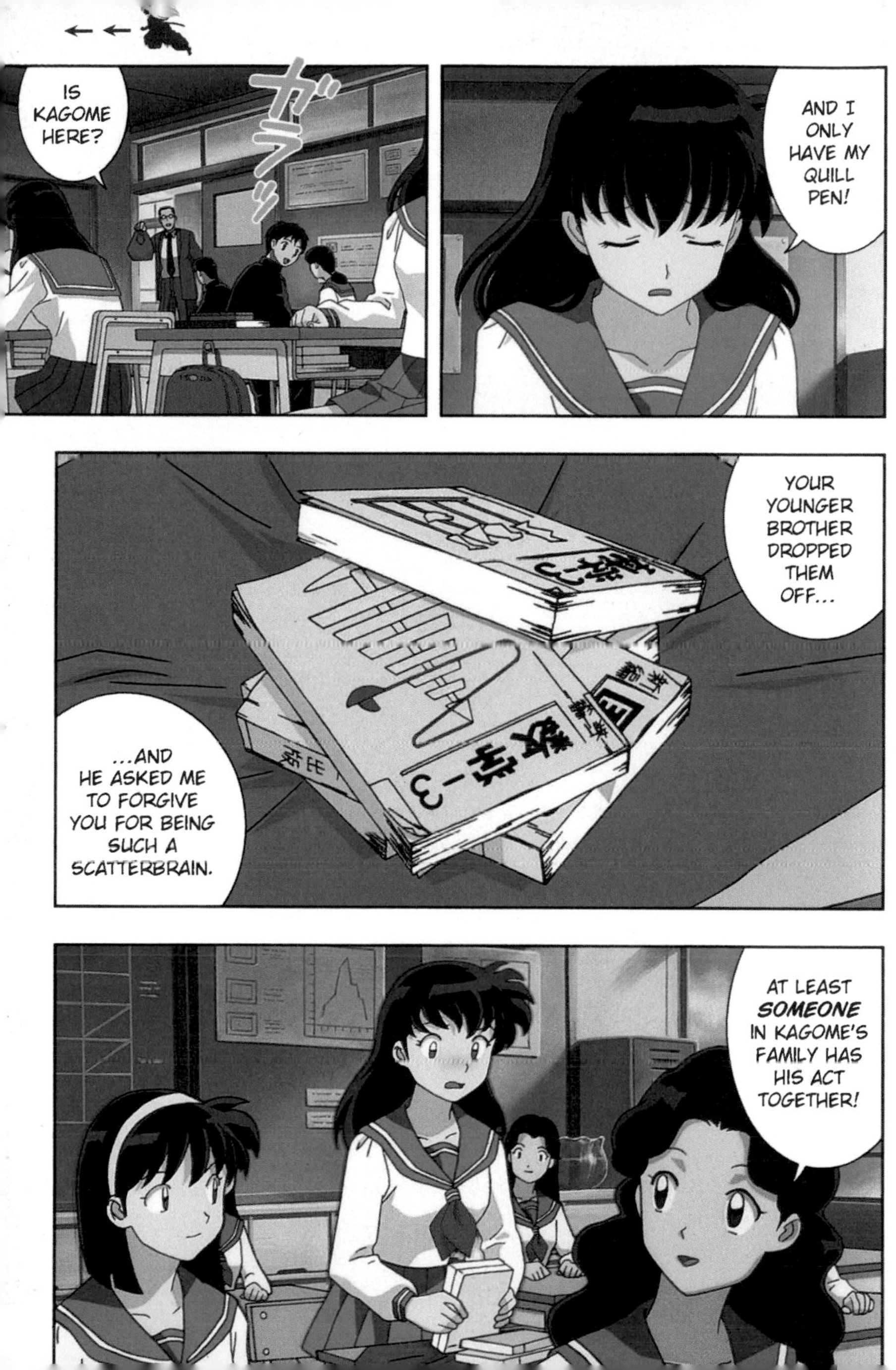
AND I ONLY HAVE MY QUILL PEN!
IS KAGOME HERE?
ガラッ
YOUR YOUNGER BROTHER DROPPED THEM OFF...
...AND HE ASKED ME TO FORGIVE YOU FOR BEING SUCH A SCATTERBRAIN.
AT LEAST **SOMEONE** IN KAGOME'S FAMILY HAS HIS ACT TOGETHER!

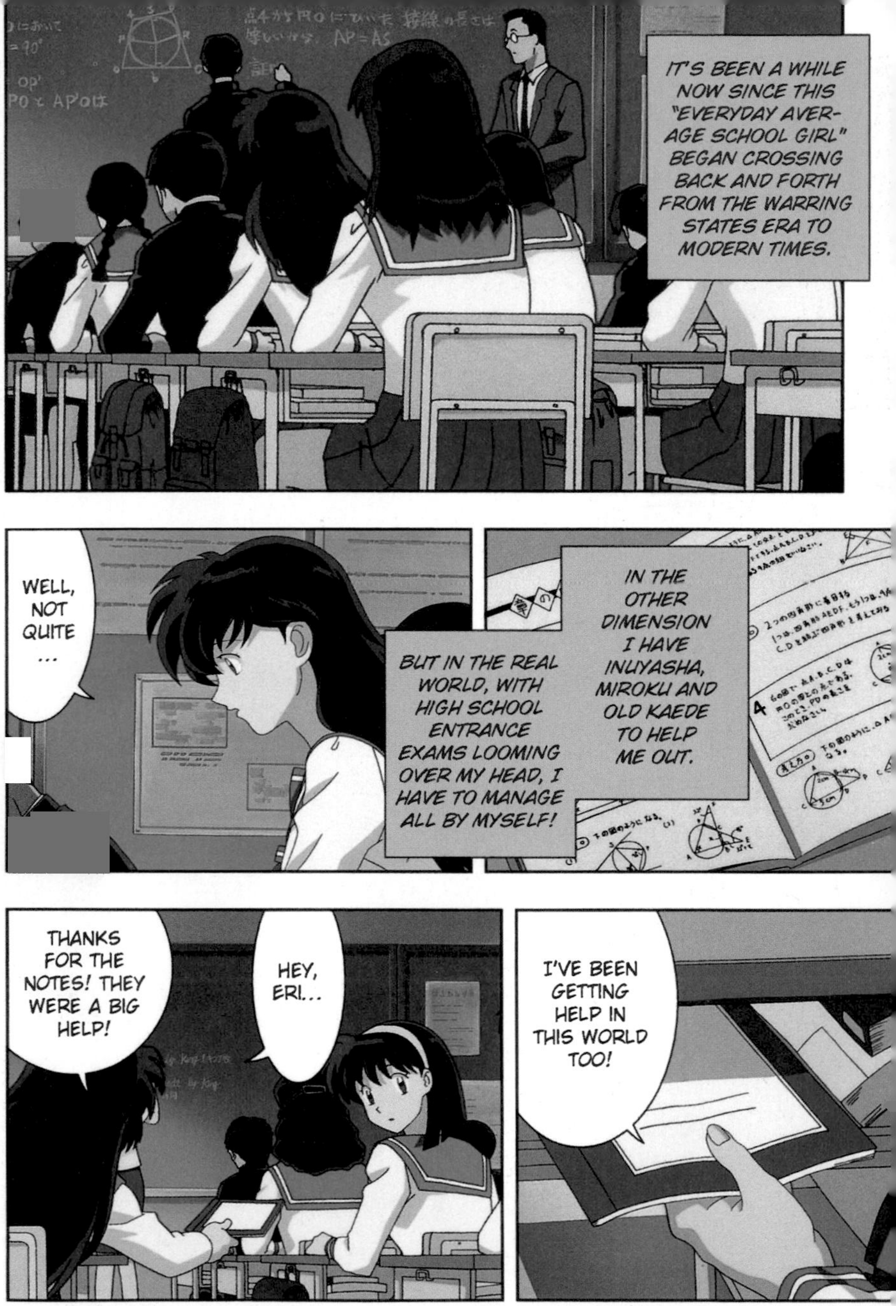
IT'S BEEN A WHILE NOW SINCE THIS "EVERYDAY AVER-AGE SCHOOL GIRL" BEGAN CROSSING BACK AND FORTH FROM THE WARRING STATES ERA TO MODERN TIMES.
IN THE OTHER DIMENSION I HAVE INUYASHA, MIROKU AND OLD KAEDE TO HELP ME OUT.
BUT IN THE REAL WORLD, WITH HIGH SCHOOL ENTRANCE EXAMS LOOMING OVER MY HEAD, I HAVE TO MANAGE ALL BY MYSELF!
WELL, NOT QUITE...
I'VE BEEN GETTING HELP IN THIS WORLD TOO!
HEY, ERI...
THANKS FOR THE NOTES! THEY WERE A BIG HELP!

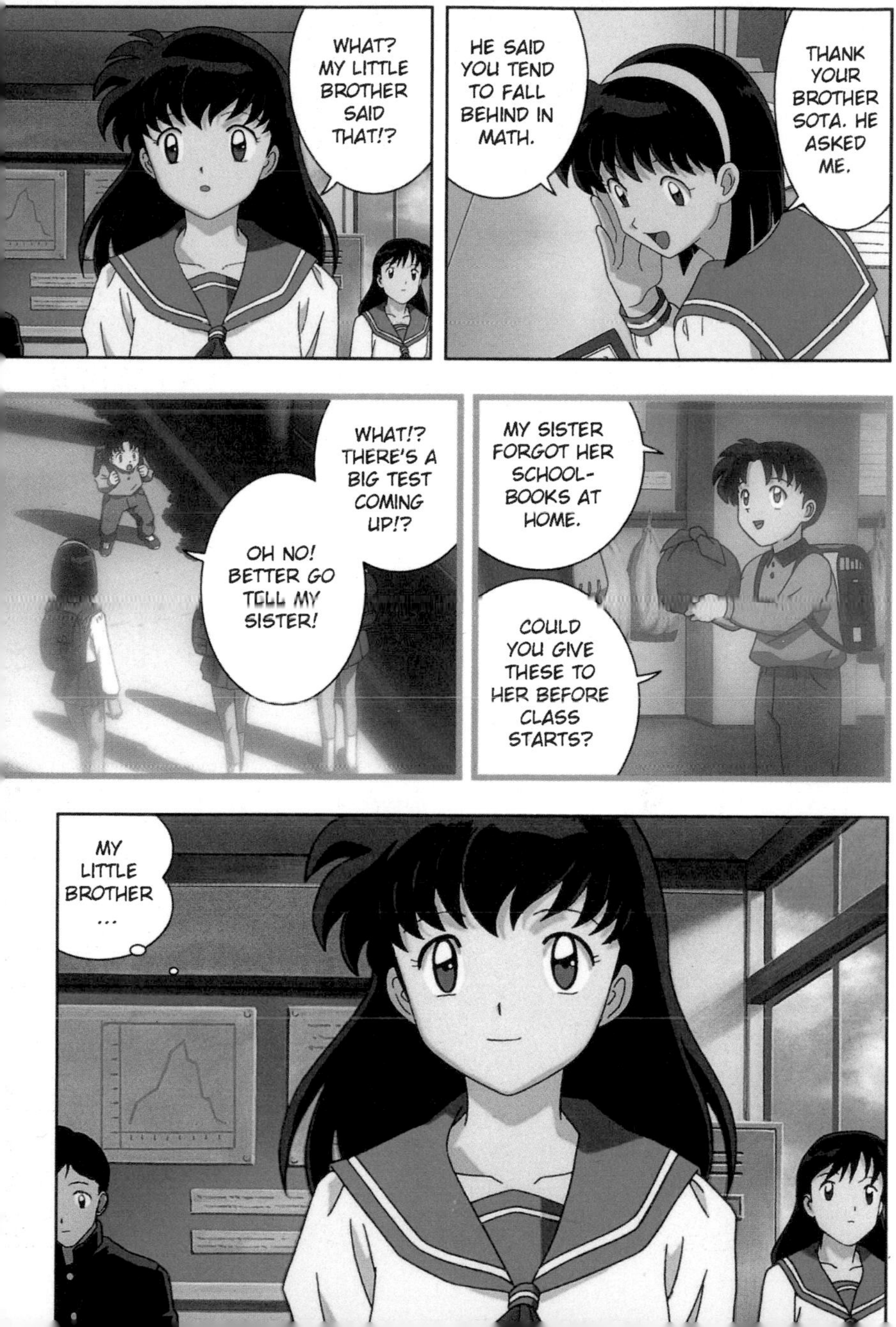
THANK YOUR BROTHER SOTA. HE ASKED ME.
HE SAID YOU TEND TO FALL BEHIND IN MATH.
WHAT? MY LITTLE BROTHER SAID THAT!?
MY SISTER FORGOT HER SCHOOL-BOOKS AT HOME.
COULD YOU GIVE THESE TO HER BEFORE CLASS STARTS?
WHAT!? THERE'S A BIG TEST COMING UP!?
OH NO! BETTER GO TELL MY SISTER!
MY LITTLE BROTHER ...

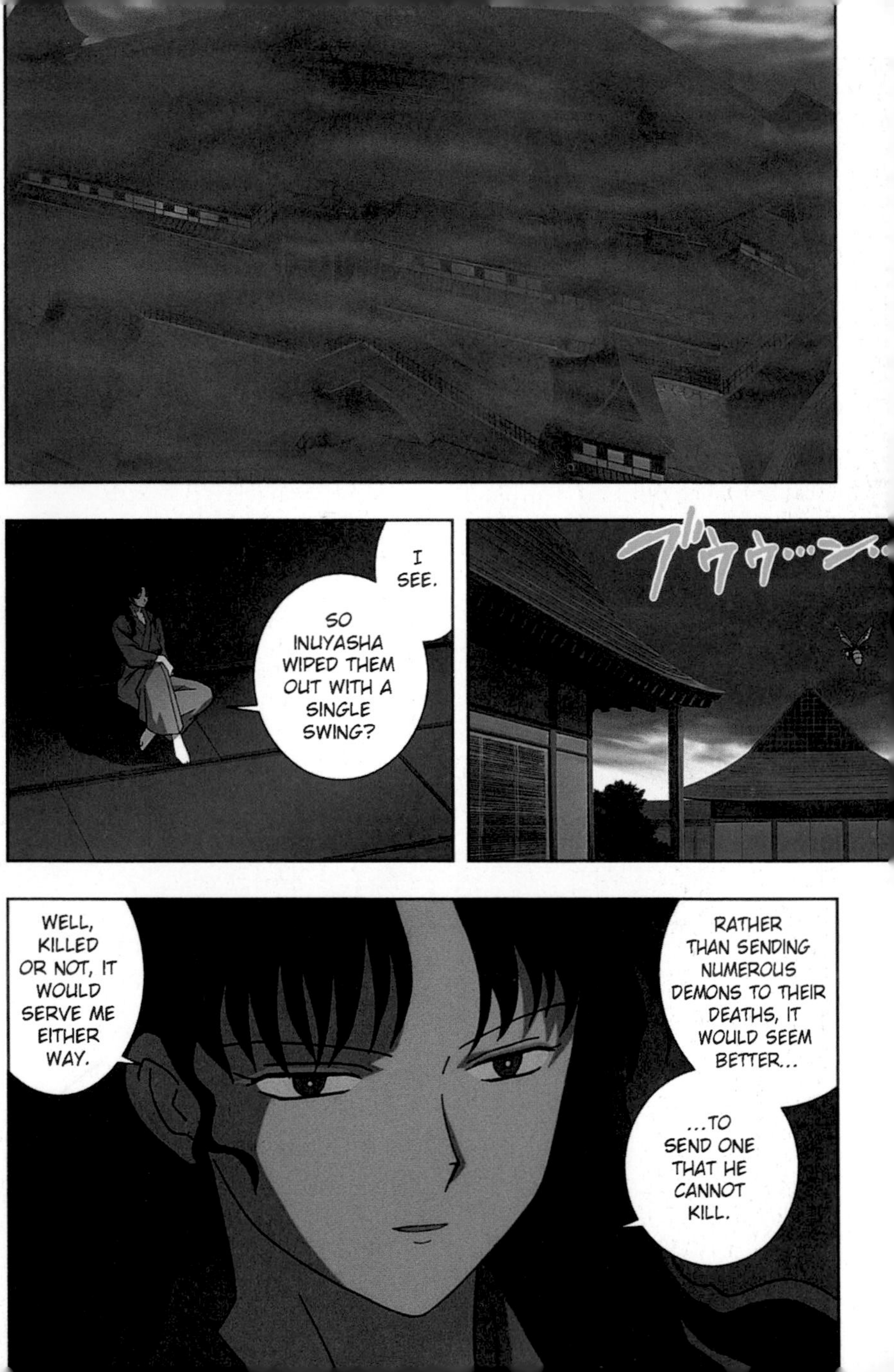
ブウウ…ン…
I SEE.
SO INUYASHA WIPED THEM OUT WITH A SINGLE SWING?
RATHER THAN SENDING NUMEROUS DEMONS TO THEIR DEATHS, IT WOULD SEEM BETTER...
...TO SEND ONE THAT HE CANNOT KILL.
WELL, KILLED OR NOT, IT WOULD SERVE ME EITHER WAY.

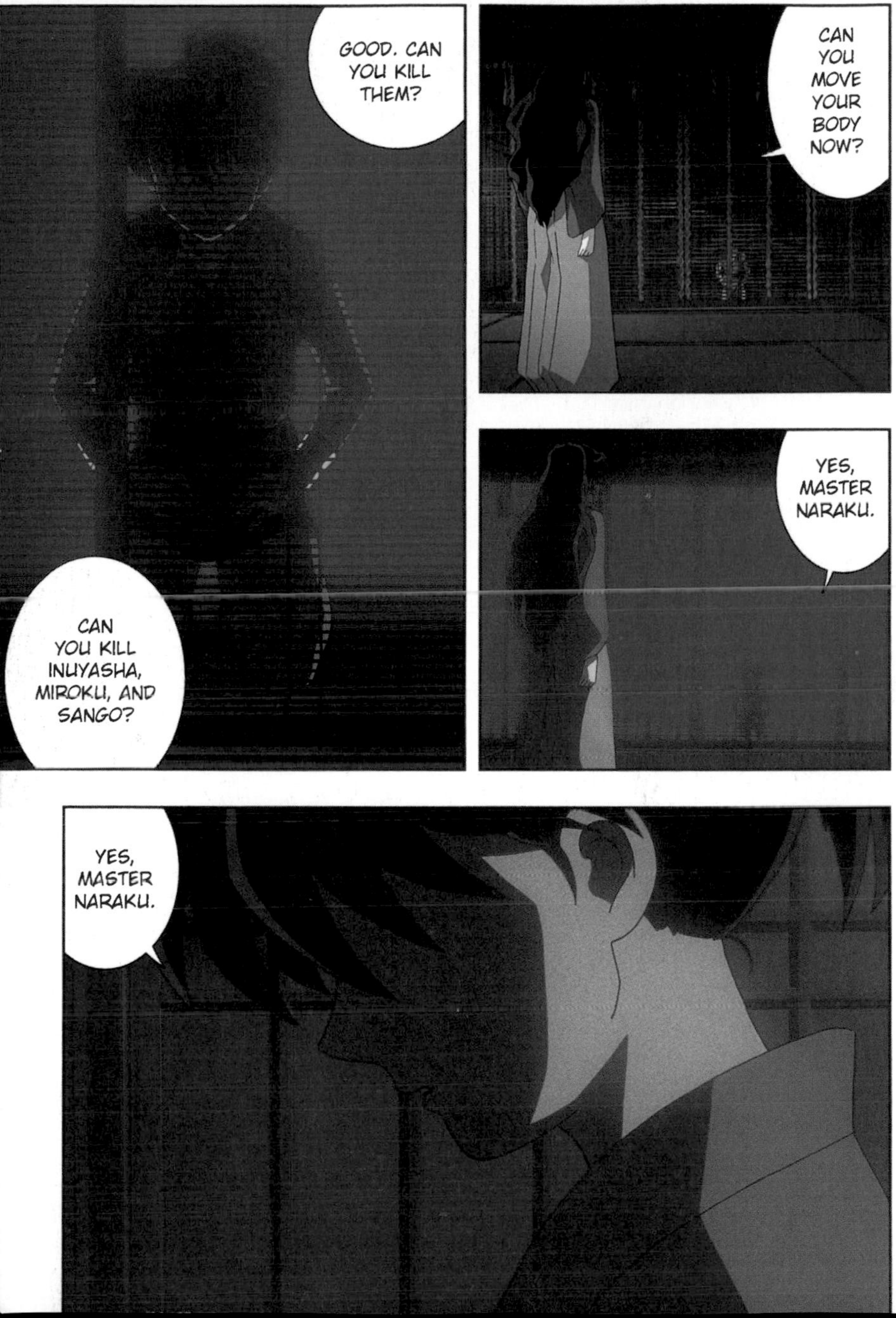
CAN YOU MOVE YOUR BODY NOW?
YES, MASTER NARAKU.
GOOD. CAN YOU KILL THEM?
CAN YOU KILL INUYASHA, MIROKU, AND SANGO?
YES, MASTER NARAKU.

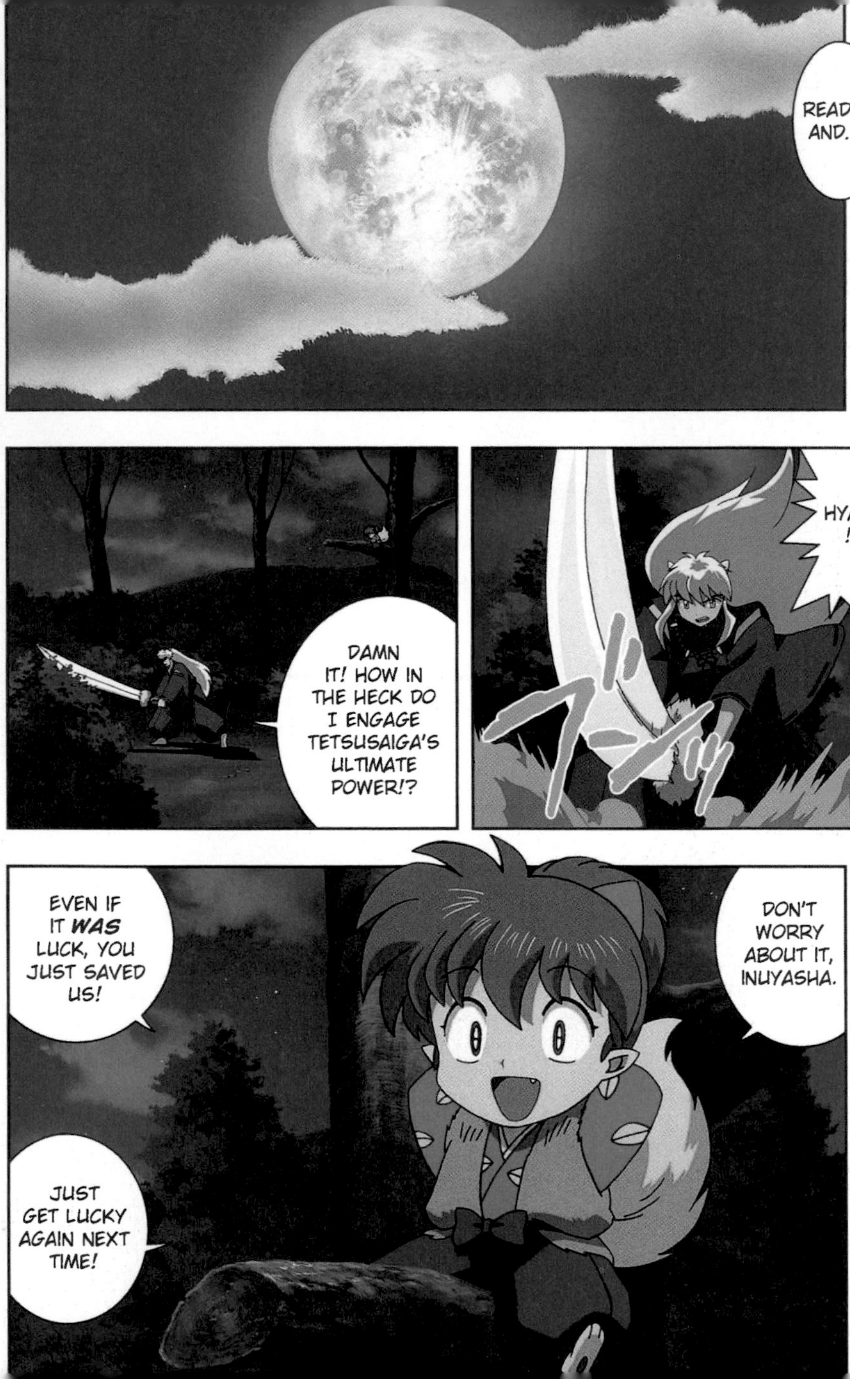
READY? AND...
HYAH!
DAMN IT! HOW IN THE HECK DO I ENGAGE TETSUSAIGA'S ULTIMATE POWER!?
DON'T WORRY ABOUT IT, INUYASHA.
EVEN IF IT *WAS* LUCK, YOU JUST SAVED US!
JUST GET LUCKY AGAIN NEXT TIME!

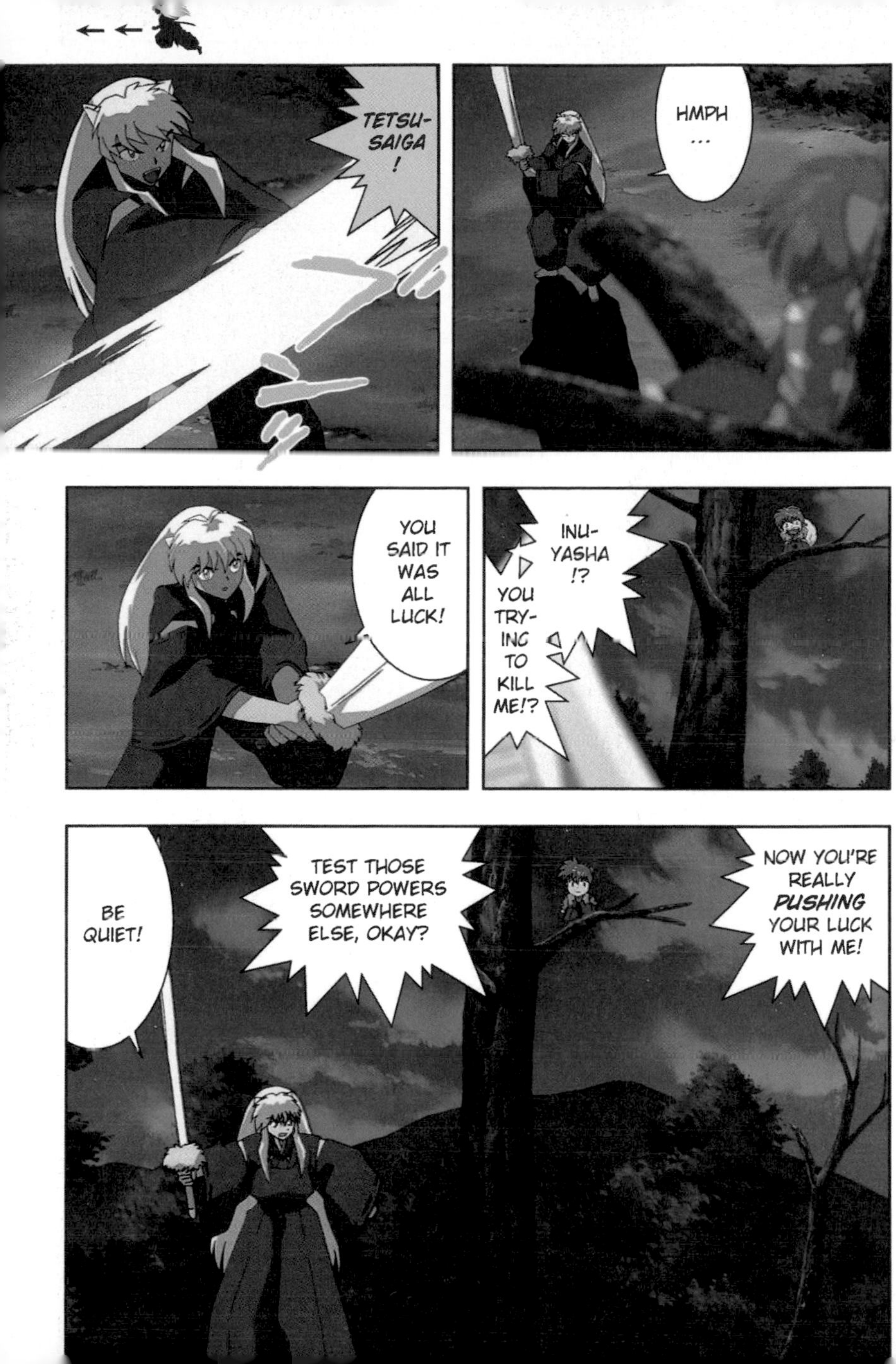
HMPH ...
TETSU-SAIGA!
INU-YASHA!?
YOU TRY-ING TO KILL ME!?
YOU SAID IT WAS ALL LUCK!
NOW YOU'RE REALLY ***PUSHING*** YOUR LUCK WITH ME!
TEST THOSE SWORD POWERS SOMEWHERE ELSE, OKAY?
BE QUIET!

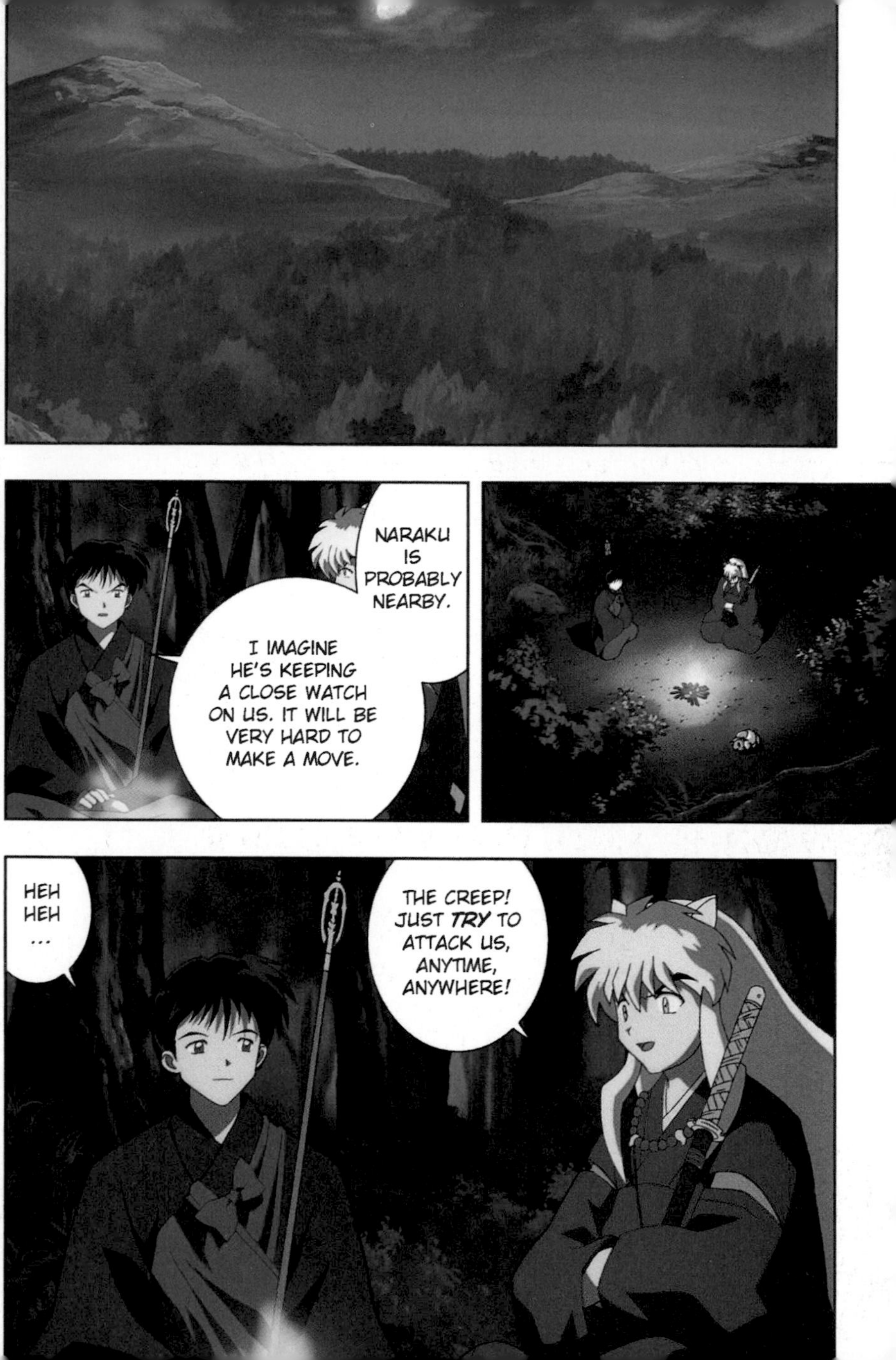
NARAKU IS PROBABLY NEARBY.
I IMAGINE HE'S KEEPING A CLOSE WATCH ON US. IT WILL BE VERY HARD TO MAKE A MOVE.
THE CREEP! JUST *TRY* TO ATTACK US, ANYTIME, ANYWHERE!
HEH HEH ...

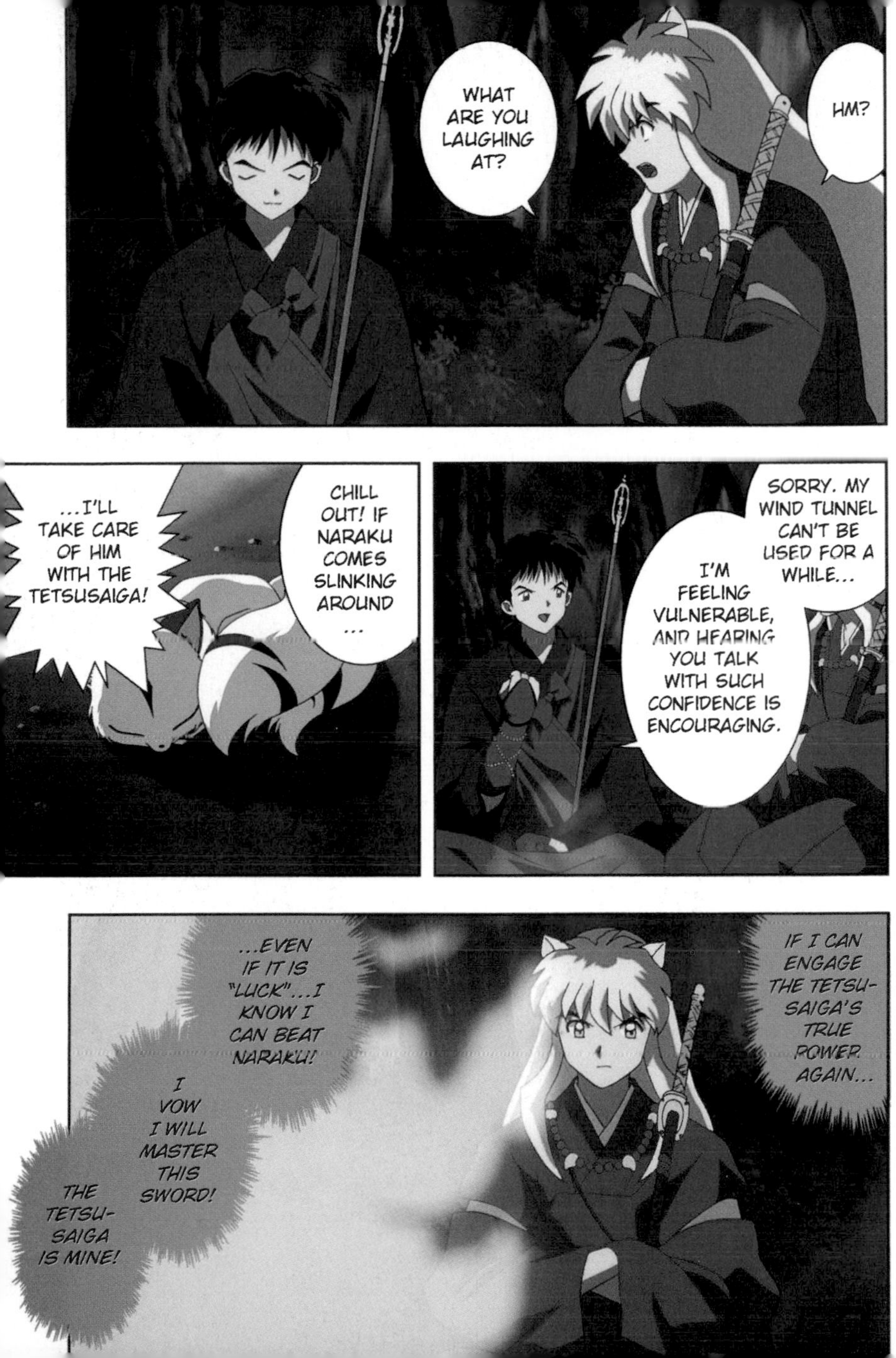
HM?
WHAT ARE YOU LAUGHING AT?
SORRY. MY WIND TUNNEL CAN'T BE USED FOR A WHILE...
I'M FEELING VULNERABLE, AND HEARING YOU TALK WITH SUCH CONFIDENCE IS ENCOURAGING.
CHILL OUT! IF NARAKU COMES SLINKING AROUND ...
...I'LL TAKE CARE OF HIM WITH THE TETSUSAIGA!
IF I CAN ENGAGE THE TETSU-SAIGA'S TRUE POWER AGAIN...
...EVEN IF IT IS "LUCK"...I KNOW I CAN BEAT NARAKU!
I VOW I WILL MASTER THIS SWORD!
THE TETSU-SAIGA IS MINE!

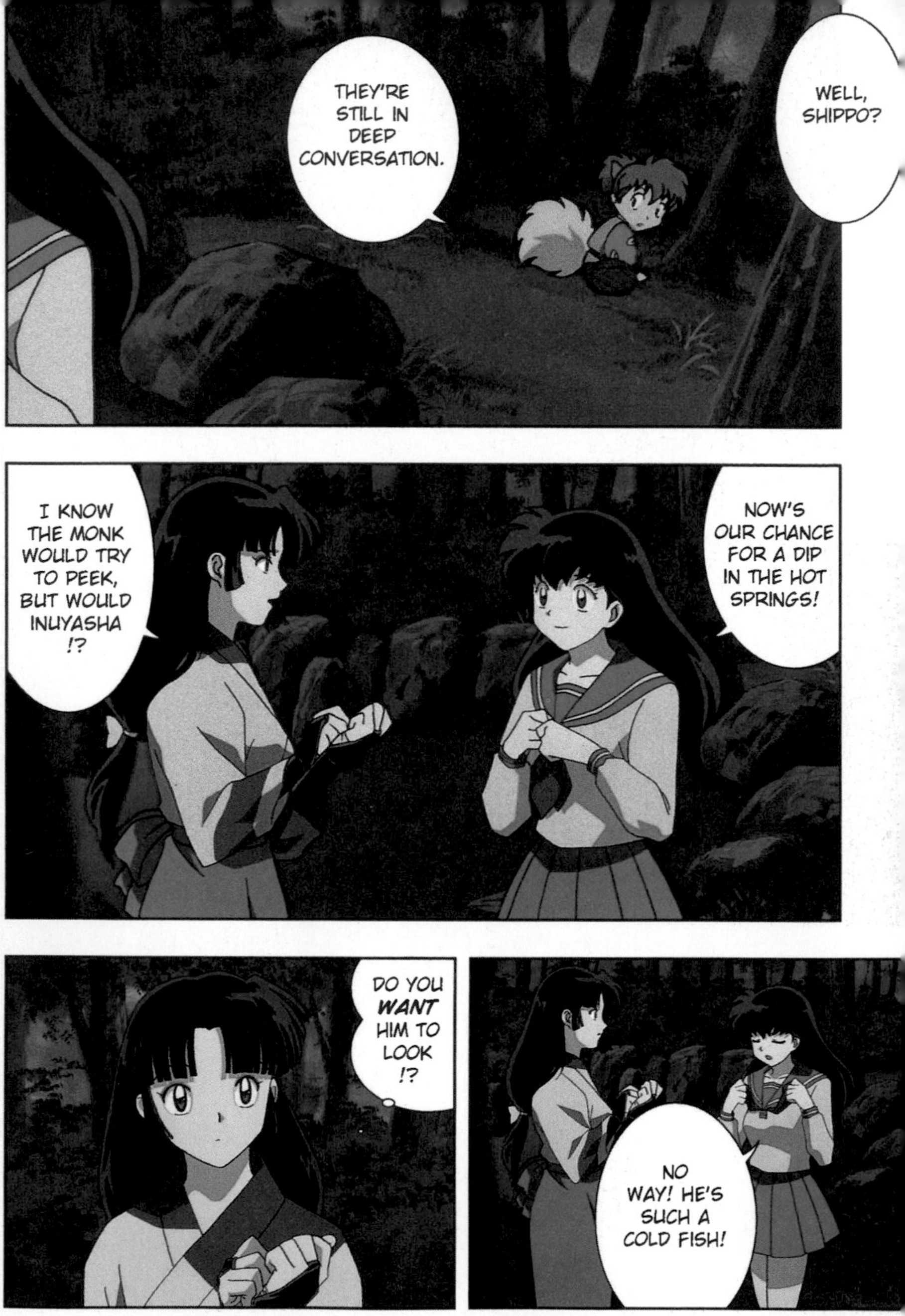

WELL, SHIPPO?
THEY'RE STILL IN DEEP CONVERSATION.
NOW'S OUR CHANCE FOR A DIP IN THE HOT SPRINGS!
I KNOW THE MONK WOULD TRY TO PEEK, BUT WOULD INUYASHA !?
NO WAY! HE'S SUCH A COLD FISH!
DO YOU ***WANT*** HIM TO LOOK !?

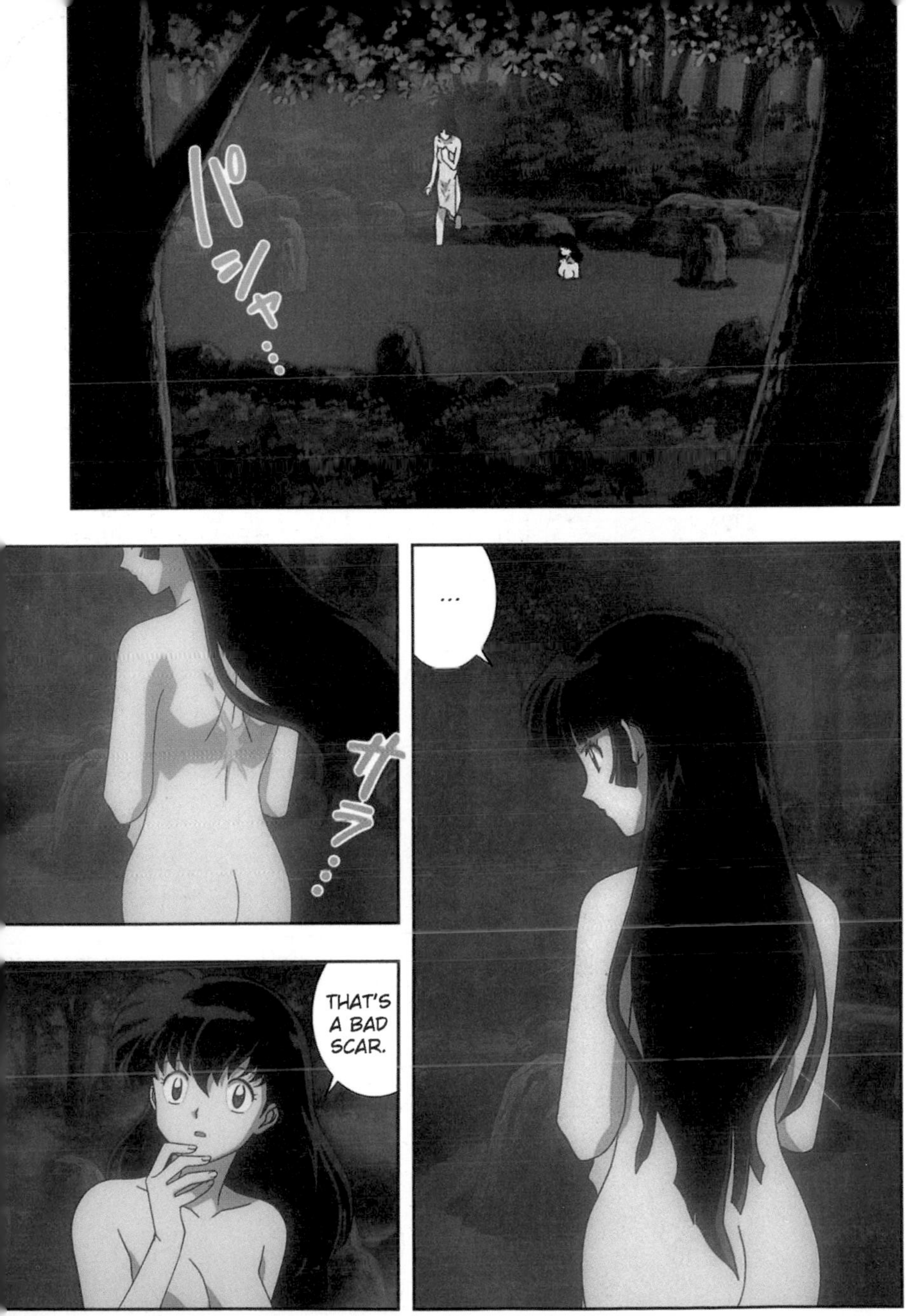
パシャ…
…
サラ…
THAT'S A BAD SCAR.

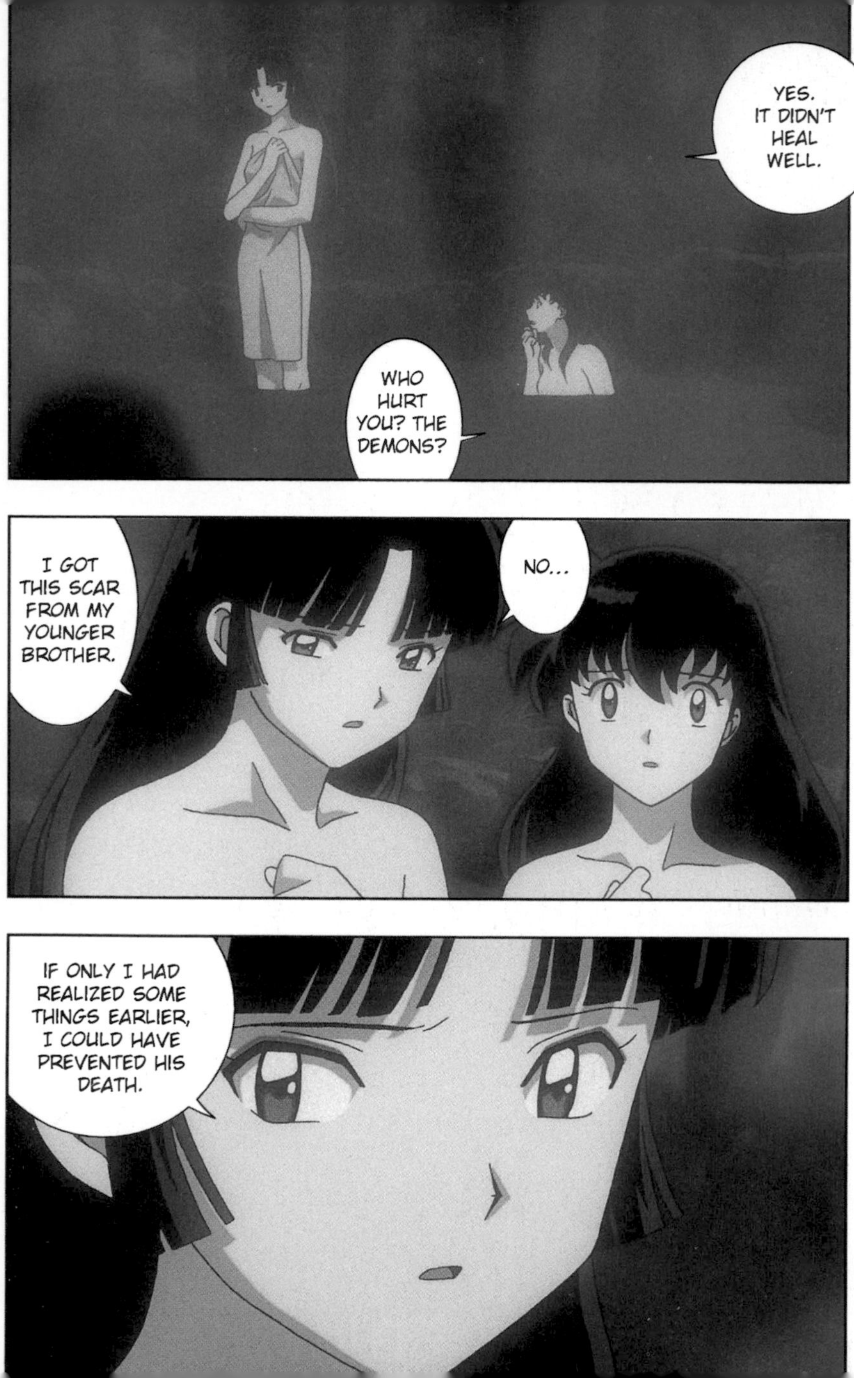
YES. IT DIDN'T HEAL WELL.
WHO HURT YOU? THE DEMONS?
NO...
I GOT THIS SCAR FROM MY YOUNGER BROTHER.
IF ONLY I HAD REALIZED SOME THINGS EARLIER, I COULD HAVE PREVENTED HIS DEATH.

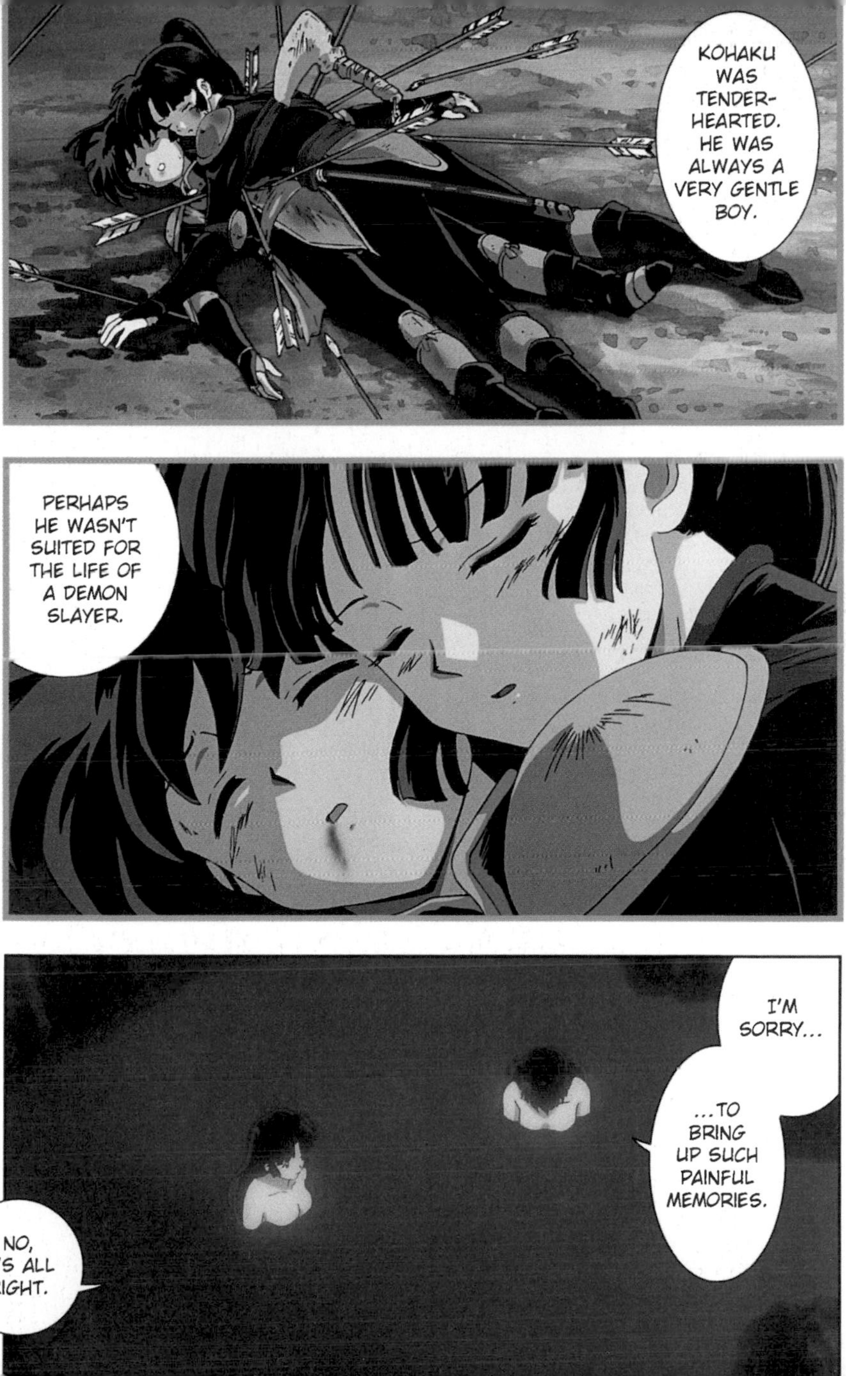
KOHAKU WAS TENDER-HEARTED. HE WAS ALWAYS A VERY GENTLE BOY.
PERHAPS HE WASN'T SUITED FOR THE LIFE OF A DEMON SLAYER.
I'M SORRY...
...TO BRING UP SUCH PAINFUL MEMORIES.
NO, IT'S ALL RIGHT.

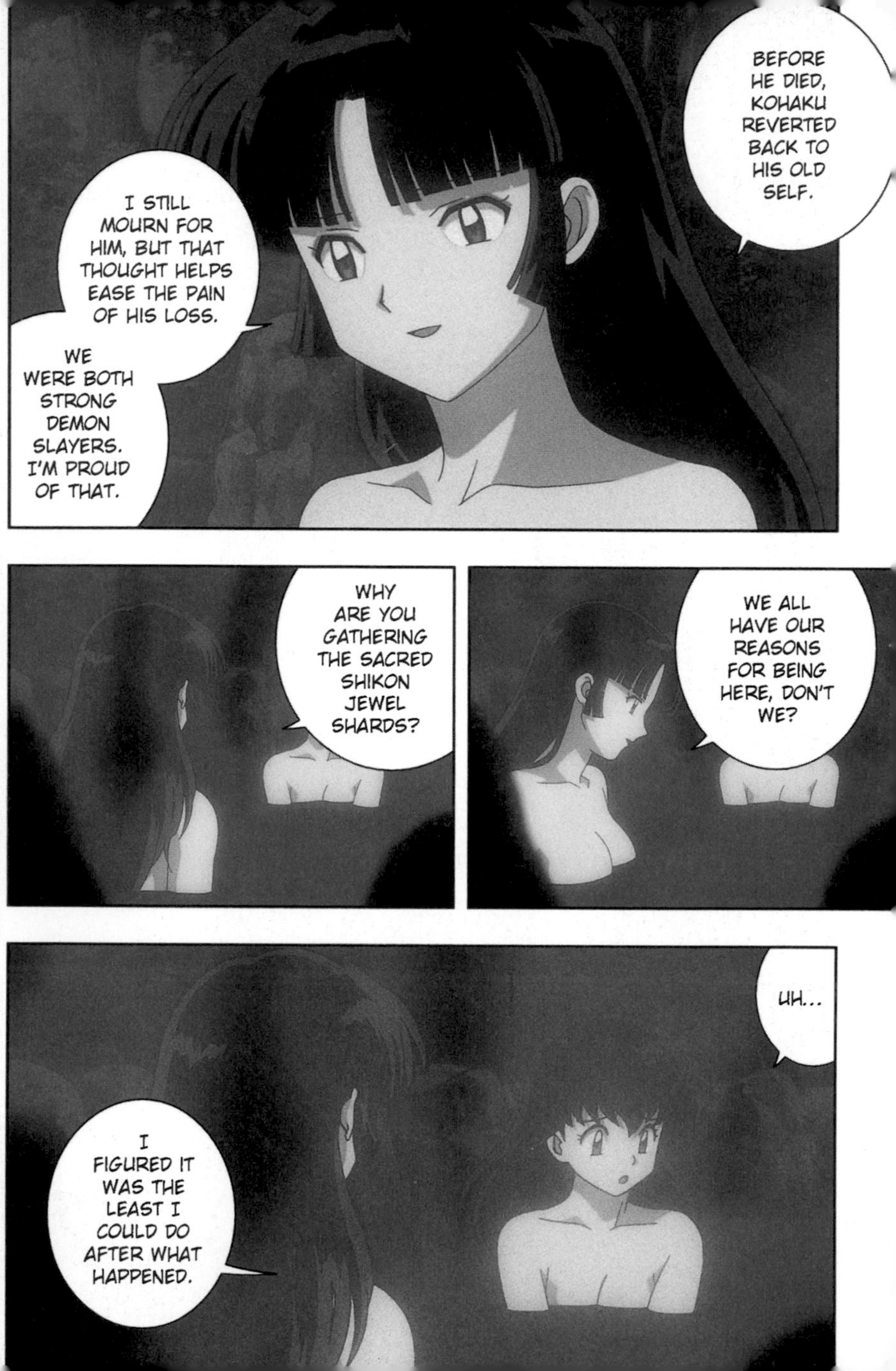
BEFORE HE DIED, KOHAKU REVERTED BACK TO HIS OLD SELF.
I STILL MOURN FOR HIM, BUT THAT THOUGHT HELPS EASE THE PAIN OF HIS LOSS.
WE WERE BOTH STRONG DEMON SLAYERS. I'M PROUD OF THAT.
WE ALL HAVE OUR REASONS FOR BEING HERE, DON'T WE?
WHY ARE YOU GATHERING THE SACRED SHIKON JEWEL SHARDS?
UH...
I FIGURED IT WAS THE LEAST I COULD DO AFTER WHAT HAPPENED.

SO DID *YOU* BREAK THE JEWEL!?
I'M SORRY. I KNOW...I REALLY BLEW IT.
I'M SURE YOU WERE JUST TRYING TO RETRIEVE IT FROM A DEMON, SO IT'S NOT YOUR FAULT.
WHAT'S AMAZING IS THAT YOU'RE THE REINCARNATION OF A PRIESTESS!

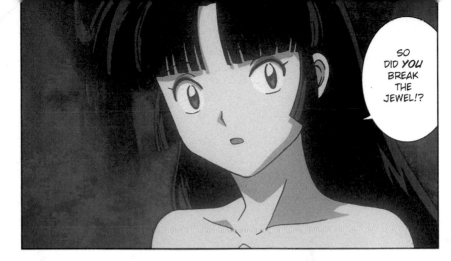

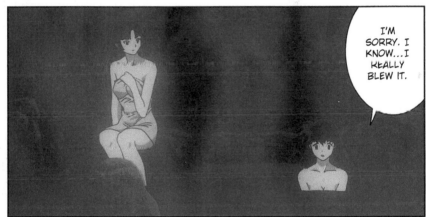

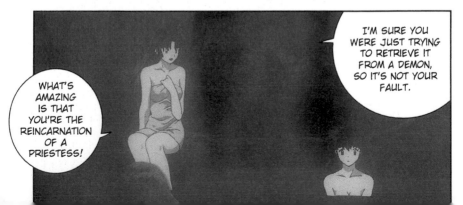

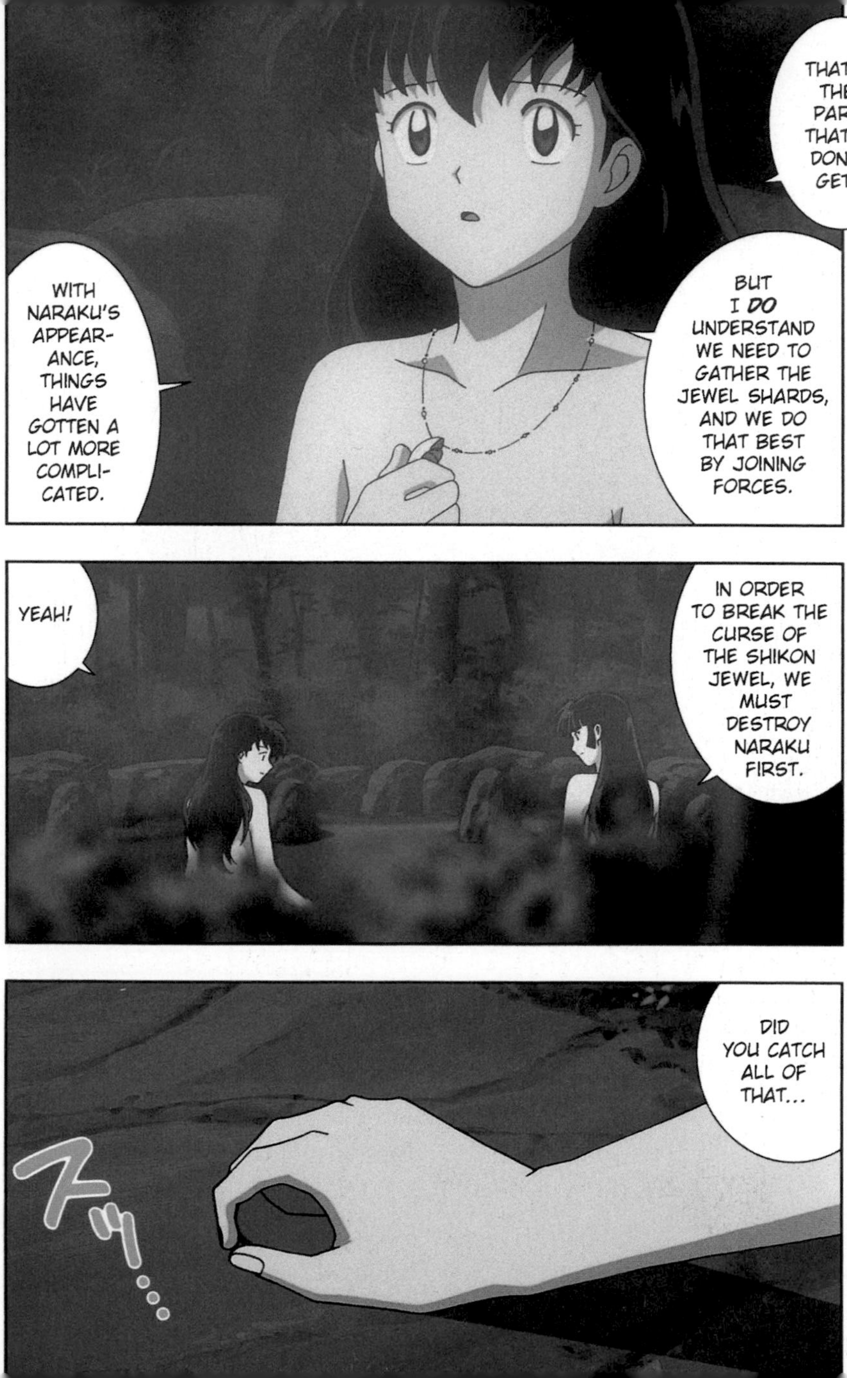
THAT'S THE PART THAT I DON'T GET.
BUT I DO UNDERSTAND WE NEED TO GATHER THE JEWEL SHARDS, AND WE DO THAT BEST BY JOINING FORCES.
WITH NARAKU'S APPEARANCE, THINGS HAVE GOTTEN A LOT MORE COMPLICATED.
IN ORDER TO BREAK THE CURSE OF THE SHIKON JEWEL, WE MUST DESTROY NARAKU FIRST.
YEAH!
DID YOU CATCH ALL OF THAT...
スッ...

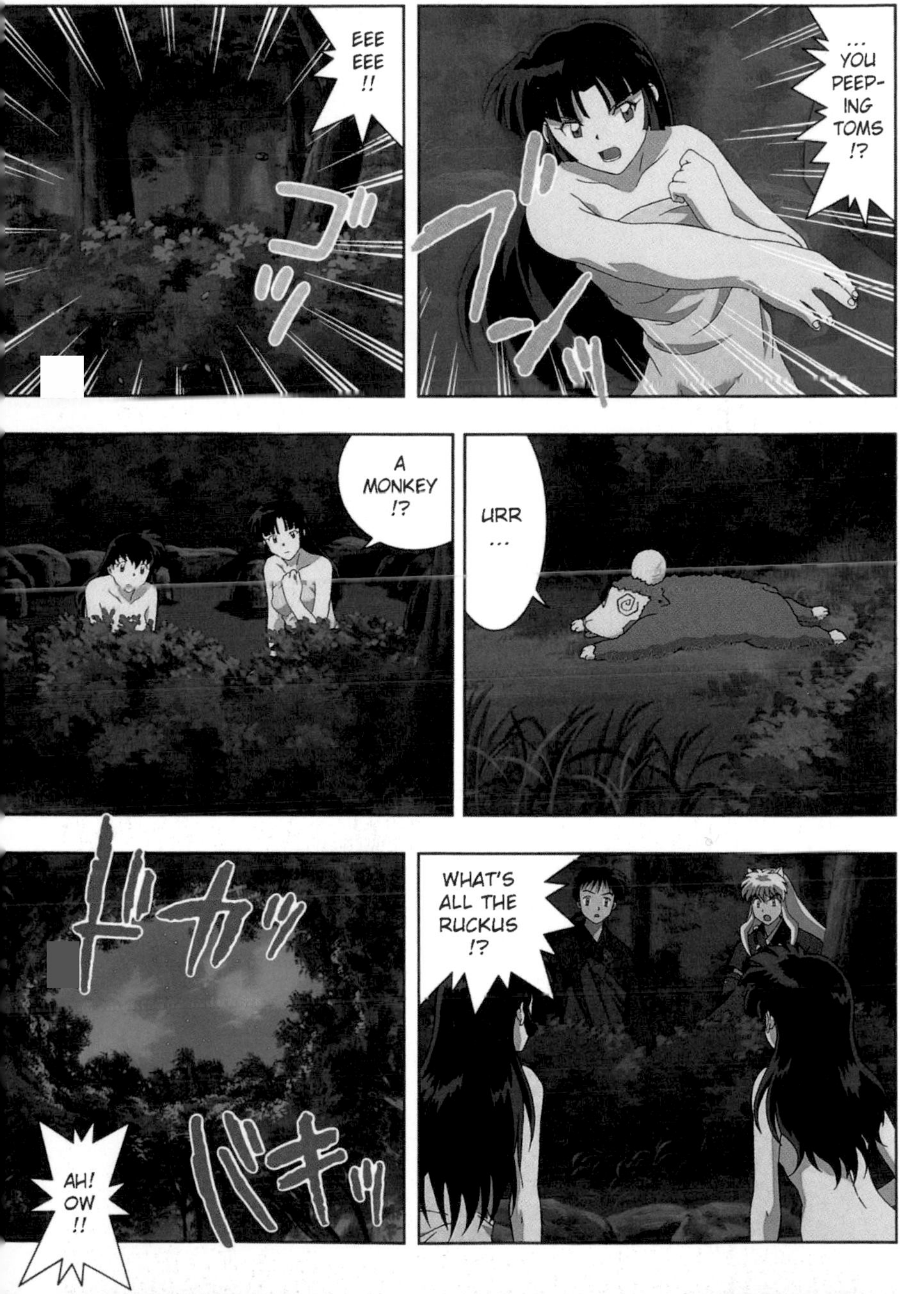

... YOU PEEP-ING TOMS !?
ブンッ
ゴッ
EEE EEE !!
URR ...
A MONKEY !?
WHAT'S ALL THE RUCKUS !?
ドカッ
バキッ
AH! OW !!

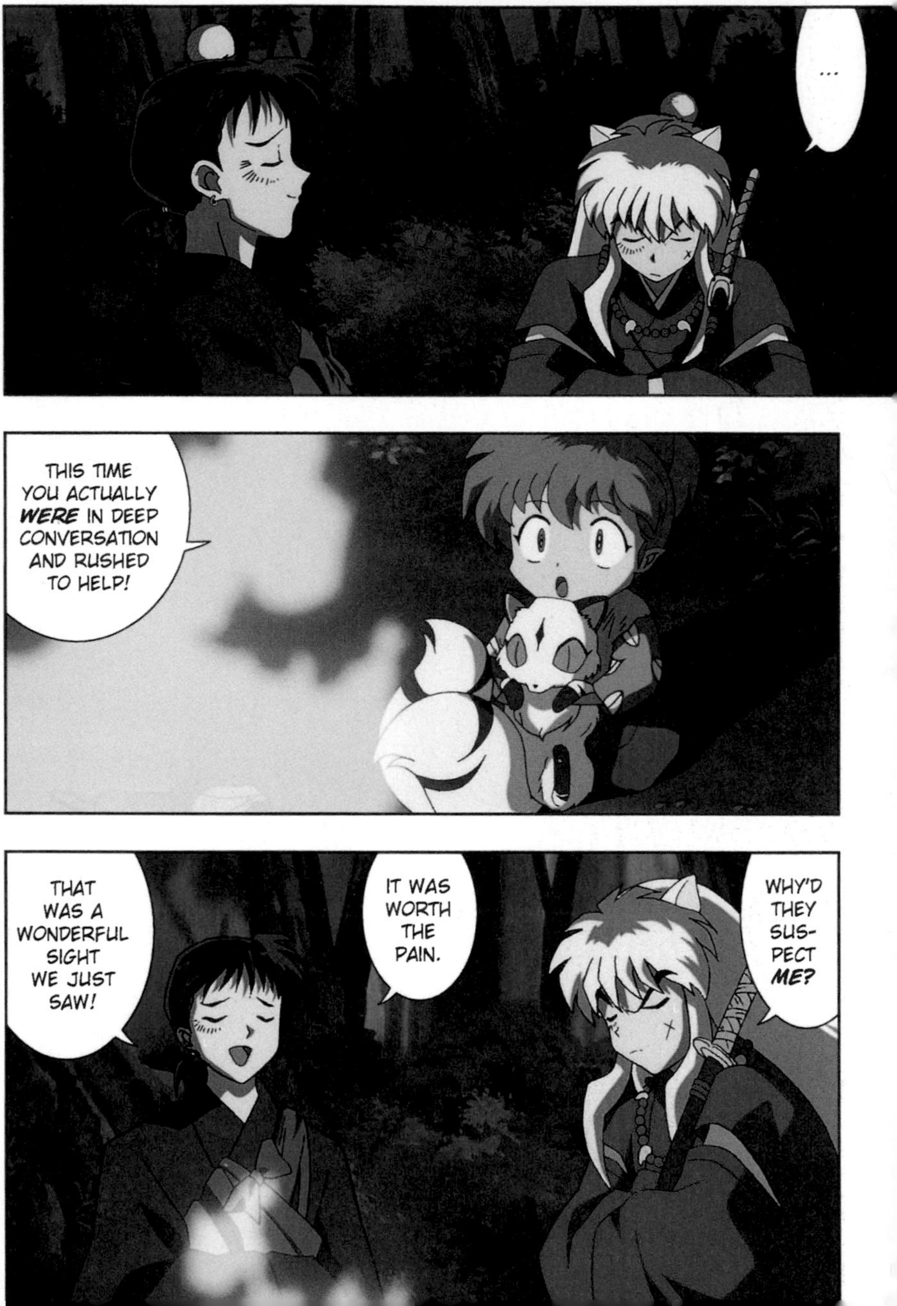
...
THIS TIME YOU ACTUALLY **WERE** IN DEEP CONVERSATION AND RUSHED TO HELP!
WHY'D THEY SUS-PECT **ME?**
IT WAS WORTH THE PAIN.
THAT WAS A WONDERFUL SIGHT WE JUST SAW!

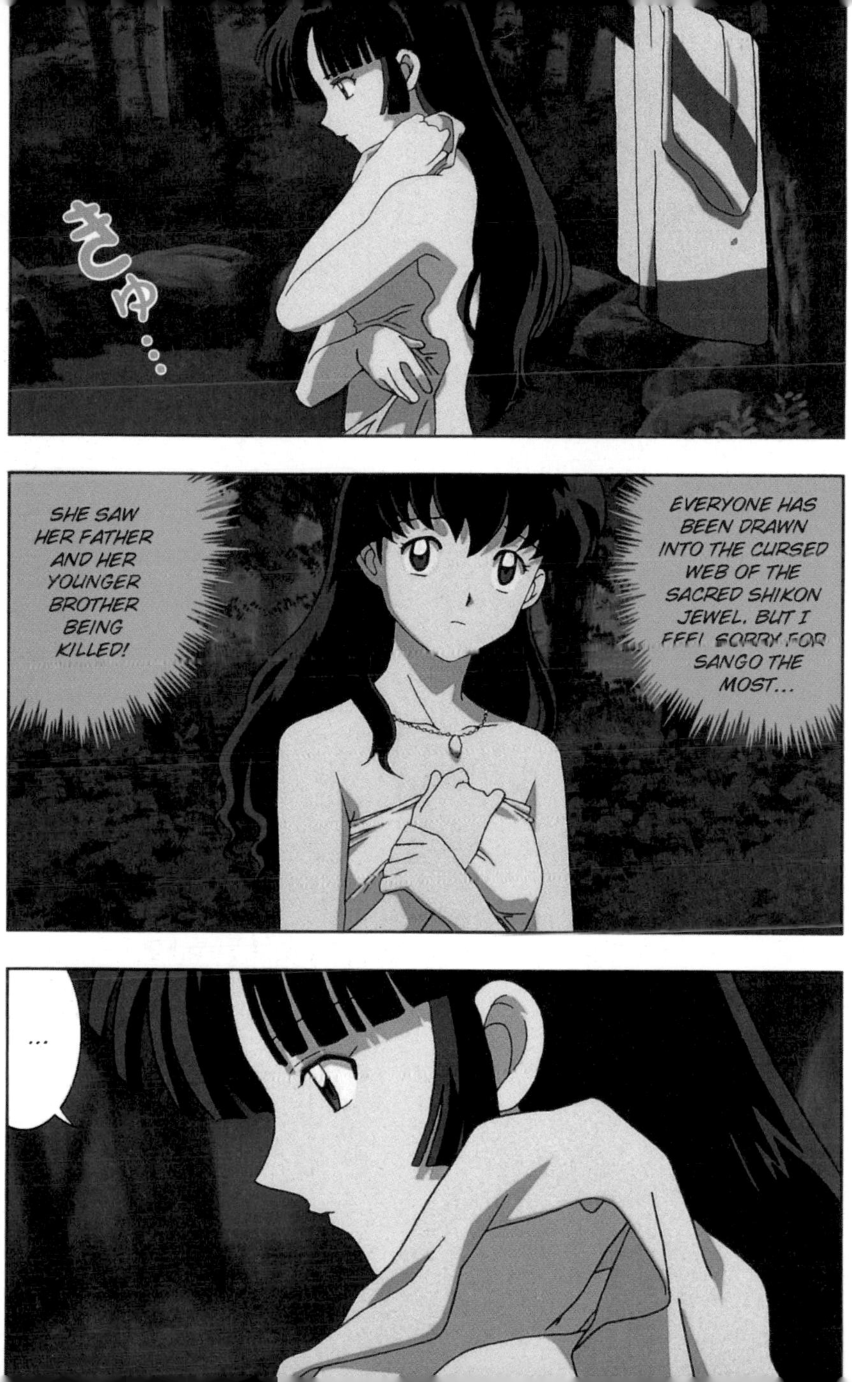
きゅ…
EVERYONE HAS BEEN DRAWN INTO THE CURSED WEB OF THE SACRED SHIKON JEWEL. BUT I FEEL SORRY FOR SANGO THE MOST...
SHE SAW HER FATHER AND HER YOUNGER BROTHER BEING KILLED!
...

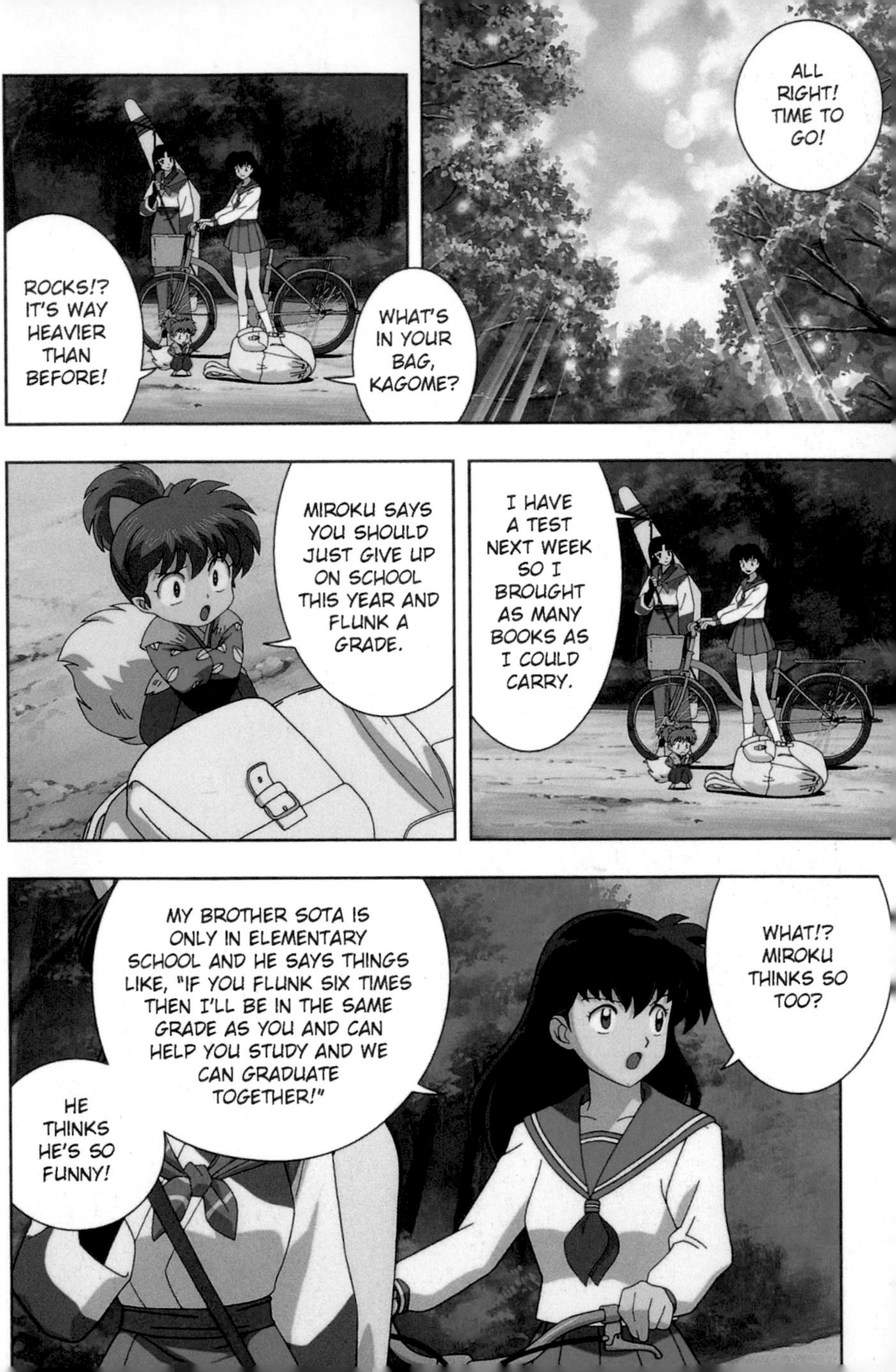
ALL RIGHT! TIME TO GO!
WHAT'S IN YOUR BAG, KAGOME?
ROCKS!? IT'S WAY HEAVIER THAN BEFORE!
I HAVE A TEST NEXT WEEK SO I BROUGHT AS MANY BOOKS AS I COULD CARRY.
MIROKU SAYS YOU SHOULD JUST GIVE UP ON SCHOOL THIS YEAR AND FLUNK A GRADE.
WHAT!? MIROKU THINKS SO TOO?
MY BROTHER SOTA IS ONLY IN ELEMENTARY SCHOOL AND HE SAYS THINGS LIKE, "IF YOU FLUNK SIX TIMES THEN I'LL BE IN THE SAME GRADE AS YOU AND CAN HELP YOU STUDY AND WE CAN GRADUATE TOGETHER!"
HE THINKS HE'S SO FUNNY!

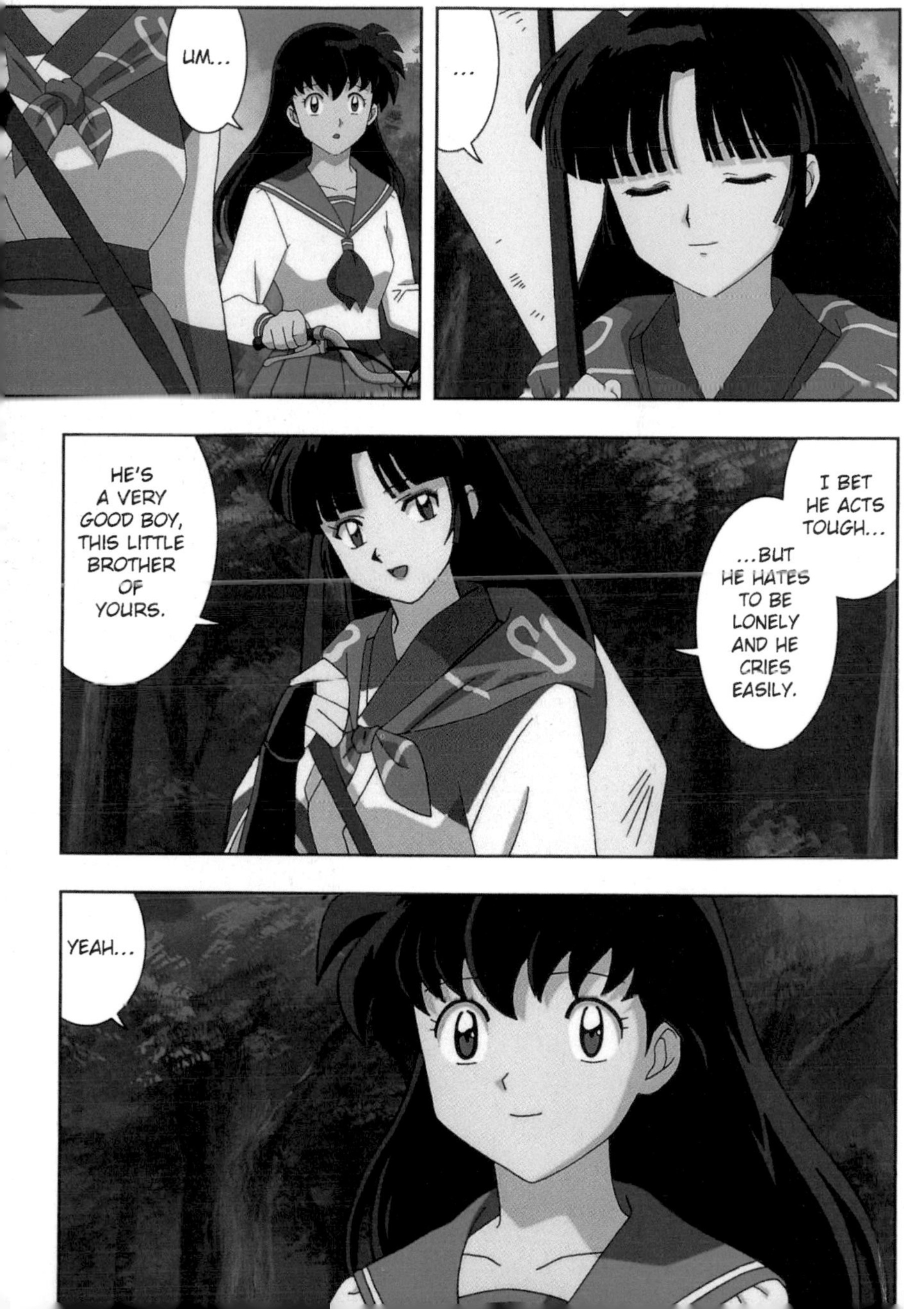
...
UM...
I BET HE ACTS TOUGH...
...BUT HE HATES TO BE LONELY AND HE CRIES EASILY.
HE'S A VERY GOOD BOY, THIS LITTLE BROTHER OF YOURS.
YEAH...

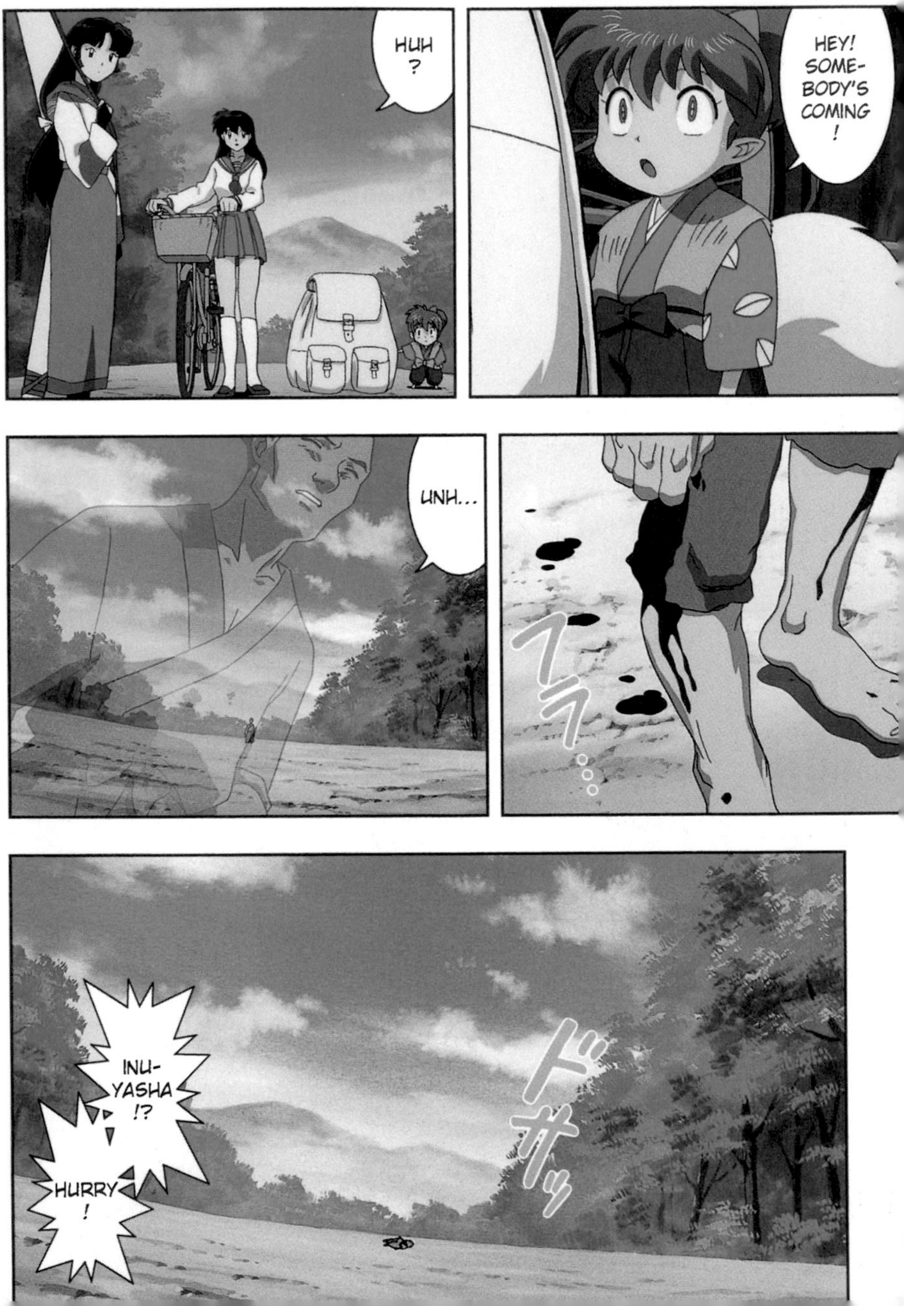
HEY! SOME-BODY'S COMING!
HUH?
フラ…
UNH...
ドサッ
INU-YASHA!?
HURRY!

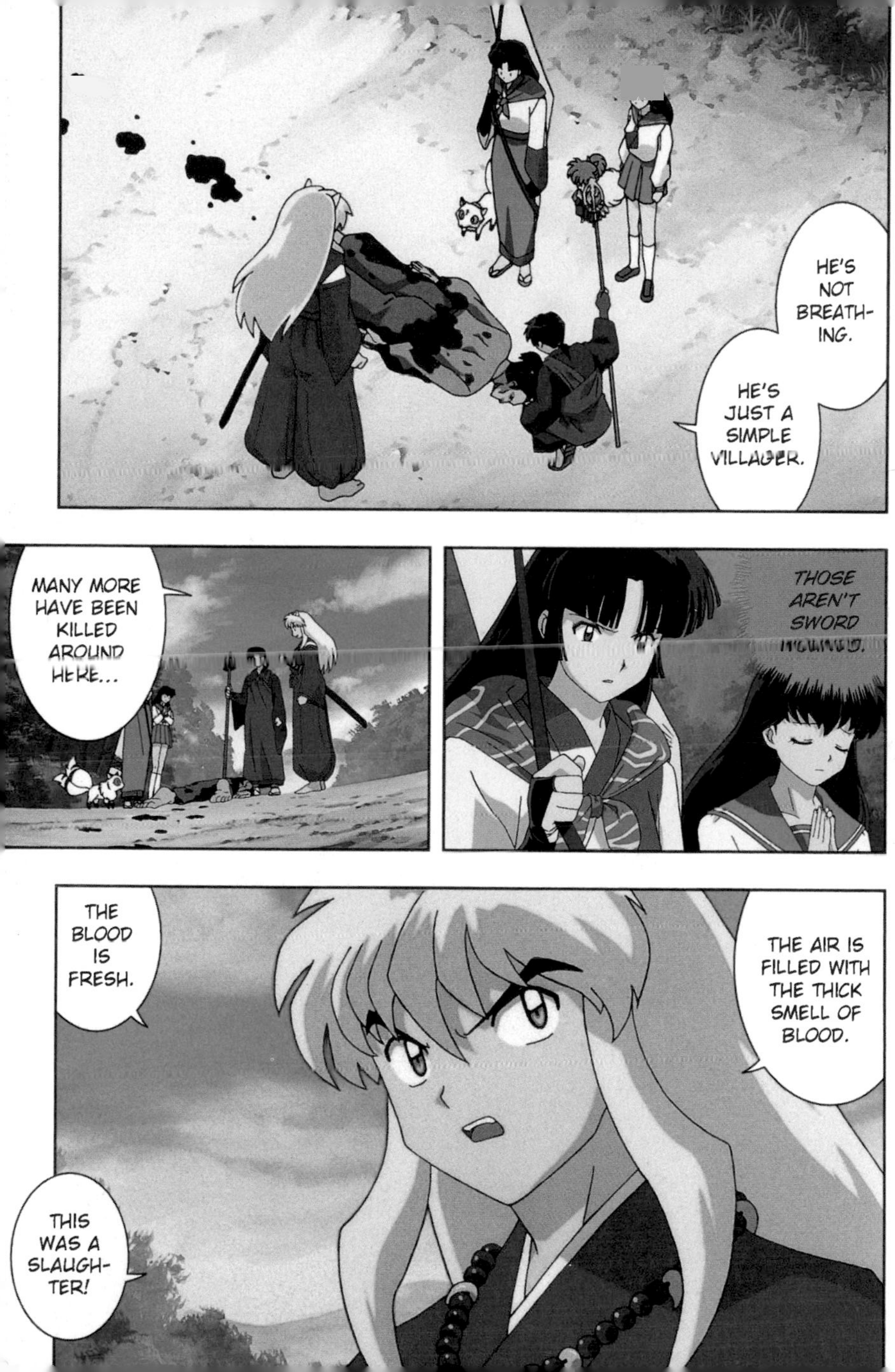
HE'S NOT BREATHING.
HE'S JUST A SIMPLE VILLAGER.
THOSE AREN'T SWORD
MANY MORE HAVE BEEN KILLED AROUND HERE...
THE AIR IS FILLED WITH THE THICK SMELL OF BLOOD.
THE BLOOD IS FRESH.
THIS WAS A SLAUGHTER!

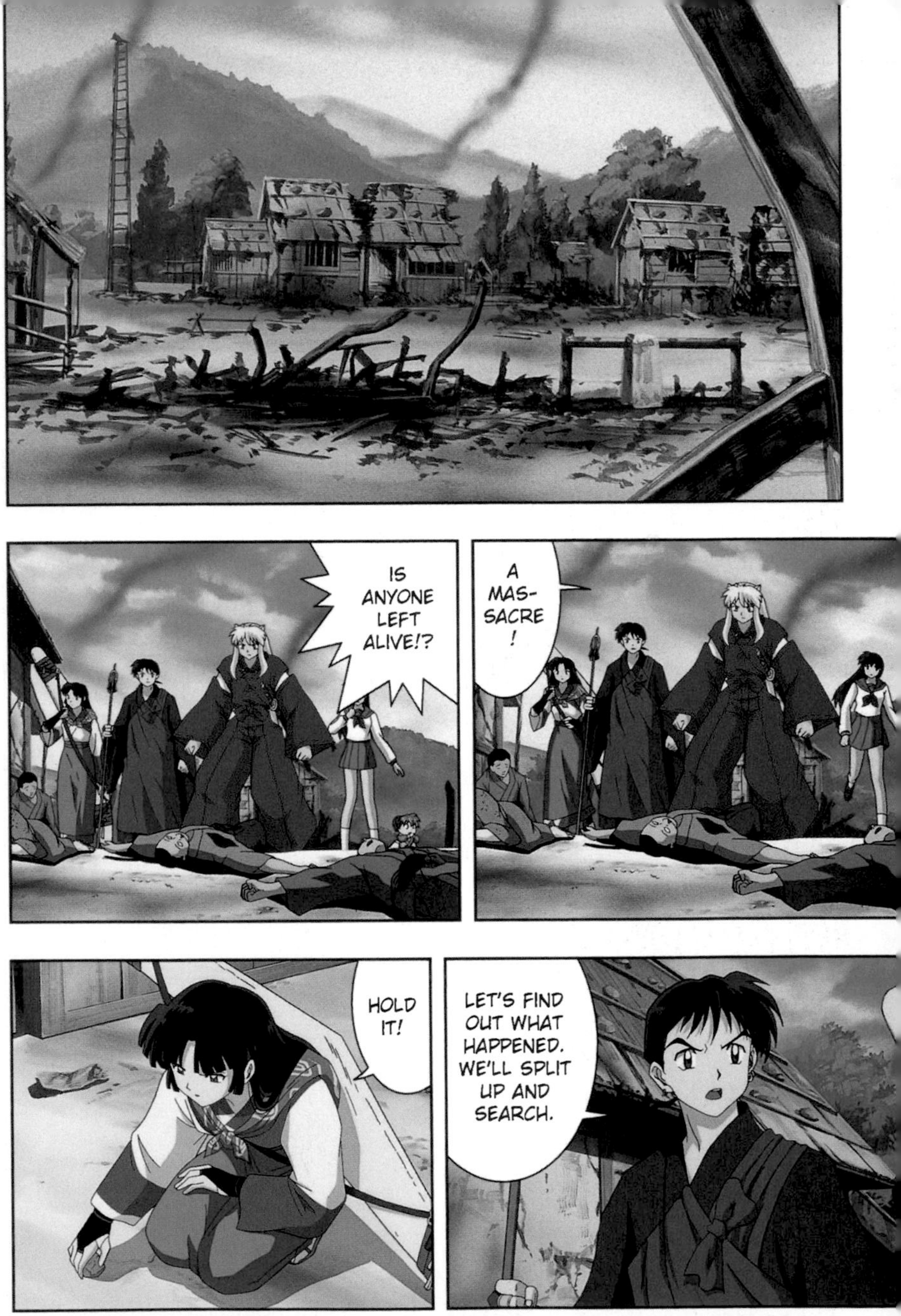
A MAS-SACRE!
IS ANYONE LEFT ALIVE!?
LET'S FIND OUT WHAT HAPPENED. WE'LL SPLIT UP AND SEARCH.
HOLD IT!

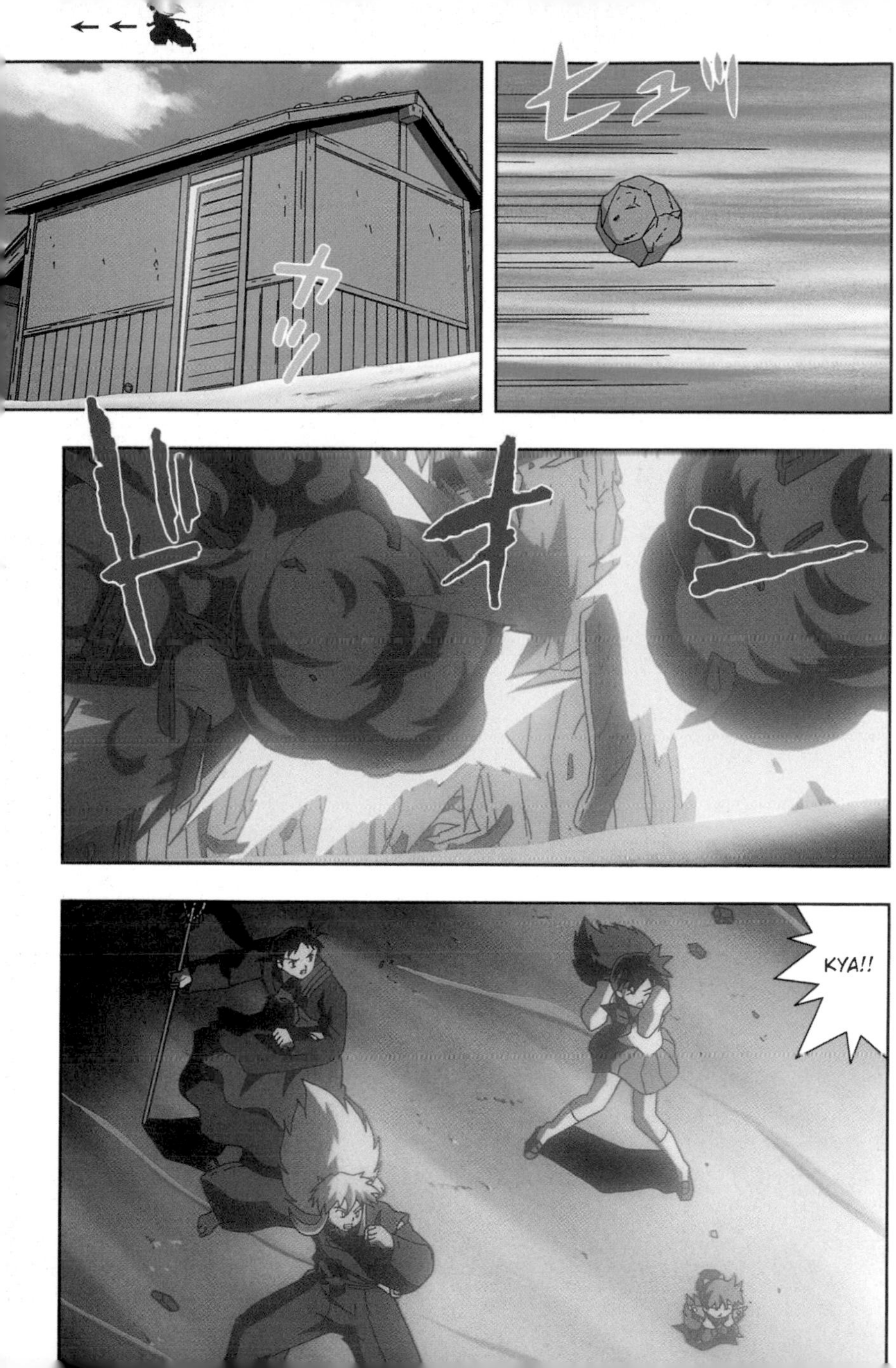
ヒュッ
カッ
ドオン
KYA!!

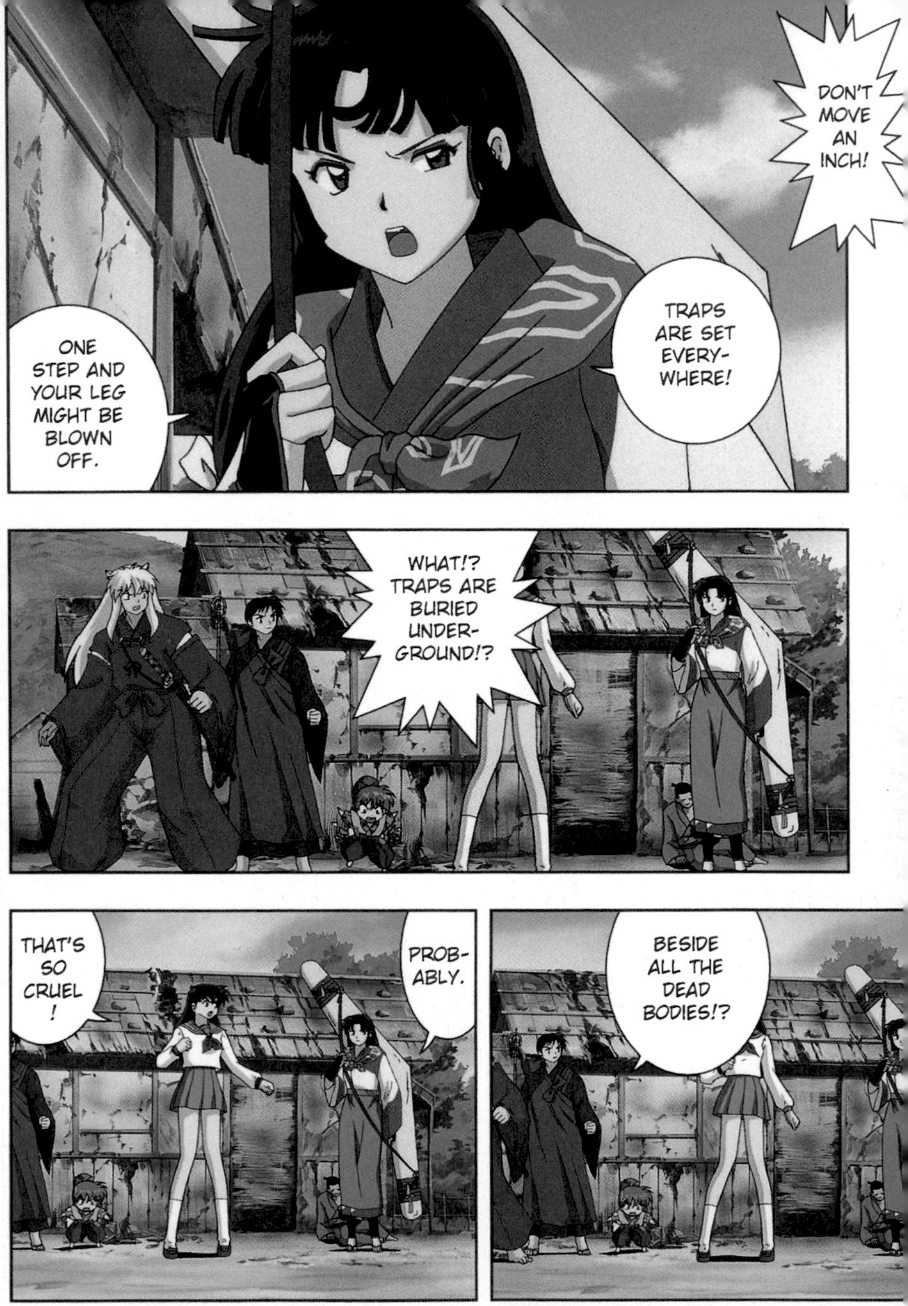

DON'T MOVE AN INCH!
TRAPS ARE SET EVERY-WHERE!
ONE STEP AND YOUR LEG MIGHT BE BLOWN OFF.
WHAT!? TRAPS ARE BURIED UNDER-GROUND!?
BESIDE ALL THE DEAD BODIES!?
PROB-ABLY.
THAT'S SO CRUEL!

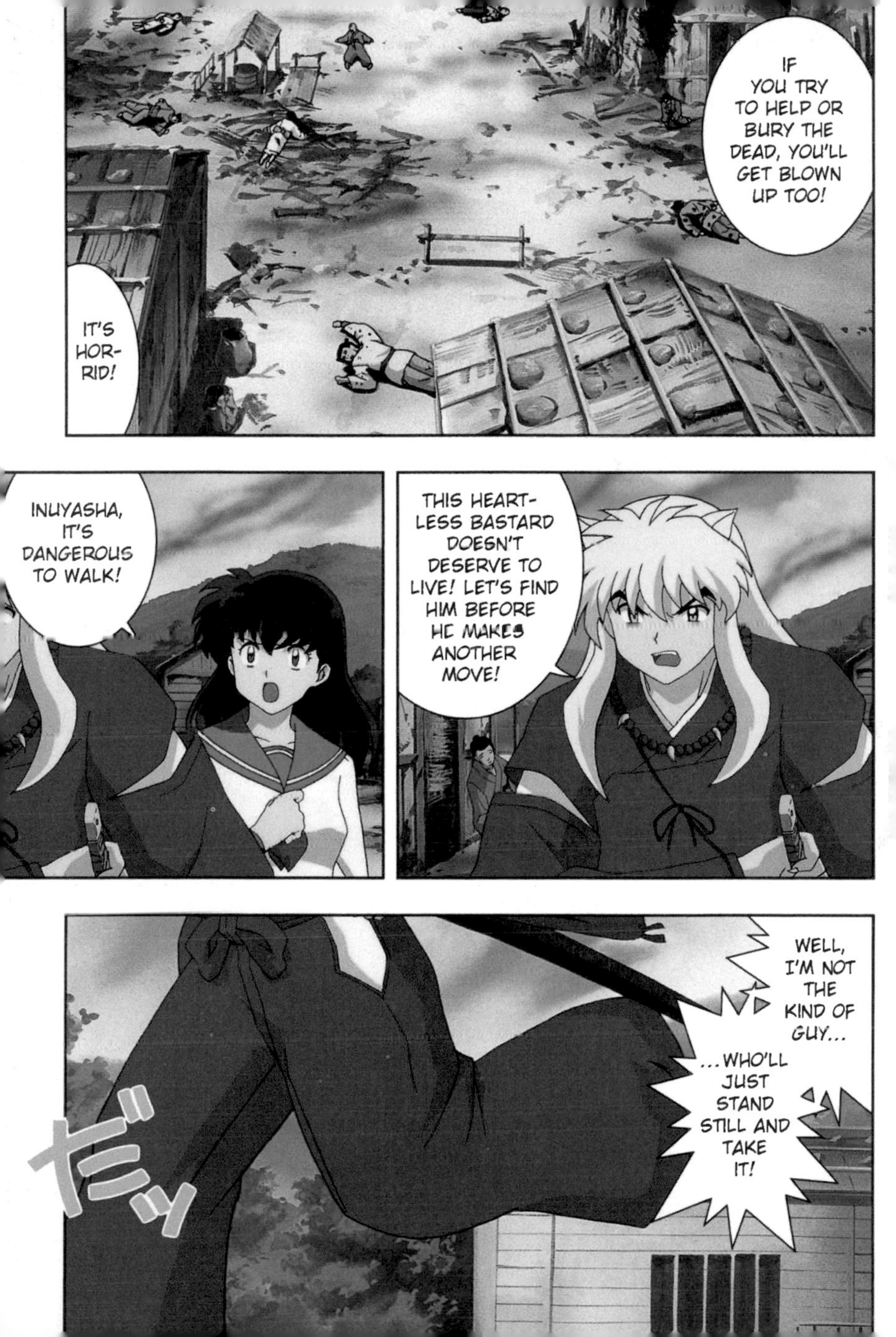
IF YOU TRY TO HELP OR BURY THE DEAD, YOU'LL GET BLOWN UP TOO!
IT'S HOR-RID!
THIS HEART-LESS BASTARD DOESN'T DESERVE TO LIVE! LET'S FIND HIM BEFORE HE MAKES ANOTHER MOVE!
INUYASHA, IT'S DANGEROUS TO WALK!
WELL, I'M NOT THE KIND OF GUY...
...WHO'LL JUST STAND STILL AND TAKE IT!

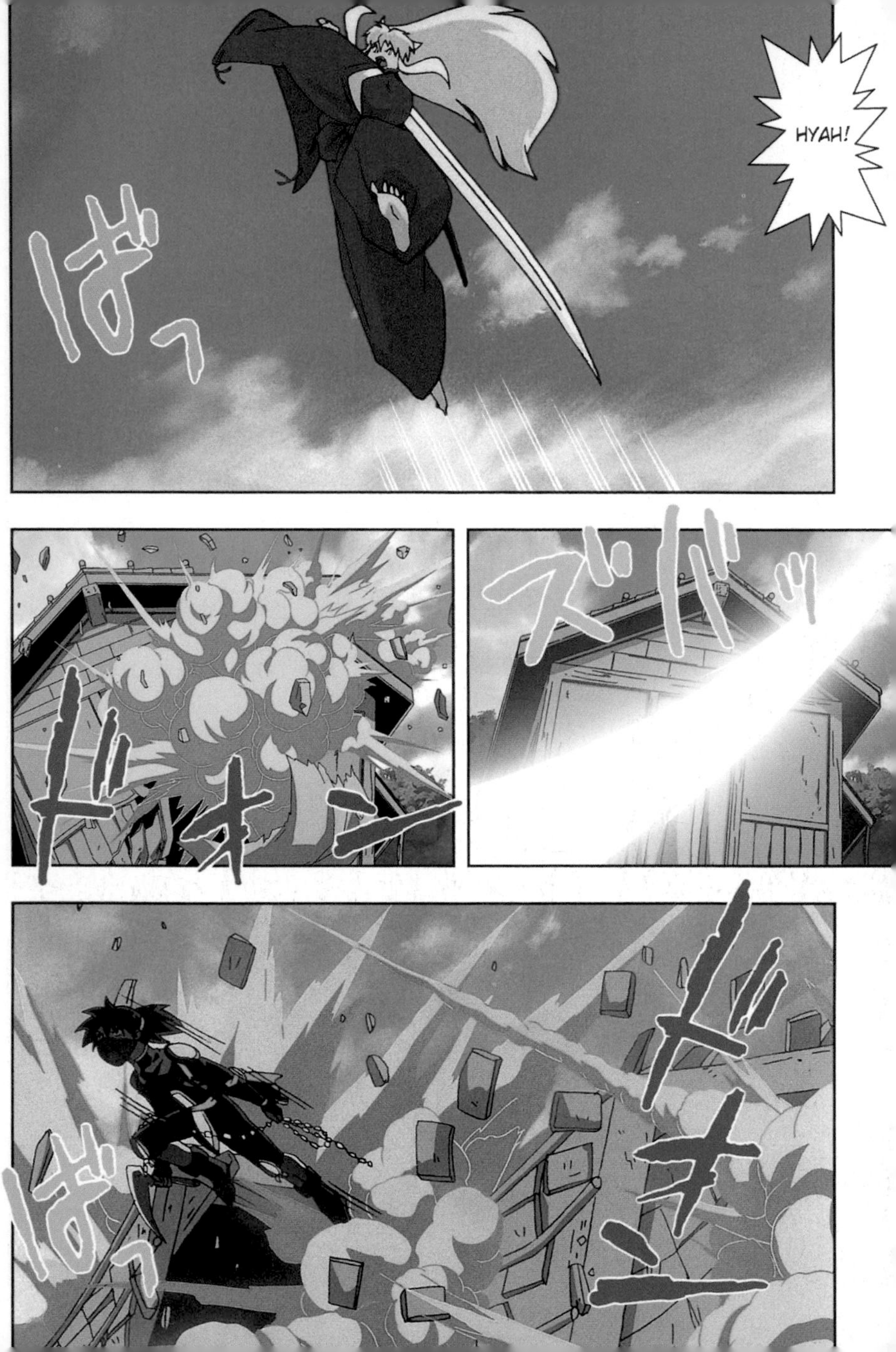
HYAH!
ばっ
ズバッ
ドォーン
ドォーン
ばっ

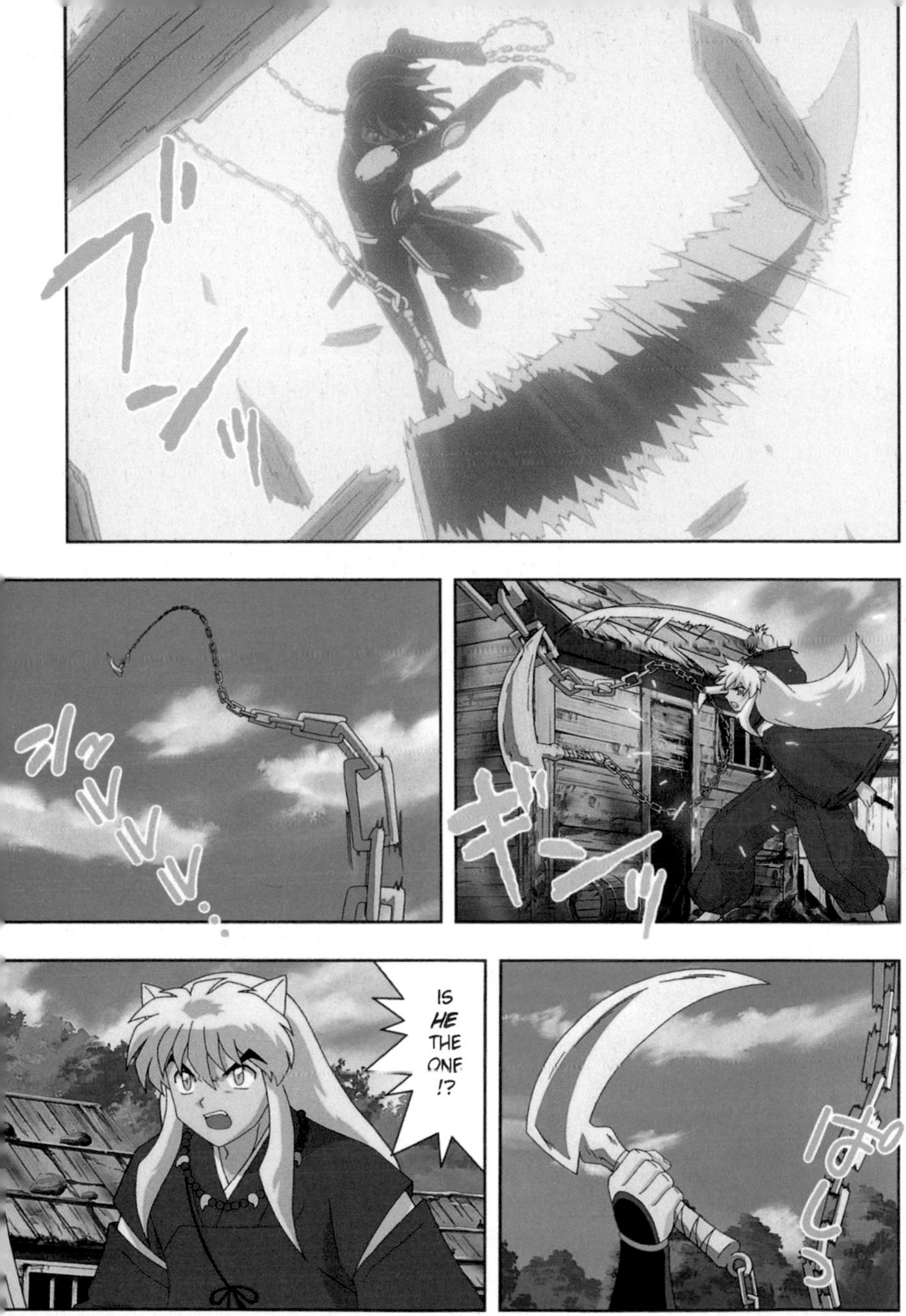
ブンッ
ギンッ
ぱしっ
IS HE THE ONE !?

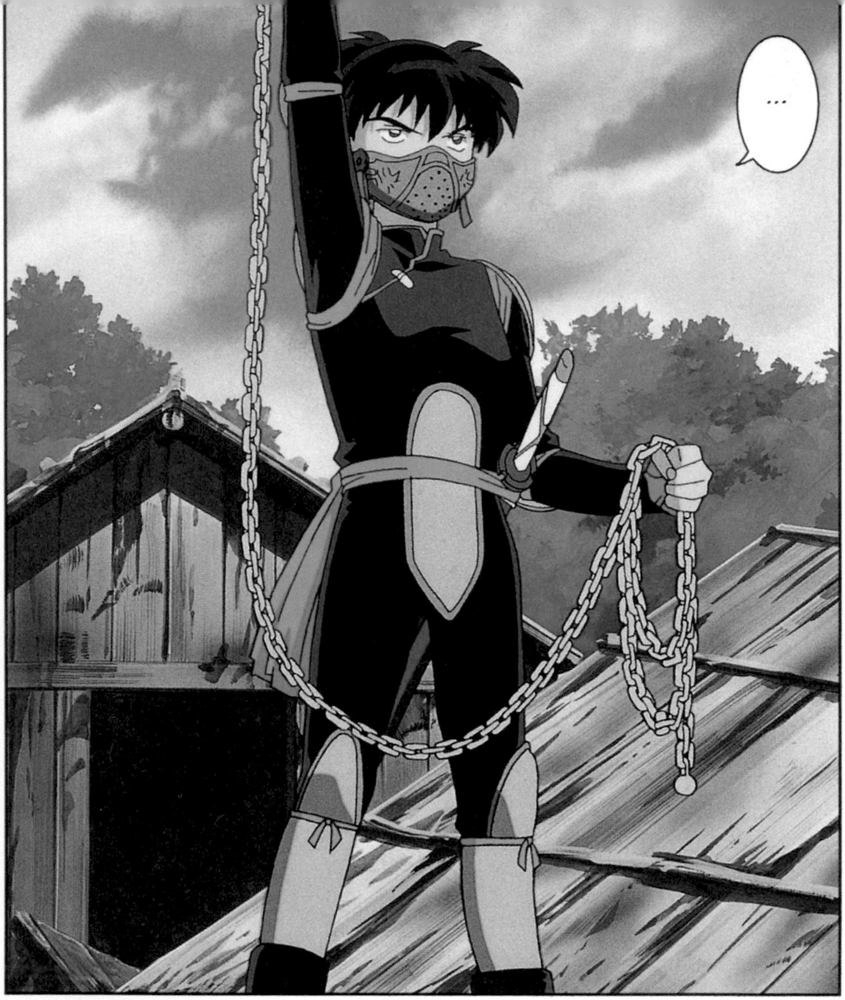
...

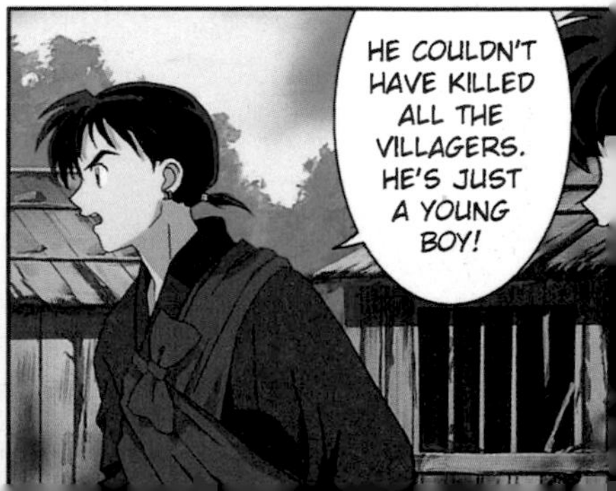
HE COULDN'T HAVE KILLED ALL THE VILLAGERS. HE'S JUST A YOUNG BOY!

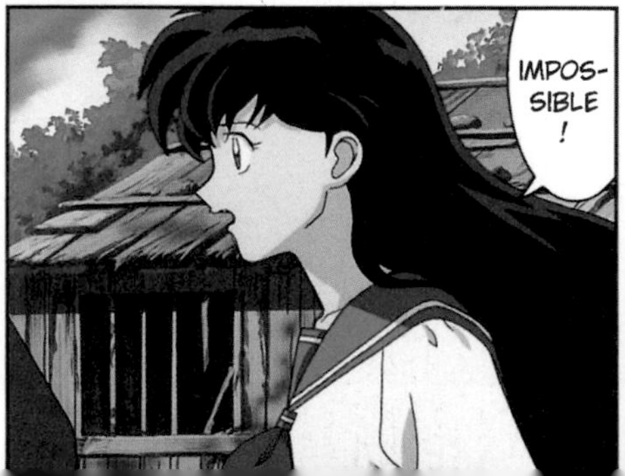
IMPOS-SIBLE!

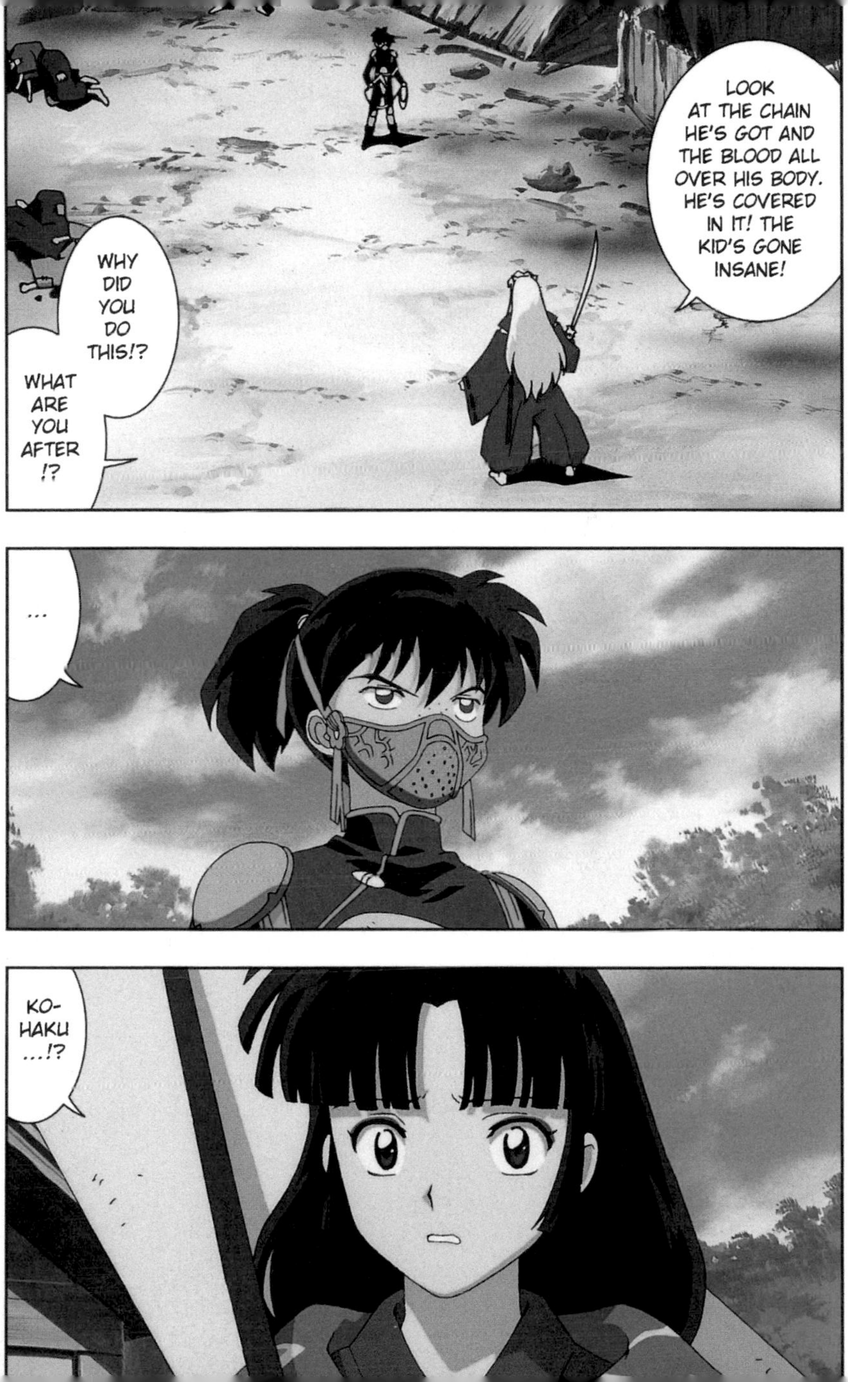
LOOK AT THE CHAIN HE'S GOT AND THE BLOOD ALL OVER HIS BODY. HE'S COVERED IN IT! THE KID'S GONE INSANE!
WHY DID YOU DO THIS!?
WHAT ARE YOU AFTER!?
...
KO-HAKU...!?

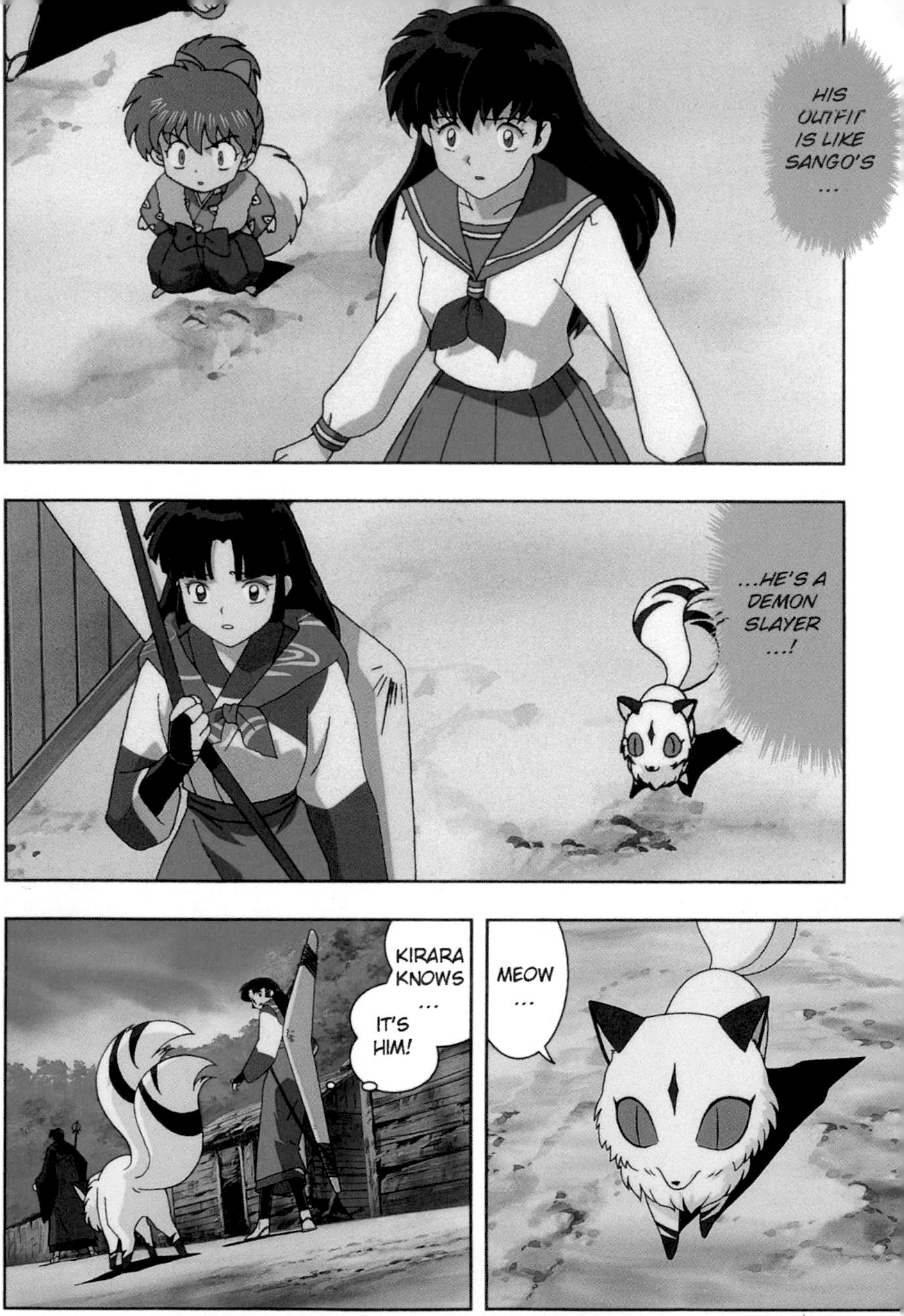
HIS OUTFIT IS LIKE SANGO'S ...
...HE'S A DEMON SLAYER ...!
MEOW ...
KIRARA KNOWS ...
IT'S HIM!

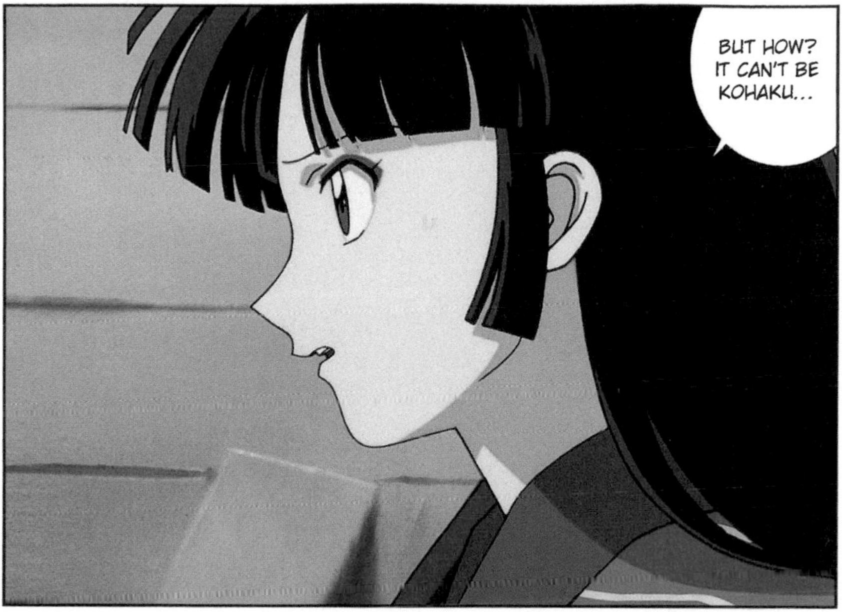
BUT HOW? IT CAN'T BE KOHAKU...
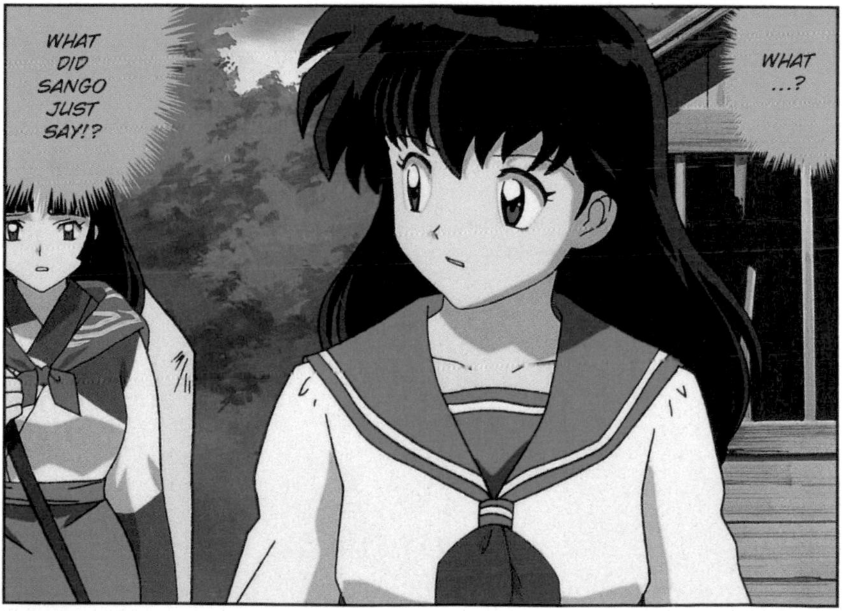
WHAT ...?
WHAT DID SANGO JUST SAY!?

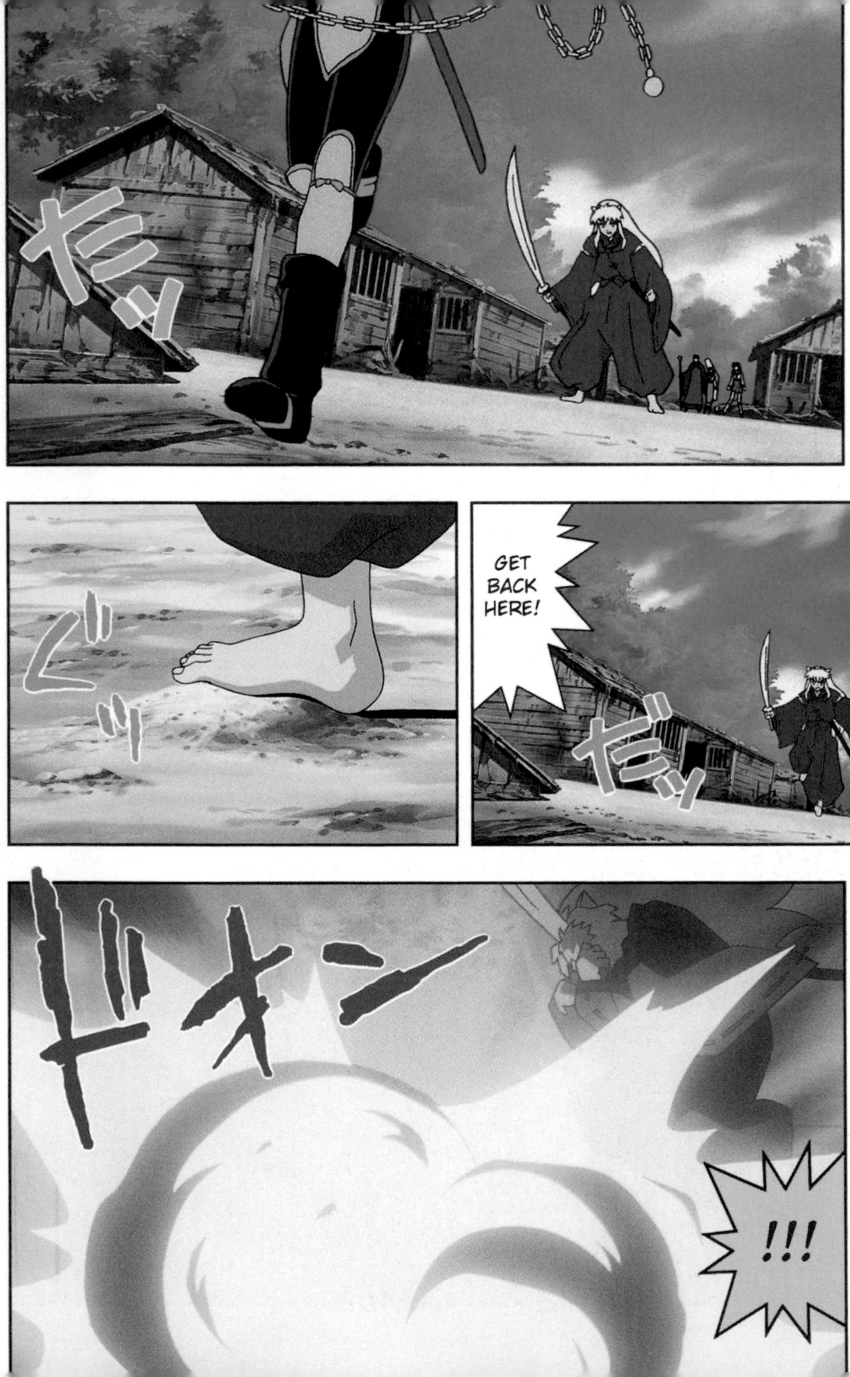
ダッ
GET BACK HERE!
ダッ
ぐッ
ドオン
!!!

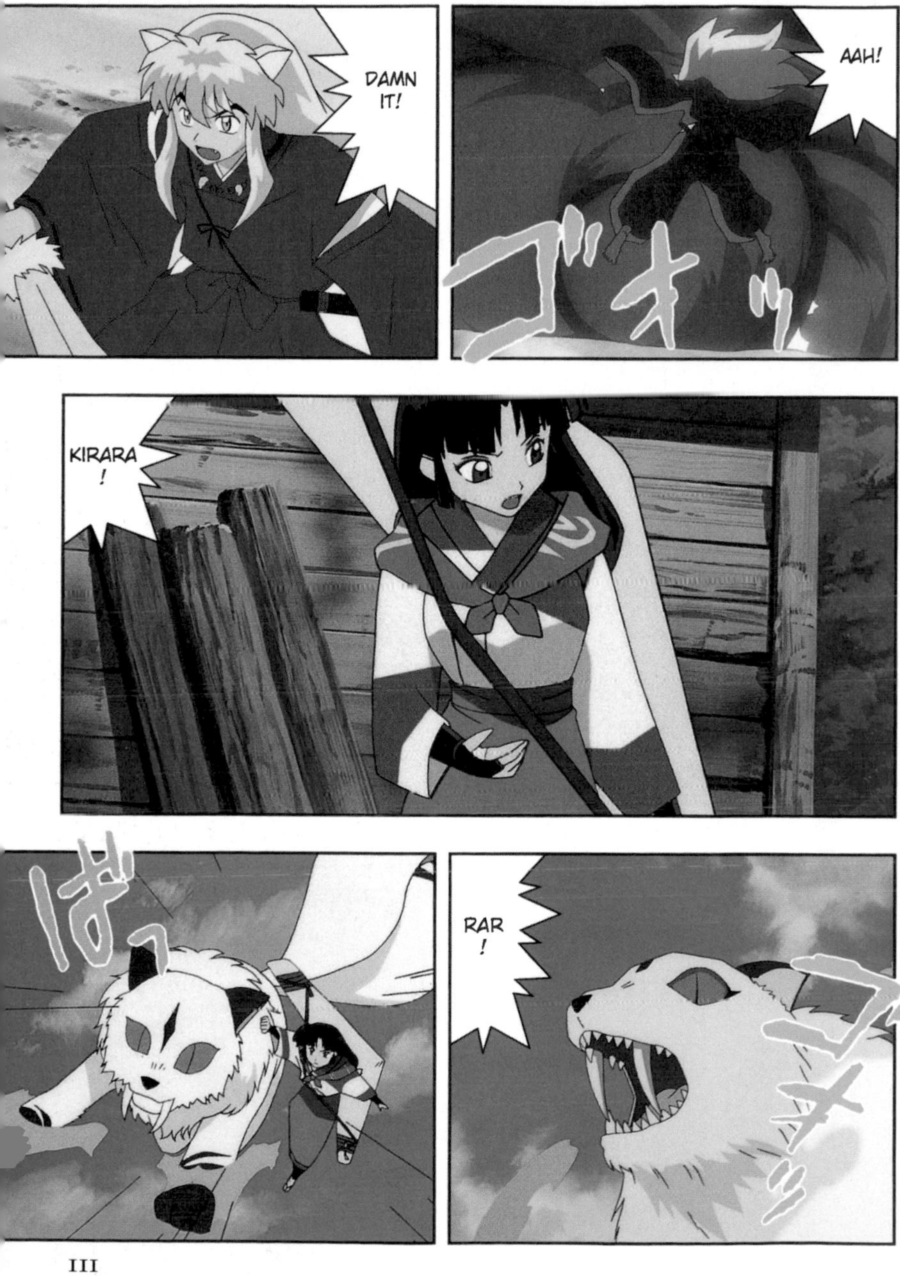
AAH!
ゴオッ
DAMN IT!
KIRARA!
RAR!

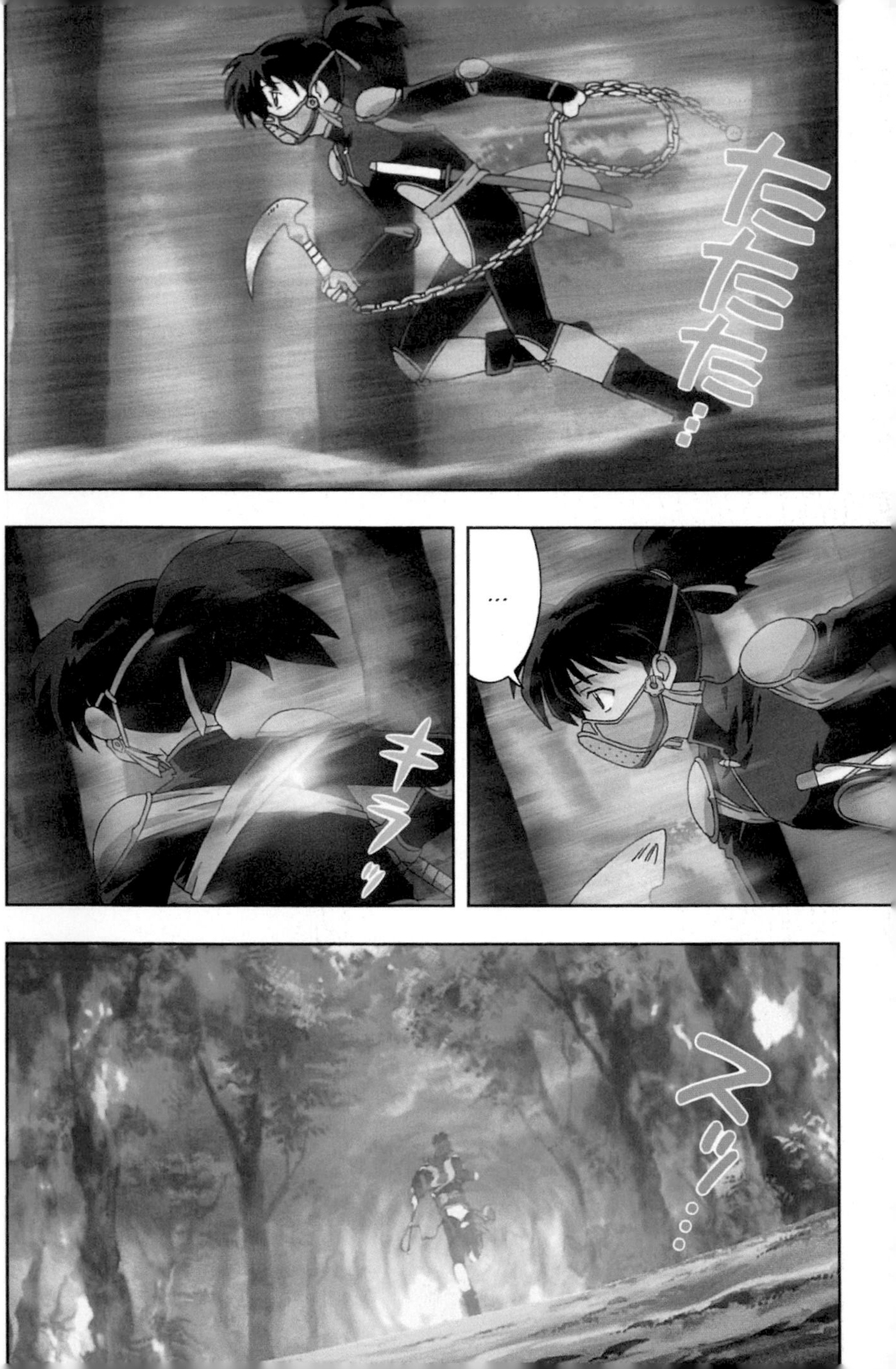
たたた…
…
キラッ
スッ…

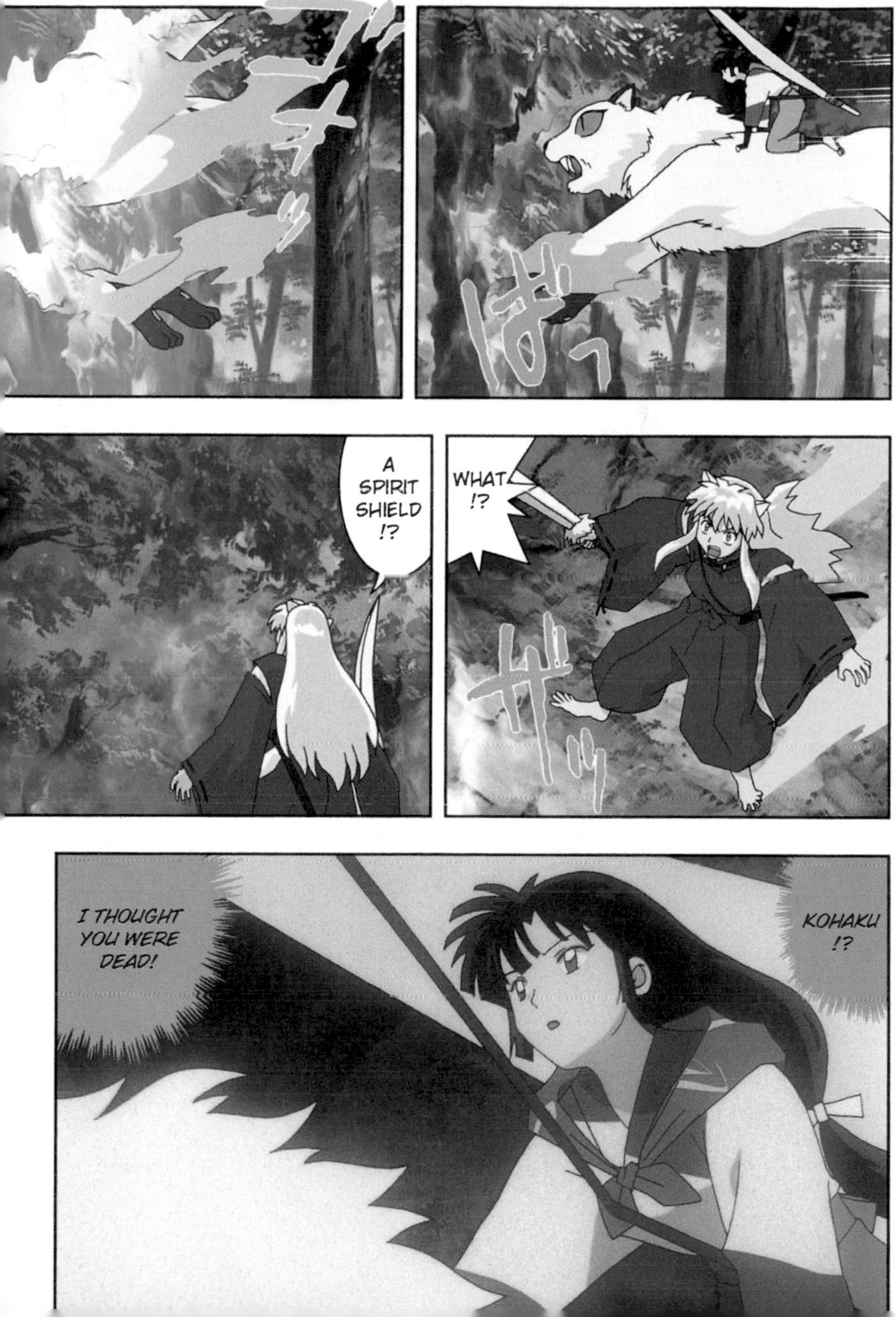
ぱっ
WHAT !?
ザッ
A SPIRIT SHIELD !?
KOHAKU !?
I THOUGHT YOU WERE DEAD!

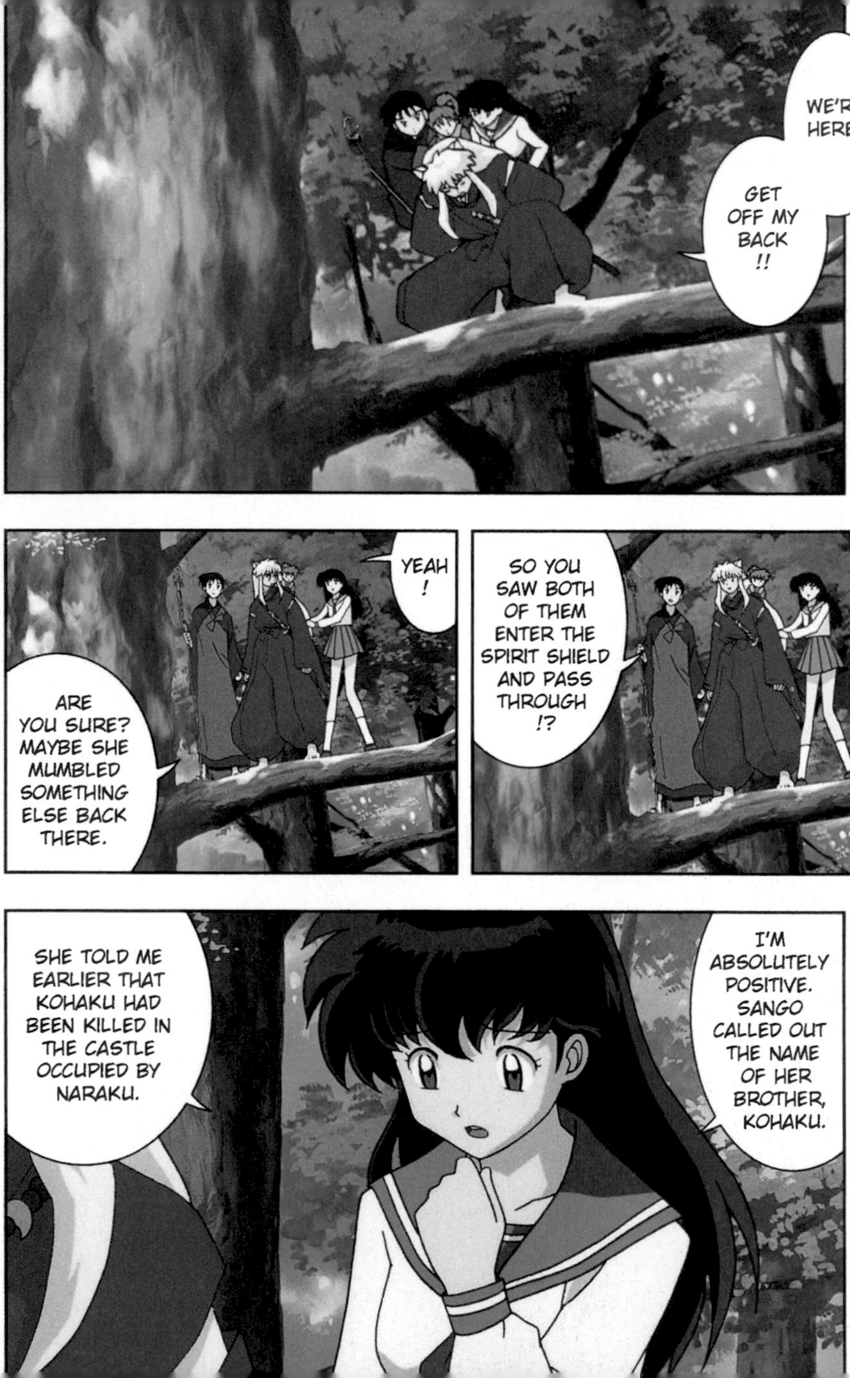
WE'RE HERE!
GET OFF MY BACK !!
SO YOU SAW BOTH OF THEM ENTER THE SPIRIT SHIELD AND PASS THROUGH !?
YEAH !
ARE YOU SURE? MAYBE SHE MUMBLED SOMETHING ELSE BACK THERE.
I'M ABSOLUTELY POSITIVE. SANGO CALLED OUT THE NAME OF HER BROTHER, KOHAKU.
SHE TOLD ME EARLIER THAT KOHAKU HAD BEEN KILLED IN THE CASTLE OCCUPIED BY NARAKU.

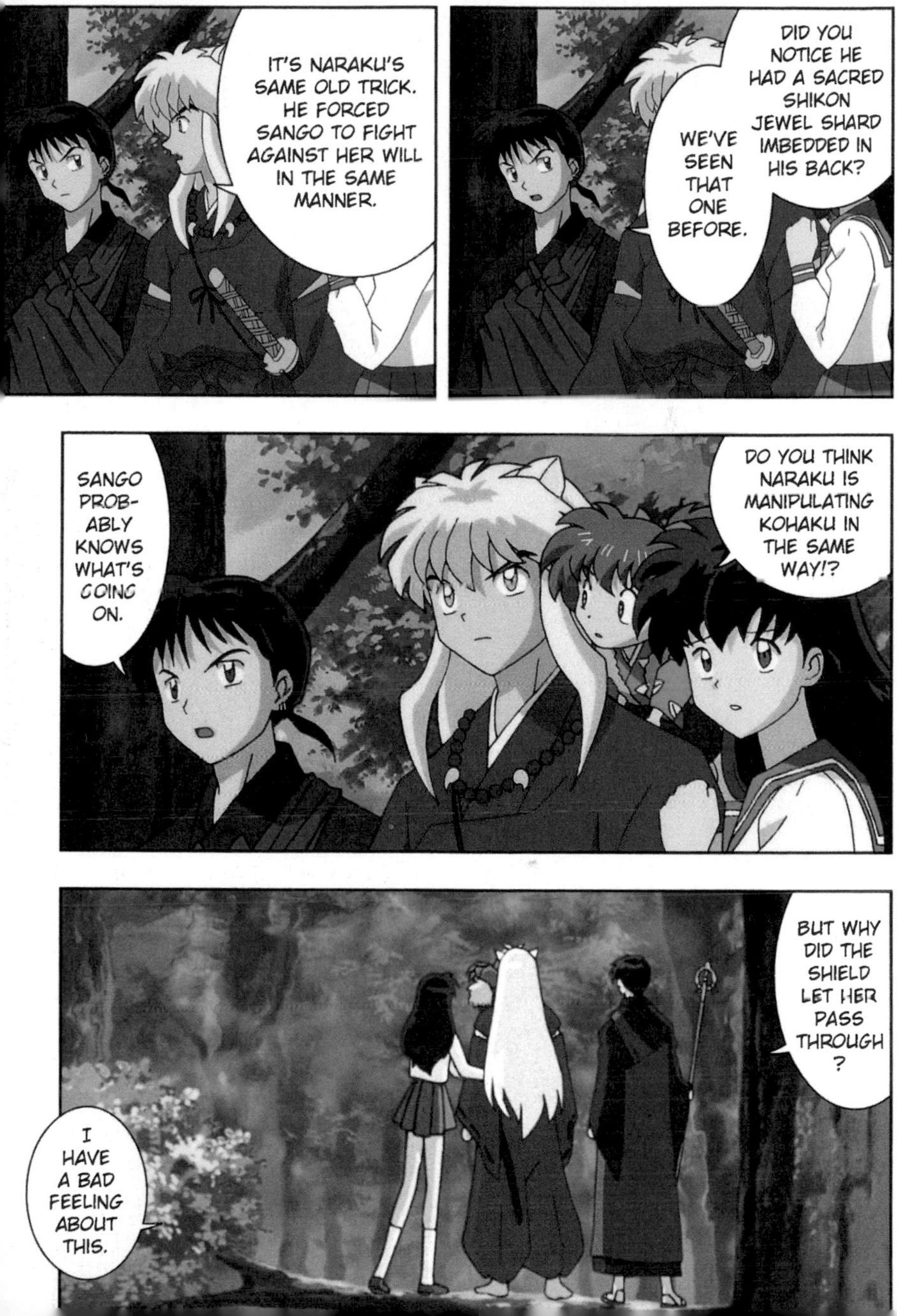
DID YOU NOTICE HE HAD A SACRED SHIKON JEWEL SHARD IMBEDDED IN HIS BACK?
WE'VE SEEN THAT ONE BEFORE.
IT'S NARAKU'S SAME OLD TRICK. HE FORCED SANGO TO FIGHT AGAINST HER WILL IN THE SAME MANNER.
DO YOU THINK NARAKU IS MANIPULATING KOHAKU IN THE SAME WAY!?
SANGO PROB-ABLY KNOWS WHAT'S GOING ON.
BUT WHY DID THE SHIELD LET HER PASS THROUGH?
I HAVE A BAD FEELING ABOUT THIS.

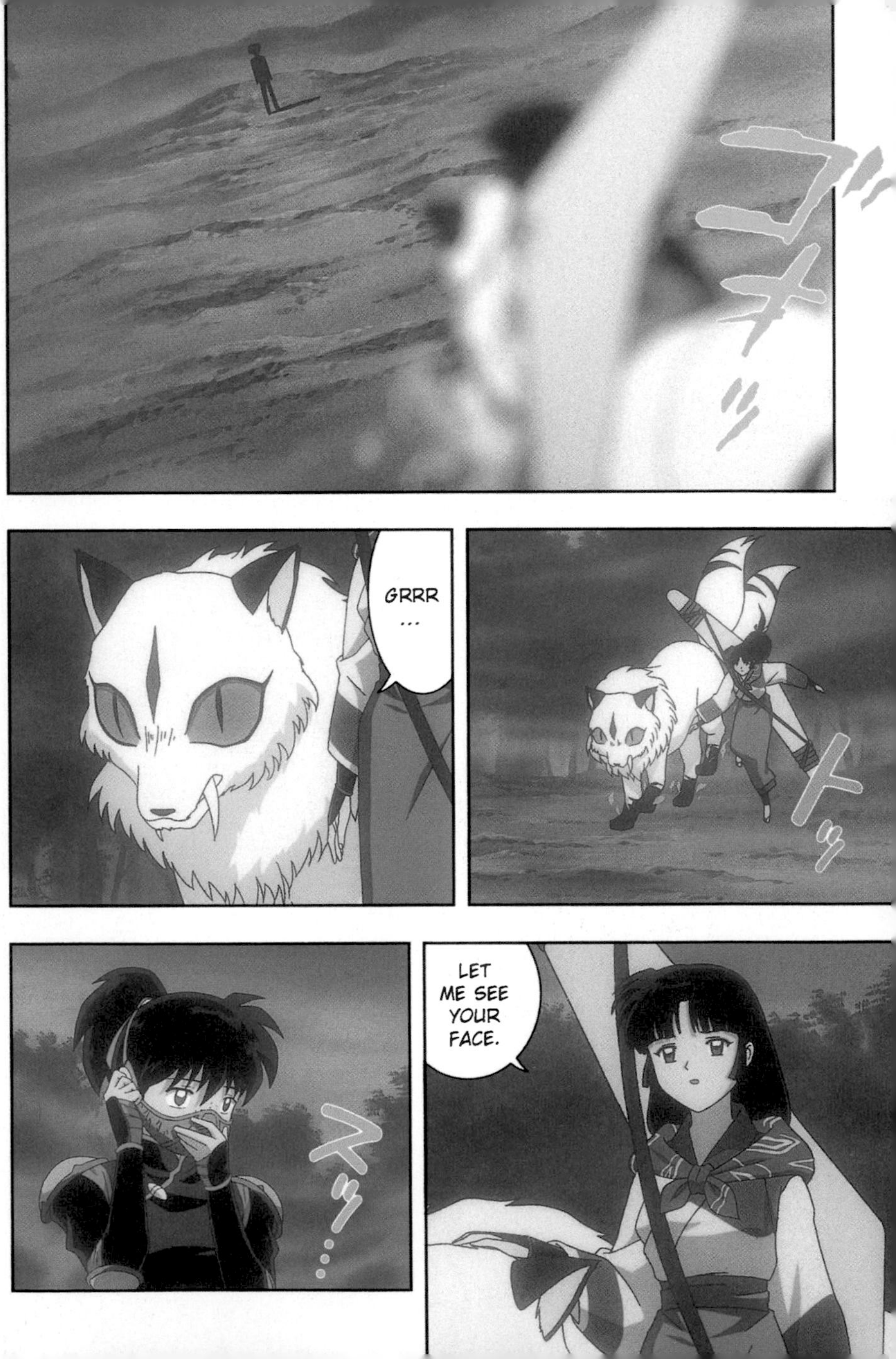
トッ
GRRR ...
LET ME SEE YOUR FACE.
スッ...

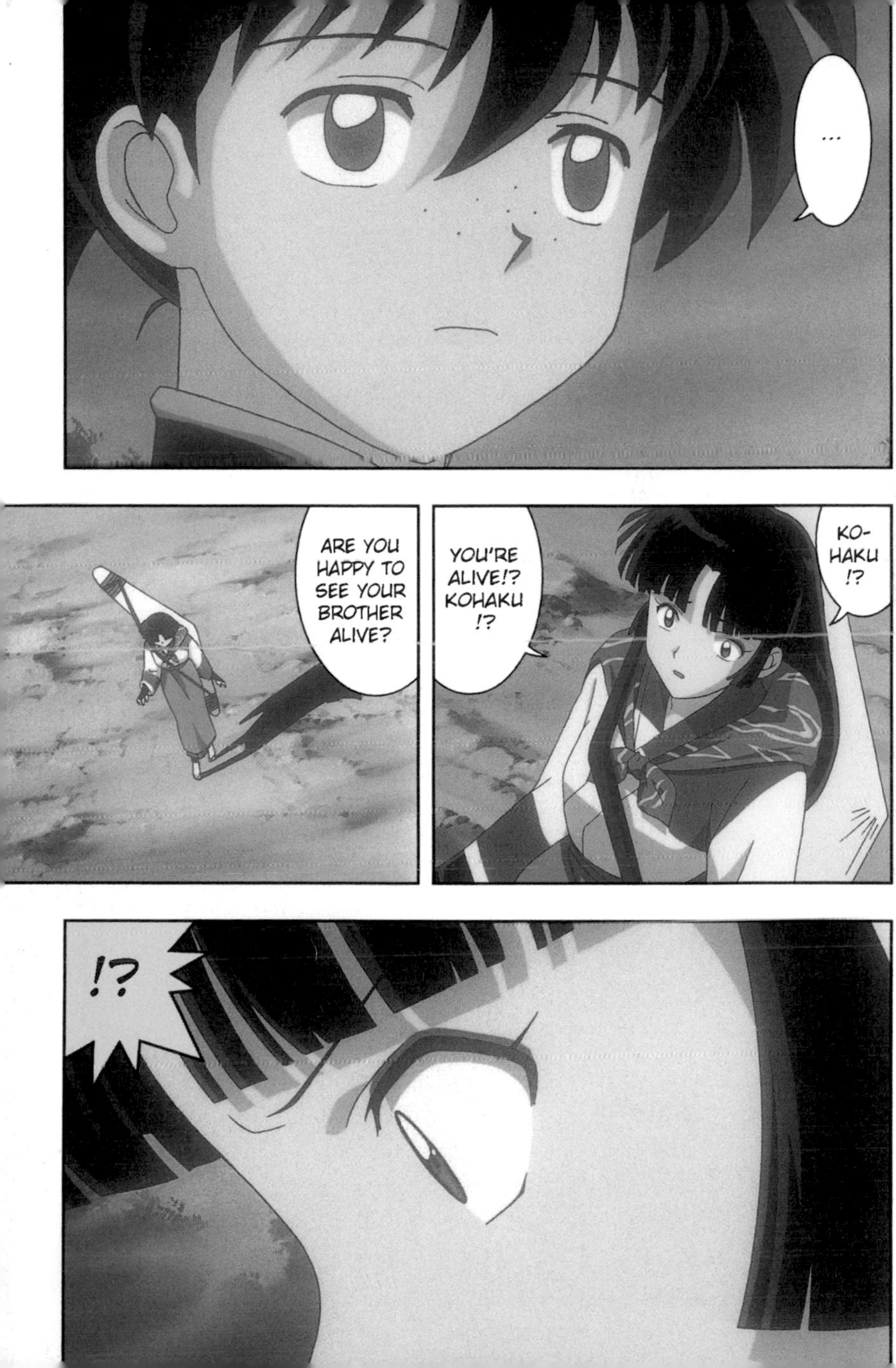
...
KO-HAKU!?
YOU'RE ALIVE!? KOHAKU!?
ARE YOU HAPPY TO SEE YOUR BROTHER ALIVE?
!?

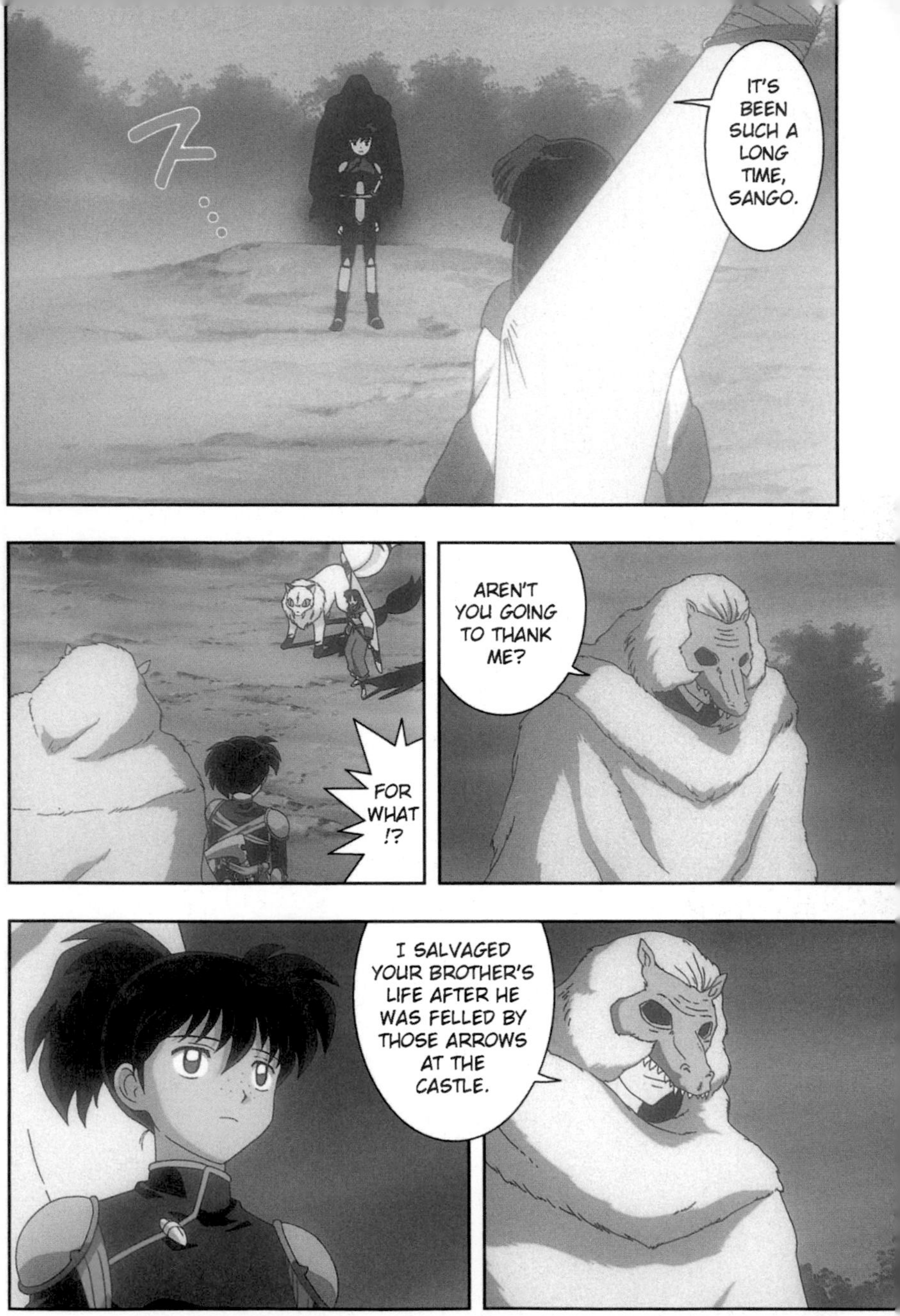
IT'S BEEN SUCH A LONG TIME, SANGO.
AREN'T YOU GOING TO THANK ME?
FOR WHAT!?
I SALVAGED YOUR BROTHER'S LIFE AFTER HE WAS FELLED BY THOSE ARROWS AT THE CASTLE.

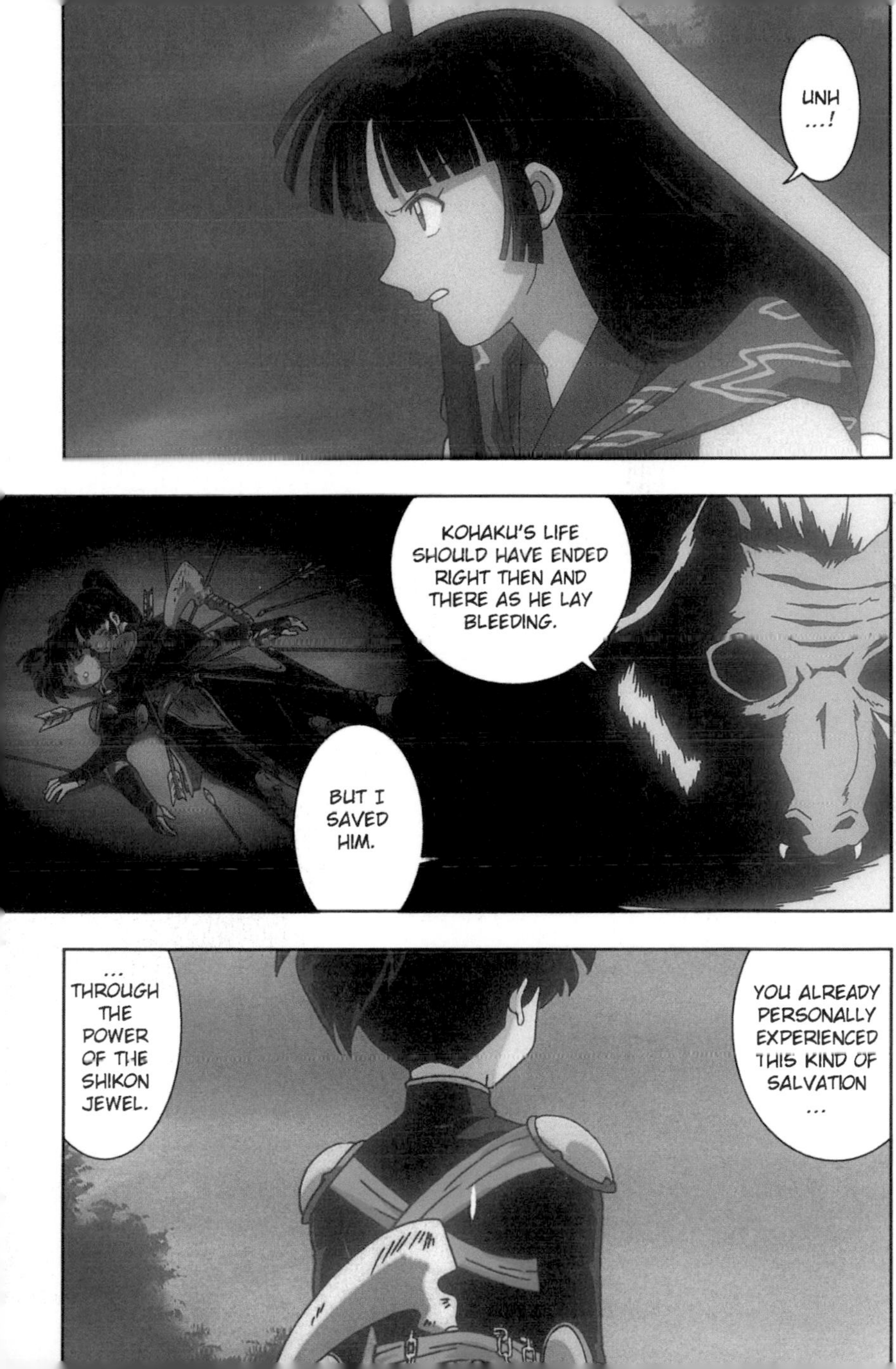
UNH ...!
KOHAKU'S LIFE SHOULD HAVE ENDED RIGHT THEN AND THERE AS HE LAY BLEEDING.
BUT I SAVED HIM.
YOU ALREADY PERSONALLY EXPERIENCED THIS KIND OF SALVATION ...
... THROUGH THE POWER OF THE SHIKON JEWEL.

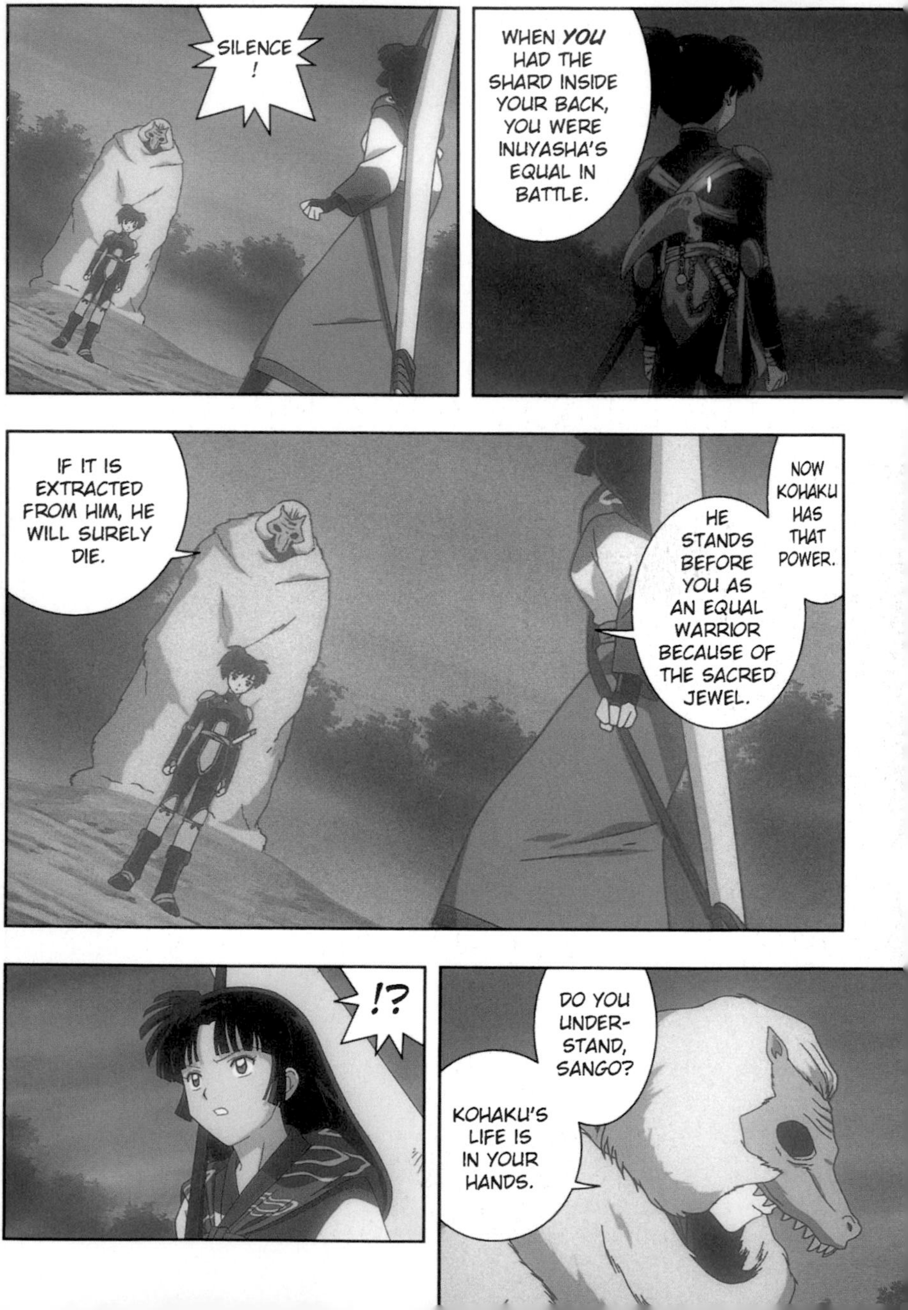
WHEN *YOU* HAD THE SHARD INSIDE YOUR BACK, YOU WERE INUYASHA'S EQUAL IN BATTLE.
SILENCE!
NOW KOHAKU HAS THAT POWER.
HE STANDS BEFORE YOU AS AN EQUAL WARRIOR BECAUSE OF THE SACRED JEWEL.
IF IT IS EXTRACTED FROM HIM, HE WILL SURELY DIE.
DO YOU UNDER-STAND, SANGO?
KOHAKU'S LIFE IS IN YOUR HANDS.
!?

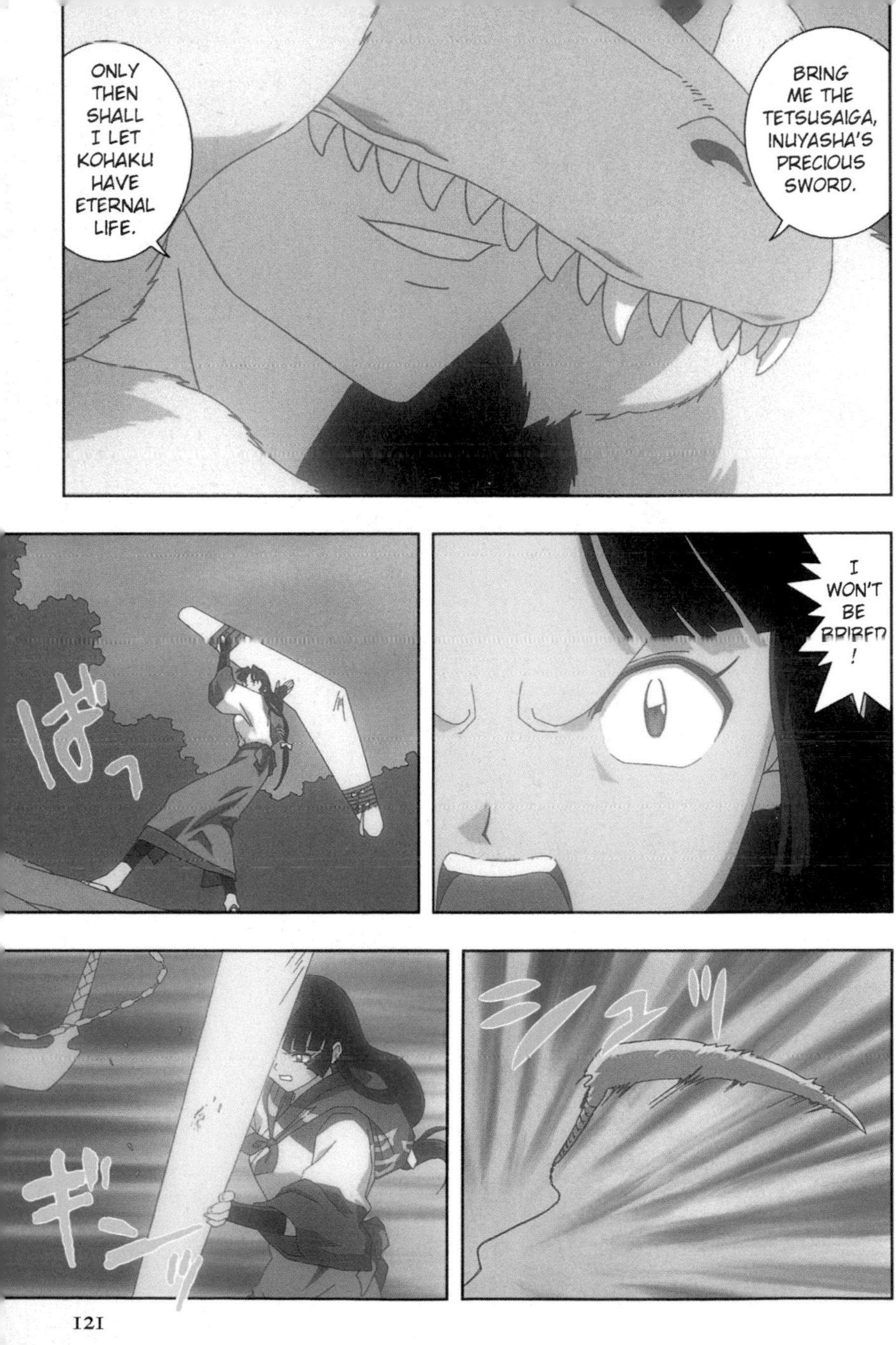
BRING ME THE TETSUSAIGA, INUYASHA'S PRECIOUS SWORD.
ONLY THEN SHALL I LET KOHAKU HAVE ETERNAL LIFE.
I WON'T BE BRIBED!
ばっ
シュヅ
ギンッ

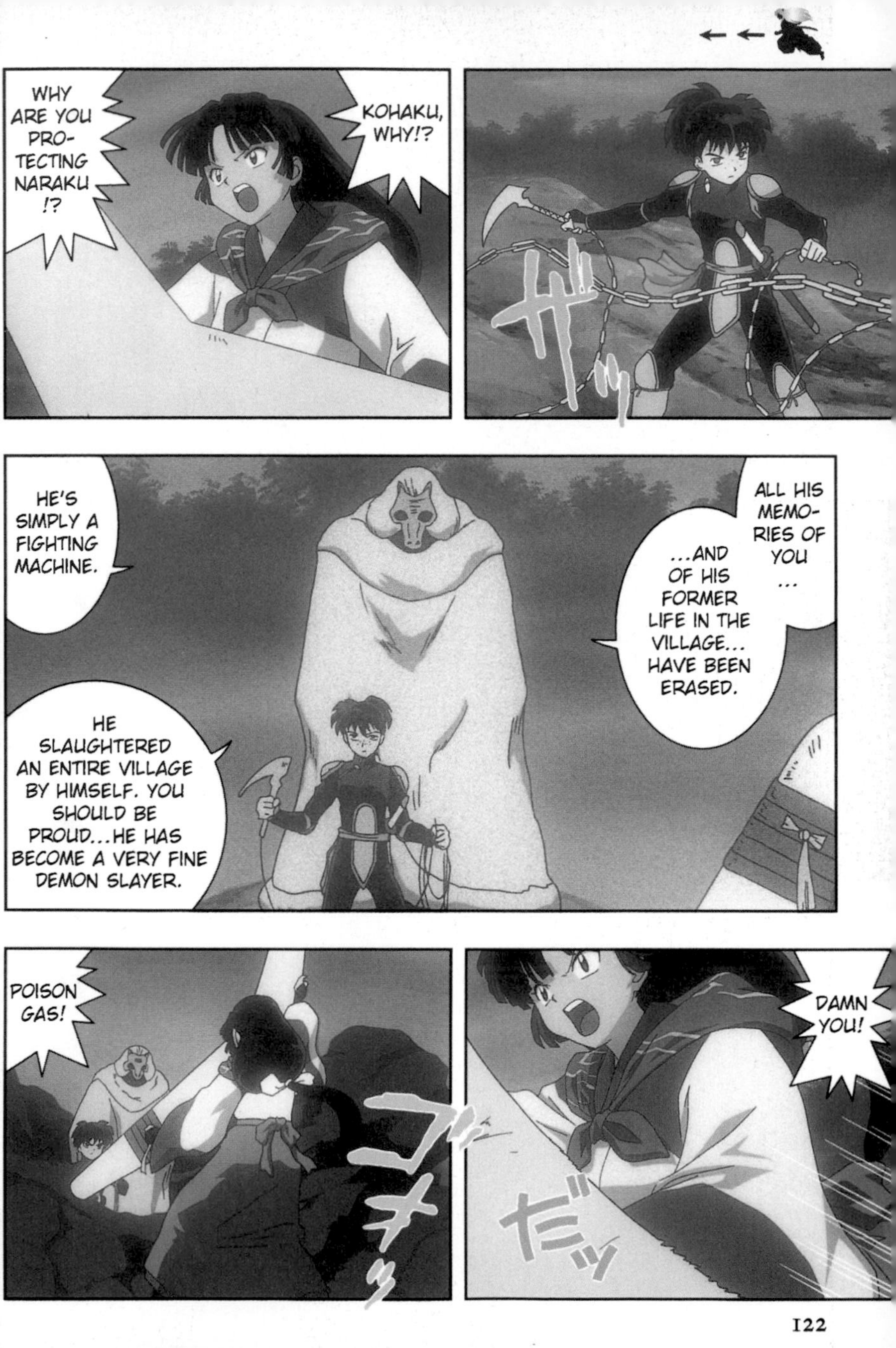
ザッ
KOHAKU, WHY!?
WHY ARE YOU PRO-TECTING NARAKU!?
ALL HIS MEMO-RIES OF YOU...
...AND OF HIS FORMER LIFE IN THE VILLAGE... HAVE BEEN ERASED.
HE'S SIMPLY A FIGHTING MACHINE.
HE SLAUGHTERED AN ENTIRE VILLAGE BY HIMSELF. YOU SHOULD BE PROUD...HE HAS BECOME A VERY FINE DEMON SLAYER.
DAMN YOU!
だッ
POISON GAS!

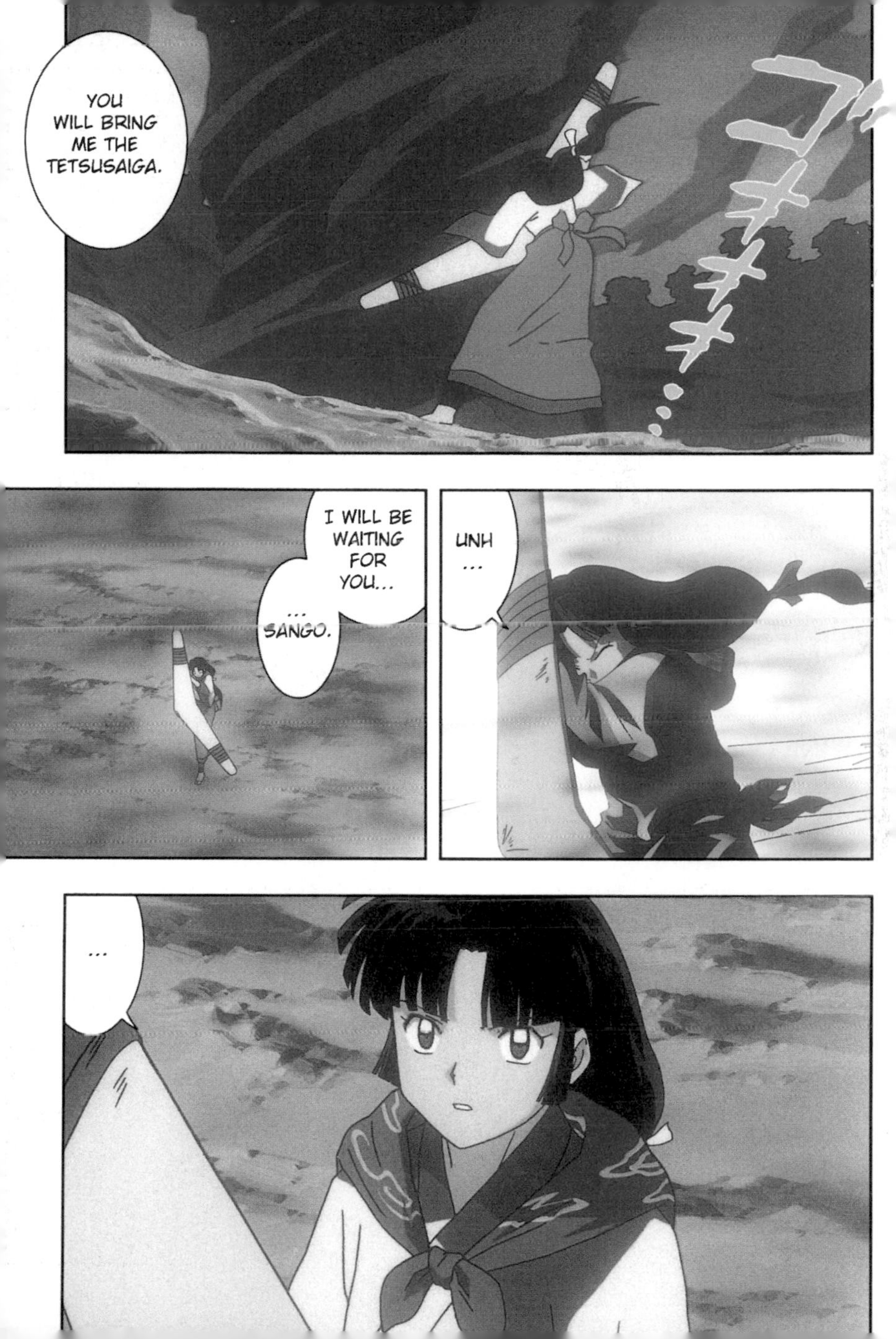
YOU WILL BRING ME THE TETSUSAIGA.
UNH ...
I WILL BE WAITING FOR YOU...
... SANGO.
...

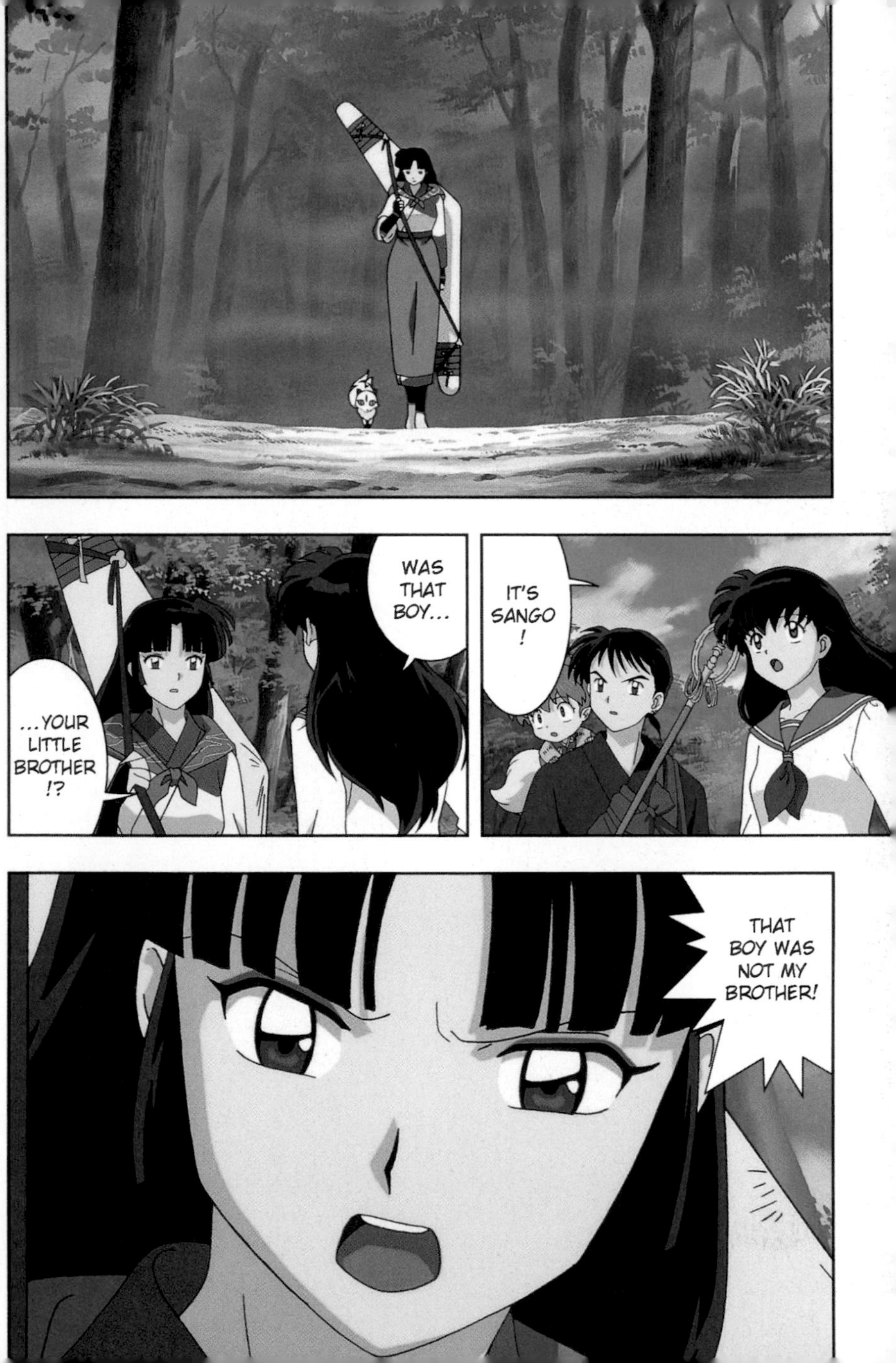
IT'S SANGO!
WAS THAT BOY...
...YOUR LITTLE BROTHER!?
THAT BOY WAS NOT MY BROTHER!

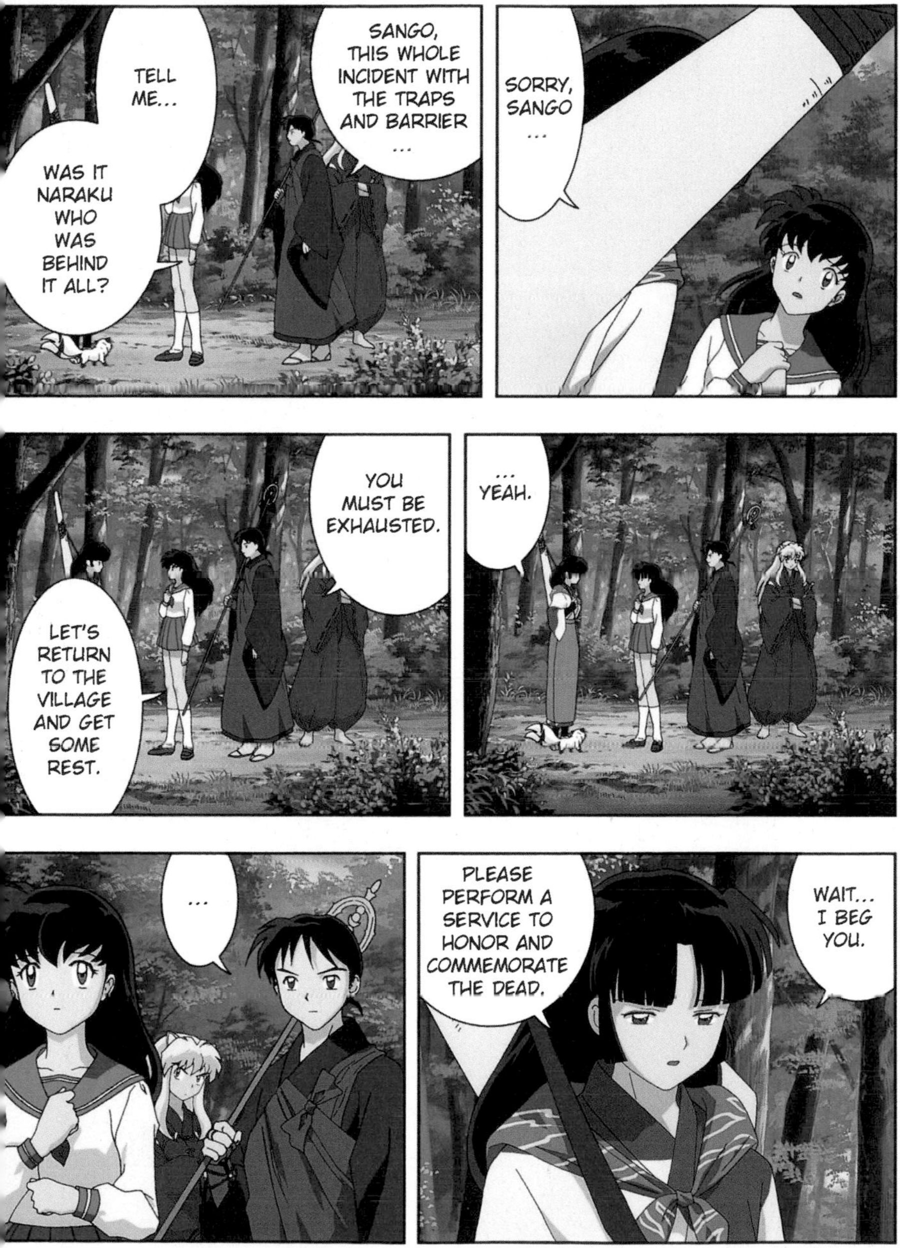
SORRY, SANGO ...
SANGO, THIS WHOLE INCIDENT WITH THE TRAPS AND BARRIER ...
TELL ME...
WAS IT NARAKU WHO WAS BEHIND IT ALL?
... YEAH.
YOU MUST BE EXHAUSTED.
LET'S RETURN TO THE VILLAGE AND GET SOME REST.
WAIT... I BEG YOU.
PLEASE PERFORM A SERVICE TO HONOR AND COMMEMORATE THE DEAD.
...

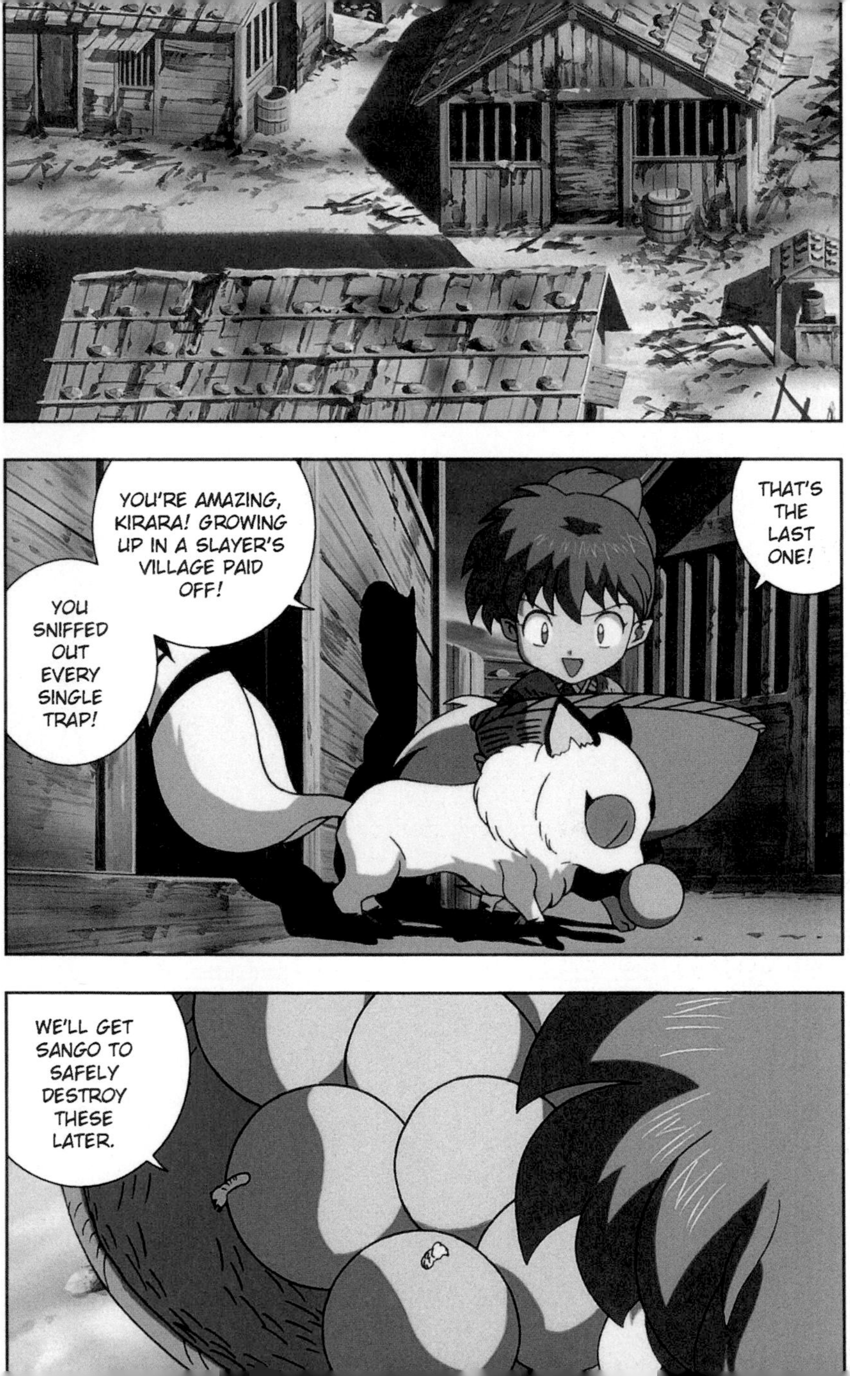
THAT'S THE LAST ONE!
YOU'RE AMAZING, KIRARA! GROWING UP IN A SLAYER'S VILLAGE PAID OFF!
YOU SNIFFED OUT EVERY SINGLE TRAP!
WE'LL GET SANGO TO SAFELY DESTROY THESE LATER.

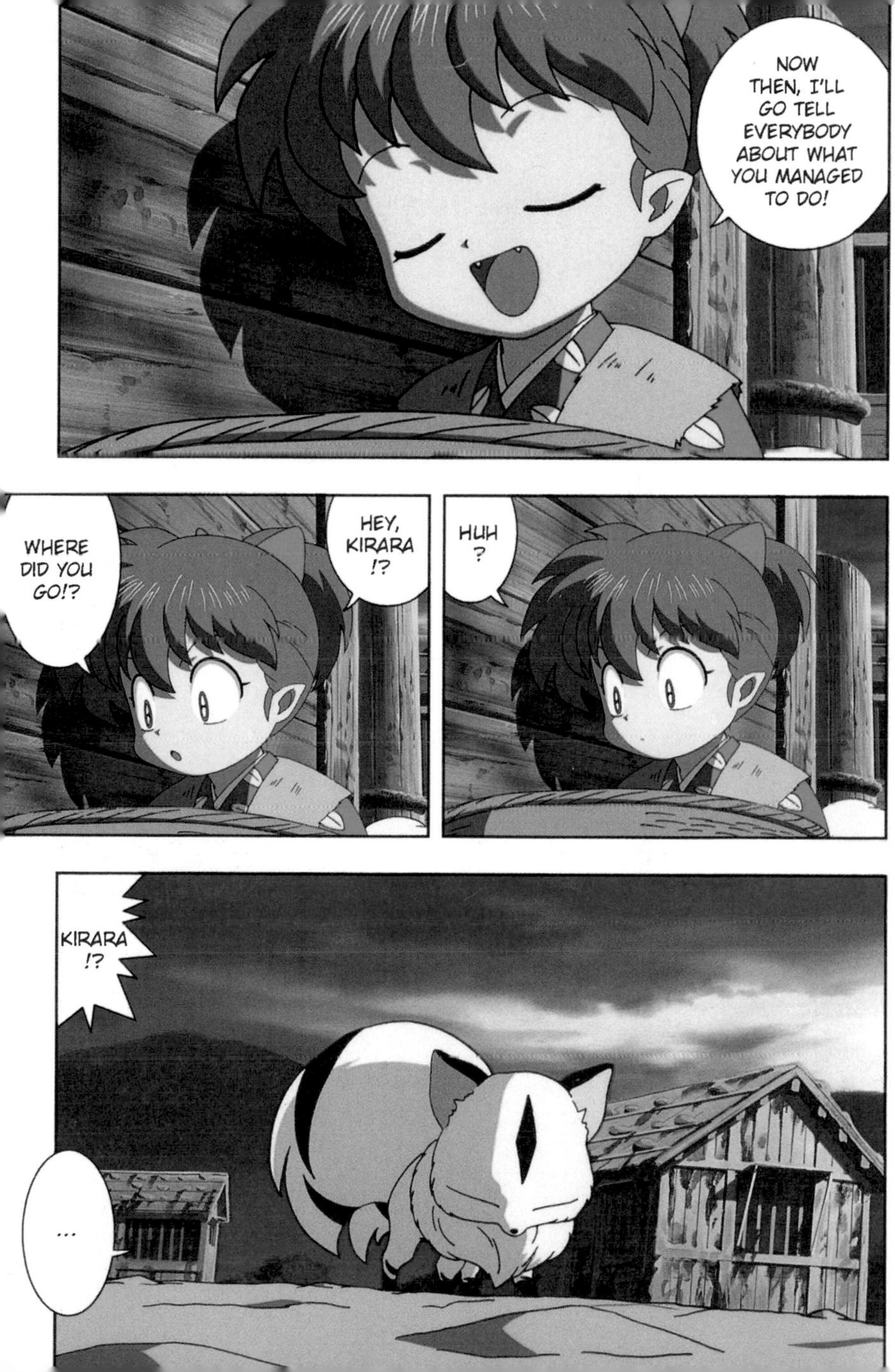
NOW THEN, I'LL GO TELL EVERYBODY ABOUT WHAT YOU MANAGED TO DO!
HUH?
HEY, KIRARA!?
WHERE DID YOU GO!?
KIRARA!?
...

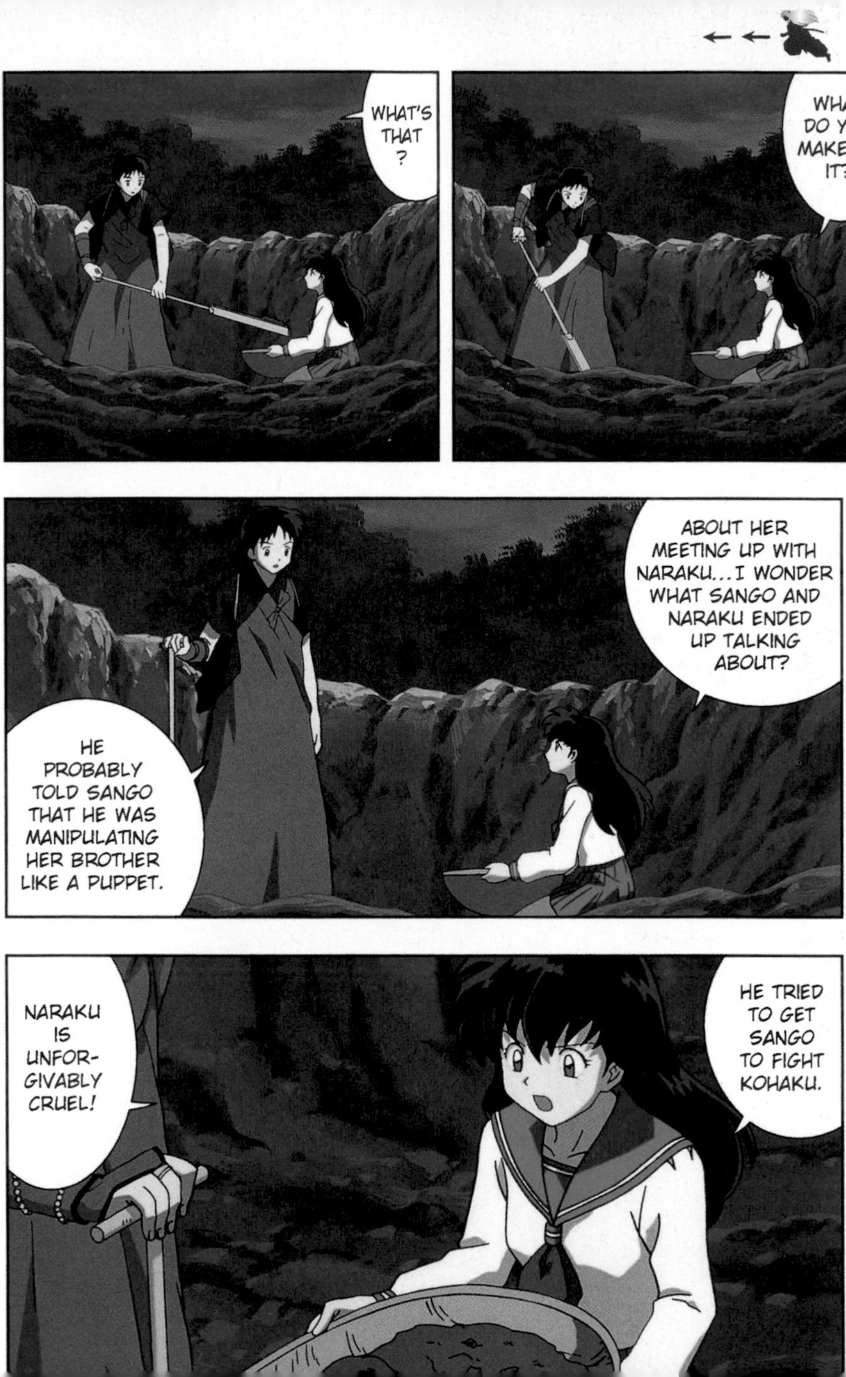
WHAT DO YOU MAKE OF IT?
WHAT'S THAT?
ABOUT HER MEETING UP WITH NARAKU...I WONDER WHAT SANGO AND NARAKU ENDED UP TALKING ABOUT?
HE PROBABLY TOLD SANGO THAT HE WAS MANIPULATING HER BROTHER LIKE A PUPPET.
HE TRIED TO GET SANGO TO FIGHT KOHAKU.
NARAKU IS UNFORGIVABLY CRUEL!

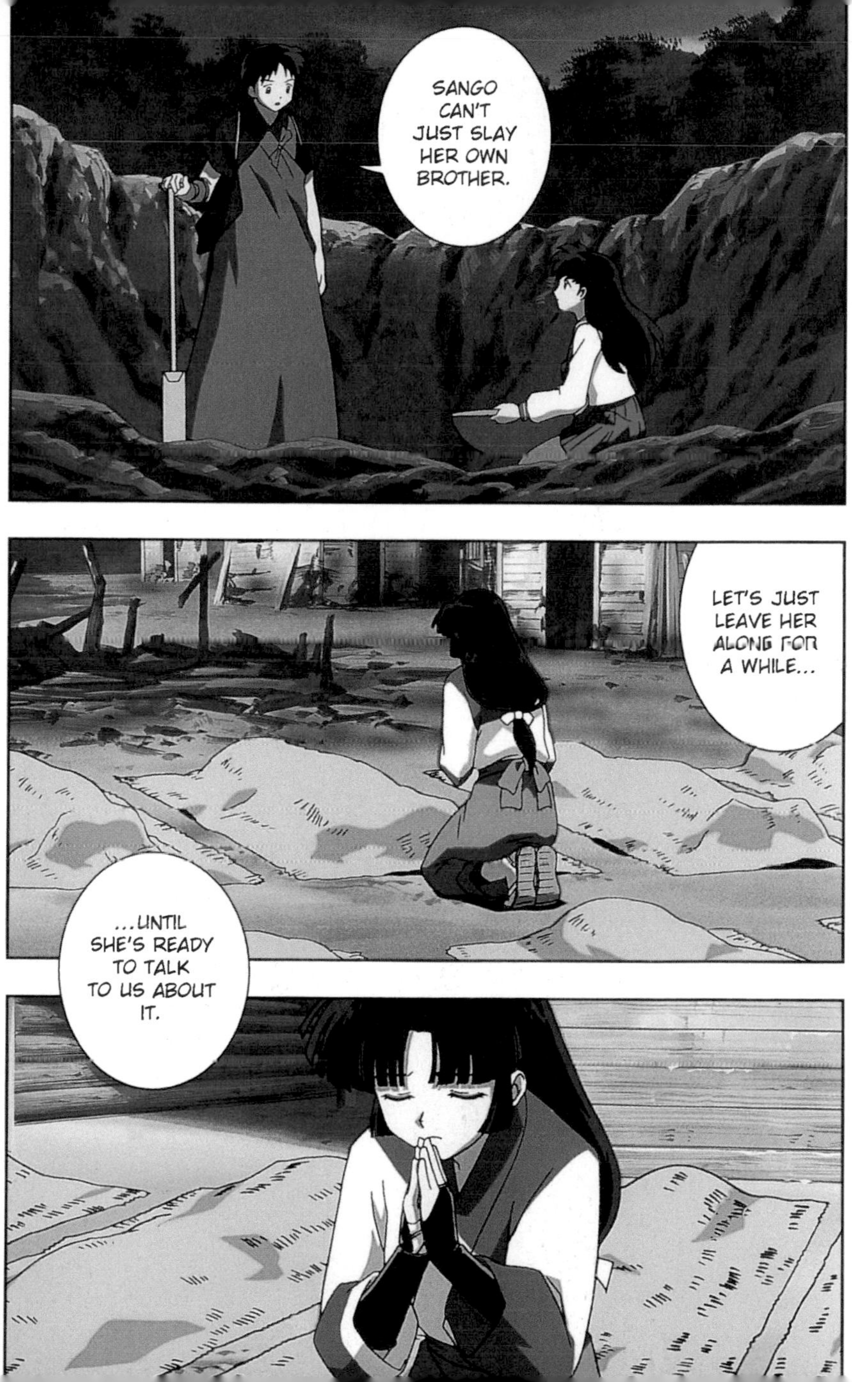
SANGO CAN'T JUST SLAY HER OWN BROTHER.
LET'S JUST LEAVE HER ALONG FOR A WHILE...
...UNTIL SHE'S READY TO TALK TO US ABOUT IT.

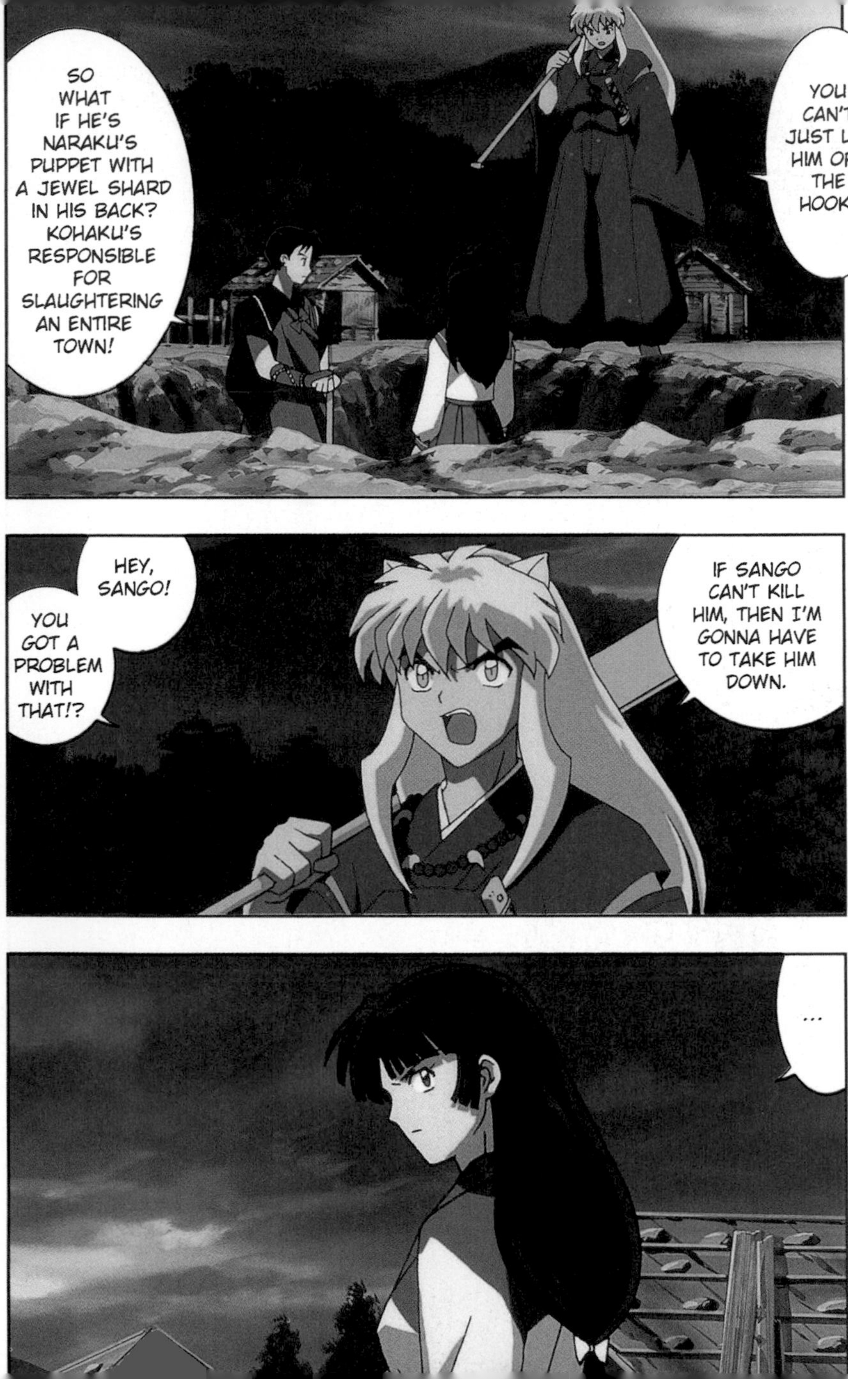
YOU CAN'T JUST LET HIM OFF THE HOOK!
SO WHAT IF HE'S NARAKU'S PUPPET WITH A JEWEL SHARD IN HIS BACK? KOHAKU'S RESPONSIBLE FOR SLAUGHTERING AN ENTIRE TOWN!
IF SANGO CAN'T KILL HIM, THEN I'M GONNA HAVE TO TAKE HIM DOWN.
HEY, SANGO!
YOU GOT A PROBLEM WITH THAT!?
...

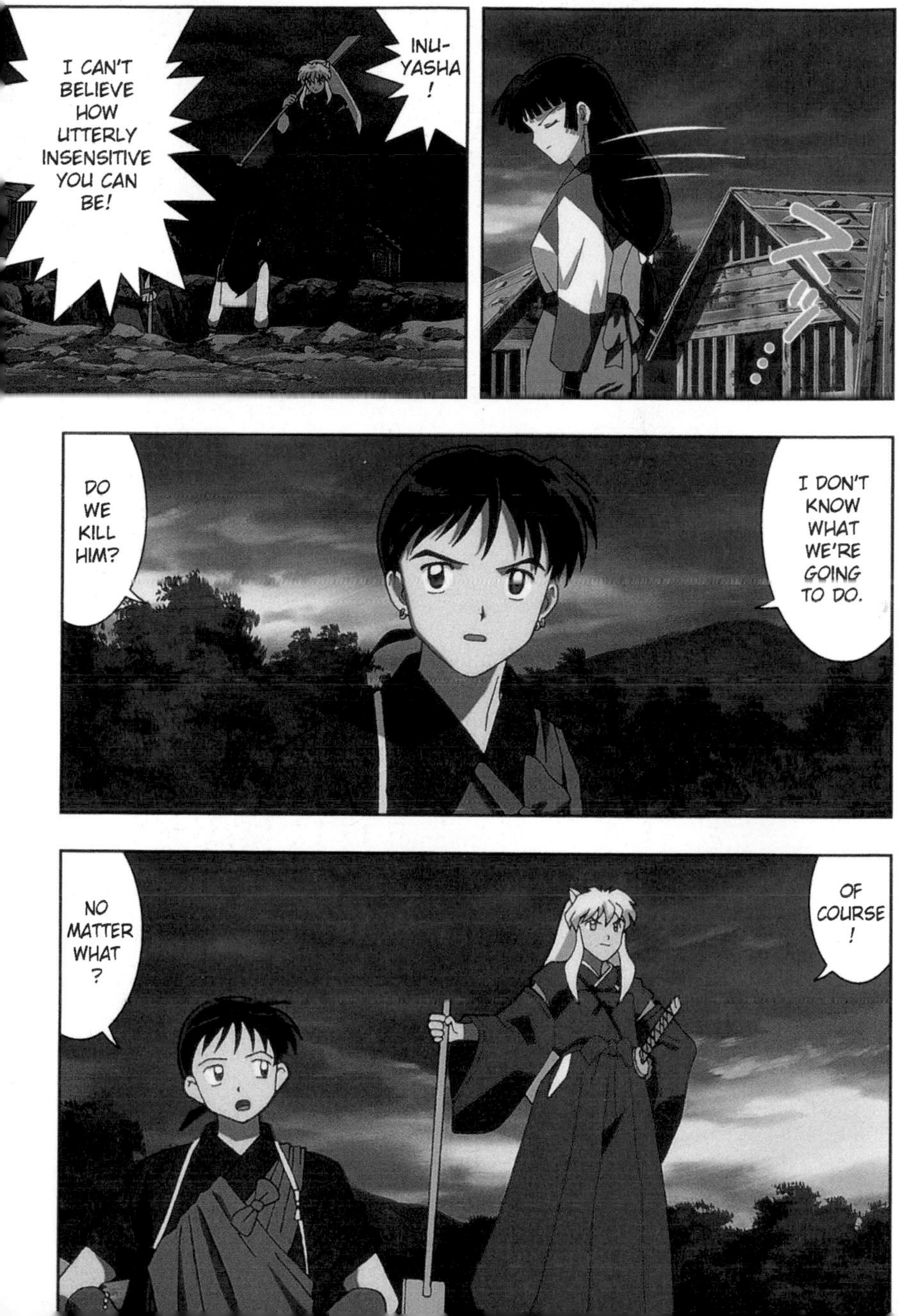
スッ
INU-YASHA!
I CAN'T BELIEVE HOW UTTERLY INSENSITIVE YOU CAN BE!
I DON'T KNOW WHAT WE'RE GOING TO DO.
DO WE KILL HIM?
OF COURSE!
NO MATTER WHAT?

YEAH! THINK ABOUT IT!

NARAKU SENT SANGO'S "ZOMBIE SHARD PUPPET" BROTHER 'CAUSE HE THOUGHT WE'D BE TOO SENTIMENTAL AND WIMPY ABOUT IT TO KILL HIM OFF.

THERE'S NO WAY I'LL FALL FOR THAT!

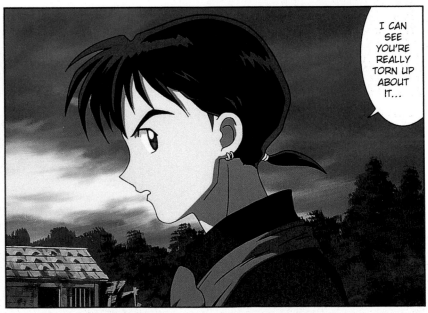

I CAN SEE YOU'RE REALLY TORN UP ABOUT IT...

132

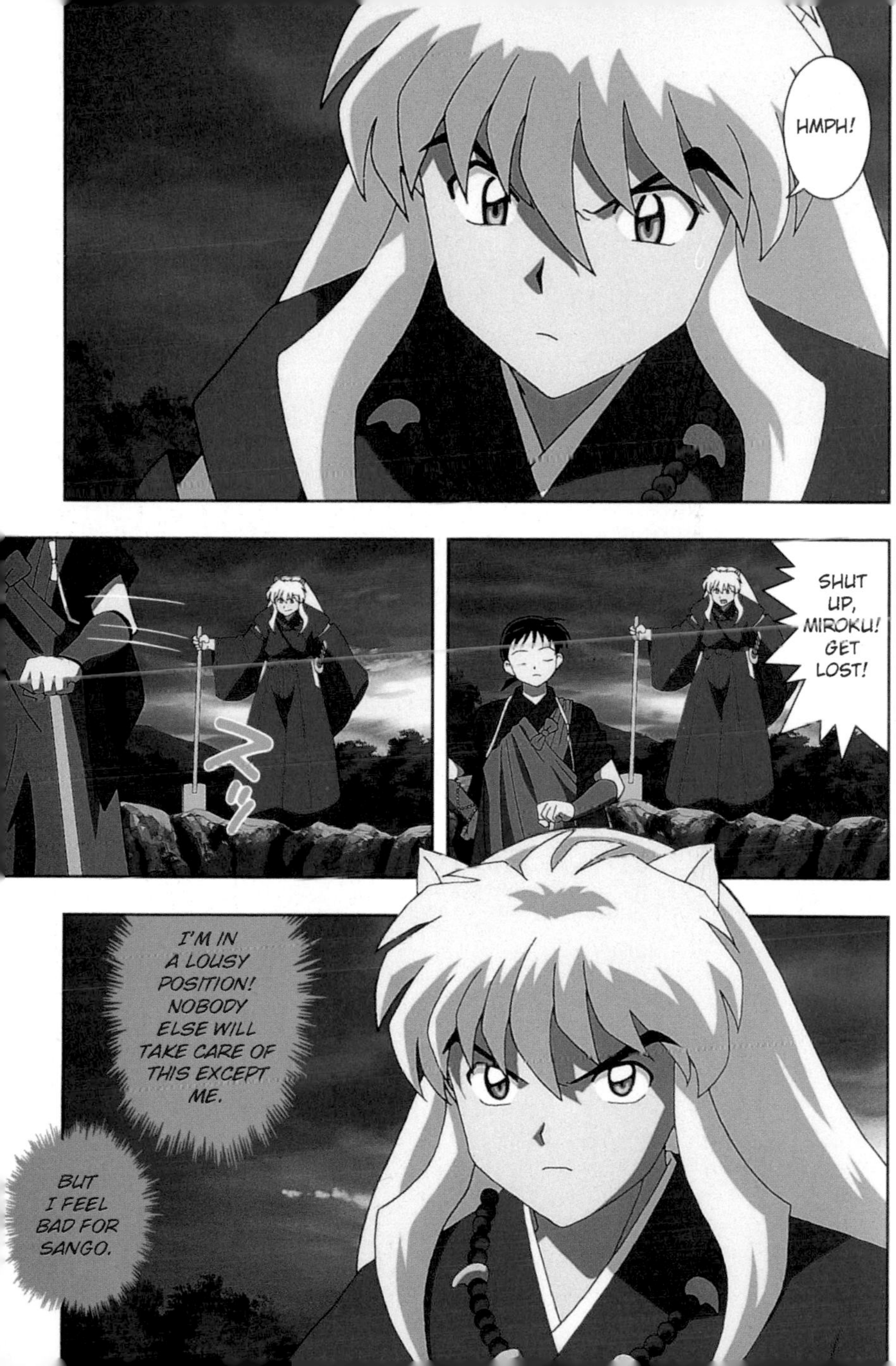
HMPH!
SHUT UP, MIROKU! GET LOST!
スッ
I'M IN A LOUSY POSITION! NOBODY ELSE WILL TAKE CARE OF THIS EXCEPT ME.
BUT I FEEL BAD FOR SANGO.

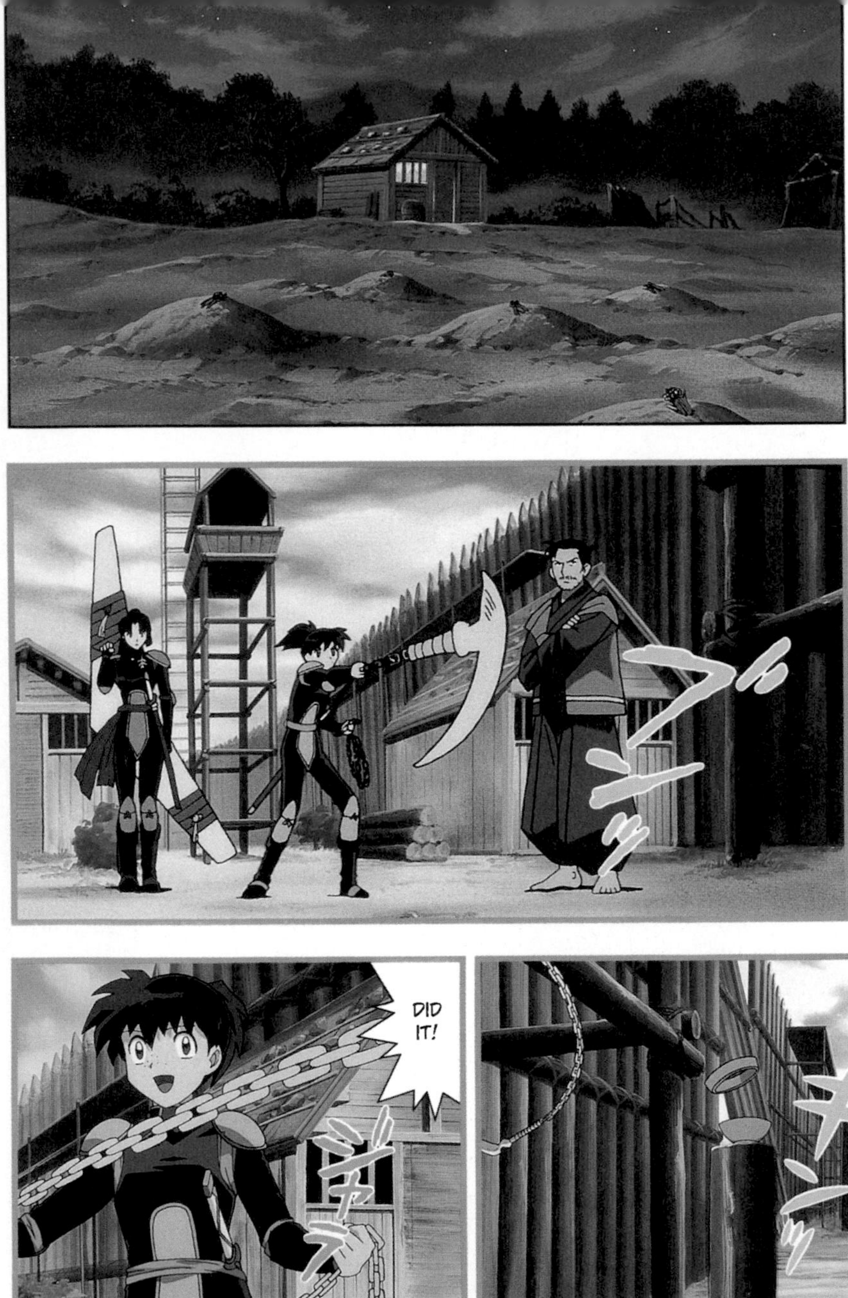
ブンッ
キンッ
DID IT!
ジャラ

AH
!!

KOHAKU
!

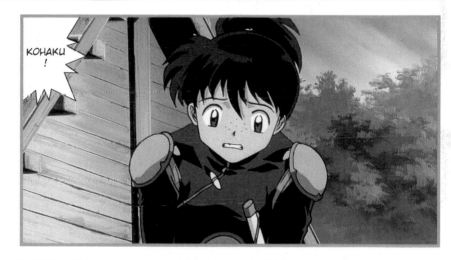

YOU'RE
NOT
TRYING
HARD
ENOUGH
!

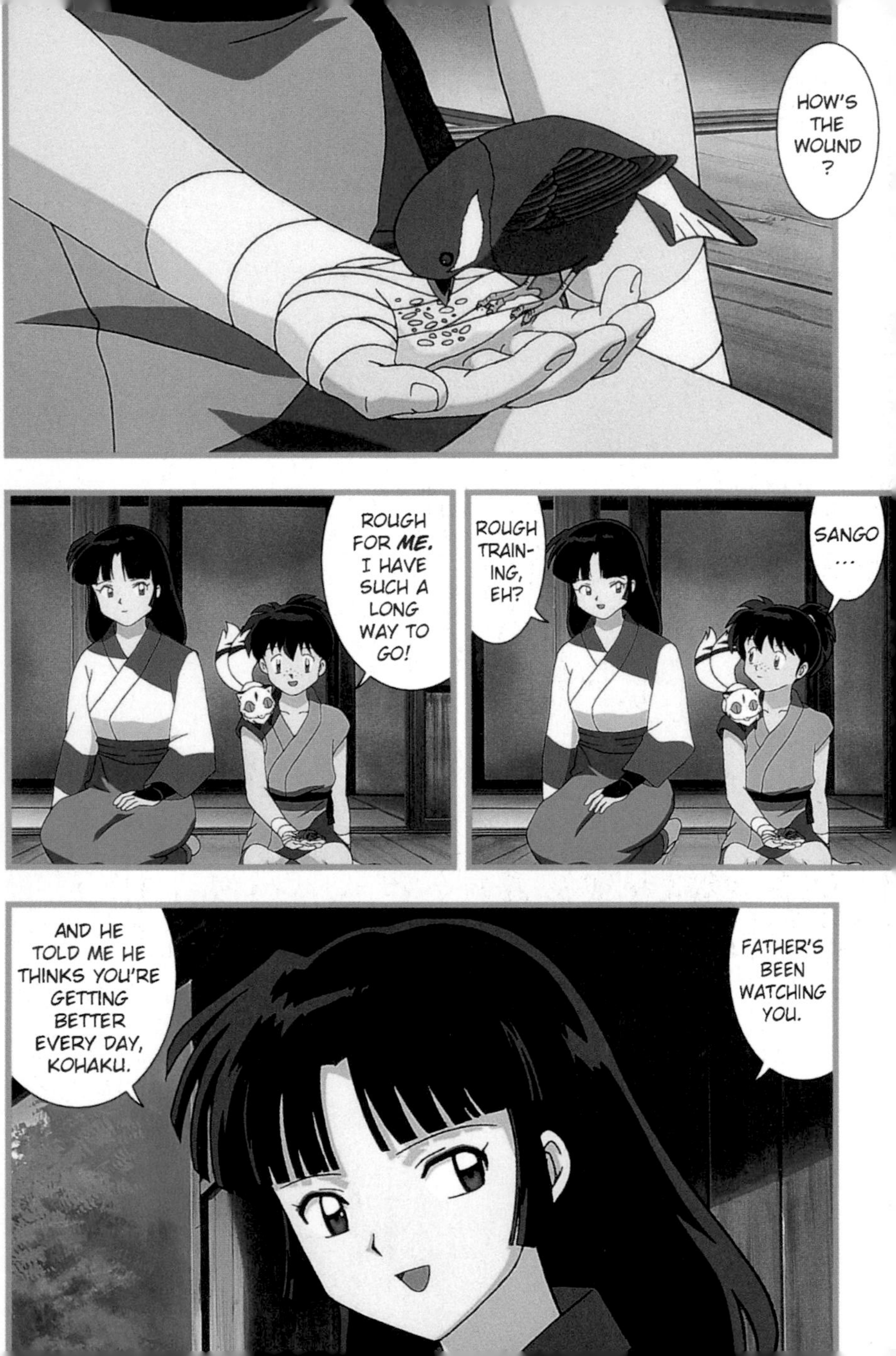
HOW'S THE WOUND ?
SANGO ...
ROUGH TRAIN-ING, EH?
ROUGH FOR **ME.** I HAVE SUCH A LONG WAY TO GO!
FATHER'S BEEN WATCHING YOU.
AND HE TOLD ME HE THINKS YOU'RE GETTING BETTER EVERY DAY, KOHAKU.

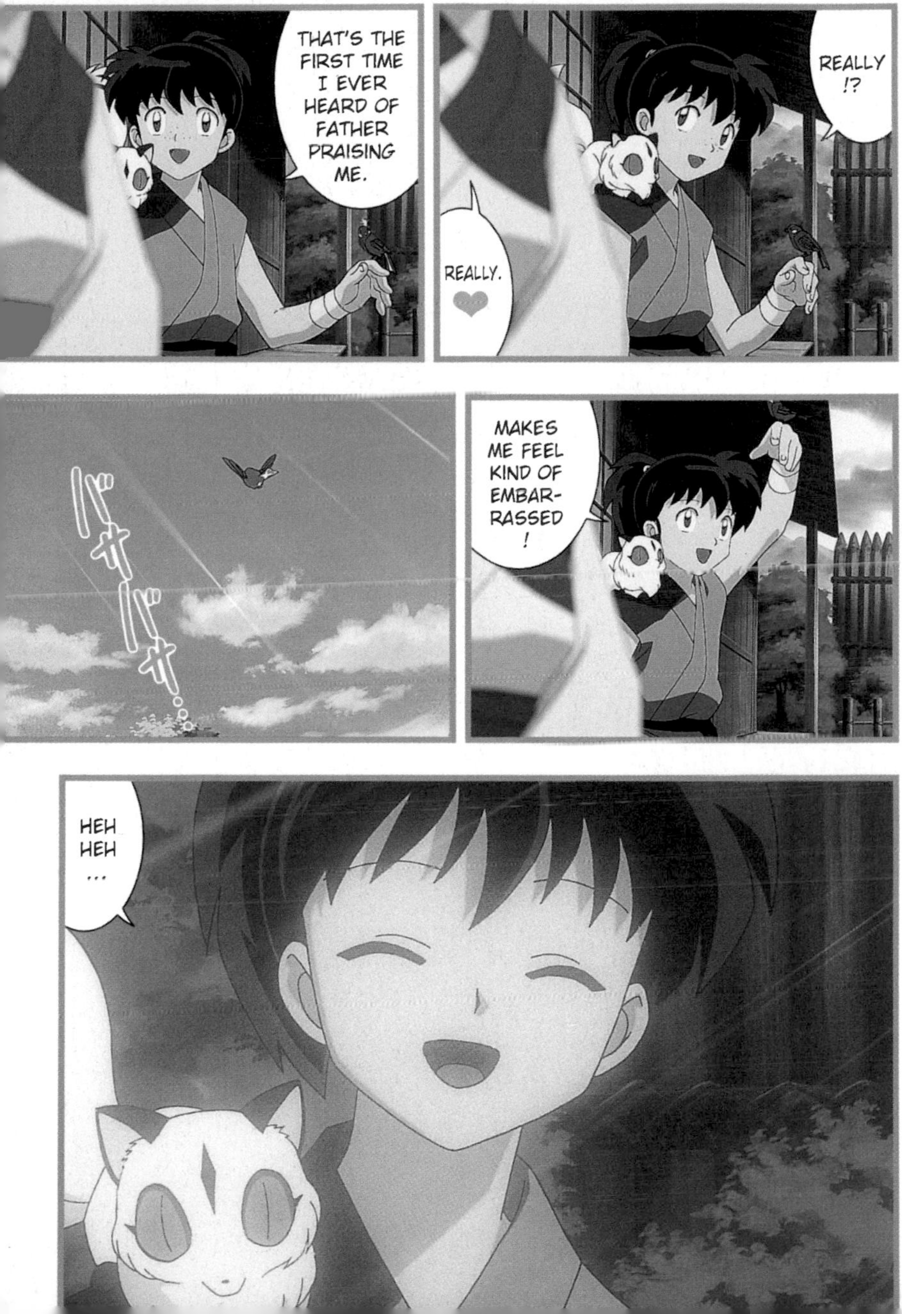
REALLY !?
REALLY.
THAT'S THE FIRST TIME I EVER HEARD OF FATHER PRAISING ME.
MAKES ME FEEL KIND OF EMBARRASSED!
バサバサ
HEH HEH...

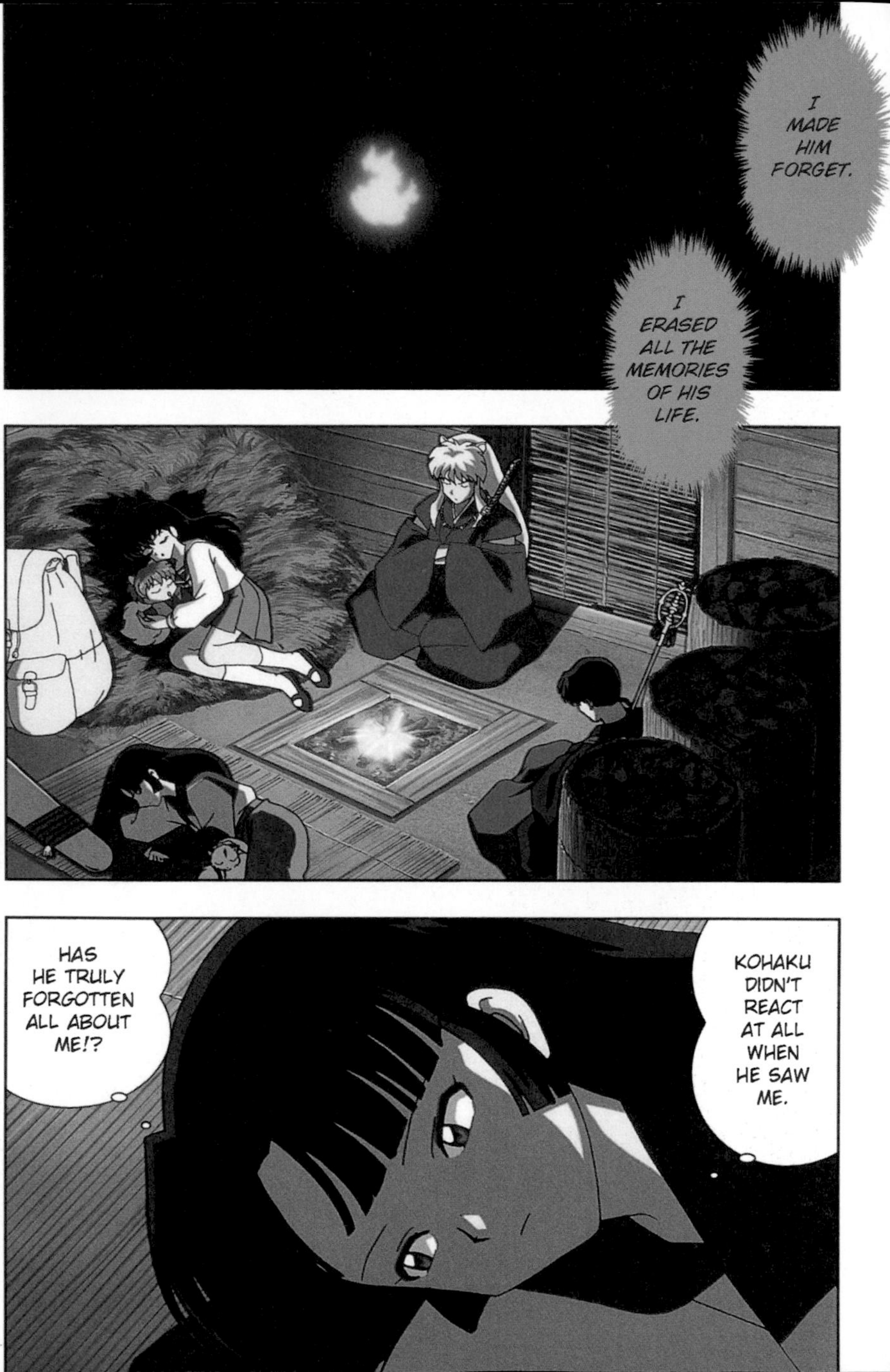
I MADE HIM FORGET.
I ERASED ALL THE MEMORIES OF HIS LIFE.
KOHAKU DIDN'T REACT AT ALL WHEN HE SAW ME.
HAS HE TRULY FORGOTTEN ALL ABOUT ME!?

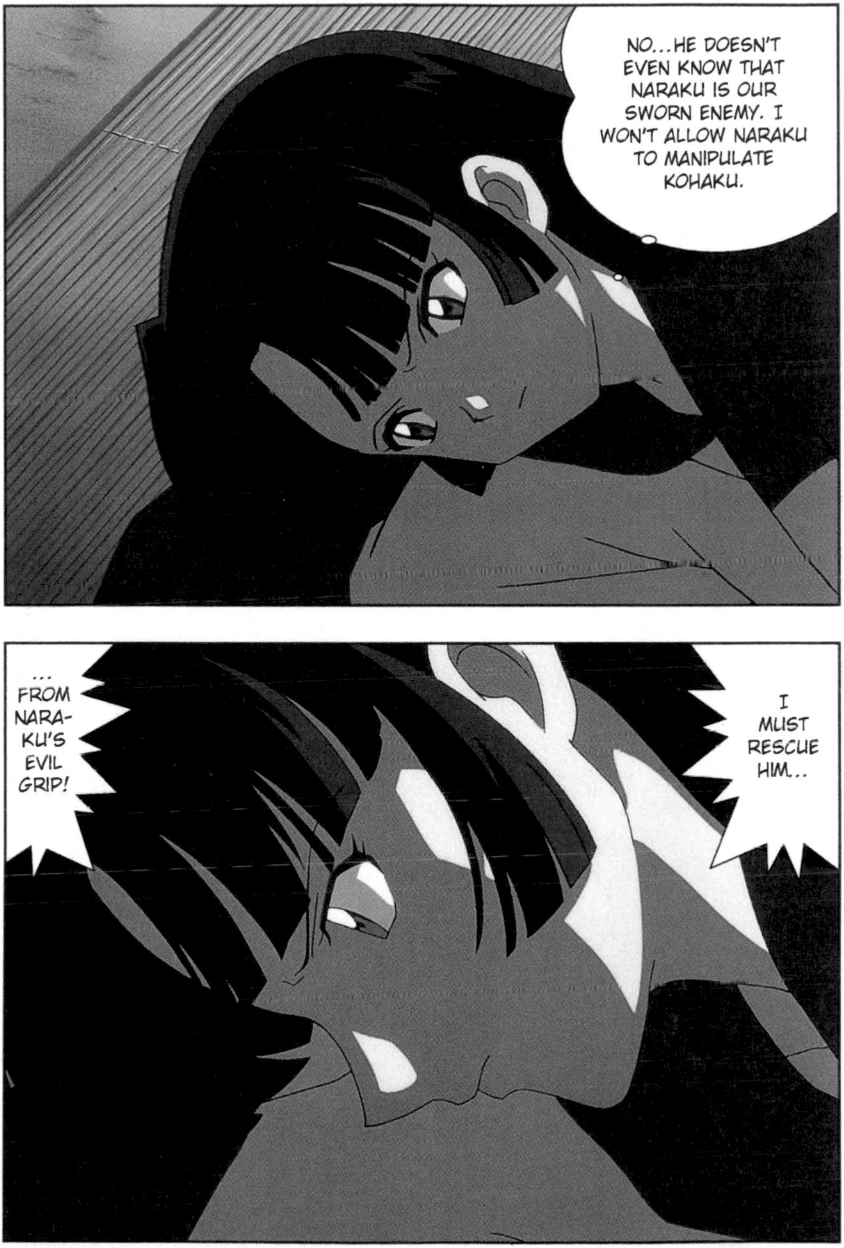
NO...HE DOESN'T EVEN KNOW THAT NARAKU IS OUR SWORN ENEMY. I WON'T ALLOW NARAKU TO MANIPULATE KOHAKU.
I MUST RESCUE HIM...
...FROM NARA-KU'S EVIL GRIP!

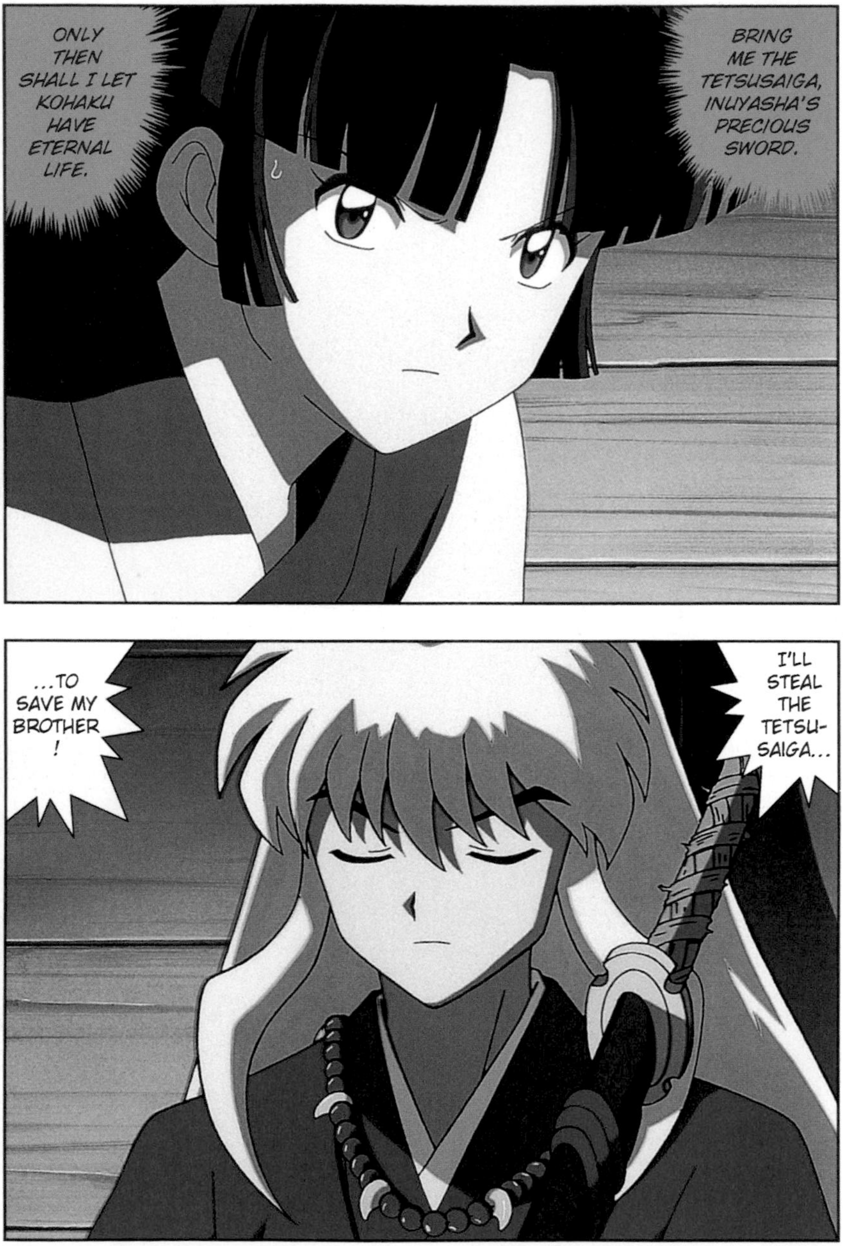
BRING ME THE TETSUSAIGA, INUYASHA'S PRECIOUS SWORD.
ONLY THEN SHALL I LET KOHAKU HAVE ETERNAL LIFE.
I'LL STEAL THE TETSU-SAIGA...
...TO SAVE MY BROTHER!

30
Tetsusaiga Is Stolen! Showdown at Naraku's Castle!

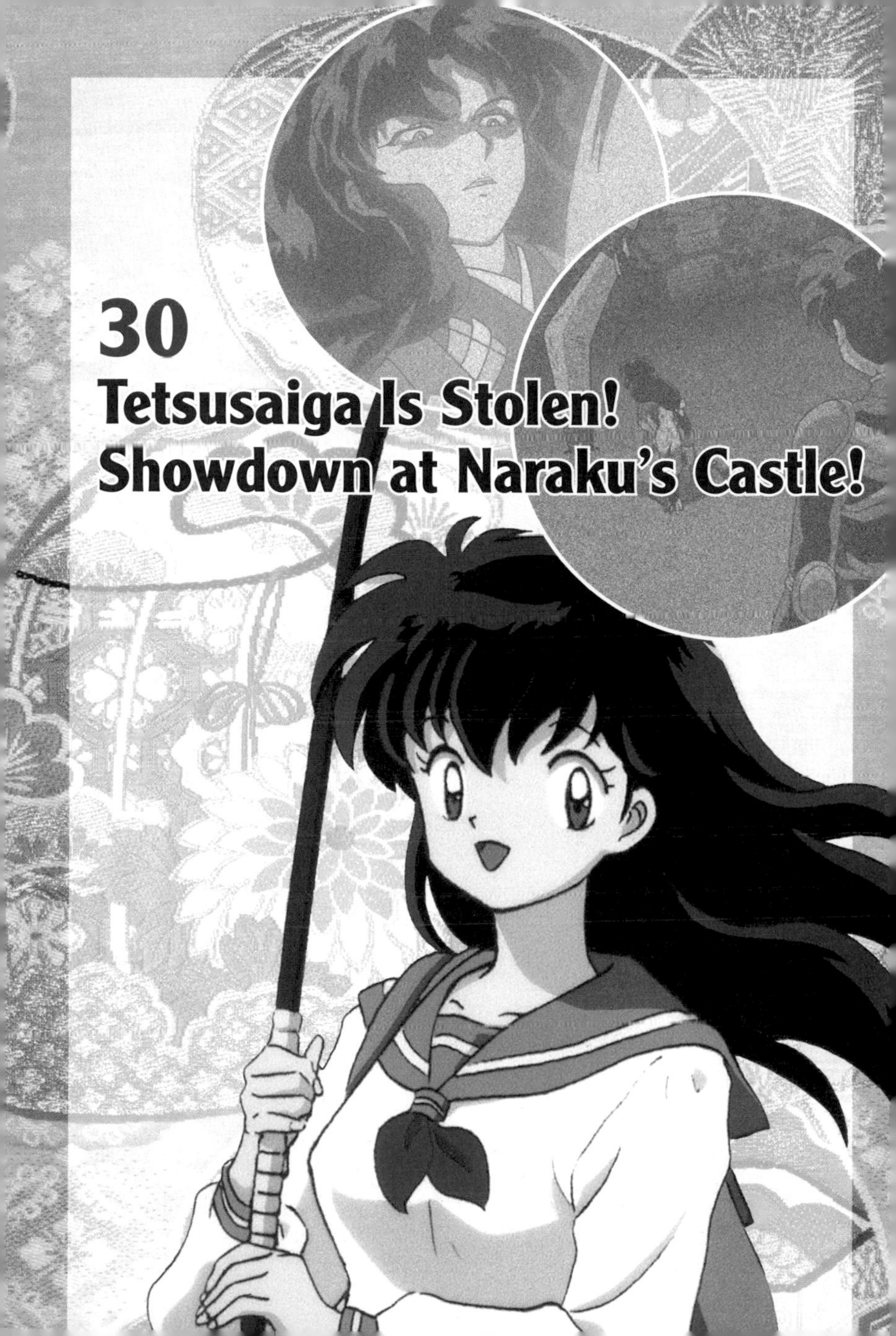

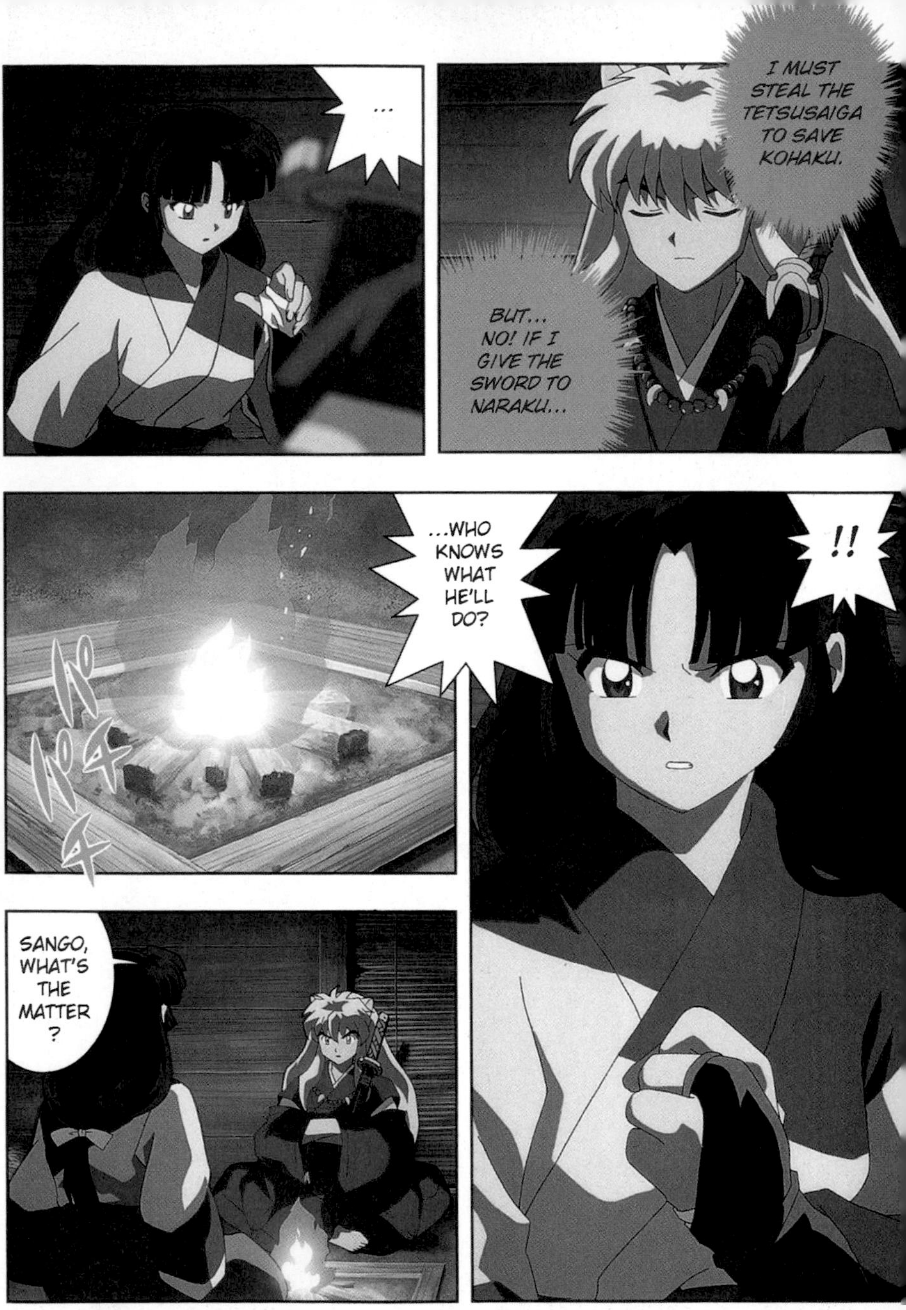

I MUST STEAL THE TETSUSAIGA TO SAVE KOHAKU.
BUT... NO! IF I GIVE THE SWORD TO NARAKU...
...
!!
...WHO KNOWS WHAT HE'LL DO?
パチ パチ
SANGO, WHAT'S THE MATTER ?

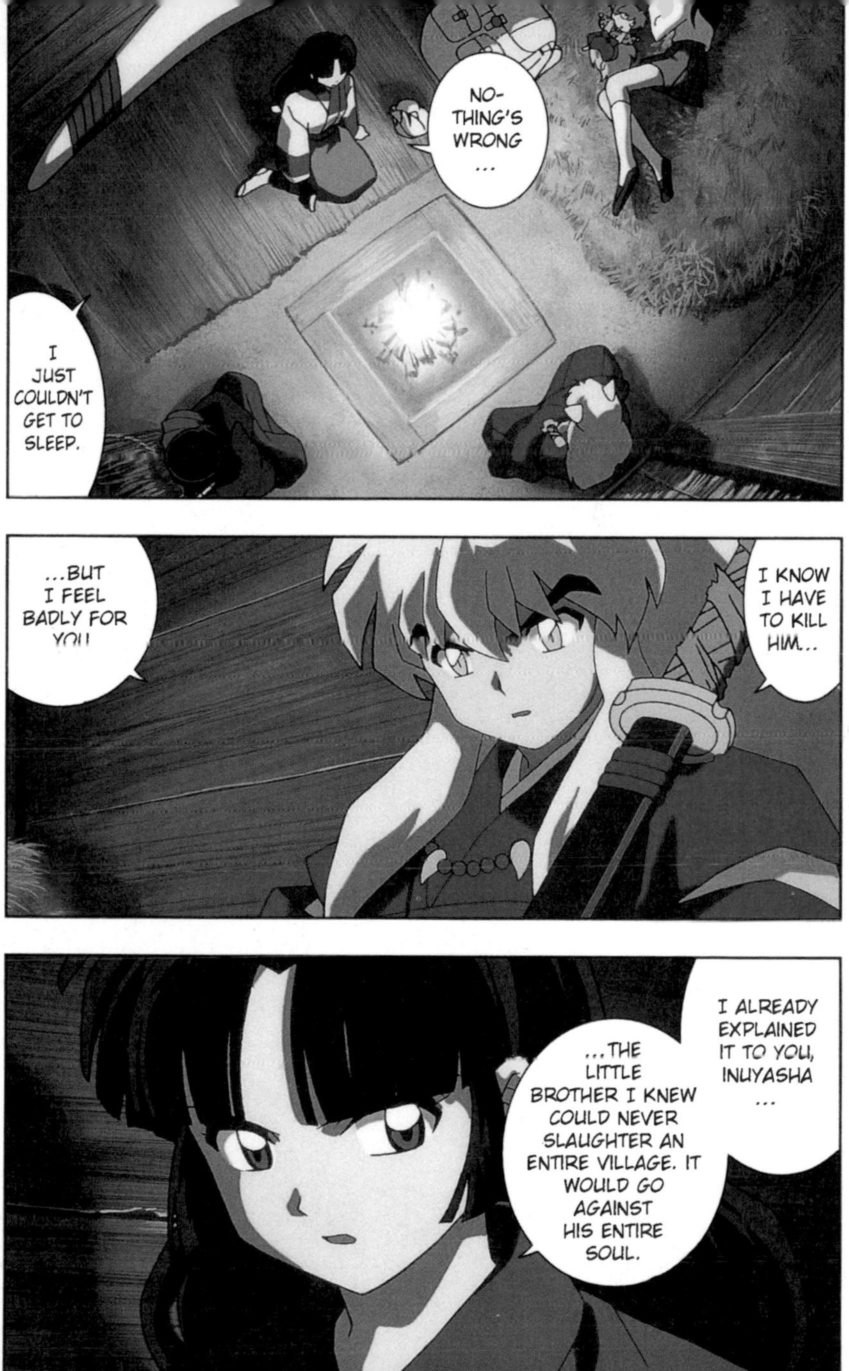
NO-THING'S WRONG ...
I JUST COULDN'T GET TO SLEEP.
I KNOW I HAVE TO KILL HIM...
...BUT I FEEL BADLY FOR YOU.
I ALREADY EXPLAINED IT TO YOU, INUYASHA ...
...THE LITTLE BROTHER I KNEW COULD NEVER SLAUGHTER AN ENTIRE VILLAGE. IT WOULD GO AGAINST HIS ENTIRE SOUL.

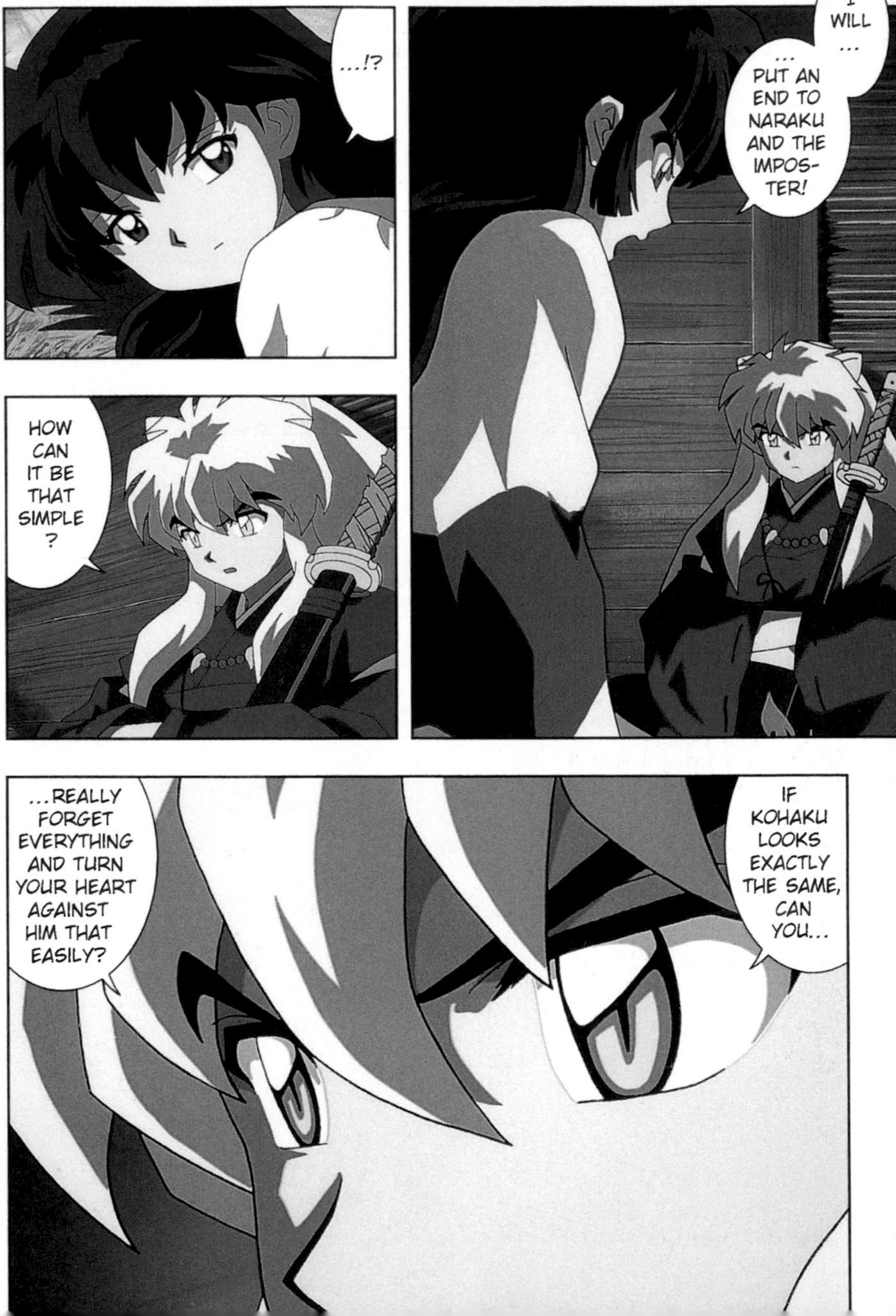
I WILL... ...PUT AN END TO NARAKU AND THE IMPOSTER!
...!?
HOW CAN IT BE THAT SIMPLE?
IF KOHAKU LOOKS EXACTLY THE SAME, CAN YOU...
...REALLY FORGET EVERYTHING AND TURN YOUR HEART AGAINST HIM THAT EASILY?

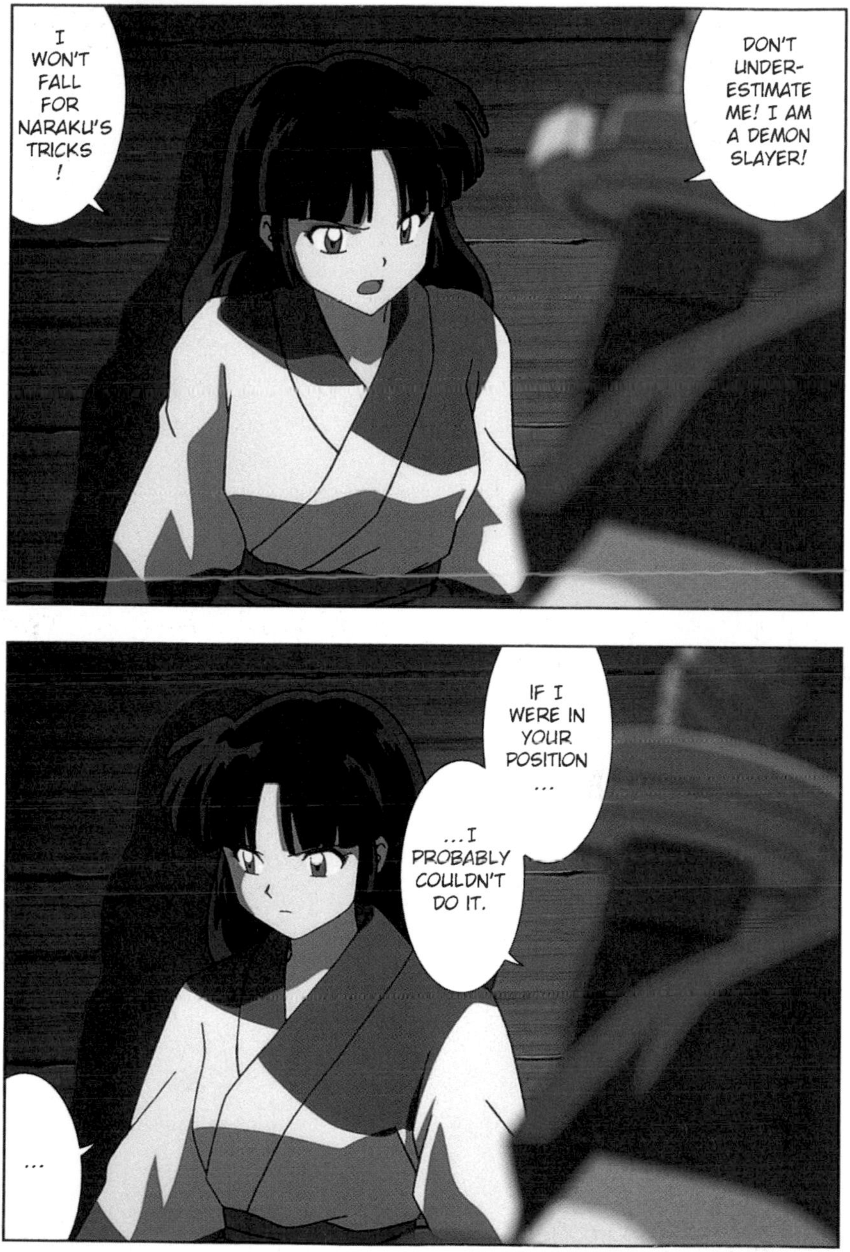
DON'T UNDER-ESTIMATE ME! I AM A DEMON SLAYER!
I WON'T FALL FOR NARAKU'S TRICKS!
IF I WERE IN YOUR POSITION...
...I PROBABLY COULDN'T DO IT.
...

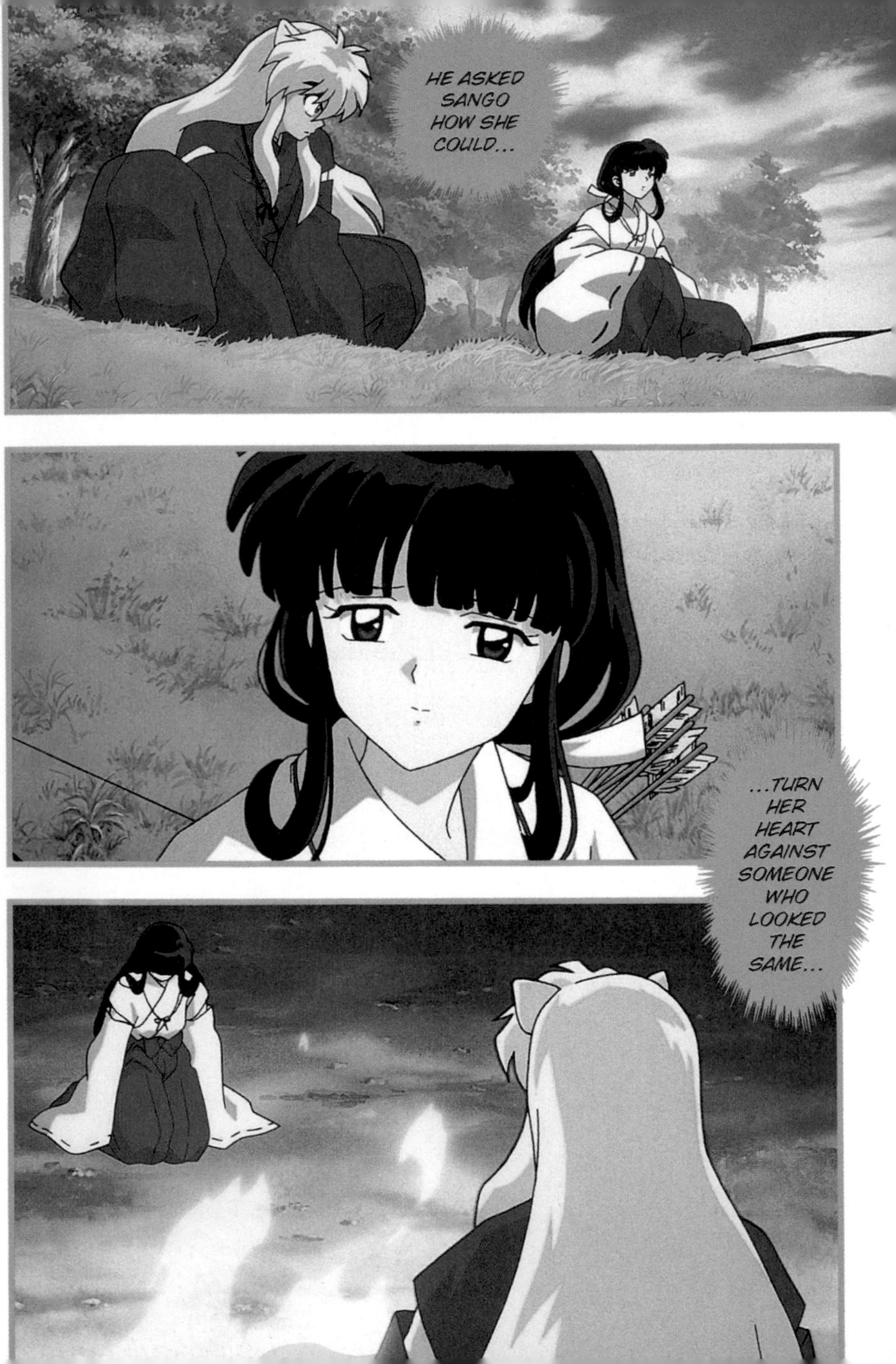
HE ASKED SANGO HOW SHE COULD...
...TURN HER HEART AGAINST SOMEONE WHO LOOKED THE SAME...

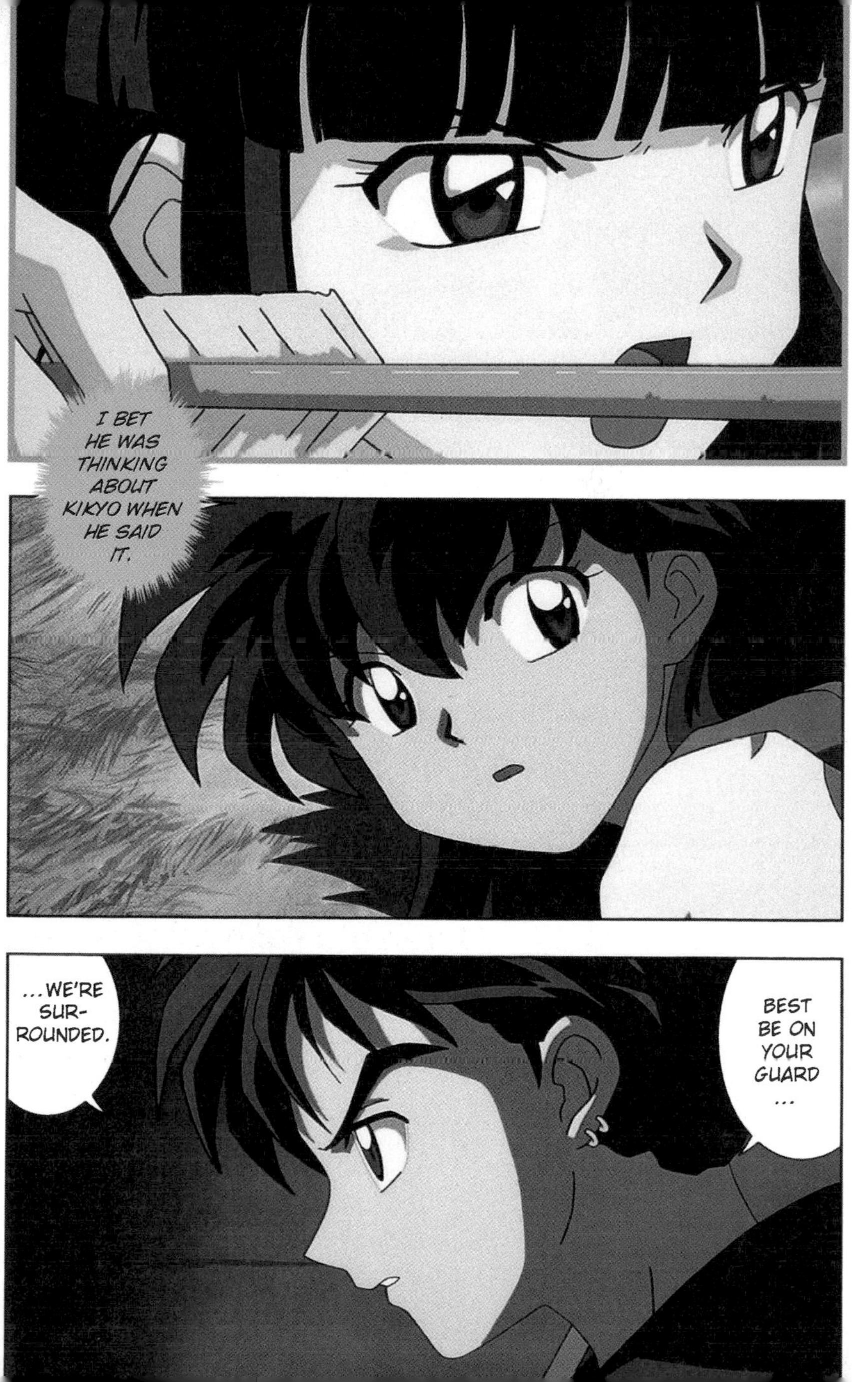
I BET HE WAS THINKING ABOUT KIKYO WHEN HE SAID IT.
BEST BE ON YOUR GUARD ...
...WE'RE SUR-ROUNDED.

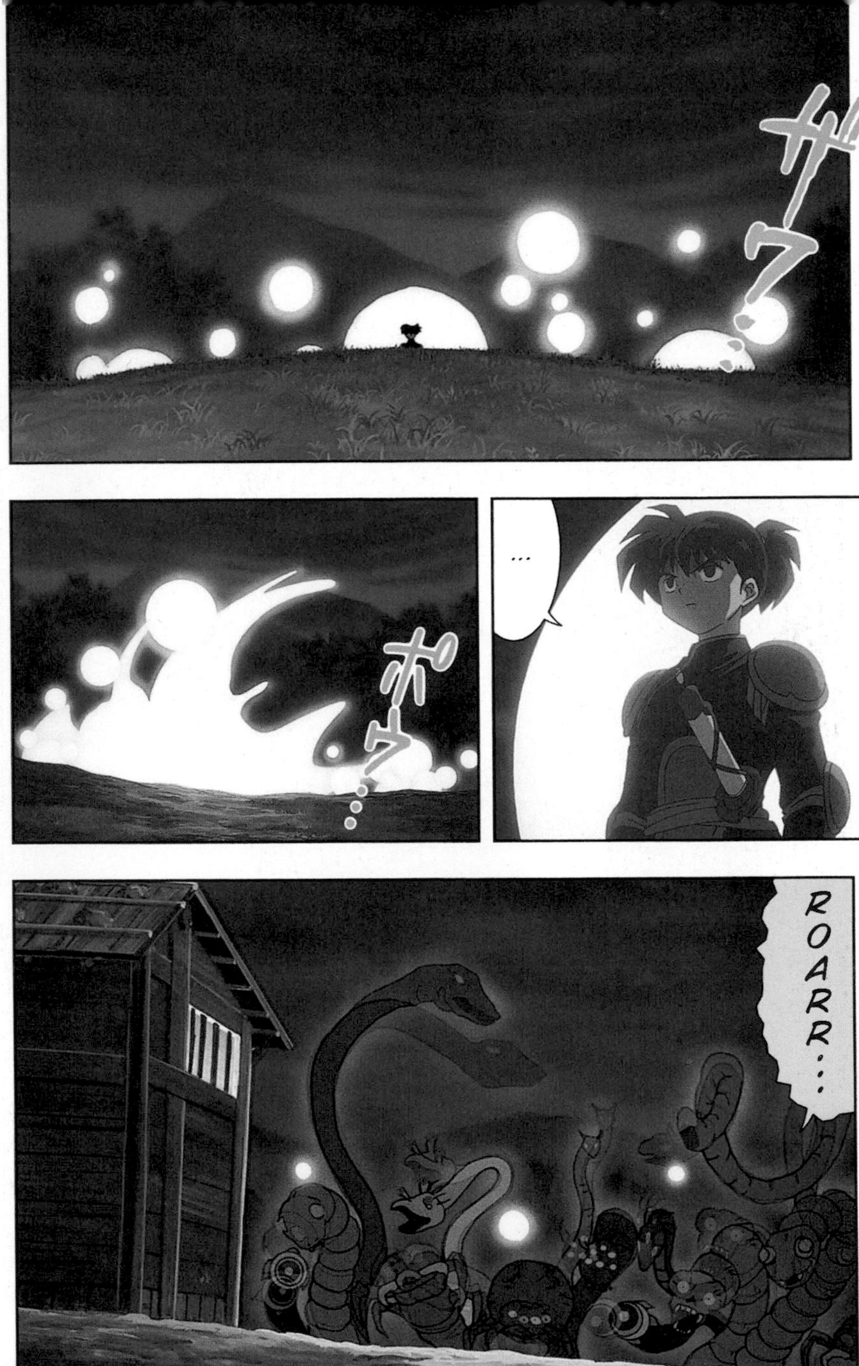
ザワ…
...
ポウ…
ROARR...

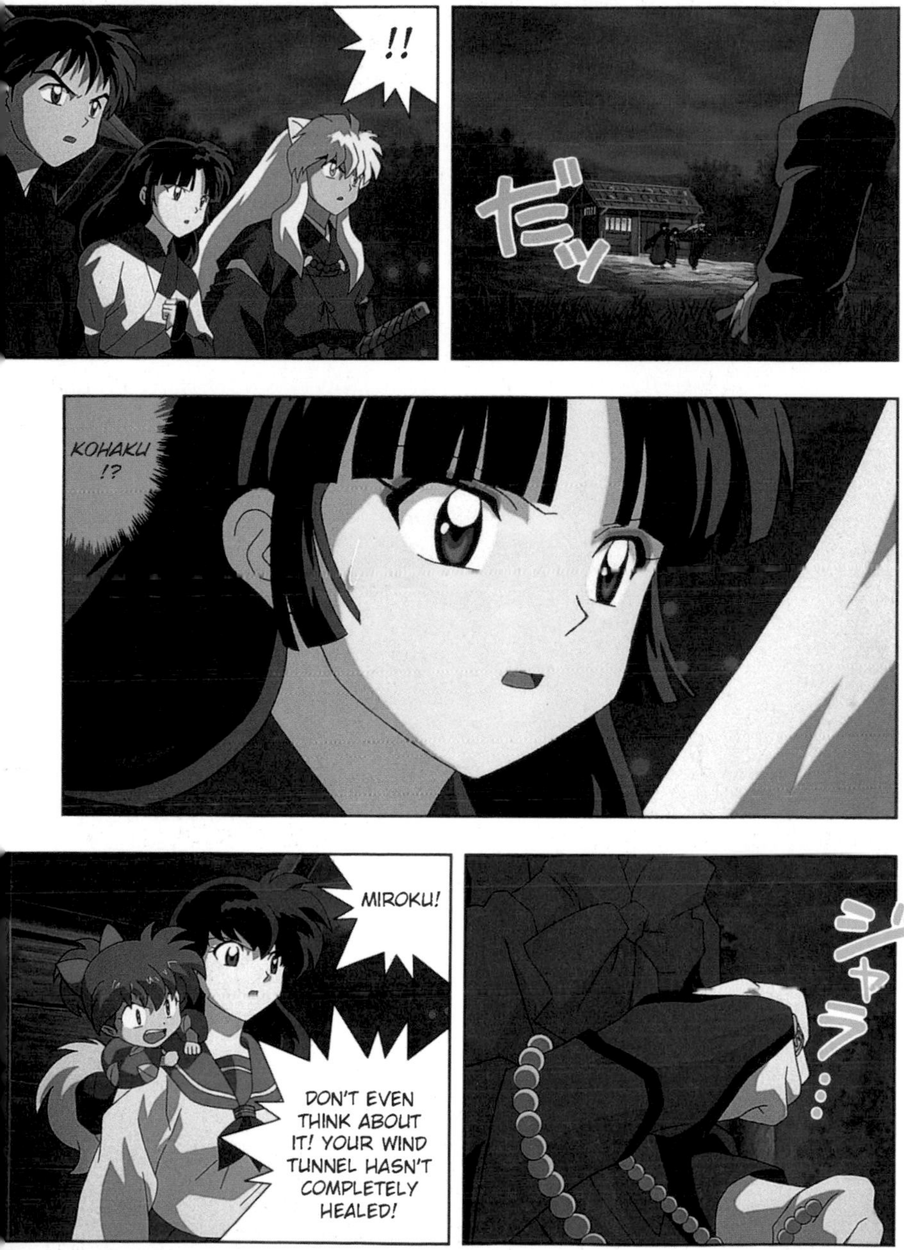
ダッ
!!
KOHAKU !?
ジャラ…
MIROKU!
DON'T EVEN THINK ABOUT IT! YOUR WIND TUNNEL HASN'T COMPLETELY HEALED!

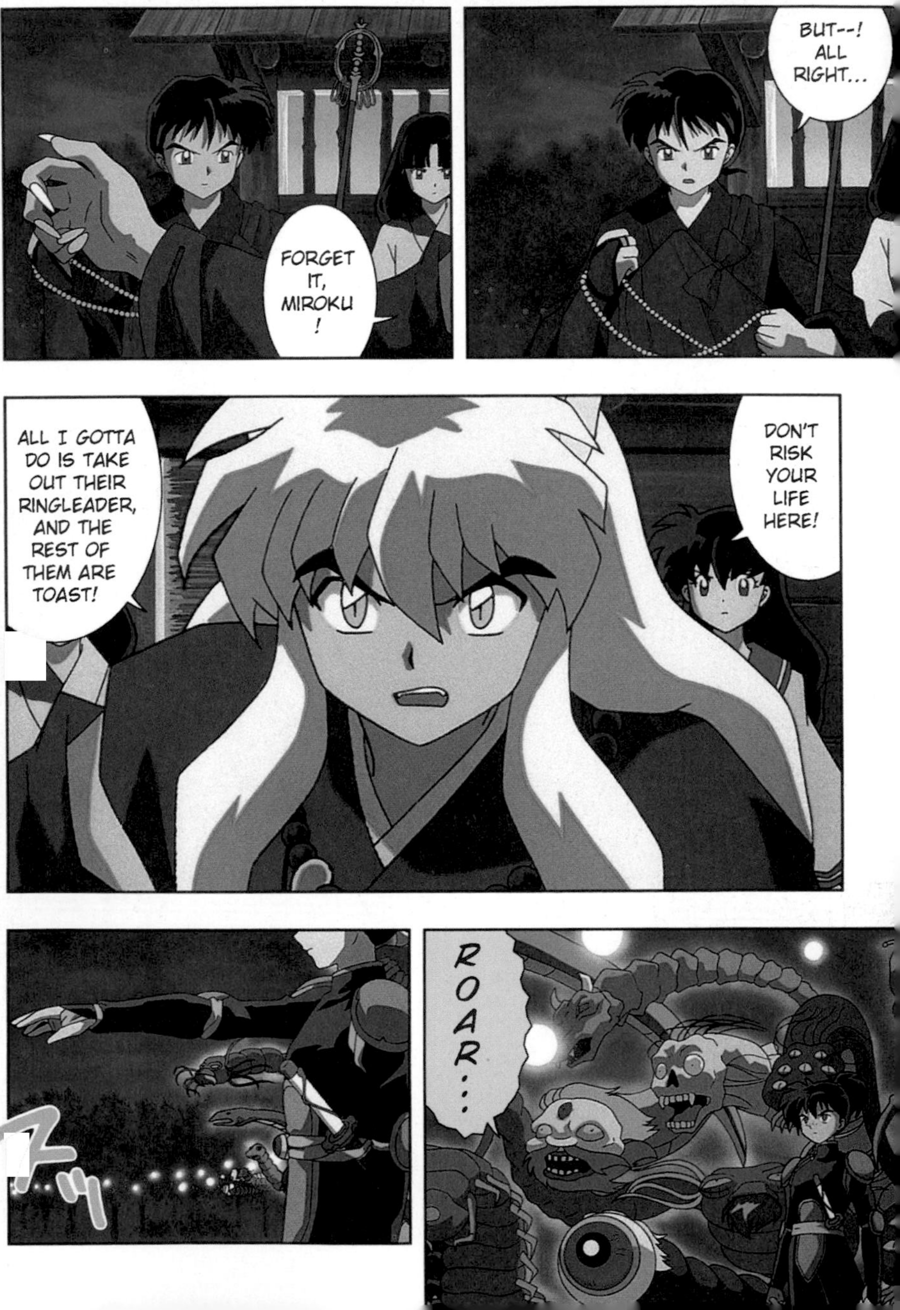
BUT--! ALL RIGHT...
FORGET IT, MIROKU!
DON'T RISK YOUR LIFE HERE!
ALL I GOTTA DO IS TAKE OUT THEIR RINGLEADER, AND THE REST OF THEM ARE TOAST!
ROAR...

GET LOST, YOU PACK OF RODENTS !!

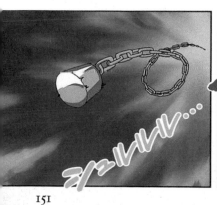

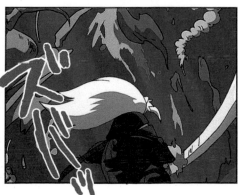

!?

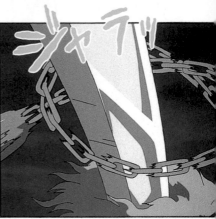

YOU'RE GONNA NEED TO FIGHT BETTER THAN *THAT* TO TAKE ME OUT!

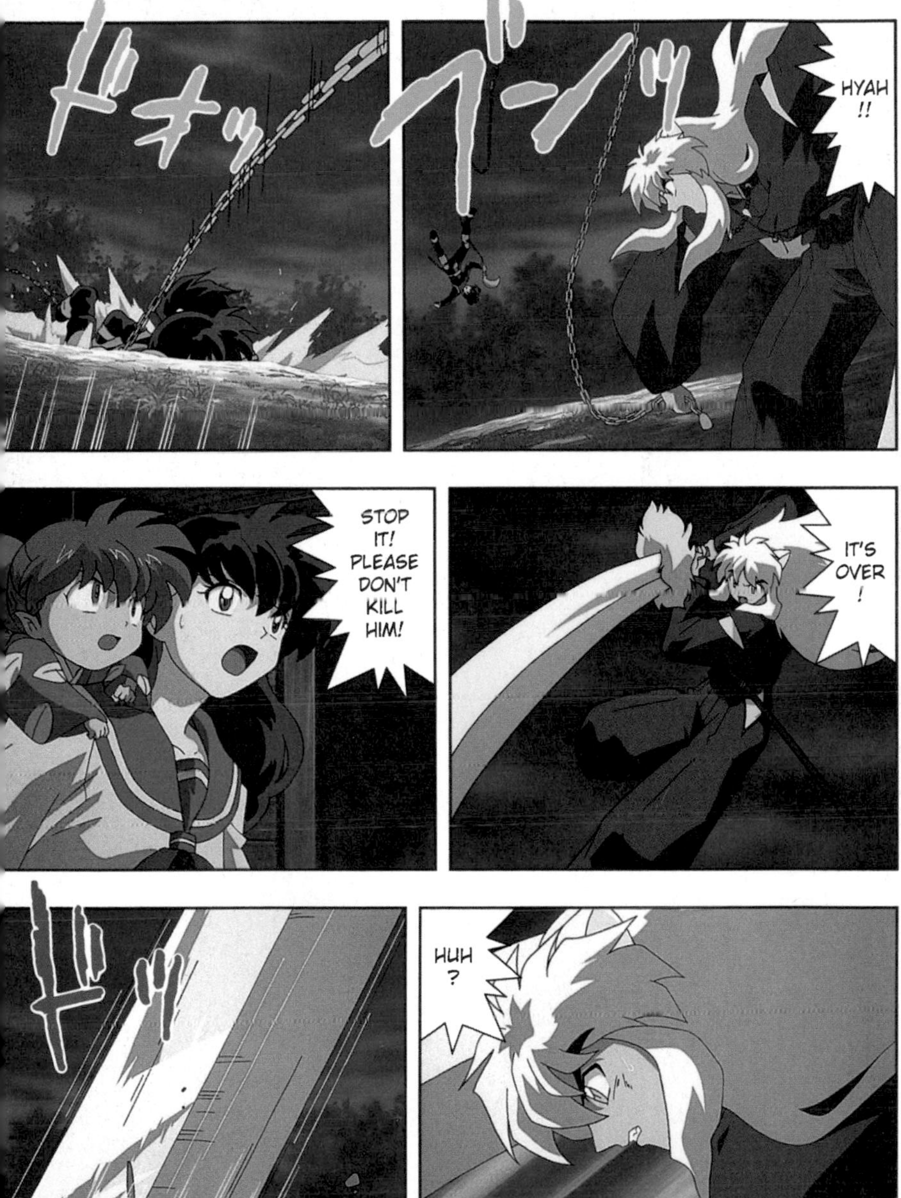
HYAH!!
IT'S OVER!
STOP IT! PLEASE DON'T KILL HIM!
HUH?

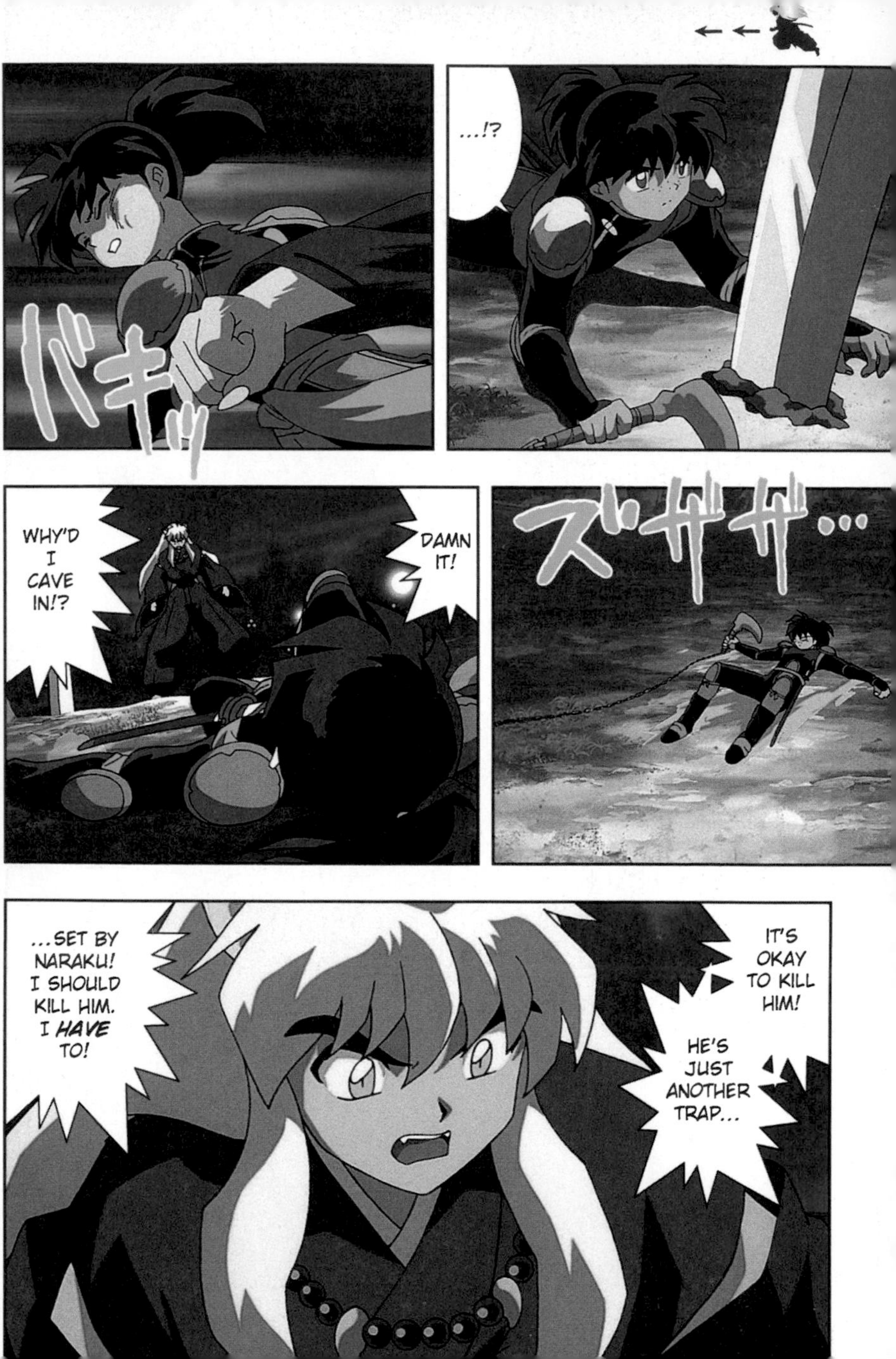
…!?
バキッ
ズザザ…
DAMN IT!
WHY'D I CAVE IN!?
IT'S OKAY TO KILL HIM!
HE'S JUST ANOTHER TRAP…
…SET BY NARAKU! I SHOULD KILL HIM. I *HAVE* TO!

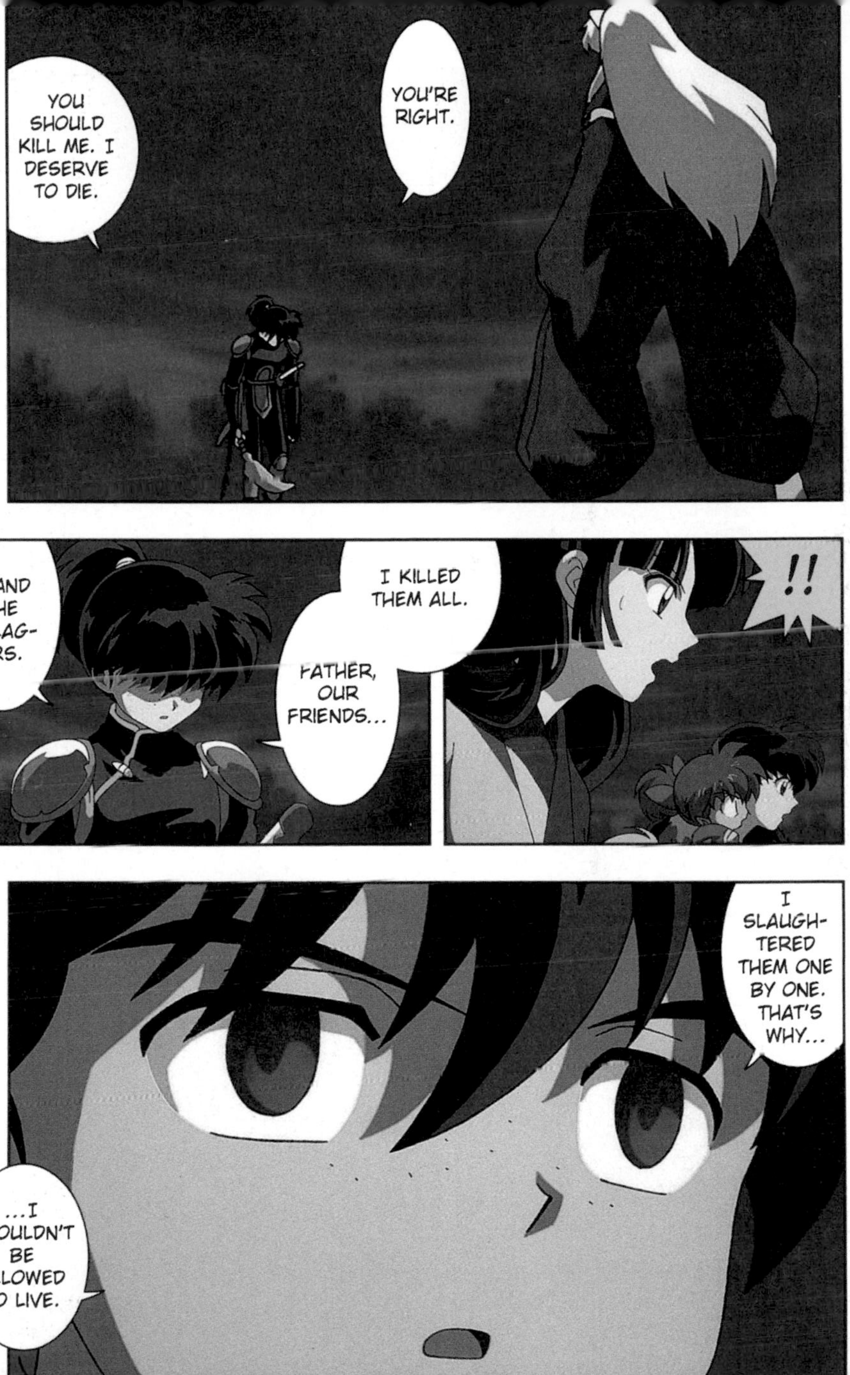
YOU'RE RIGHT.
YOU SHOULD KILL ME. I DESERVE TO DIE.
!!
I KILLED THEM ALL.
FATHER, OUR FRIENDS...
...AND THE VILLAGERS.
I SLAUGHTERED THEM ONE BY ONE. THAT'S WHY...
...I SHOULDN'T BE ALLOWED TO LIVE.

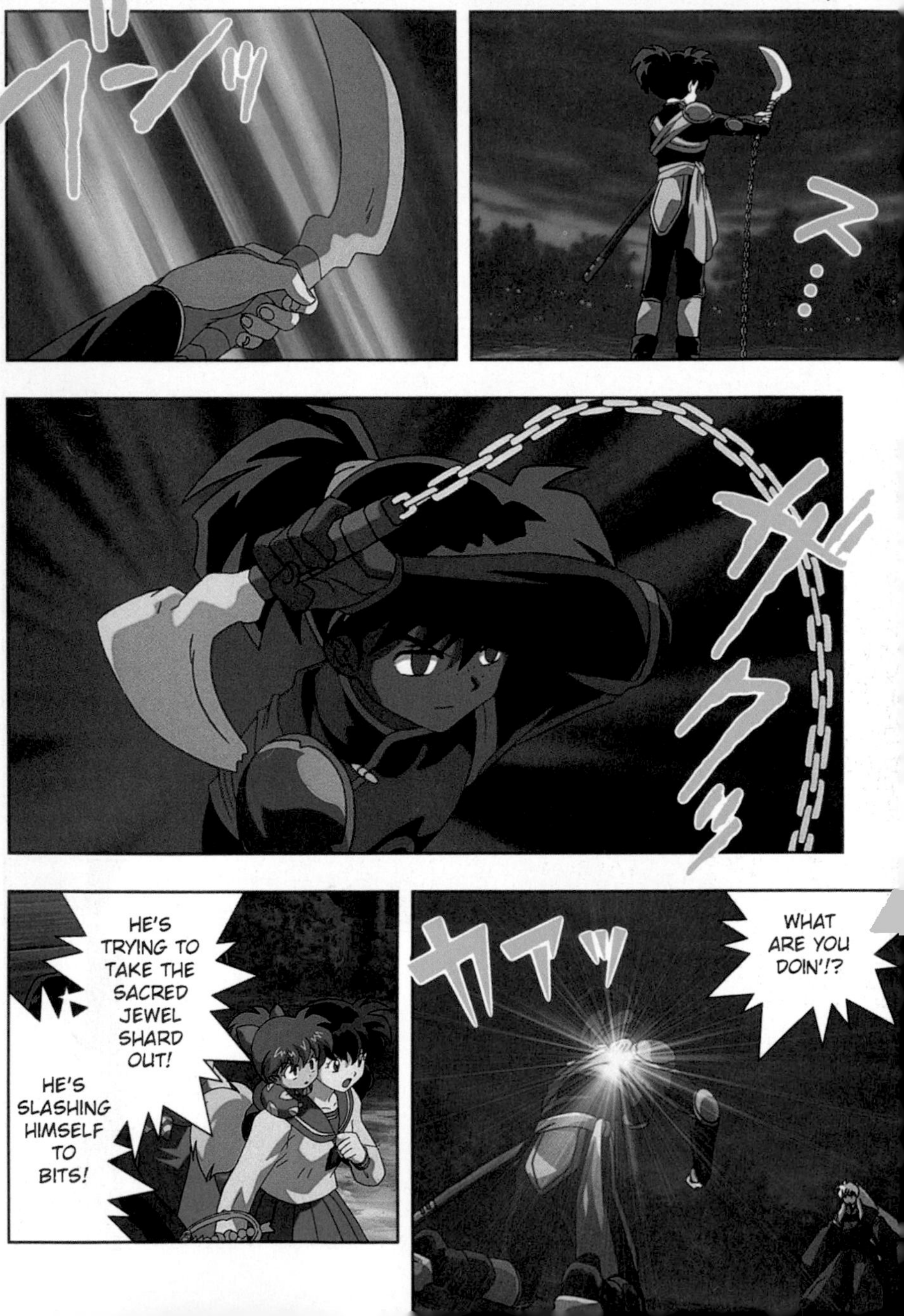
ス…
ブーンッ
ザクッ
カァッ
WHAT ARE YOU DOIN'!?
HE'S TRYING TO TAKE THE SACRED JEWEL SHARD OUT!
HE'S SLASHING HIMSELF TO BITS!

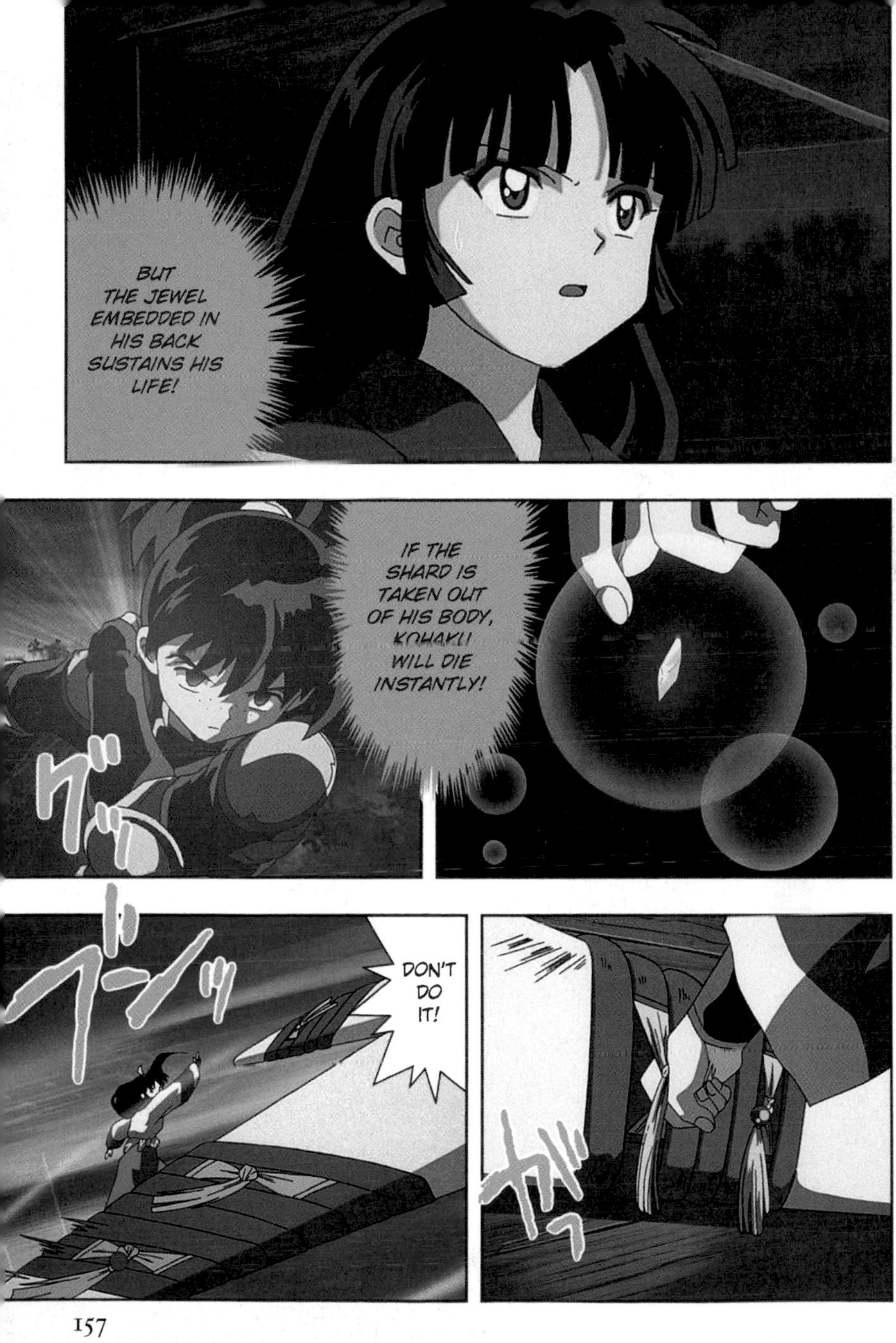
BUT THE JEWEL EMBEDDED IN HIS BACK SUSTAINS HIS LIFE!
IF THE SHARD IS TAKEN OUT OF HIS BODY, KOHAKU WILL DIE INSTANTLY!
DON'T DO IT!

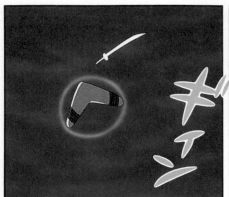

SANGO
!?

WHAT ARE
YOU DOING,
SANGO!?

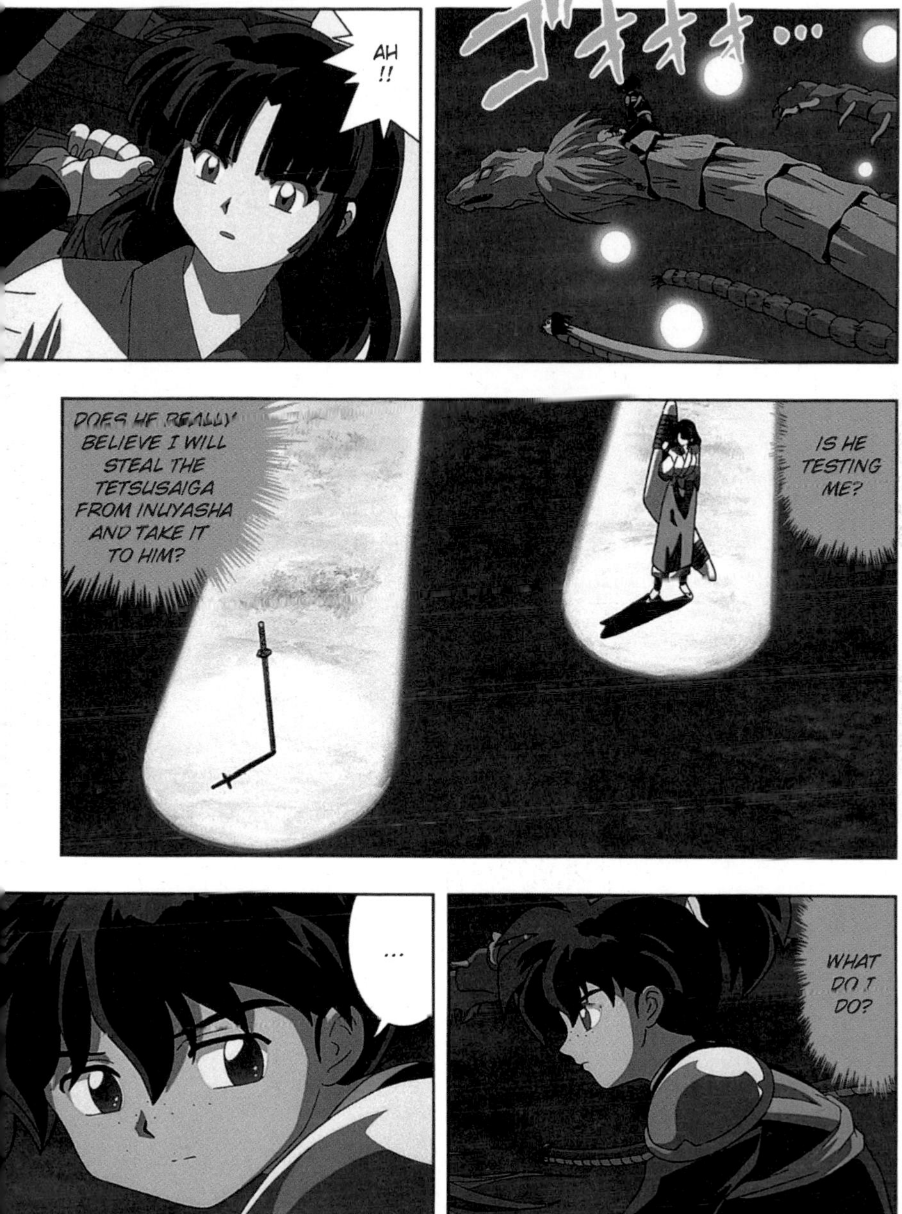
ゴォォォ…
AH !!
IS HE TESTING ME?
DOES HE REALLY BELIEVE I WILL STEAL THE TETSUSAIGA FROM INUYASHA AND TAKE IT TO HIM?
WHAT DO I DO?
...

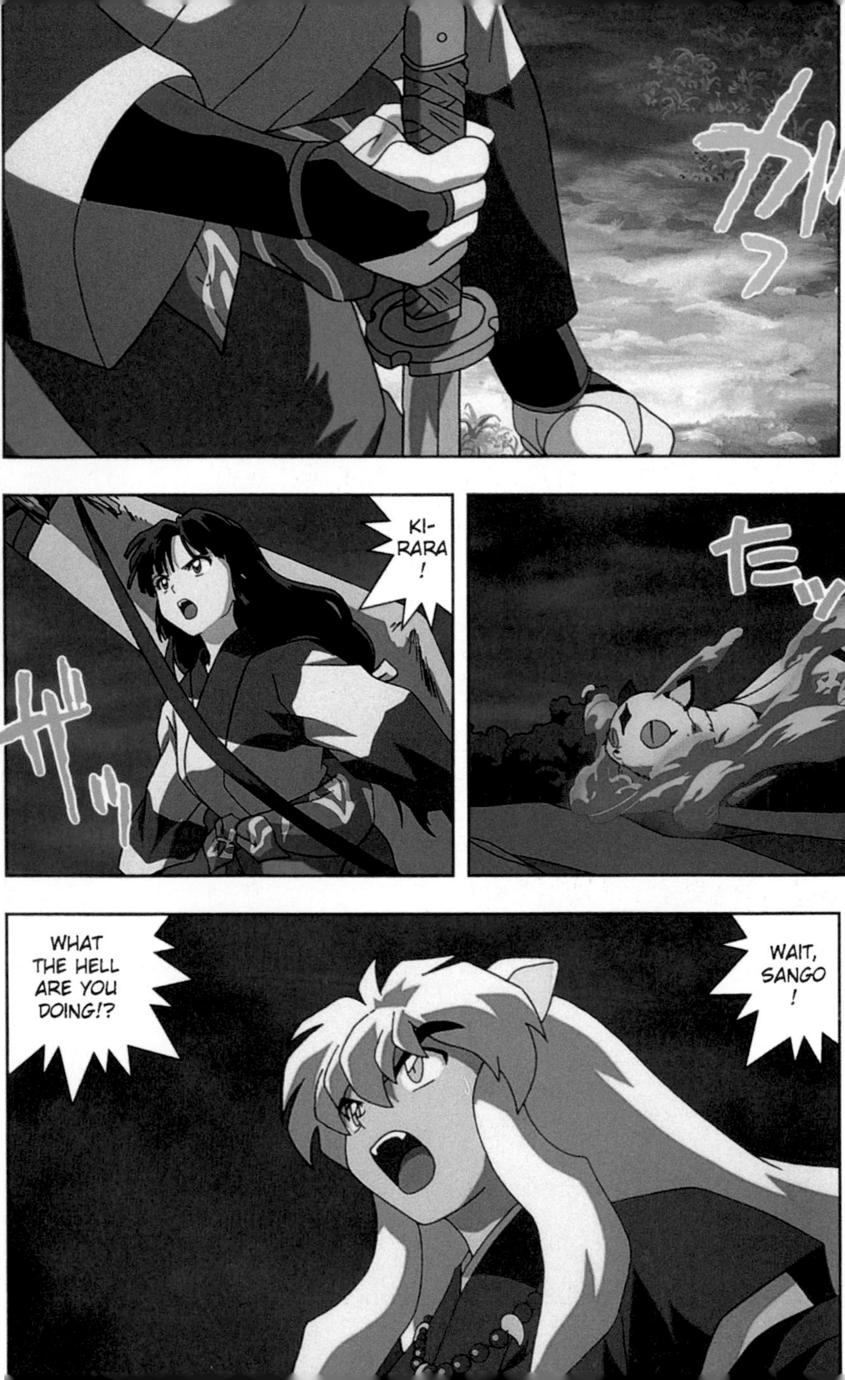
カッ
たッ
KI-RARA!
ザッ
WAIT, SANGO!
WHAT THE HELL ARE YOU DOING!?

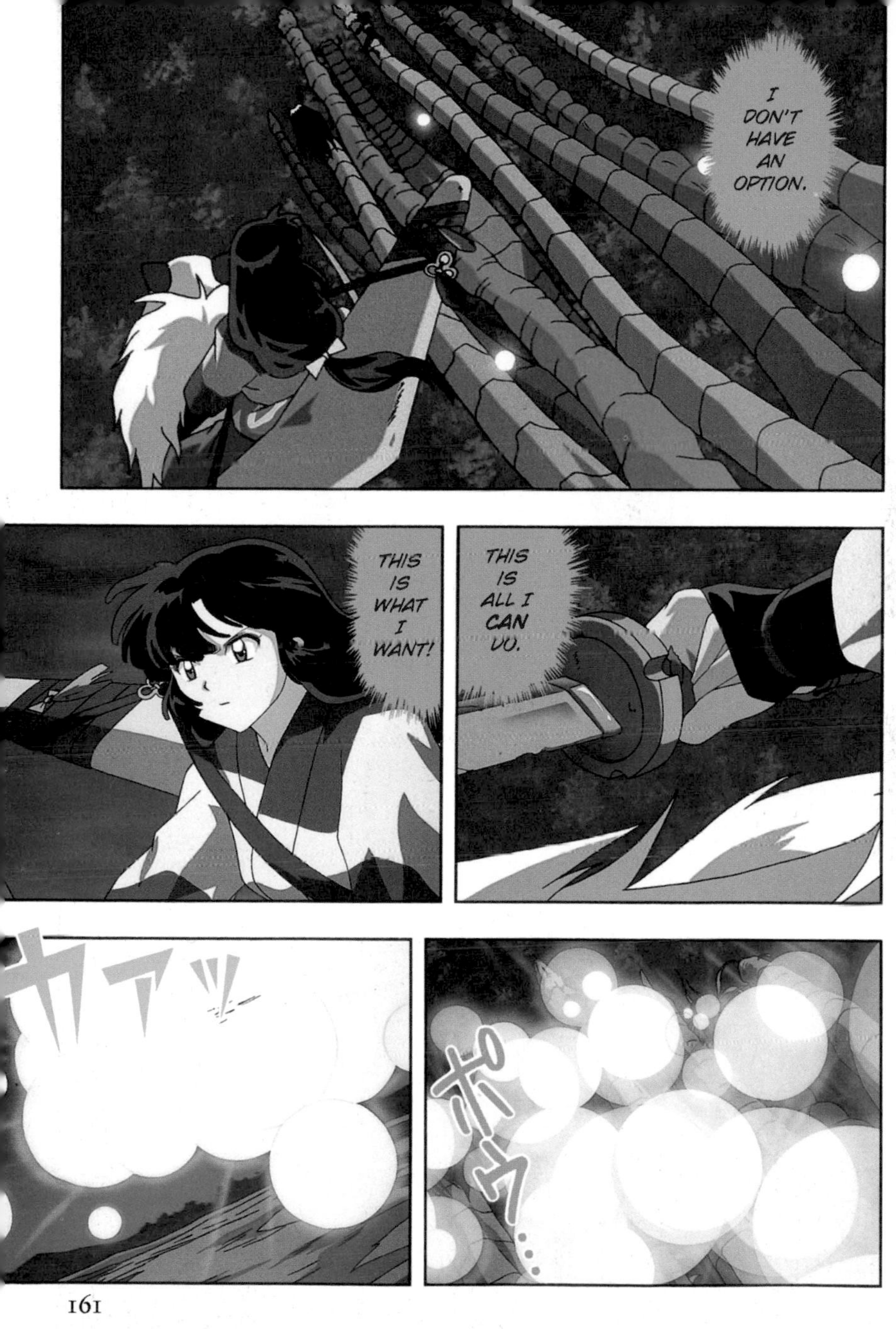
I DON'T HAVE AN OPTION.
THIS IS ALL I CAN DO.
THIS IS WHAT I WANT!
ポォゥ…
カァッ!!

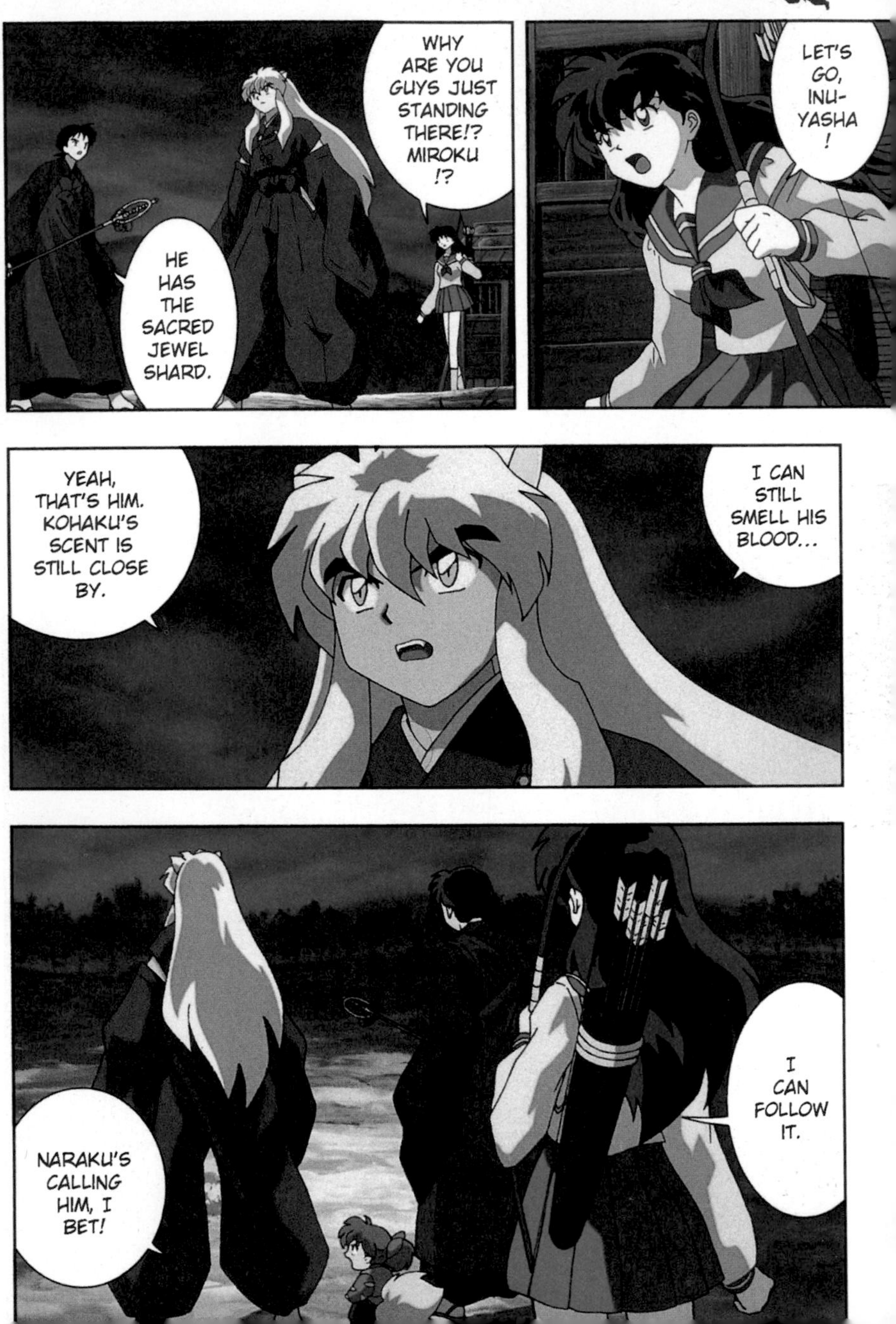
LET'S GO, INU-YASHA!
WHY ARE YOU GUYS JUST STANDING THERE!? MIROKU!?
HE HAS THE SACRED JEWEL SHARD.
I CAN STILL SMELL HIS BLOOD...
YEAH, THAT'S HIM. KOHAKU'S SCENT IS STILL CLOSE BY.
I CAN FOLLOW IT.
NARAKU'S CALLING HIM, I BET!

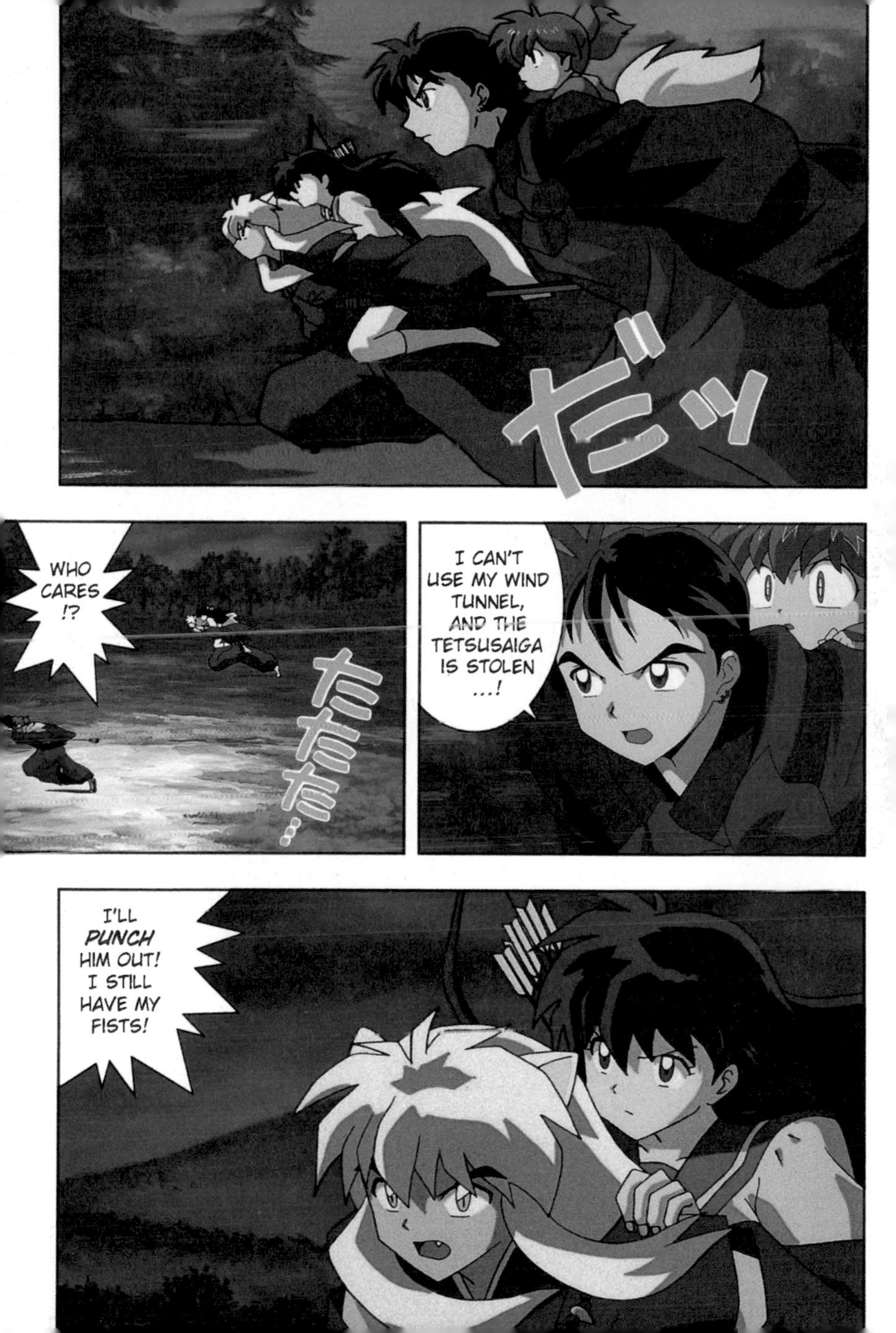
ダッ
I CAN'T USE MY WIND TUNNEL, AND THE TETSUSAIGA IS STOLEN ...!
WHO CARES !?
たたた…
I'LL *PUNCH* HIM OUT! I STILL HAVE MY FISTS!

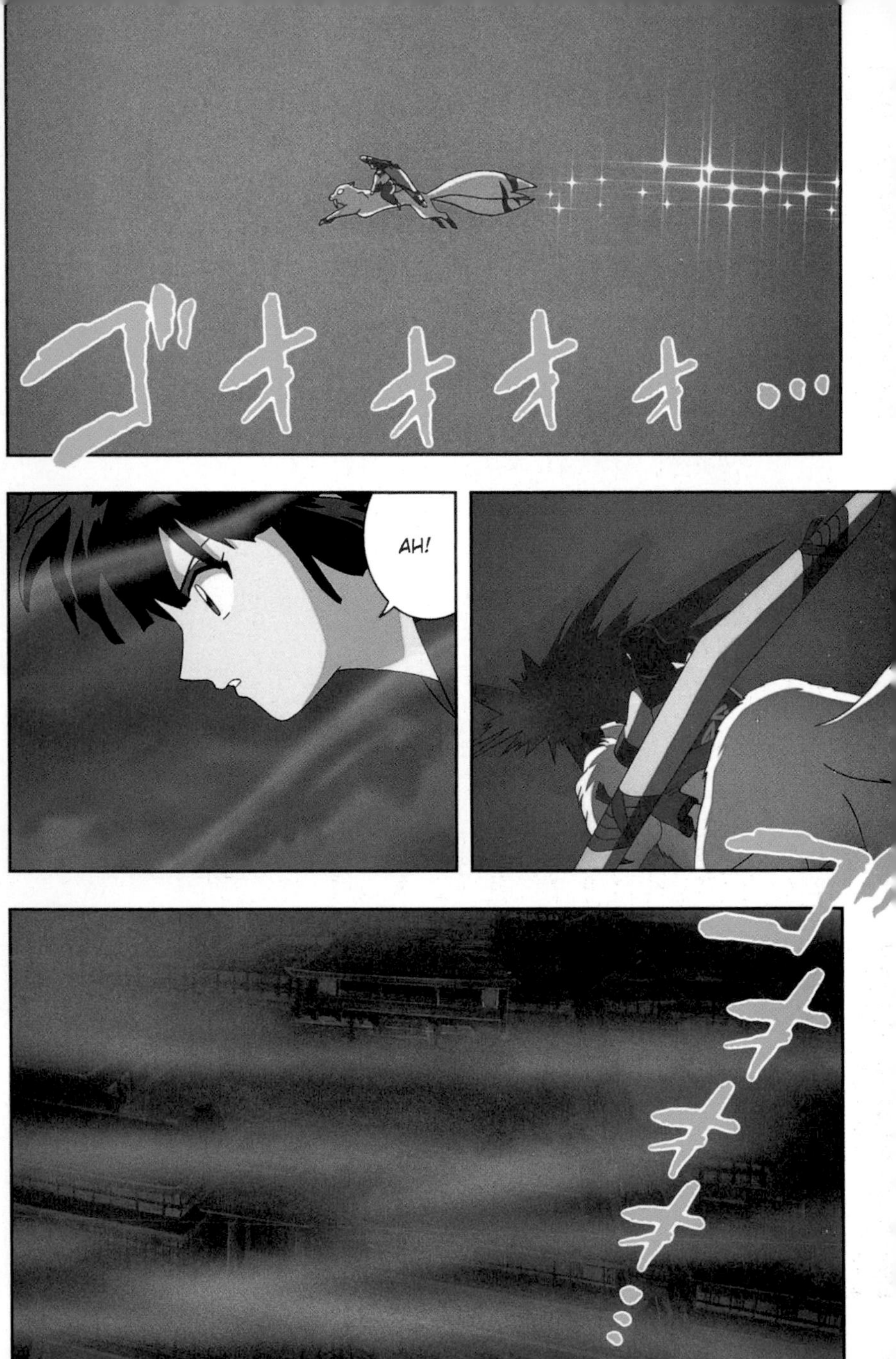
ゴォォォォ…
AH!
ゴォォォ…

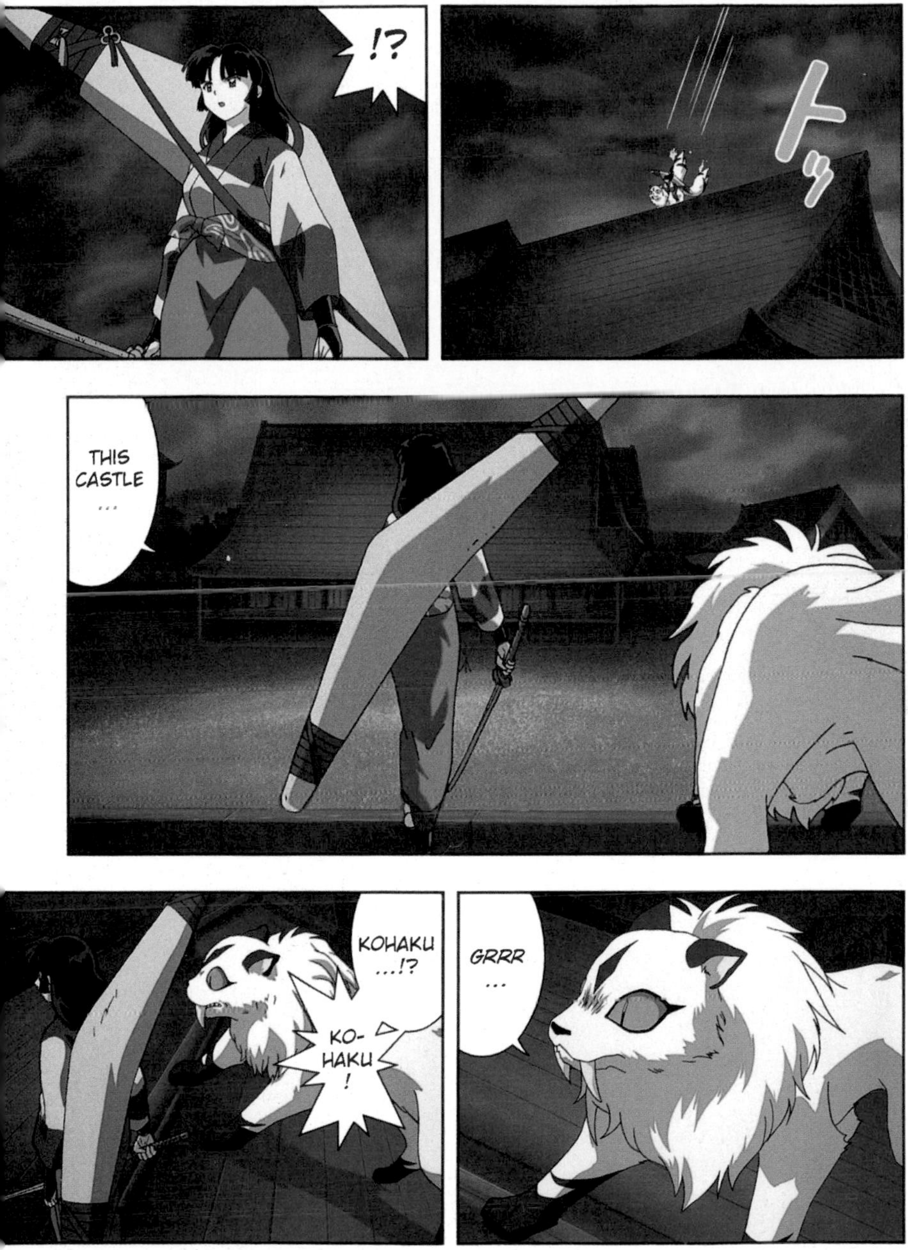
トッ
!?
THIS CASTLE ...
GRRR ...
KOHAKU ...!?
KO-HAKU !

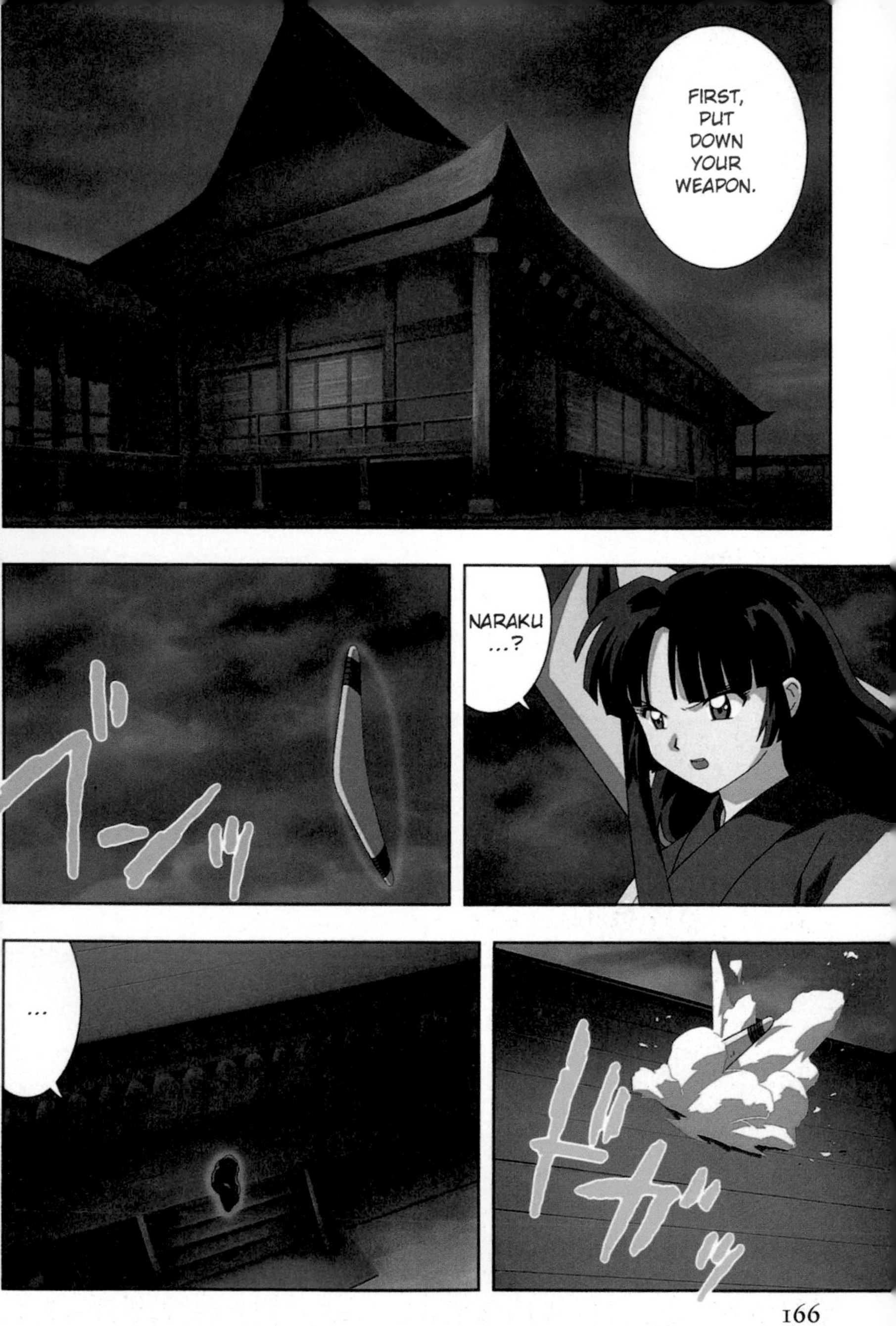
FIRST, PUT DOWN YOUR WEAPON.
NARAKU ...?
ブンッ
ドガッ
...

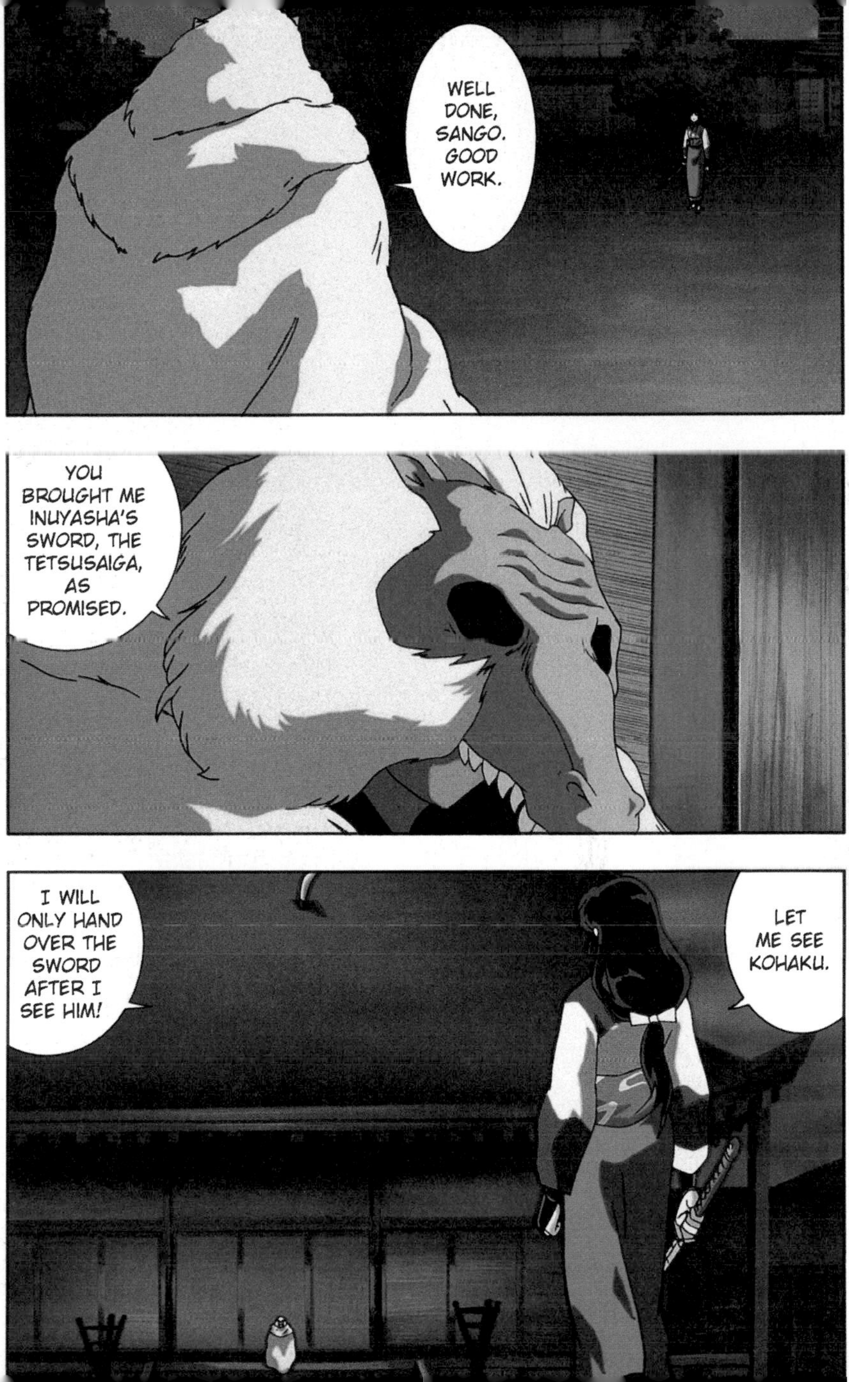
WELL DONE, SANGO. GOOD WORK.
YOU BROUGHT ME INUYASHA'S SWORD, THE TETSUSAIGA, AS PROMISED.
LET ME SEE KOHAKU.
I WILL ONLY HAND OVER THE SWORD AFTER I SEE HIM!

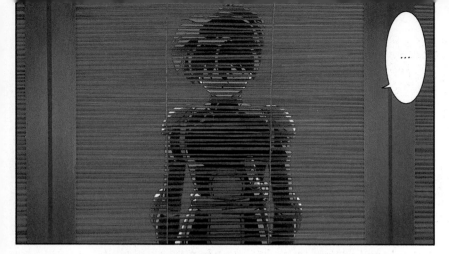

...
NA-RAKU!
TURN KOHAKU BACK TO HIS FORMER SELF IMMEDIATELY!
KILLING ME WON'T HELP...
YOU SHOULD KNOW THAT ALREADY.
THIS IS ALL THE FAULT OF THE SACRED SHIKON JEWEL.

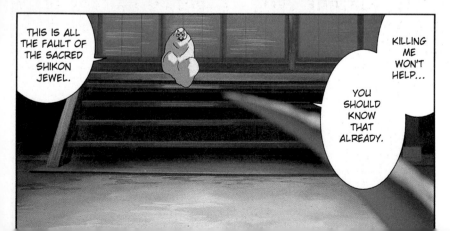

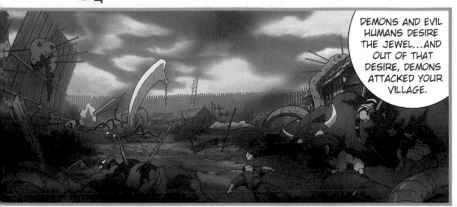

DEMONS AND EVIL HUMANS DESIRE THE JEWEL...AND OUT OF THAT DESIRE, DEMONS ATTACKED YOUR VILLAGE.

THAT'S WHY YOUR FATHER WAS KILLED. THAT'S WHY YOUR BROTHER KOHAKU'S SOUL NOW WANDERS IN DARKNESS.

IT'S ALL PART OF THE CURSE OF THE SACRED JEWEL.

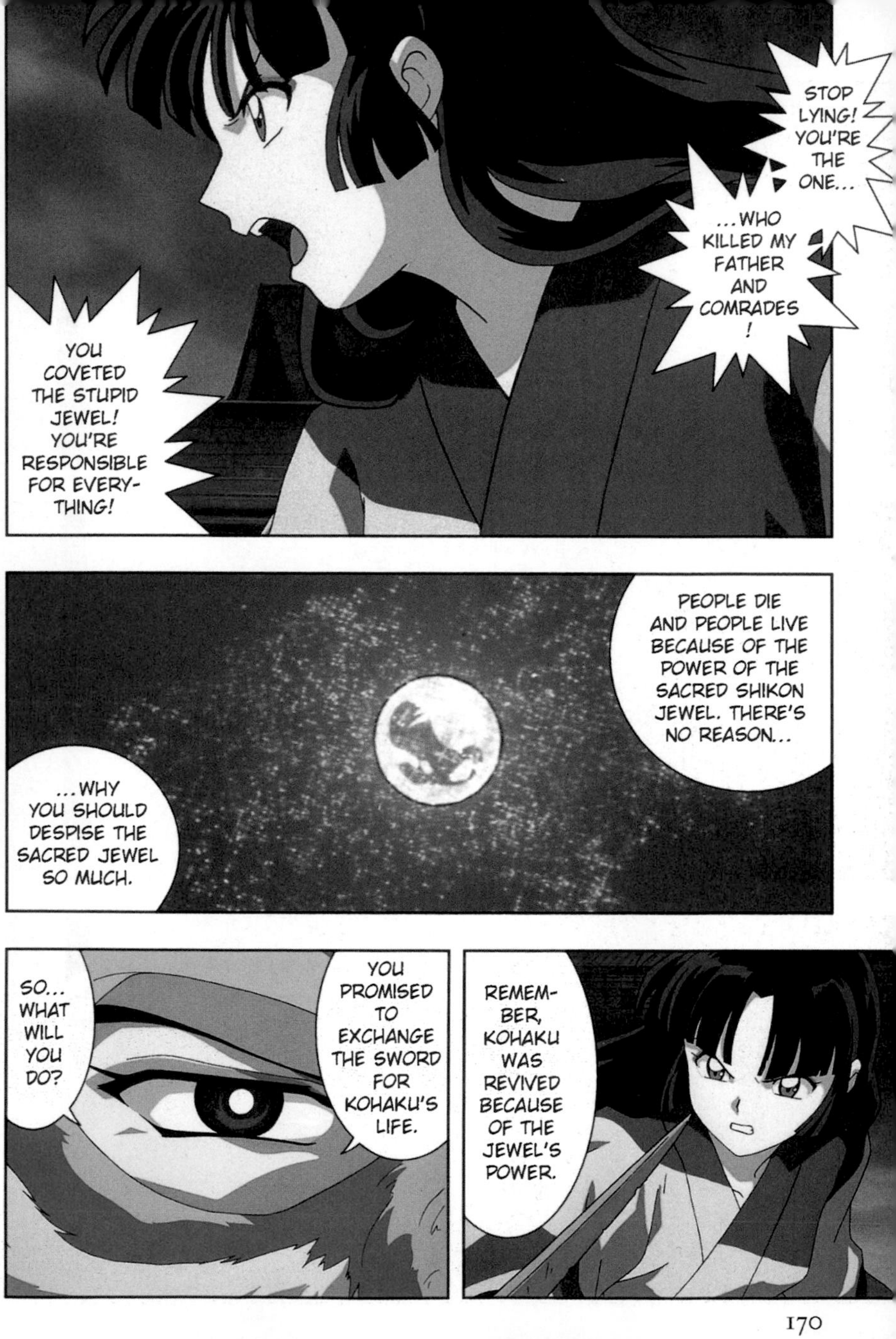
STOP LYING! YOU'RE THE ONE...
...WHO KILLED MY FATHER AND COMRADES!
YOU COVETED THE STUPID JEWEL! YOU'RE RESPONSIBLE FOR EVERY-THING!
PEOPLE DIE AND PEOPLE LIVE BECAUSE OF THE POWER OF THE SACRED SHIKON JEWEL. THERE'S NO REASON...
...WHY YOU SHOULD DESPISE THE SACRED JEWEL SO MUCH.
REMEM-BER, KOHAKU WAS REVIVED BECAUSE OF THE JEWEL'S POWER.
YOU PROMISED TO EXCHANGE THE SWORD FOR KOHAKU'S LIFE.
SO... WHAT WILL YOU DO?

HERE IT IS !!

YOU WANT MY ANSWER !?

HYAH !!

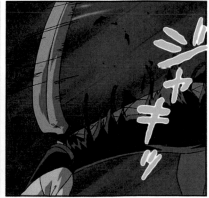

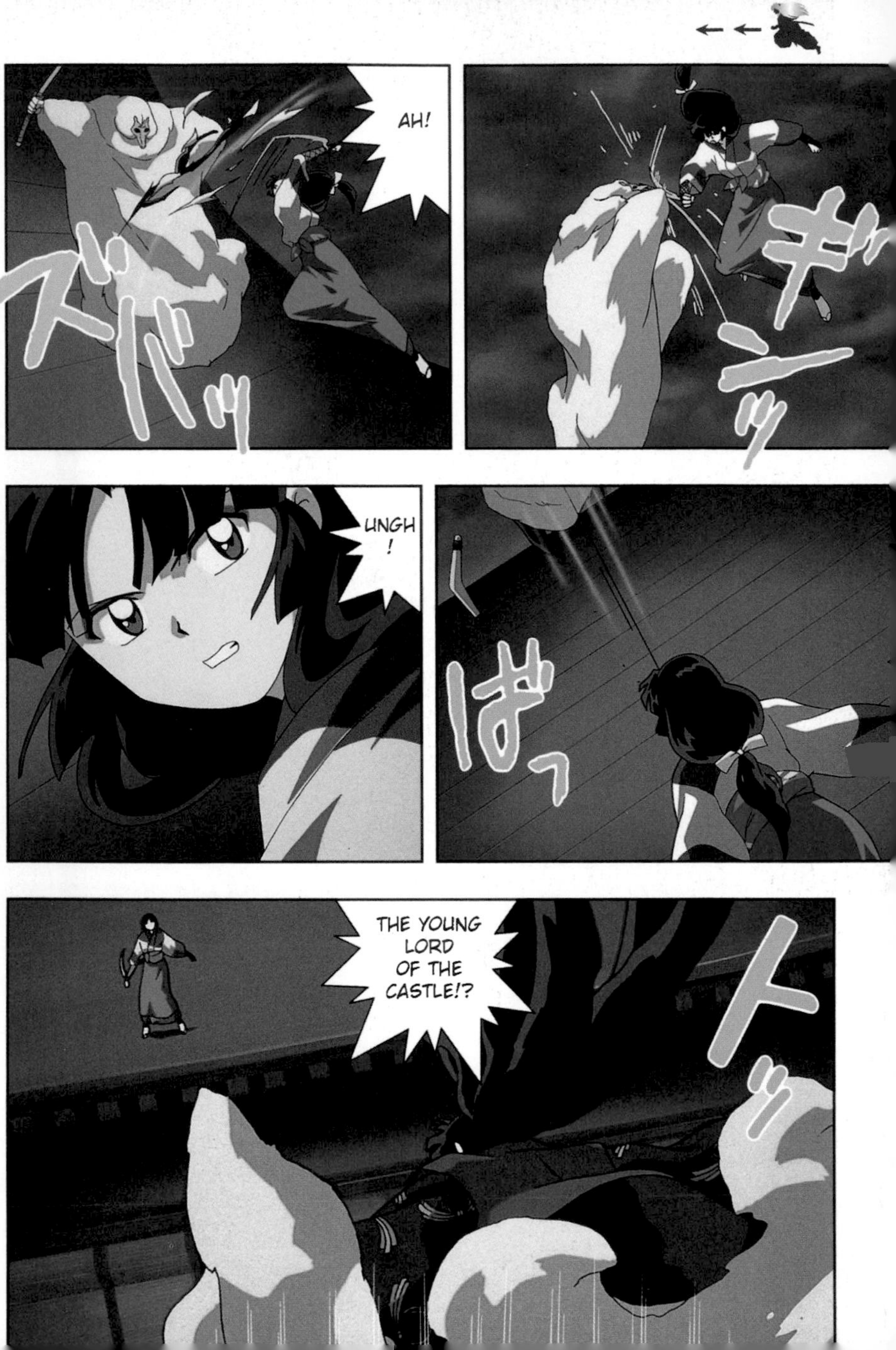
ギーンッ
AH!
ズバッ
ぱっ
UNGH !
THE YOUNG LORD OF THE CASTLE!?
トッ

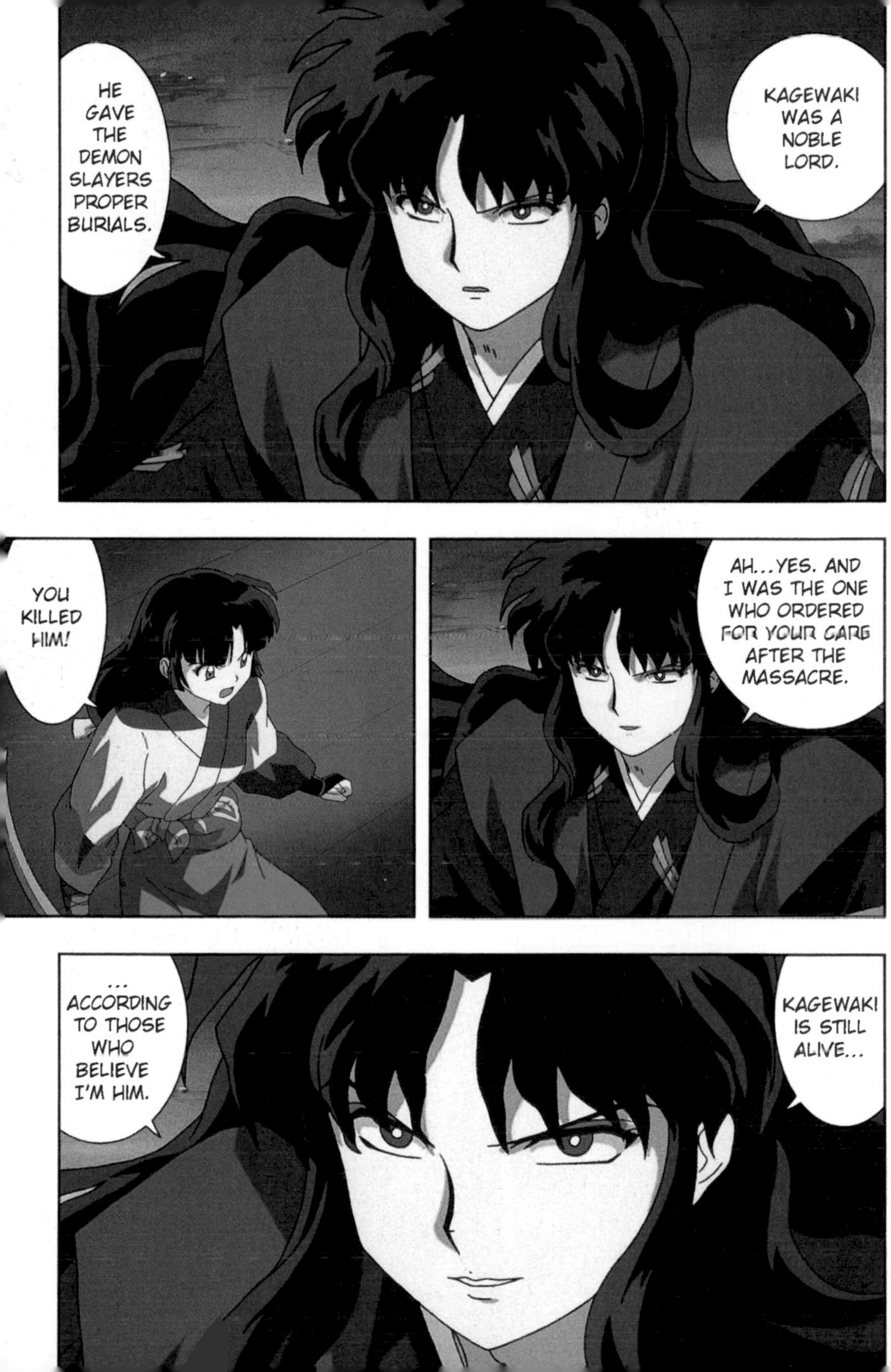
KAGEWAKI WAS A NOBLE LORD.
HE GAVE THE DEMON SLAYERS PROPER BURIALS.
AH...YES. AND I WAS THE ONE WHO ORDERED FOR YOUR CARE AFTER THE MASSACRE.
YOU KILLED HIM!
KAGEWAKI IS STILL ALIVE...
...ACCORDING TO THOSE WHO BELIEVE I'M HIM.

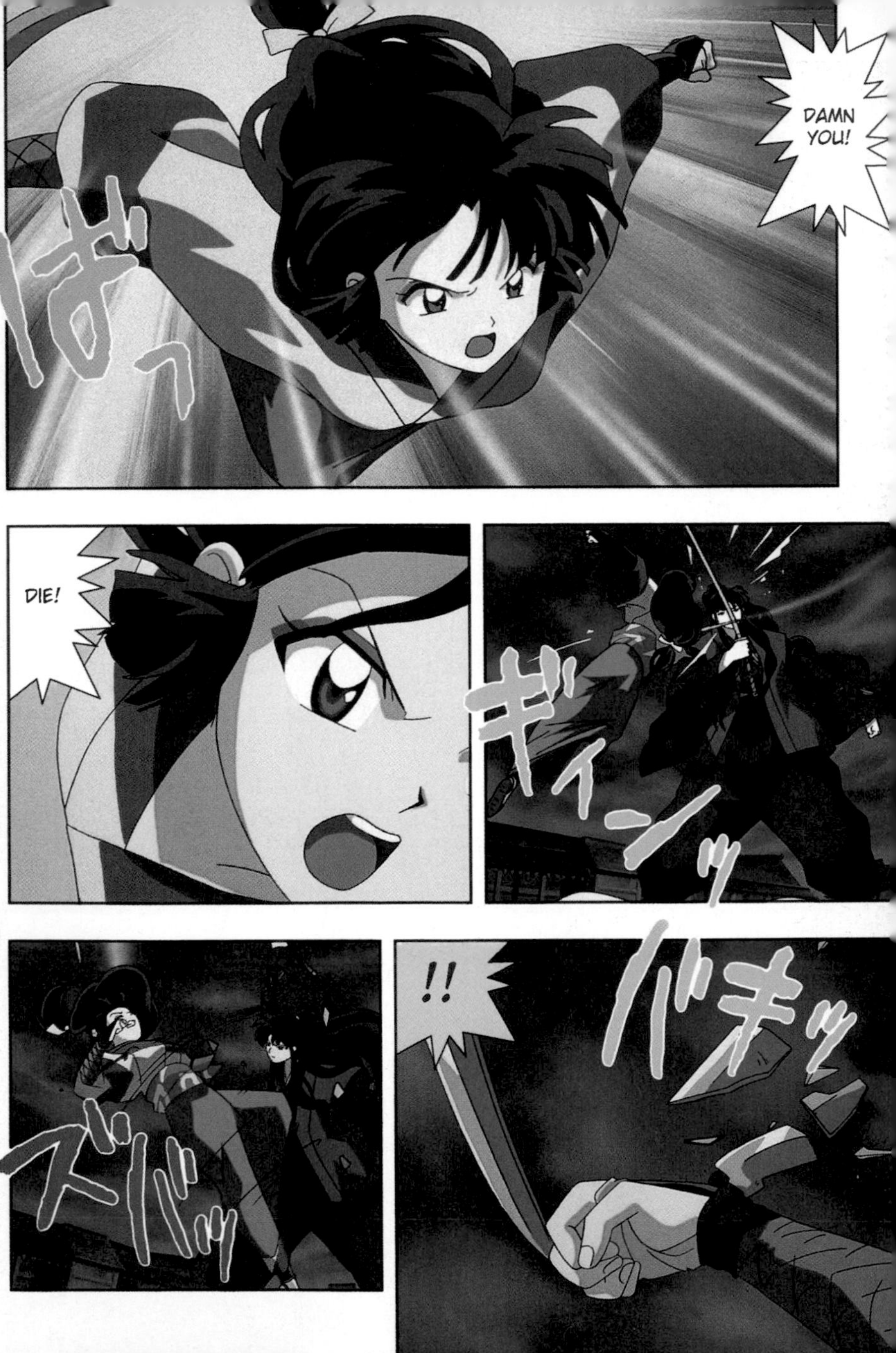
DAMN YOU!
ぼっ
ギィーンッ
DIE!
!!
バキッ
ズバッ

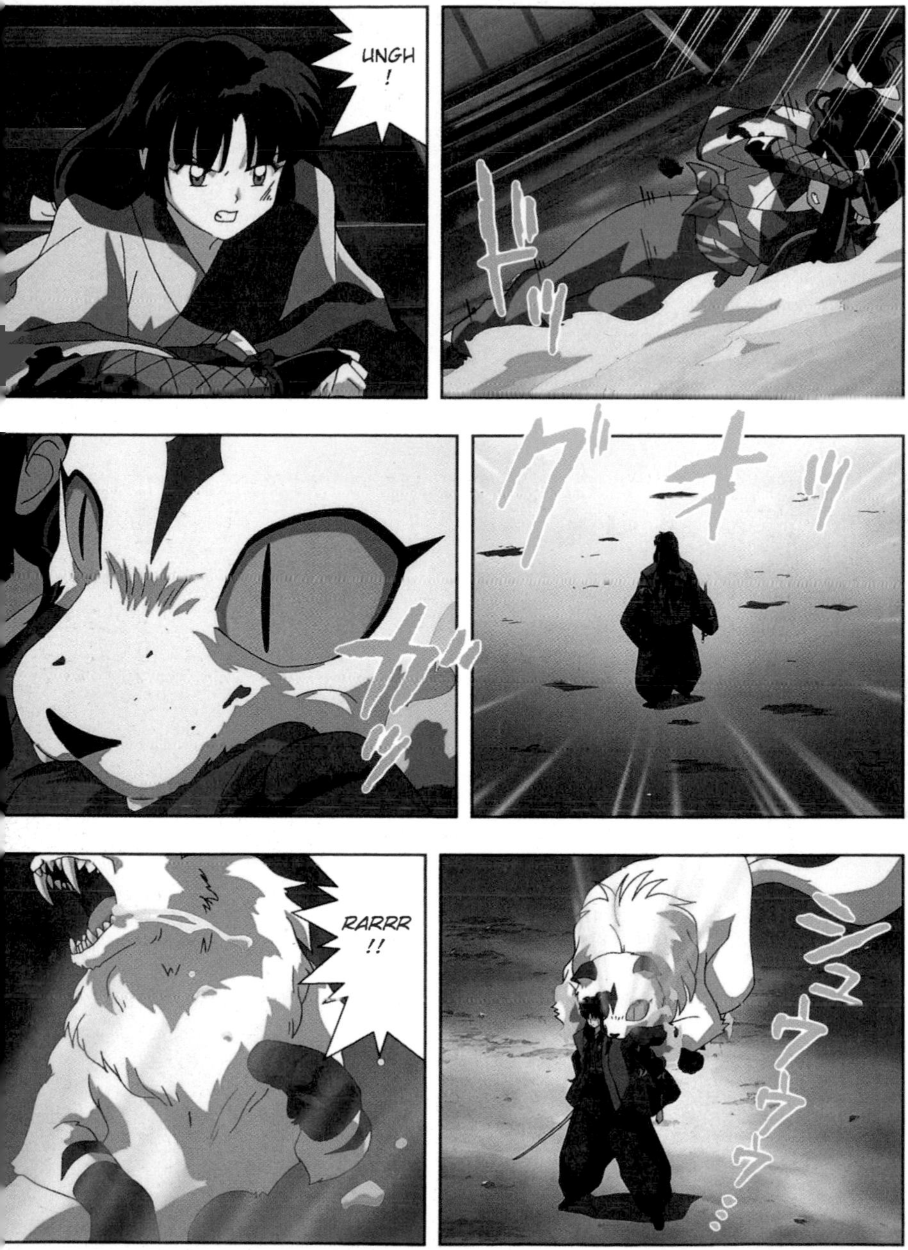
ドッ
UNGH !
グキッ
ガッ
シュウウウ…
RARRR !!

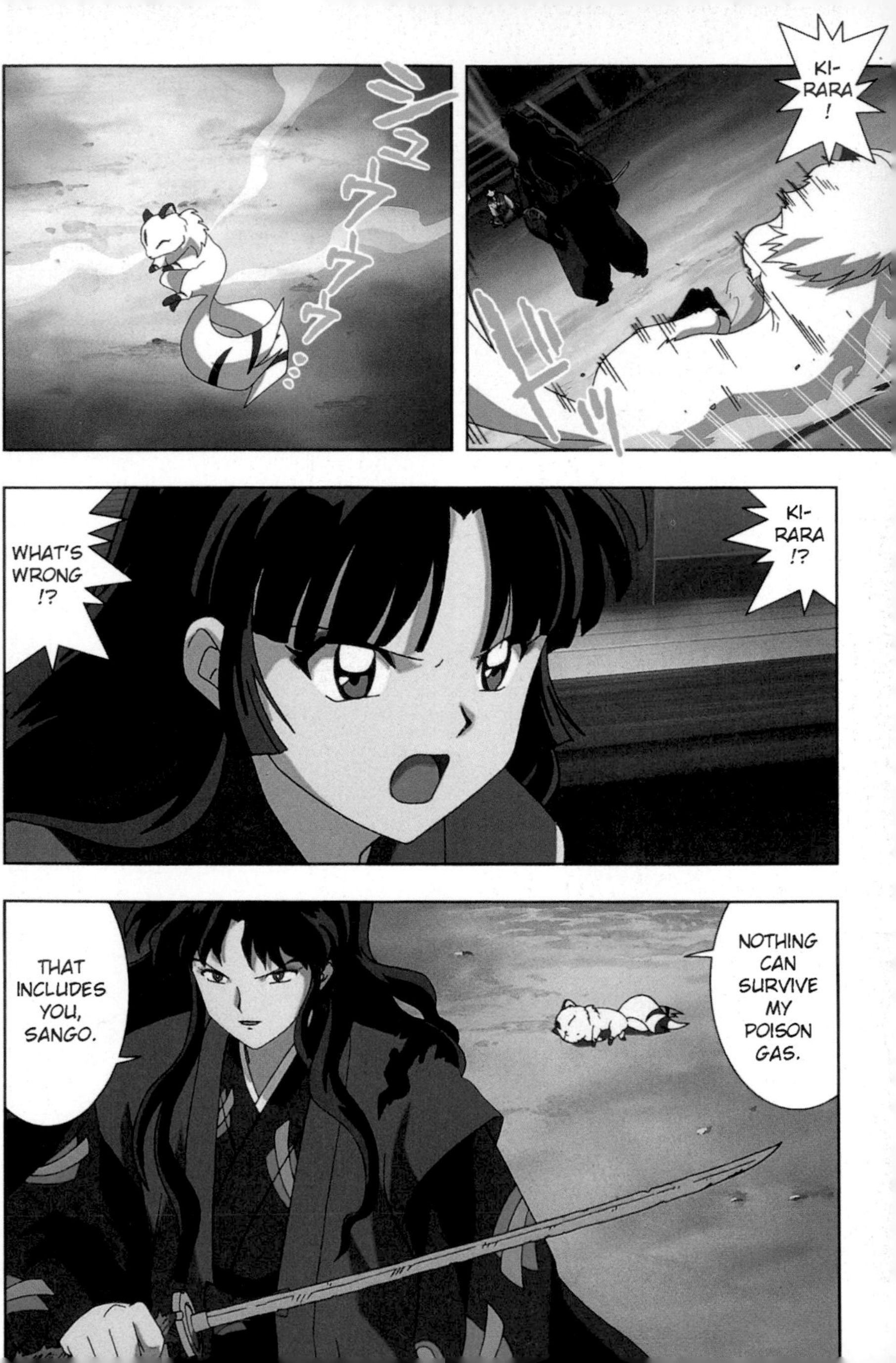
KI-RARA!
KI-RARA!?
WHAT'S WRONG!?
NOTHING CAN SURVIVE MY POISON GAS.
THAT INCLUDES YOU, SANGO.

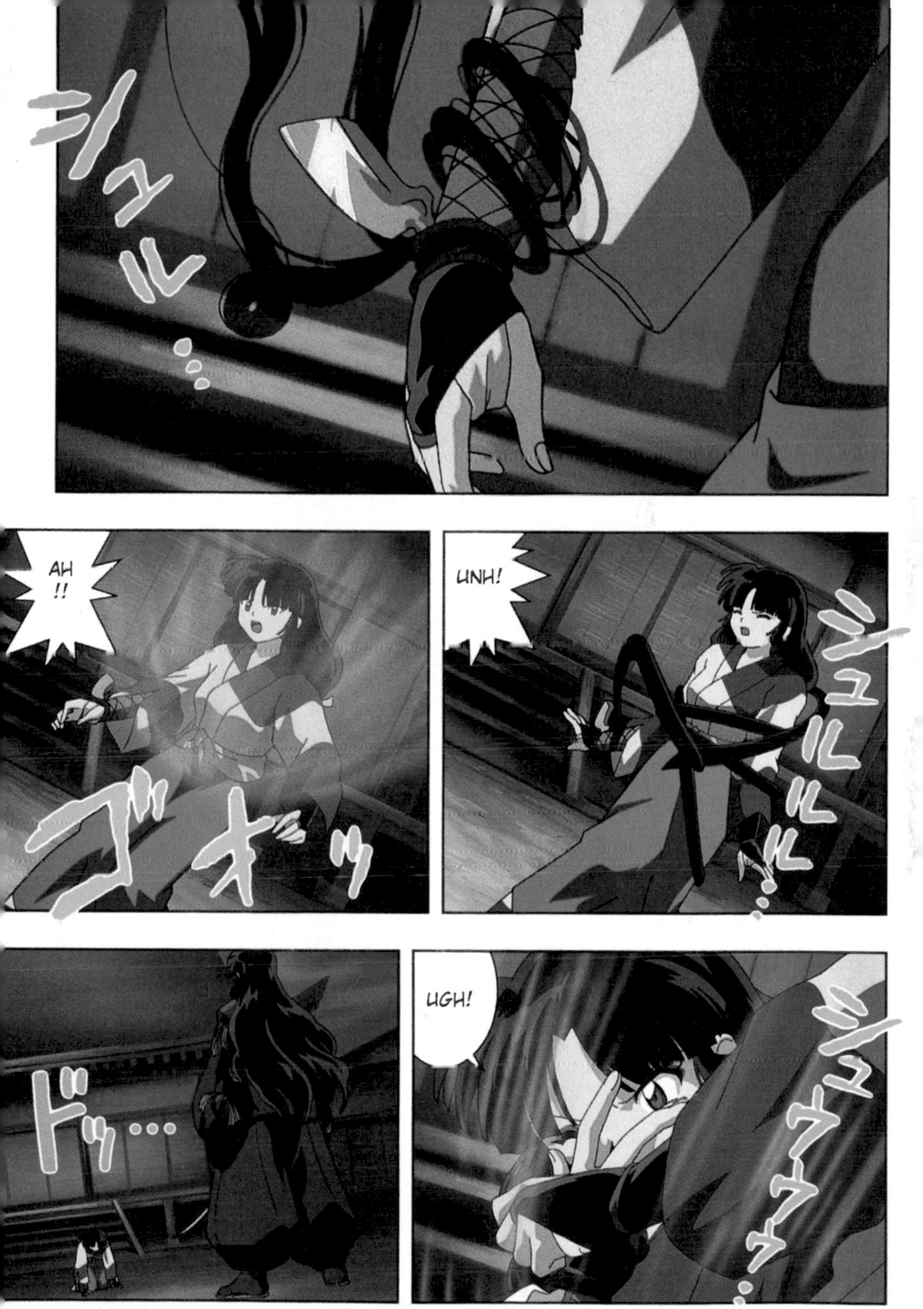
シュル…
UNH!
シュルルル…
AH !!
ゴオッ
UGH!
シュウウウ…
ドッ…

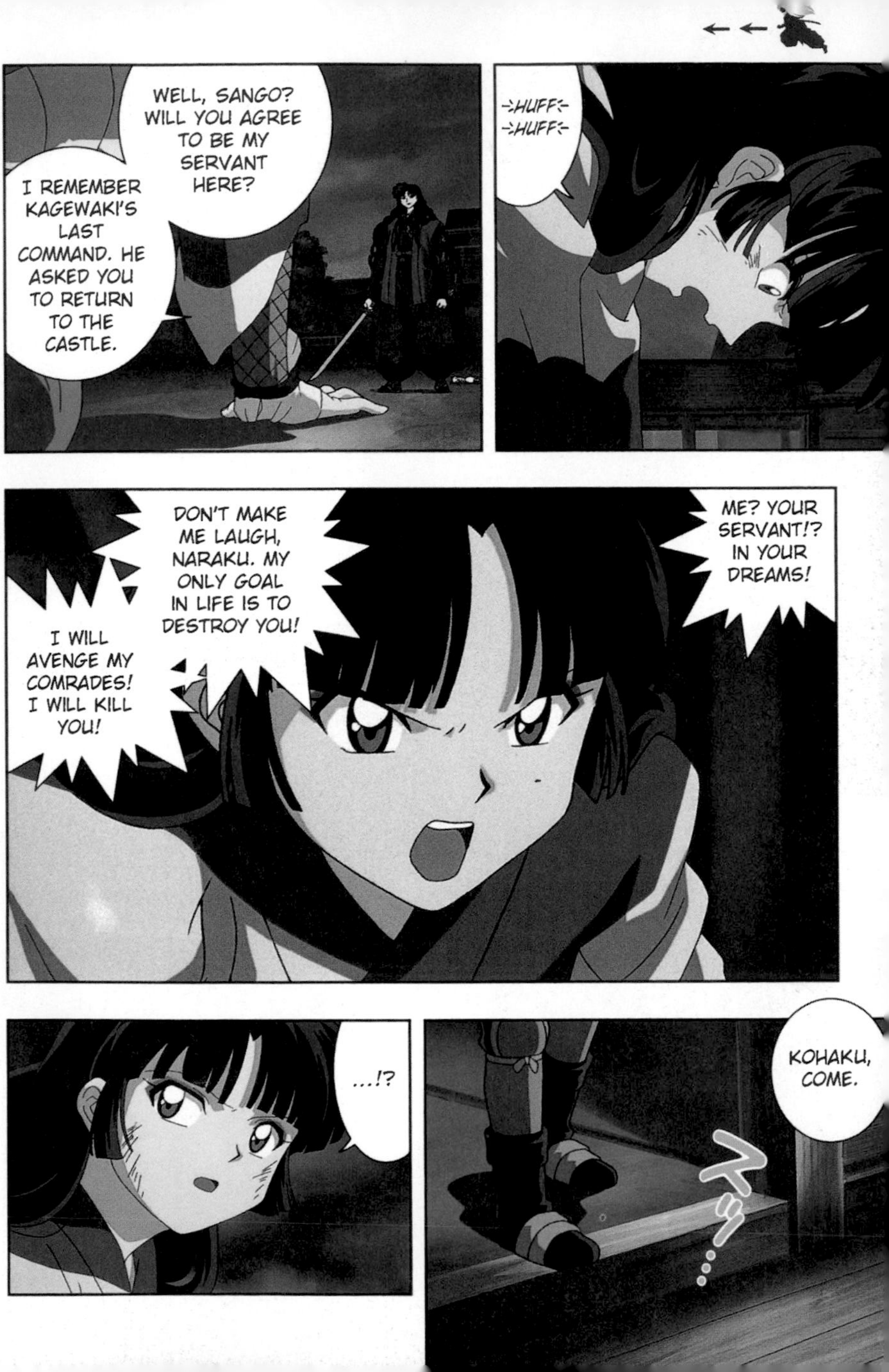

-HUFF-
-HUFF-
WELL, SANGO? WILL YOU AGREE TO BE MY SERVANT HERE?
I REMEMBER KAGEWAKI'S LAST COMMAND. HE ASKED YOU TO RETURN TO THE CASTLE.
ME? YOUR SERVANT!? IN YOUR DREAMS!
DON'T MAKE ME LAUGH, NARAKU. MY ONLY GOAL IN LIFE IS TO DESTROY YOU!
I WILL AVENGE MY COMRADES! I WILL KILL YOU!
KOHAKU, COME.
スッ...
...!?

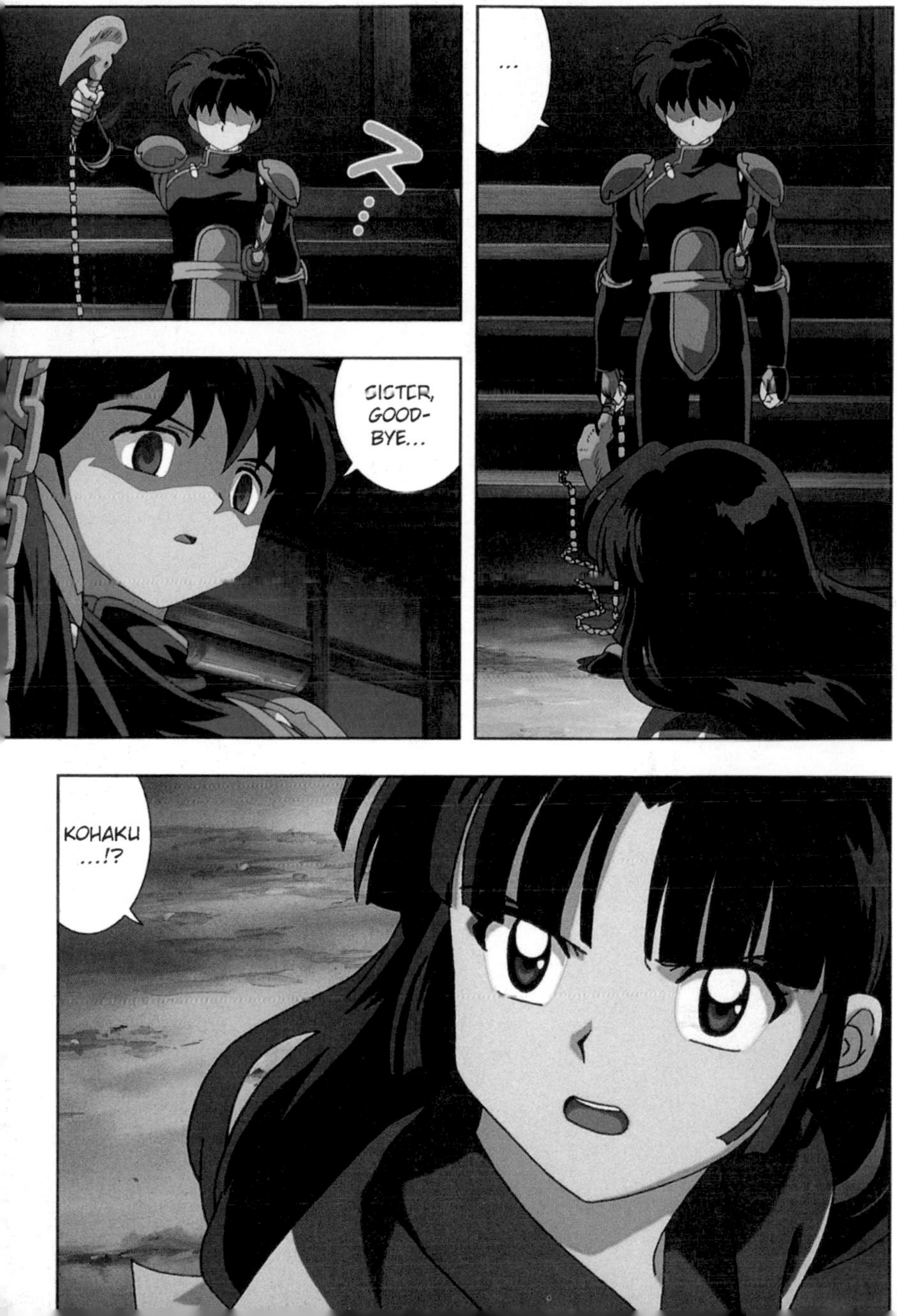
...
ス
SISTER, GOOD-BYE...
KOHAKU ...!?

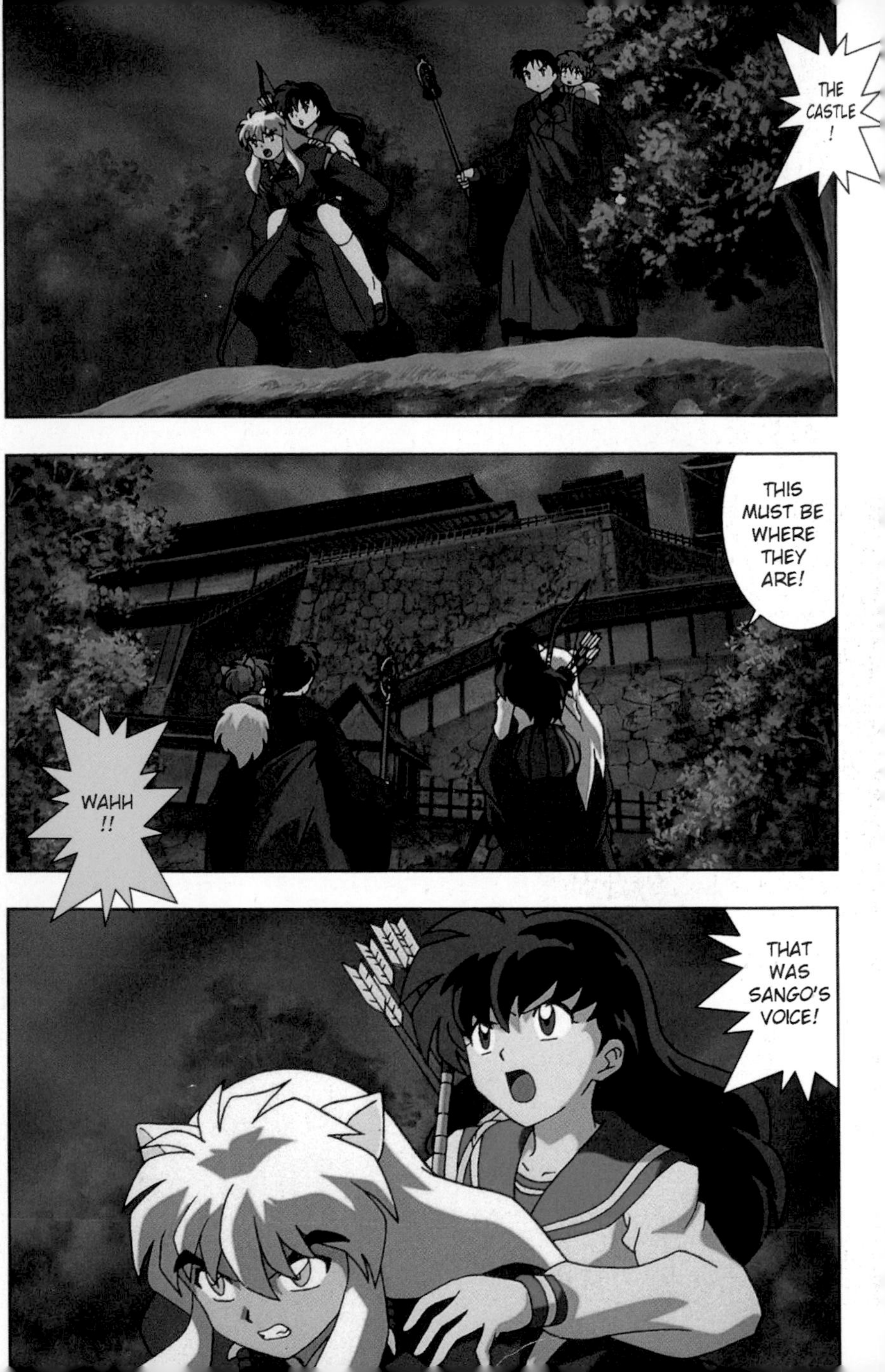
THE CASTLE !
THIS MUST BE WHERE THEY ARE!
WAHH !!
THAT WAS SANGO'S VOICE!

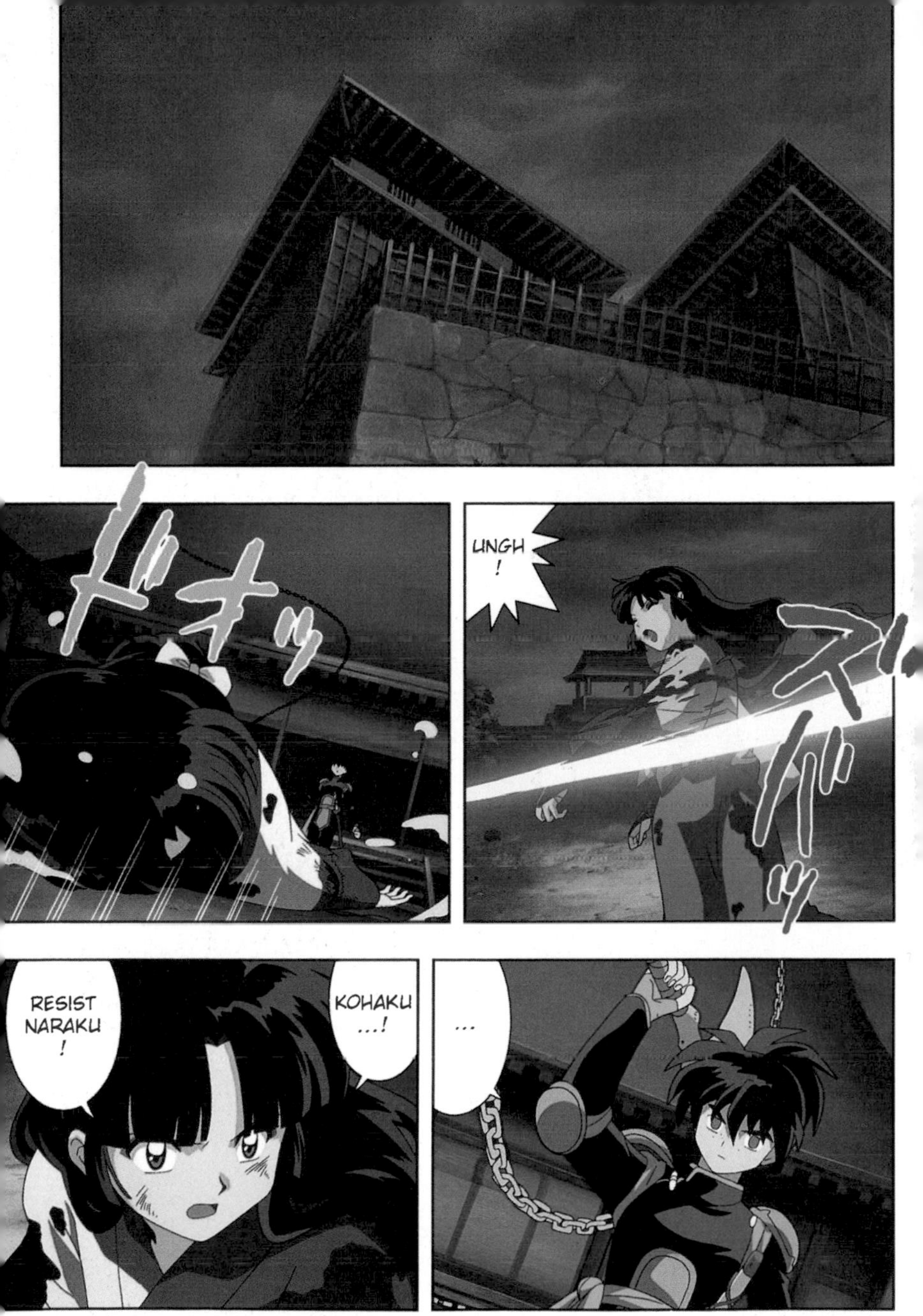
UNGH!
...
KOHAKU...!
RESIST NARAKU!

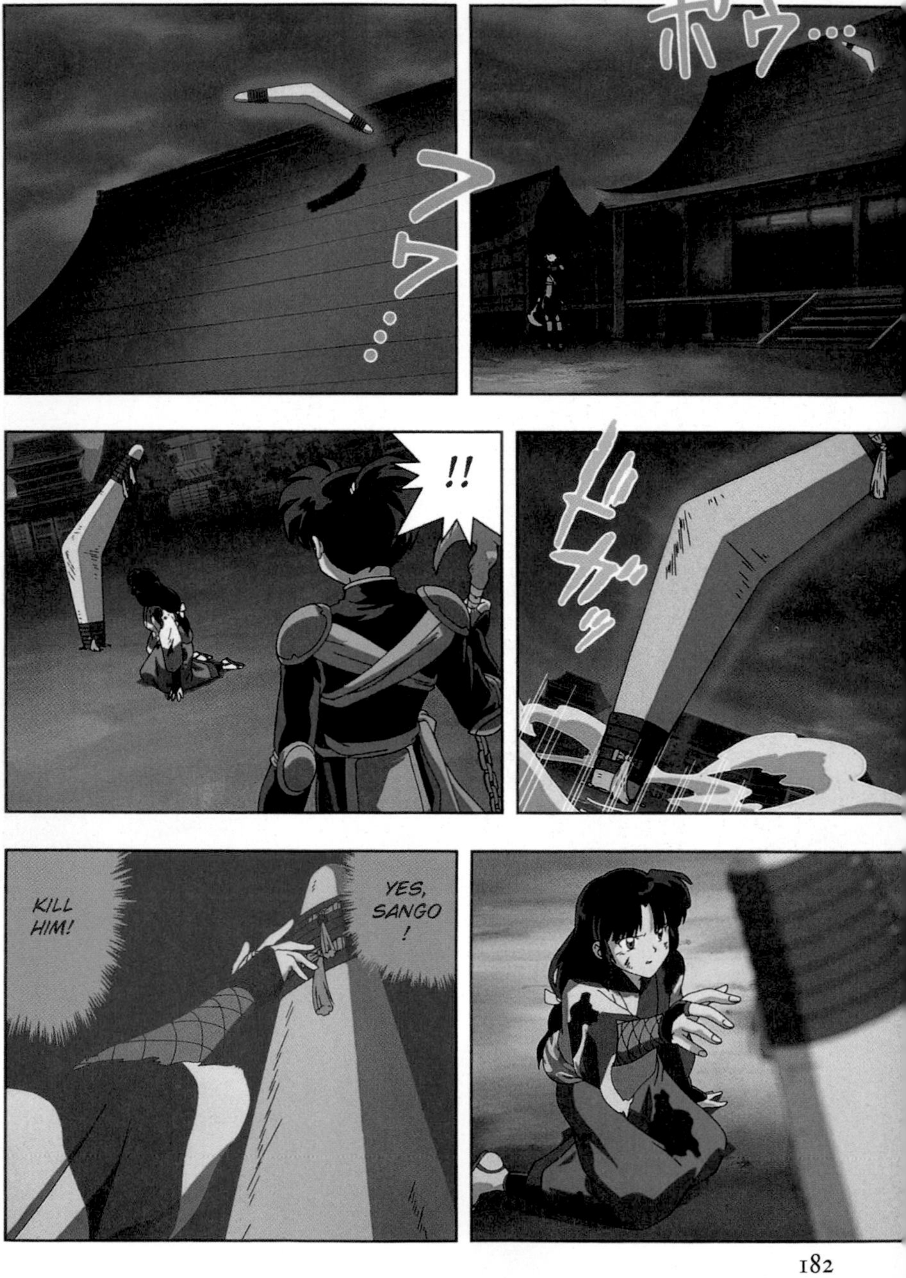
ポウ…
フワ…
ドガッ
!!
YES, SANGO!
KILL HIM!

SLAUGHTER YOUR BROTHER ...
...AND THEN BURN WITH A DESIRE TO LIVE.
PRAY TO CONTINUE WANDERING IN THE WORLD...
...AND VOW TO SURVIVE AT ANY COST.
WHEN YOU KILL KOHAKU, AND YOU ARE BATHED IN HIS BLOOD, THE SACRED JEWEL WILL GLOW BRIGHTER WITH THE POWER OF THE DARK.
THE MORE SULLIED IT IS, THE MORE BEAUTIFUL THE SACRED JEWEL BECOMES.

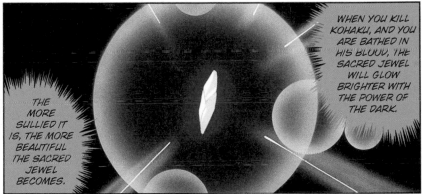

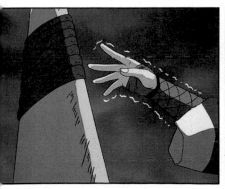

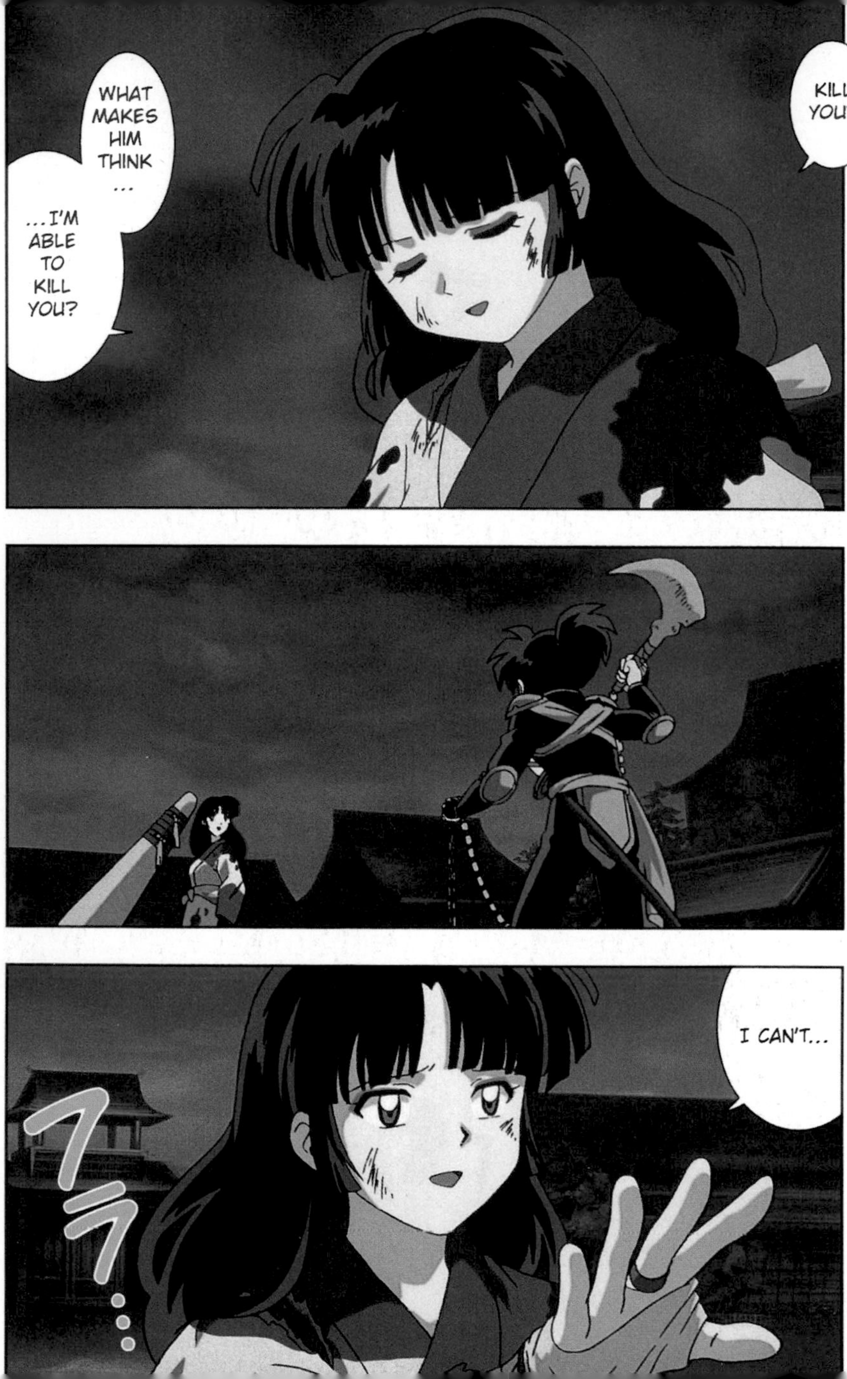
KILL YOU?
WHAT MAKES HIM THINK ...
...I'M ABLE TO KILL YOU?
I CAN'T...
フラ…

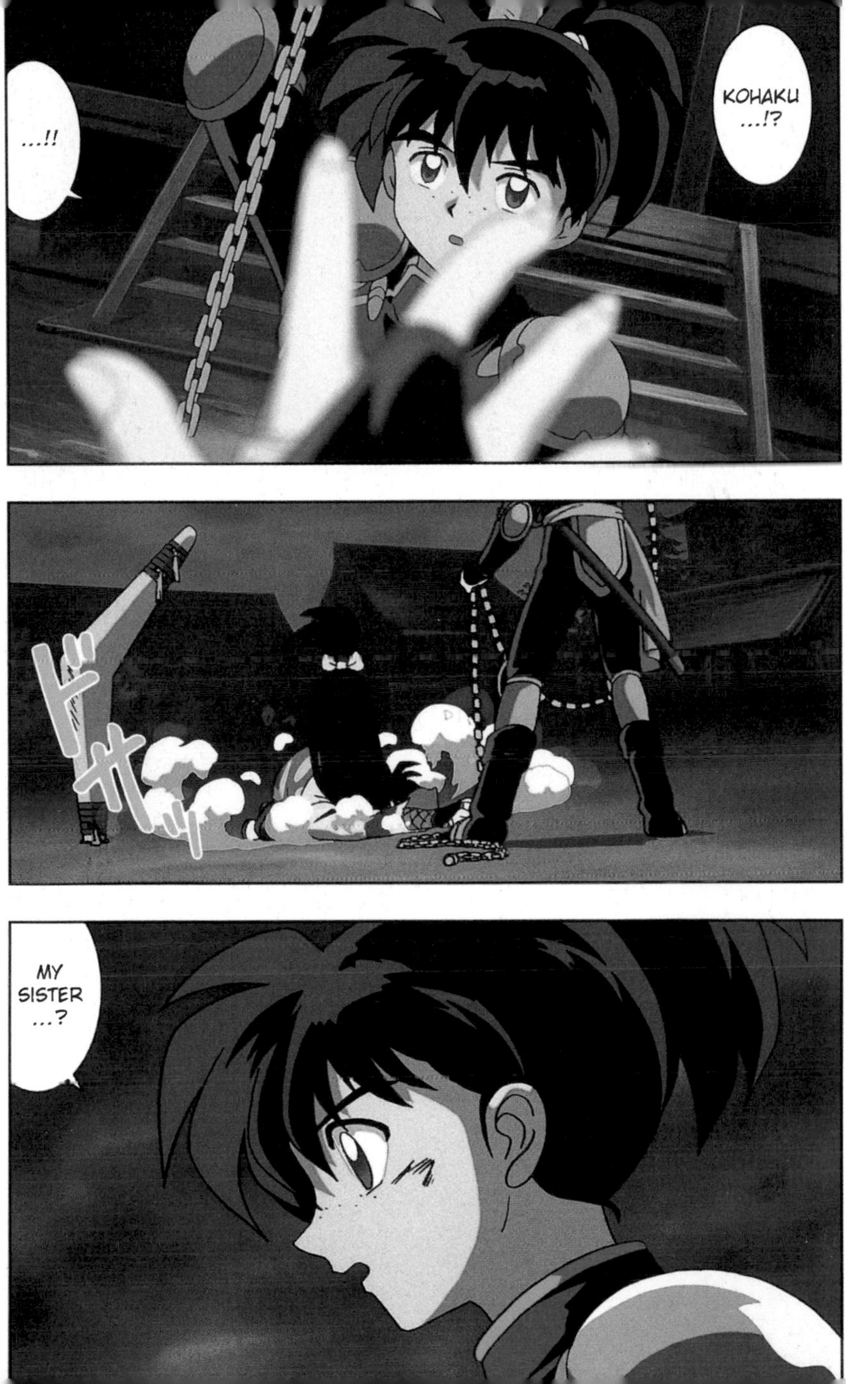
KOHAKU ...!?
...!!
ドサッ
MY SISTER ...?

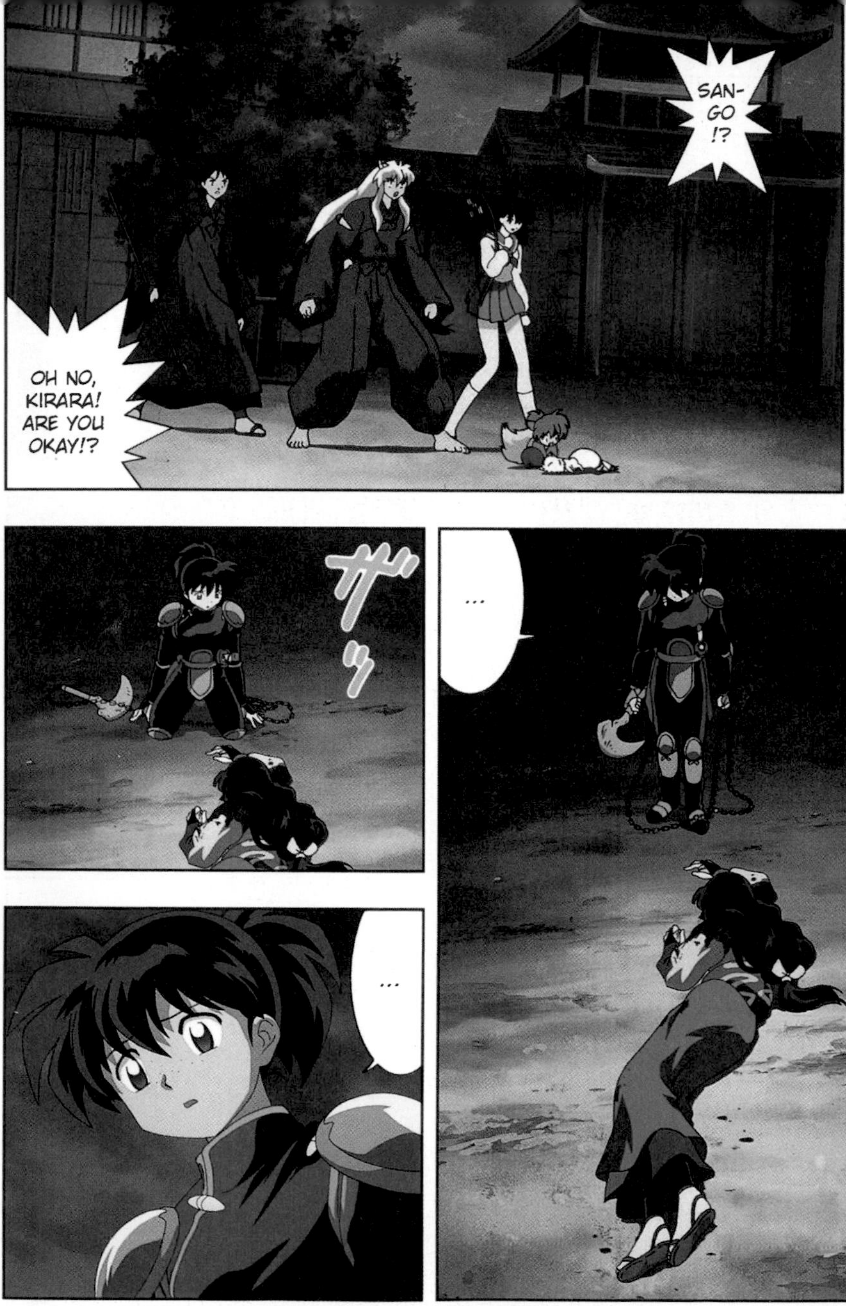
SAN-GO!?
OH NO, KIRARA! ARE YOU OKAY!?
...
ザッ
...

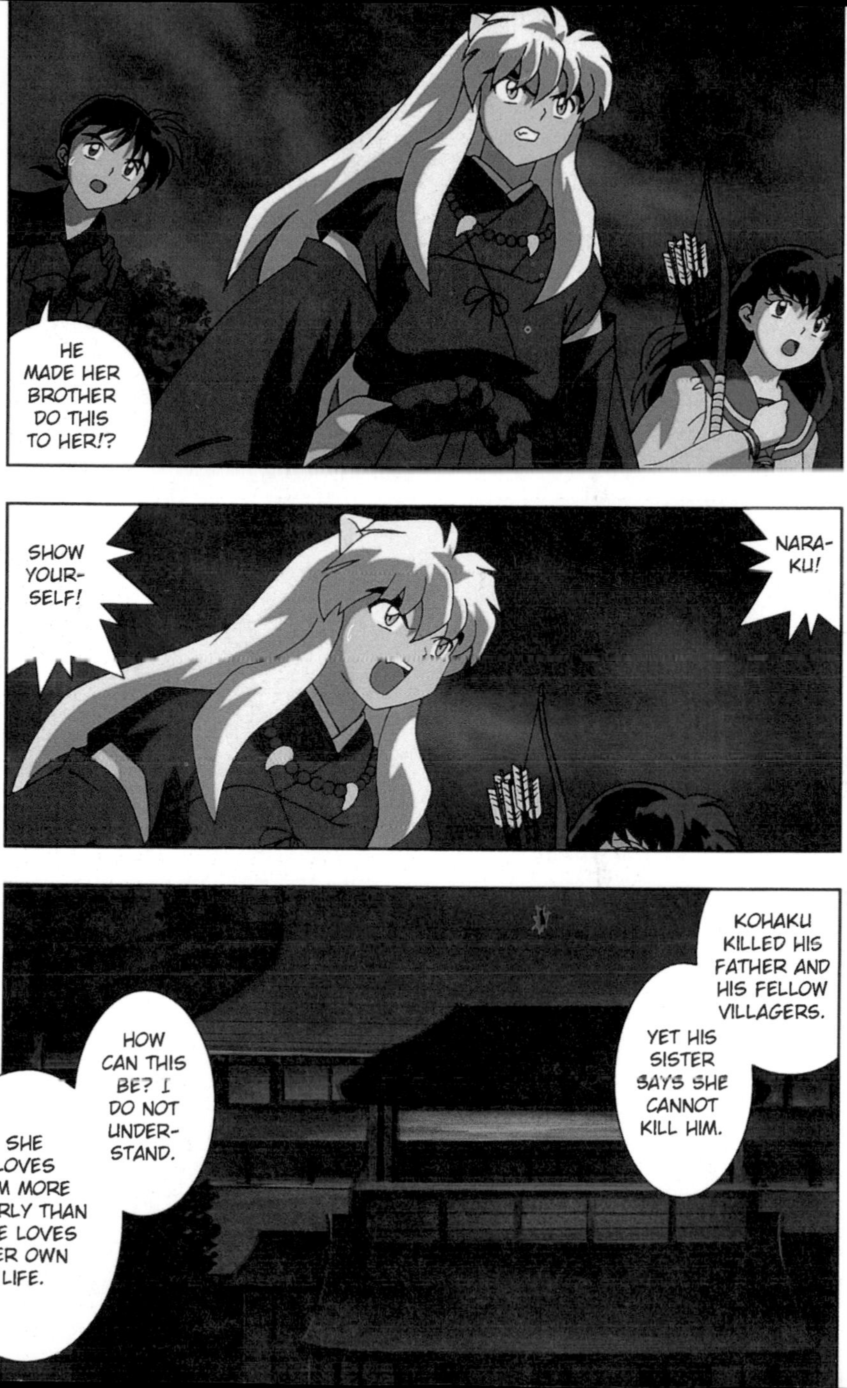
HE MADE HER BROTHER DO THIS TO HER!?
NARA-KU!
SHOW YOUR-SELF!
KOHAKU KILLED HIS FATHER AND HIS FELLOW VILLAGERS.
YET HIS SISTER SAYS SHE CANNOT KILL HIM.
HOW CAN THIS BE? I DO NOT UNDER-STAND.
SHE LOVES HIM MORE DEARLY THAN SHE LOVES HER OWN LIFE.

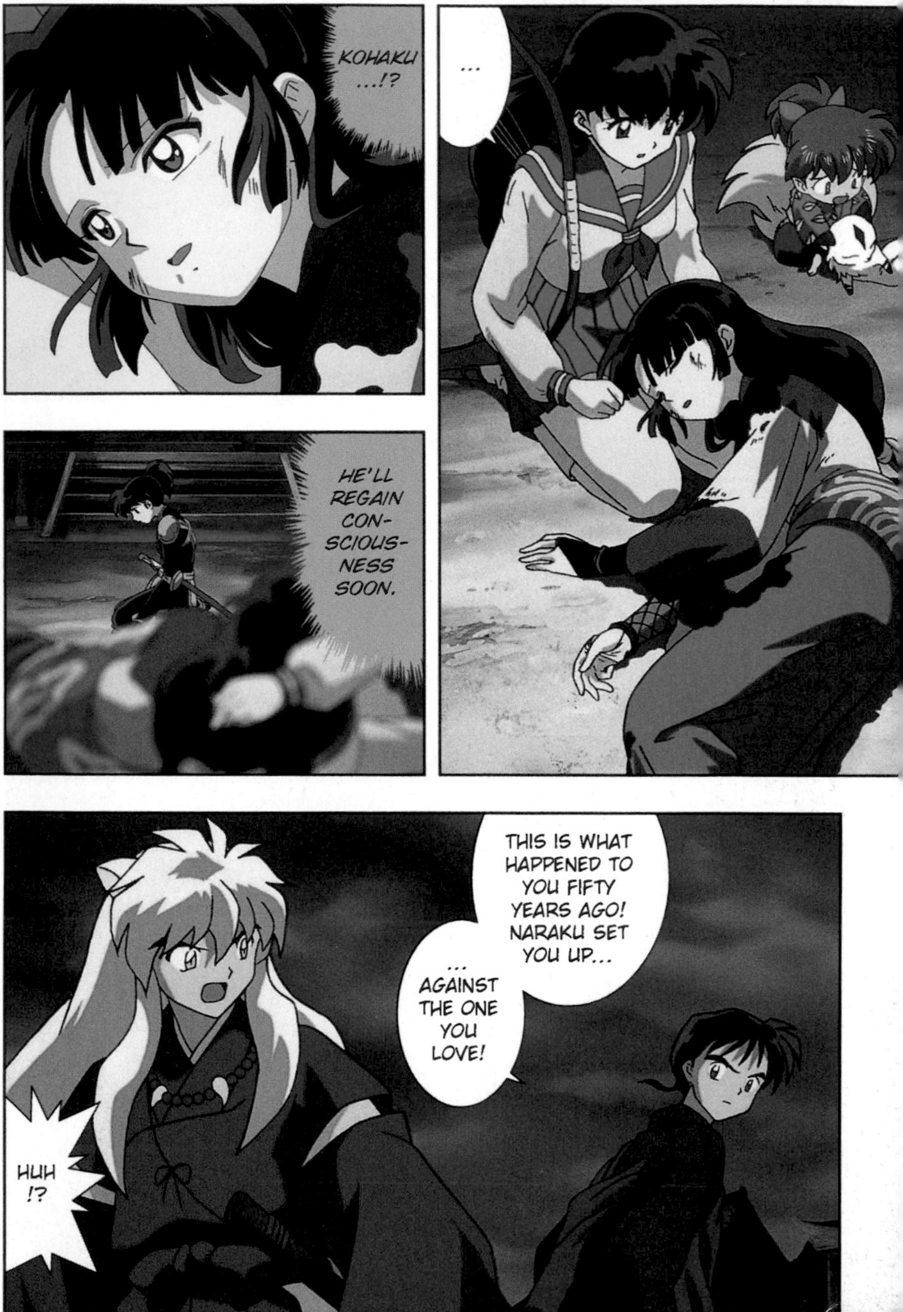
...
KOHAKU ...!?
HE'LL REGAIN CON-SCIOUS-NESS SOON.
THIS IS WHAT HAPPENED TO YOU FIFTY YEARS AGO! NARAKU SET YOU UP...
... AGAINST THE ONE YOU LOVE!
HUH !?

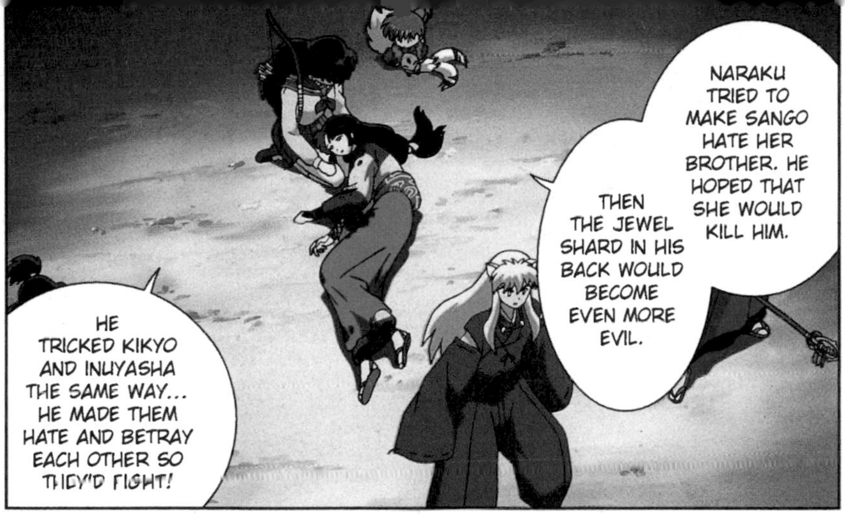
NARAKU TRIED TO MAKE SANGO HATE HER BROTHER. HE HOPED THAT SHE WOULD KILL HIM.
THEN THE JEWEL SHARD IN HIS BACK WOULD BECOME EVEN MORE EVIL.
HE TRICKED KIKYO AND INUYASHA THE SAME WAY... HE MADE THEM HATE AND BETRAY EACH OTHER SO THEY'D FIGHT!

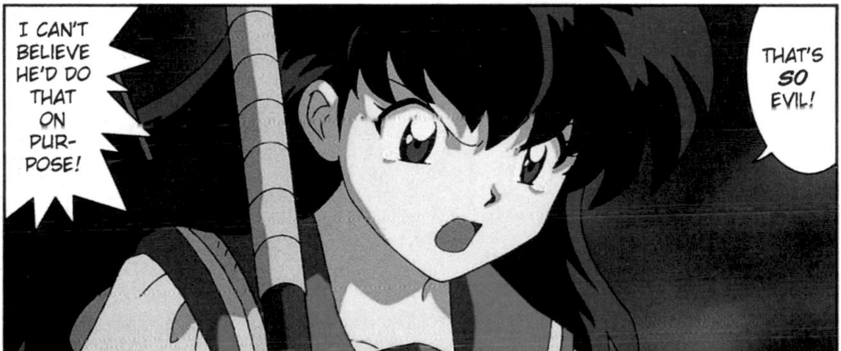
THAT'S SO EVIL!
I CAN'T BELIEVE HE'D DO THAT ON PUR-POSE!

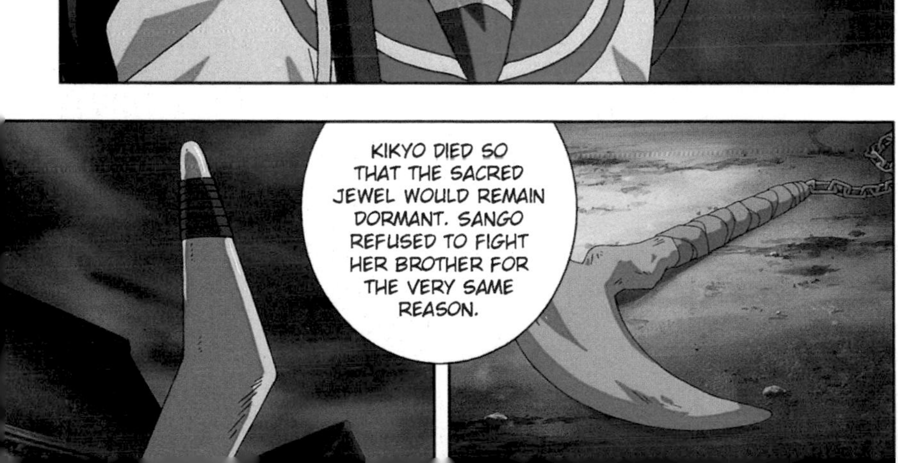
KIKYO DIED SO THAT THE SACRED JEWEL WOULD REMAIN DORMANT. SANGO REFUSED TO FIGHT HER BROTHER FOR THE VERY SAME REASON.

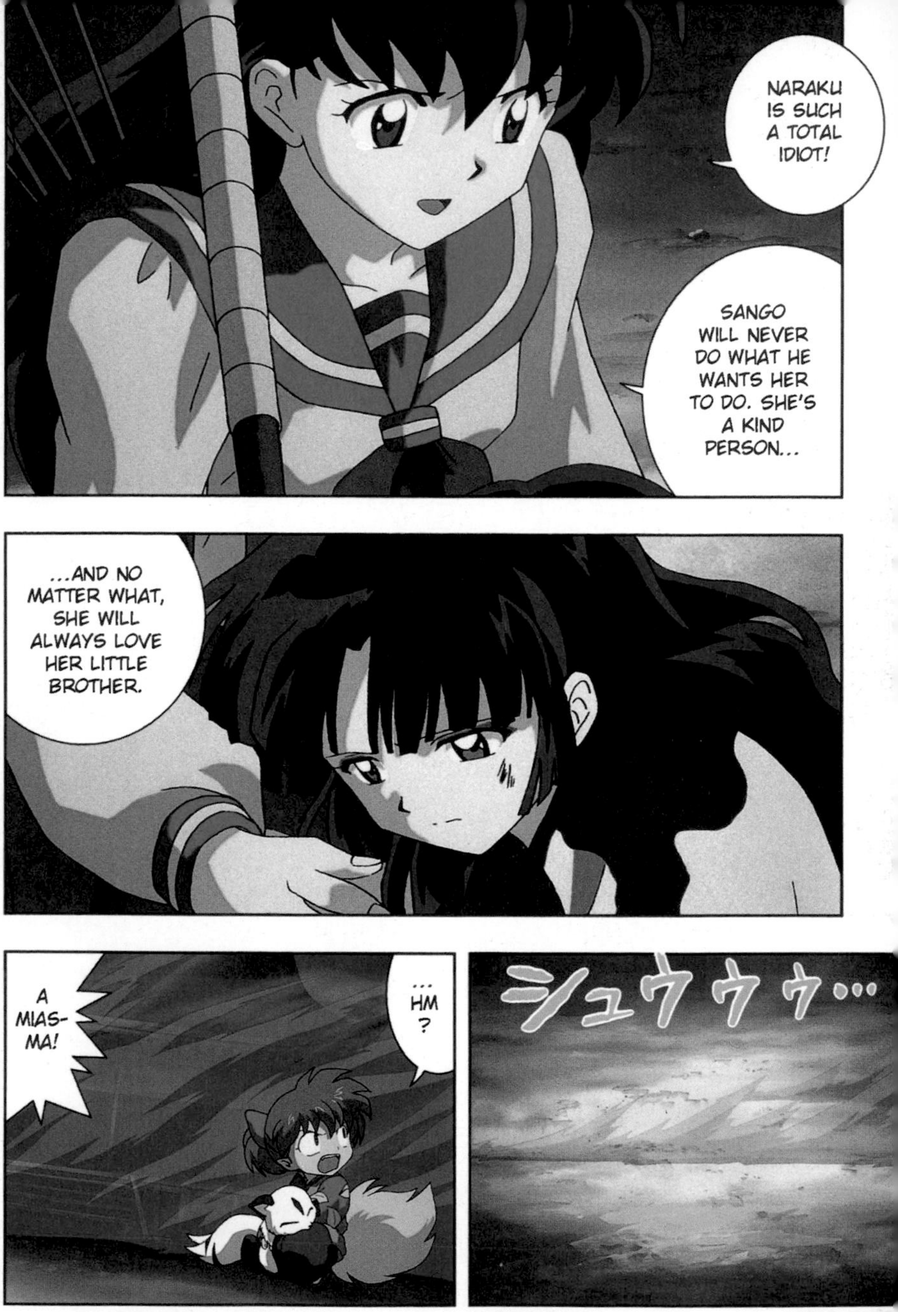
NARAKU IS SUCH A TOTAL IDIOT!
SANGO WILL NEVER DO WHAT HE WANTS HER TO DO. SHE'S A KIND PERSON...
...AND NO MATTER WHAT, SHE WILL ALWAYS LOVE HER LITTLE BROTHER.
シュウウウ…
...HM?
A MIAS-MA!

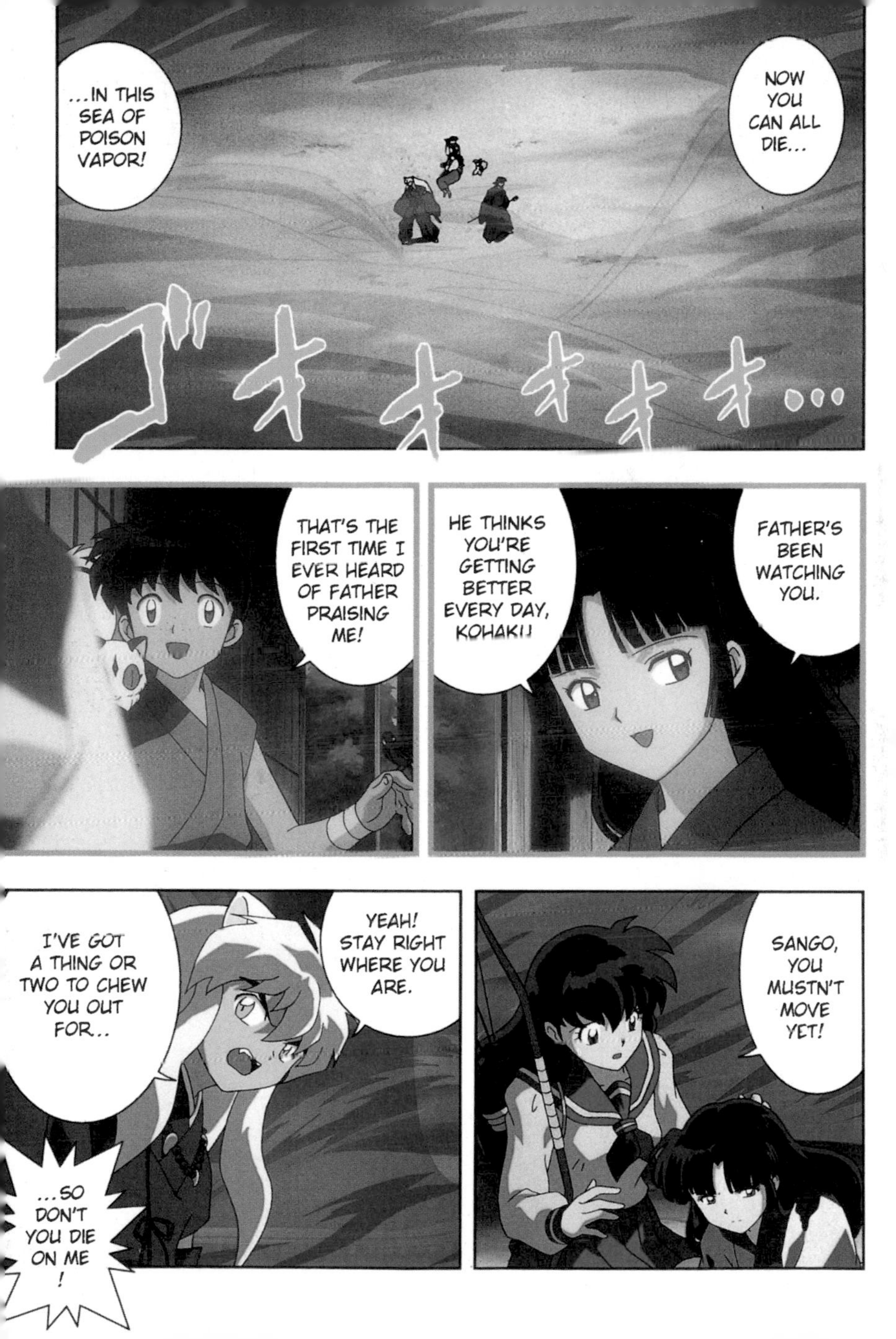
NOW YOU CAN ALL DIE...
...IN THIS SEA OF POISON VAPOR!
ゴオオオオ...
FATHER'S BEEN WATCHING YOU.
HE THINKS YOU'RE GETTING BETTER EVERY DAY, KOHAKU.
THAT'S THE FIRST TIME I EVER HEARD OF FATHER PRAISING ME!
SANGO, YOU MUSTN'T MOVE YET!
YEAH! STAY RIGHT WHERE YOU ARE.
I'VE GOT A THING OR TWO TO CHEW YOU OUT FOR...
...SO DON'T YOU DIE ON ME!

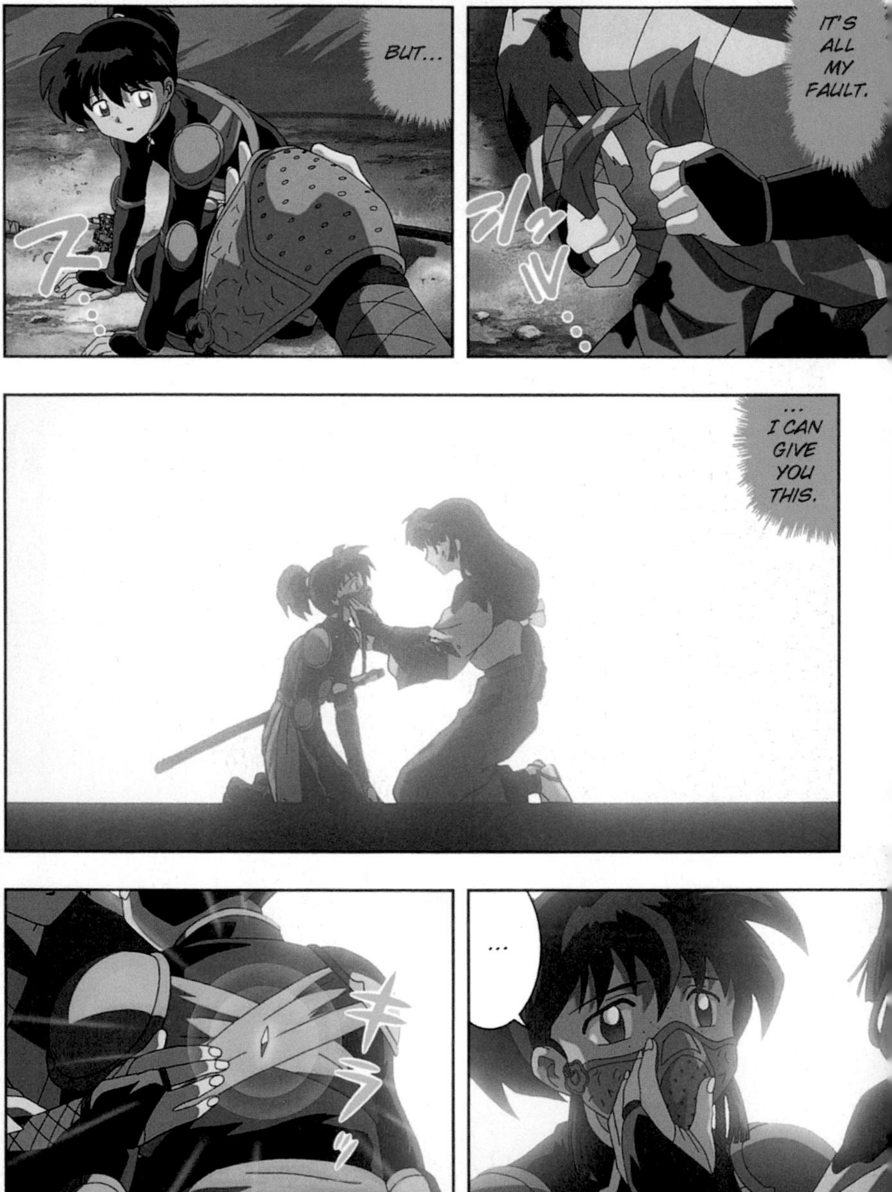
IT'S ALL MY FAULT.
BUT...
... I CAN GIVE YOU THIS.
...
キラッ

I KNOW!

NARAKU HAS JEWEL SHARDS!

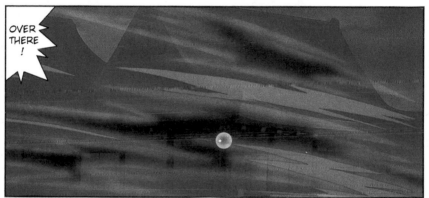

OVER THERE!

NARAKU! TAKE THIS!

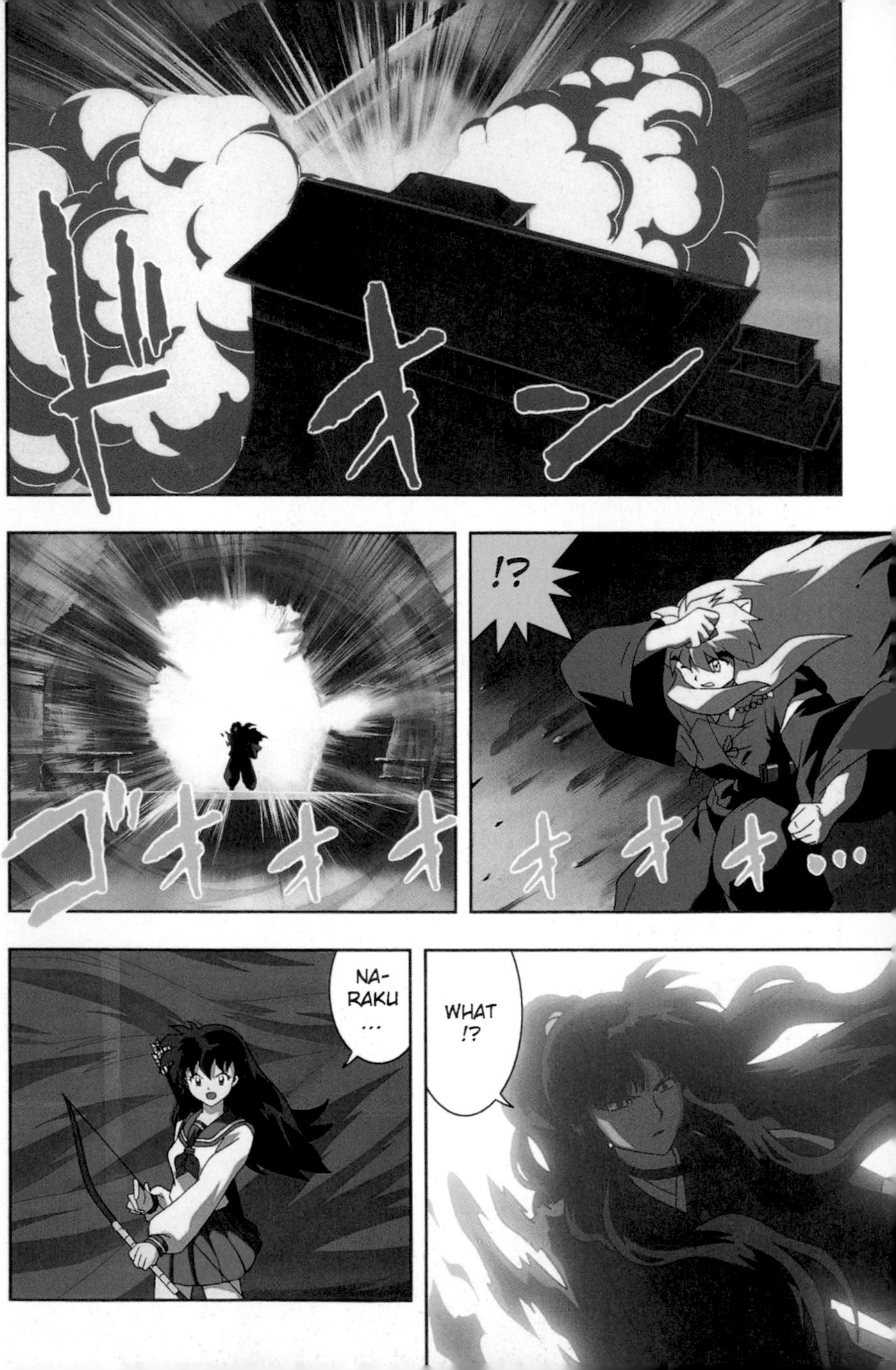
ドオーン
!?
ゴオオオオオオ…
WHAT !?
NA-RAKU ...

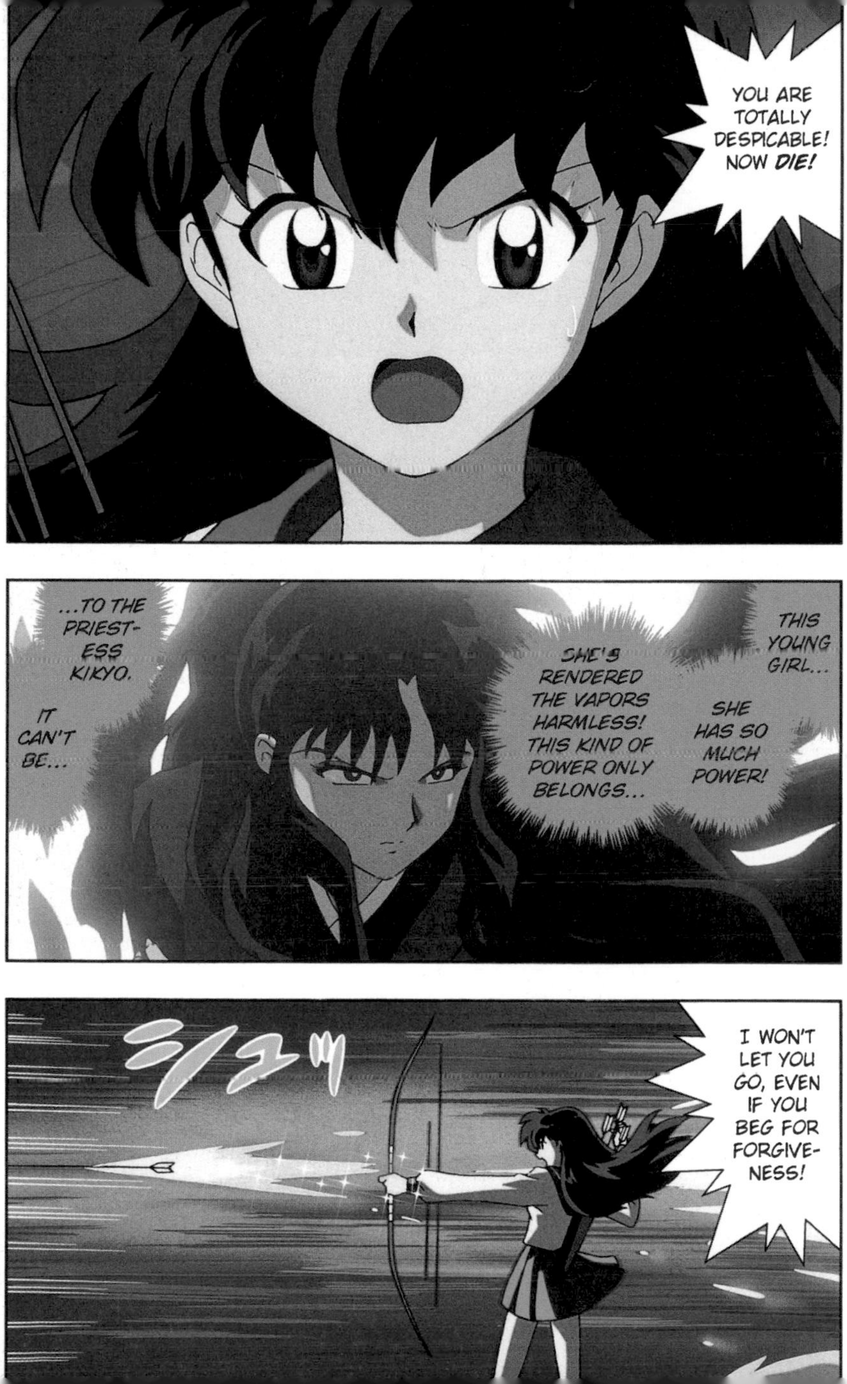
YOU ARE TOTALLY DESPICABLE! NOW *DIE!*
THIS YOUNG GIRL...
SHE HAS SO MUCH POWER!
SHE'S RENDERED THE VAPORS HARMLESS! THIS KIND OF POWER ONLY BELONGS...
...TO THE PRIEST-ESS KIKYO.
IT CAN'T BE...
シュッ
I WON'T LET YOU GO, EVEN IF YOU BEG FOR FORGIVE-NESS!

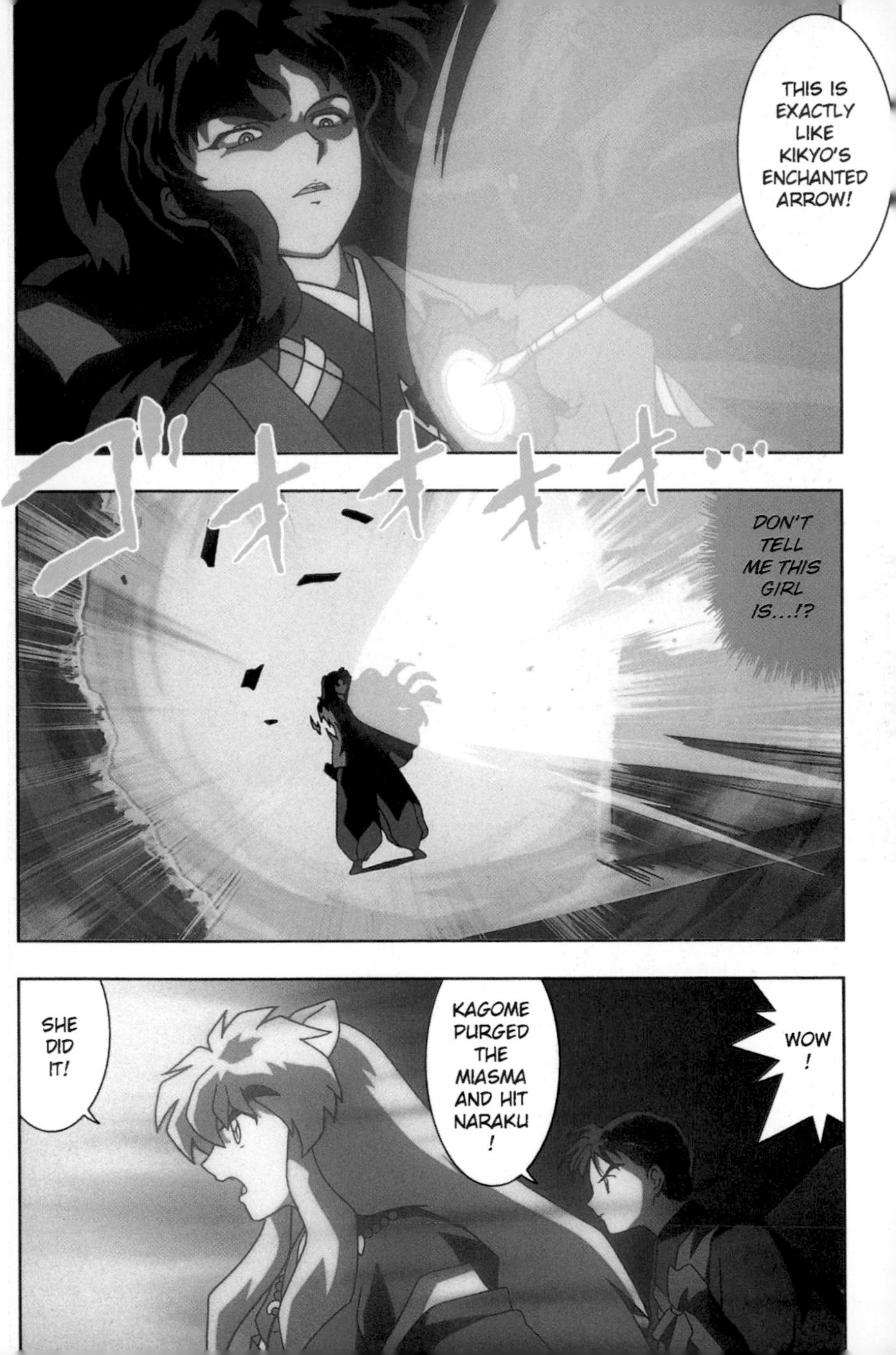
THIS IS EXACTLY LIKE KIKYO'S ENCHANTED ARROW!
ゴオオオオ…
DON'T TELL ME THIS GIRL IS...!?
WOW!
KAGOME PURGED THE MIASMA AND HIT NARAKU!
SHE DID IT!

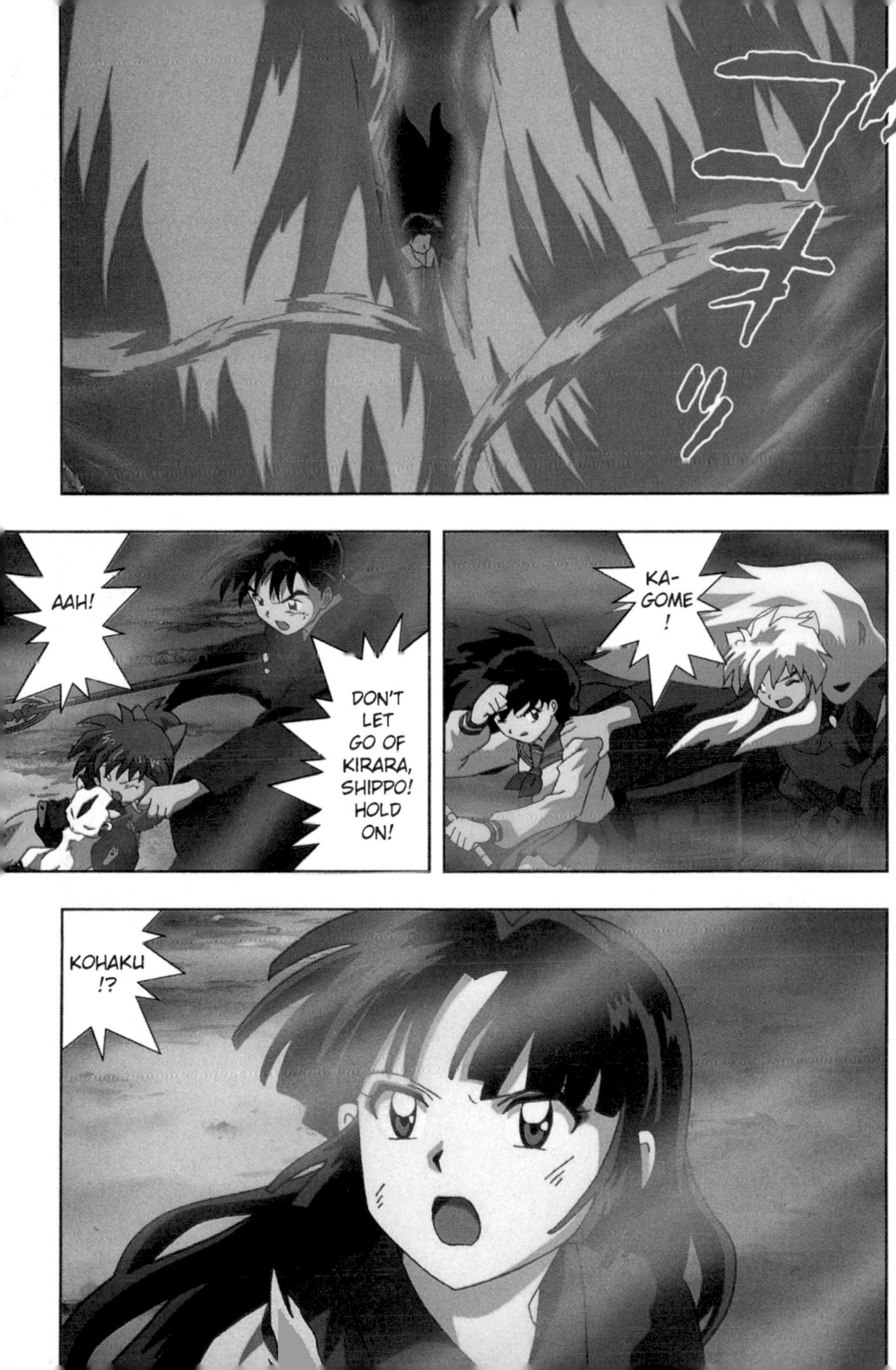
KA-GOME!
AAH!
DON'T LET GO OF KIRARA, SHIPPO! HOLD ON!
KOHAKU!?

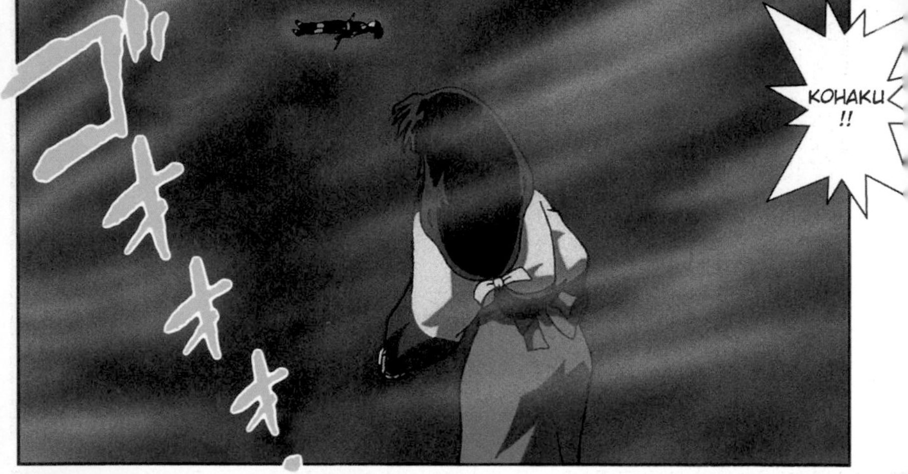
KOHAKU !!
ゴオオオオ…
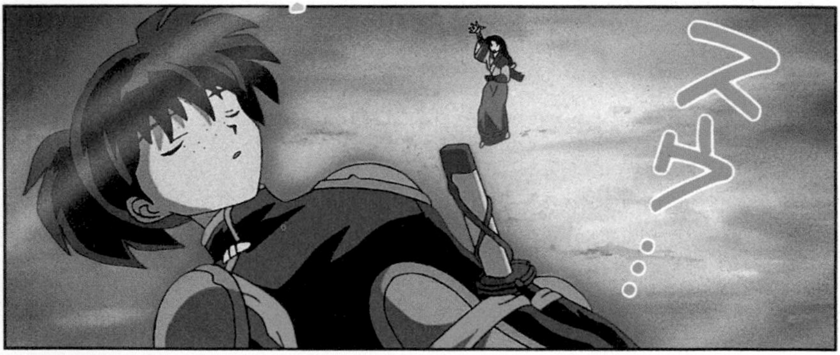
スッ…
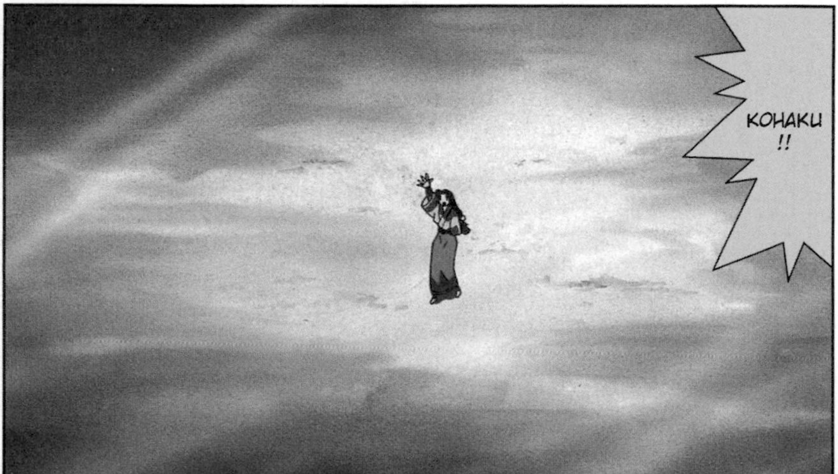
KOHAKU !!

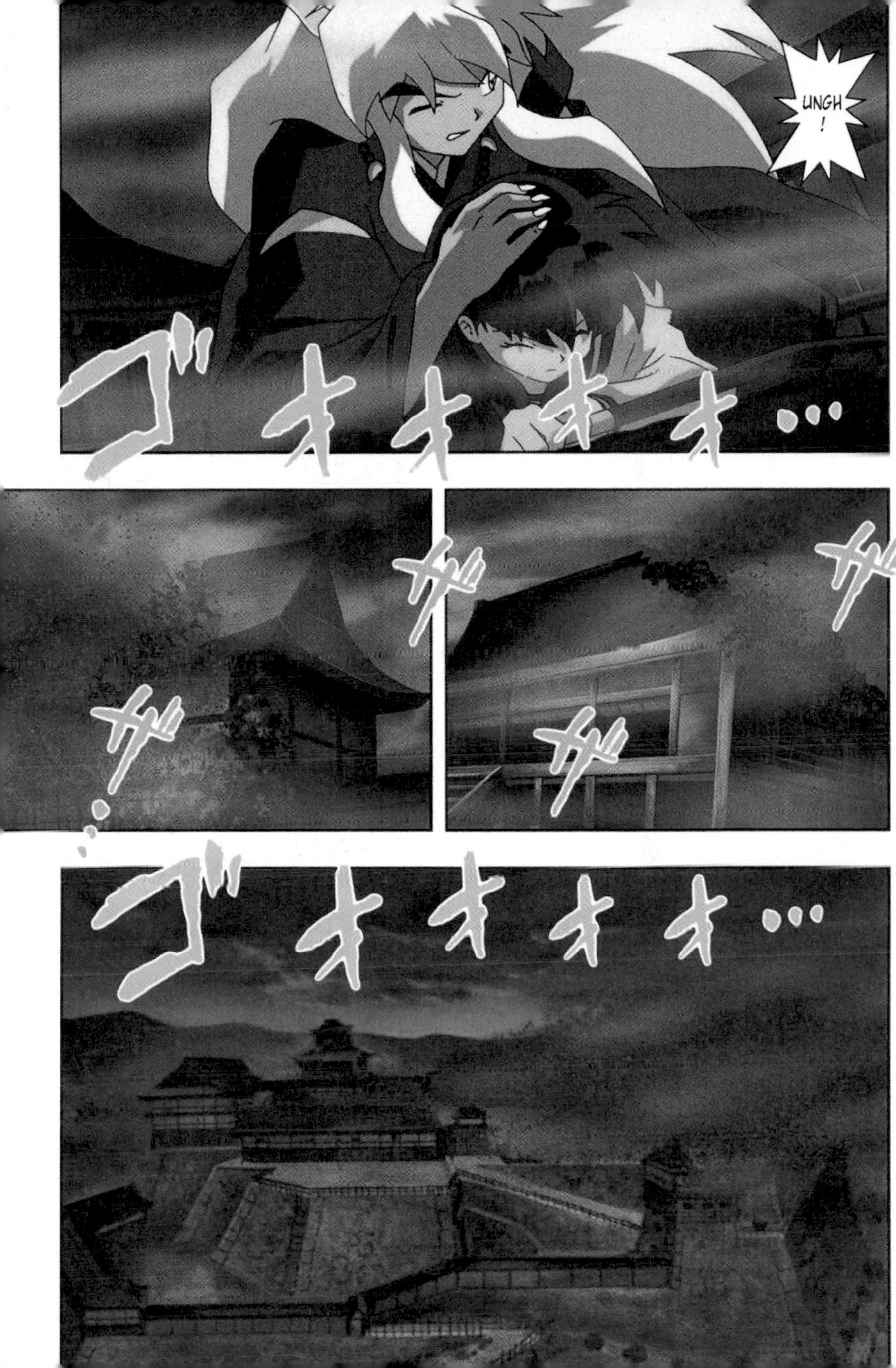
UNGH
!
ゴオオオオ…
ザ
ザ
ザ
ザ…
ゴオオオオ…

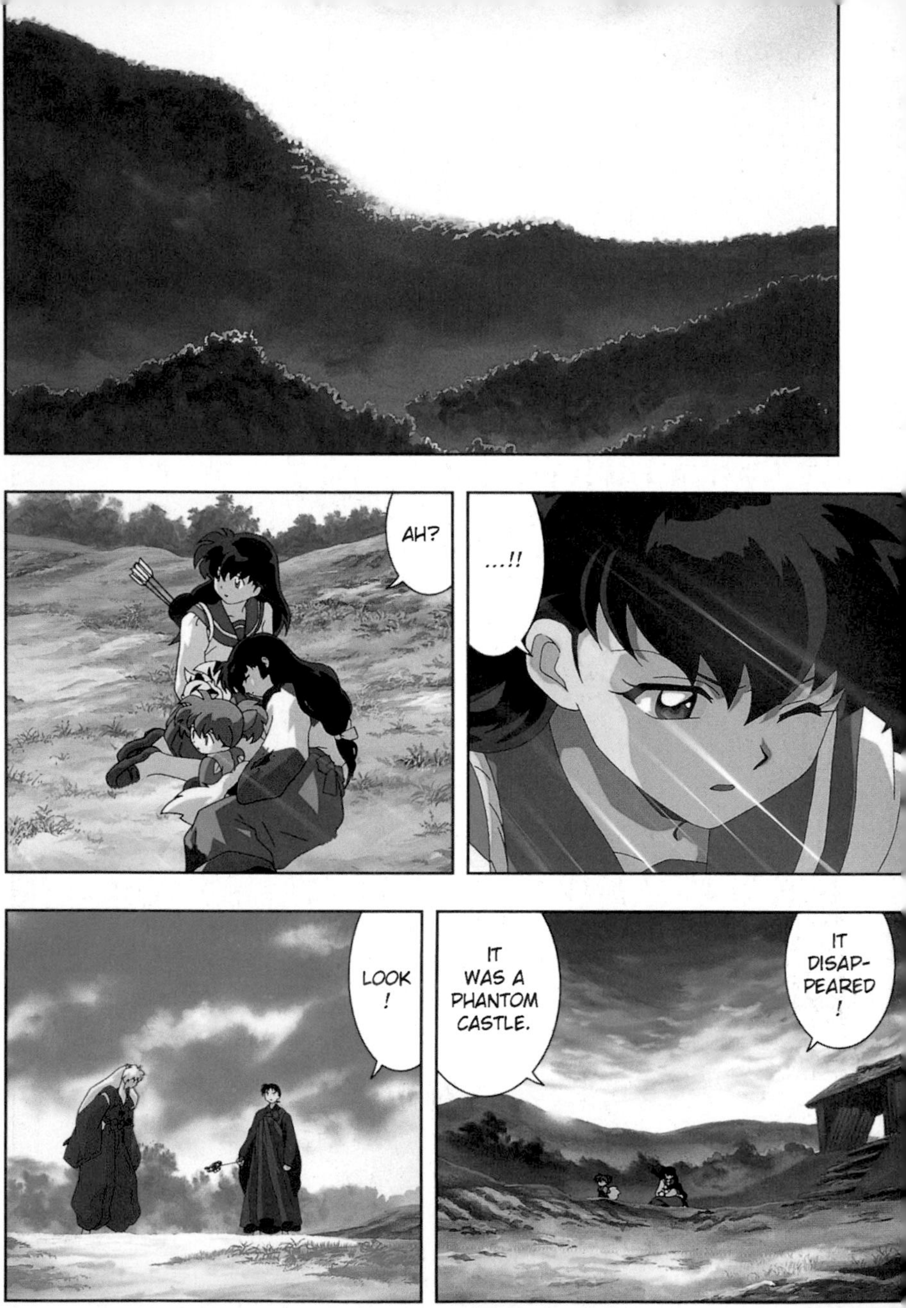
...!!
AH?
IT DISAP-PEARED!
IT WAS A PHANTOM CASTLE.
LOOK!

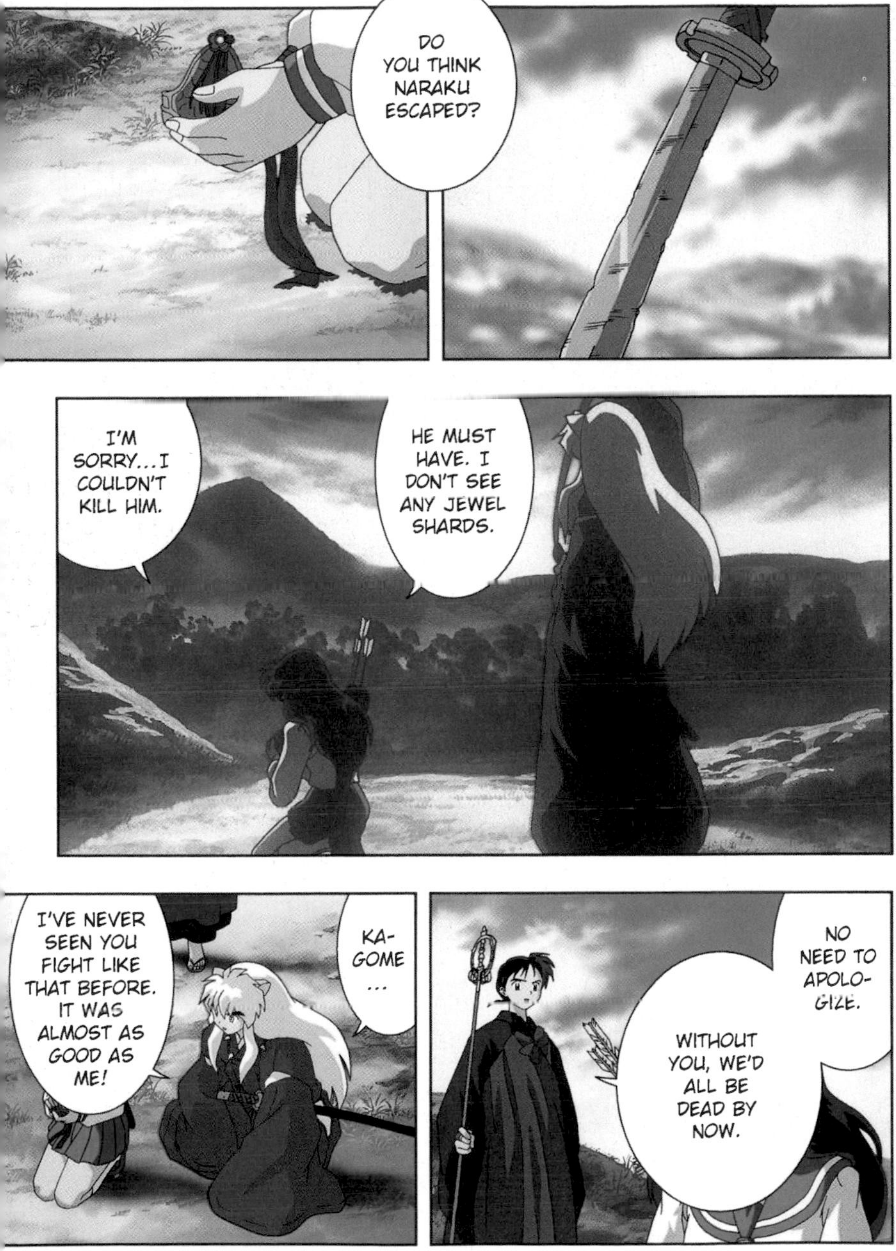
DO YOU THINK NARAKU ESCAPED?
HE MUST HAVE. I DON'T SEE ANY JEWEL SHARDS.
I'M SORRY...I COULDN'T KILL HIM.
NO NEED TO APOLO-GIZE.
WITHOUT YOU, WE'D ALL BE DEAD BY NOW.
KA-GOME...
I'VE NEVER SEEN YOU FIGHT LIKE THAT BEFORE. IT WAS ALMOST AS GOOD AS ME!

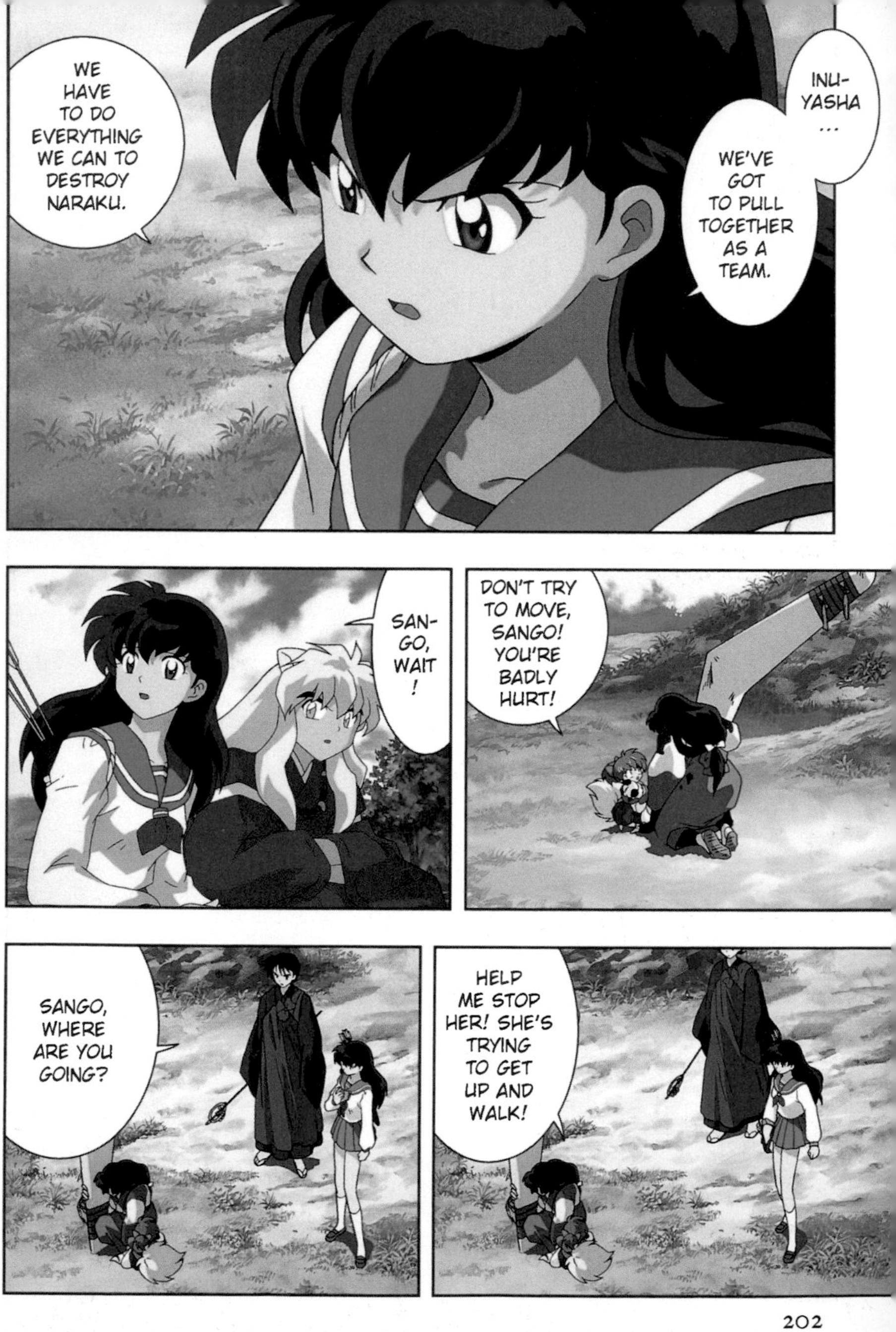
INU-YASHA ... WE'VE GOT TO PULL TOGETHER AS A TEAM.
WE HAVE TO DO EVERYTHING WE CAN TO DESTROY NARAKU.
DON'T TRY TO MOVE, SANGO! YOU'RE BADLY HURT!
SANGO, WAIT!
HELP ME STOP HER! SHE'S TRYING TO GET UP AND WALK!
SANGO, WHERE ARE YOU GOING?

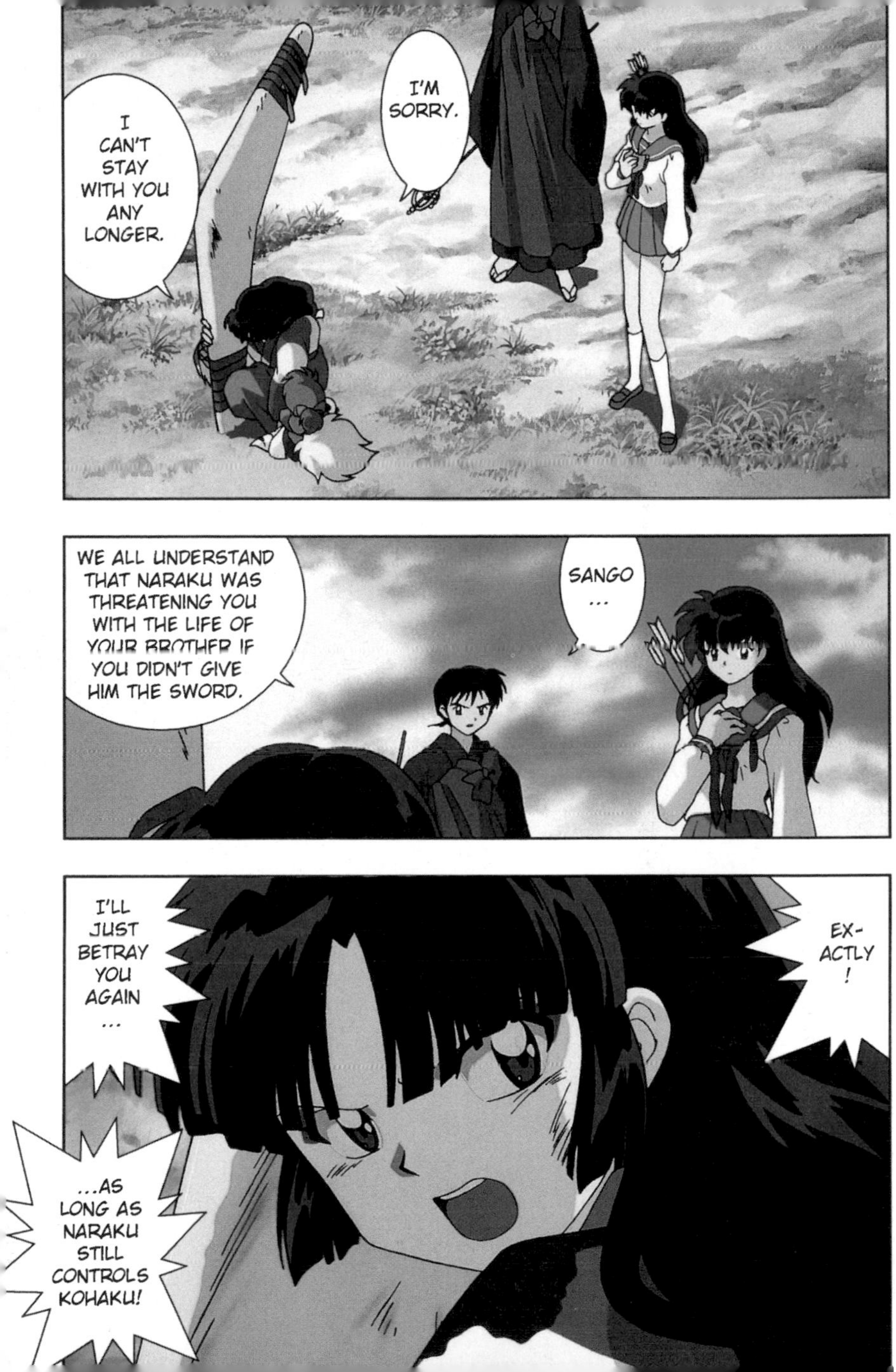
I'M SORRY.
I CAN'T STAY WITH YOU ANY LONGER.
SANGO...
WE ALL UNDERSTAND THAT NARAKU WAS THREATENING YOU WITH THE LIFE OF YOUR BROTHER IF YOU DIDN'T GIVE HIM THE SWORD.
EX-ACTLY!
I'LL JUST BETRAY YOU AGAIN...
...AS LONG AS NARAKU STILL CONTROLS KOHAKU!

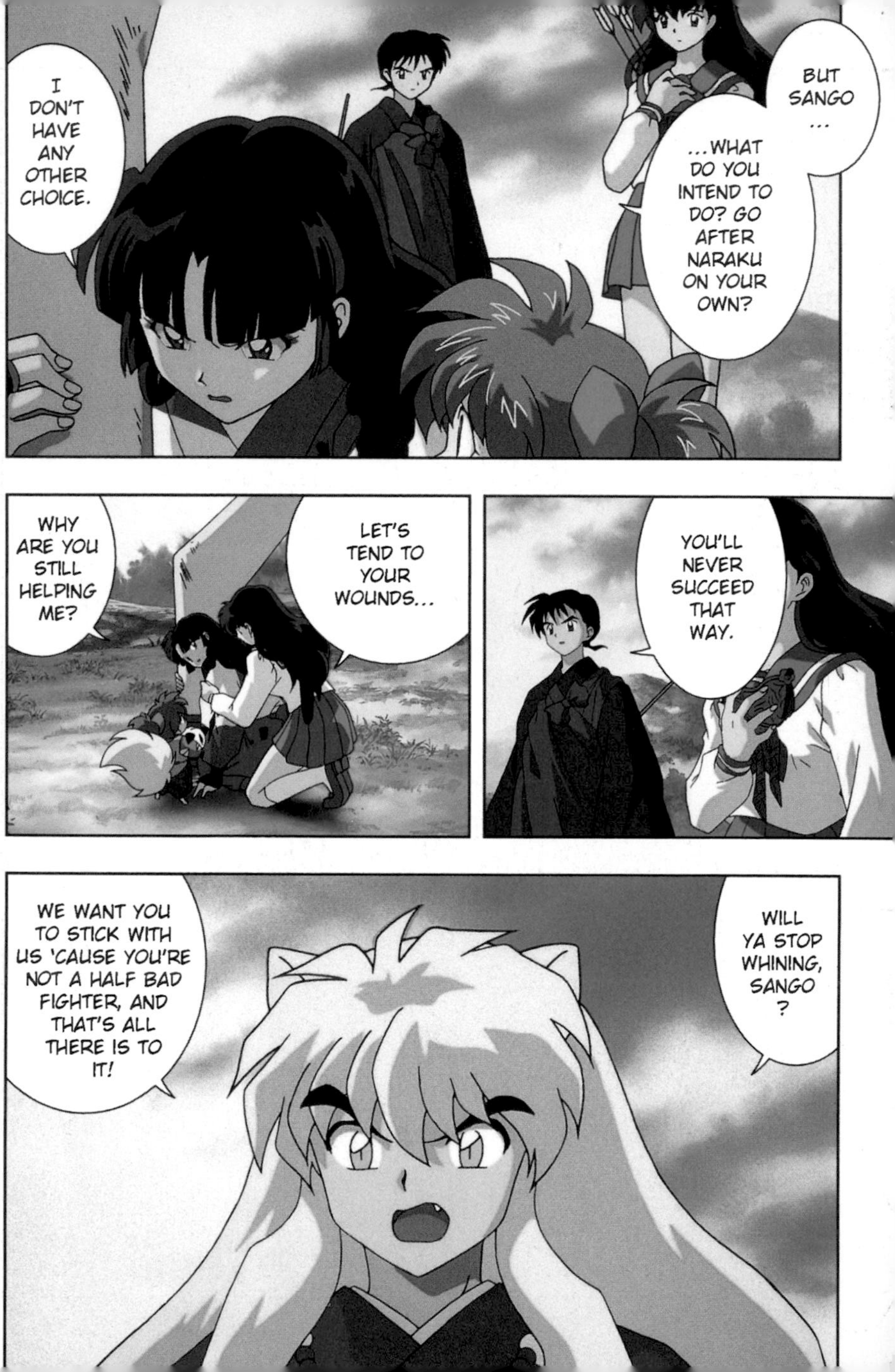
BUT SANGO ...
...WHAT DO YOU INTEND TO DO? GO AFTER NARAKU ON YOUR OWN?
I DON'T HAVE ANY OTHER CHOICE.
YOU'LL NEVER SUCCEED THAT WAY.
LET'S TEND TO YOUR WOUNDS...
WHY ARE YOU STILL HELPING ME?
WILL YA STOP WHINING, SANGO ?
WE WANT YOU TO STICK WITH US 'CAUSE YOU'RE NOT A HALF BAD FIGHTER, AND THAT'S ALL THERE IS TO IT!

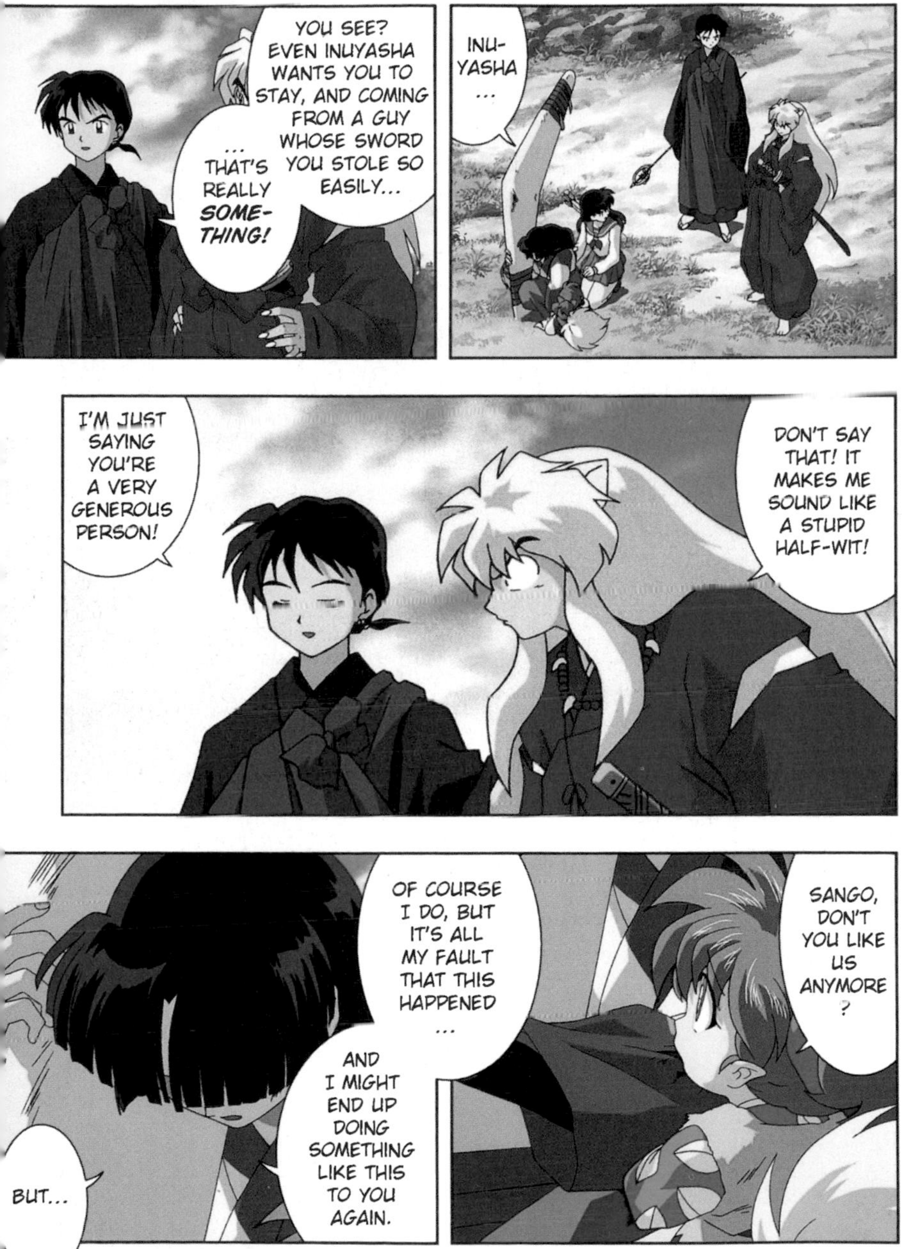
INU-YASHA ...
YOU SEE? EVEN INUYASHA WANTS YOU TO STAY, AND COMING FROM A GUY WHOSE SWORD YOU STOLE SO EASILY...
... THAT'S REALLY SOME-THING!
DON'T SAY THAT! IT MAKES ME SOUND LIKE A STUPID HALF-WIT!
I'M JUST SAYING YOU'RE A VERY GENEROUS PERSON!
SANGO, DON'T YOU LIKE US ANYMORE?
OF COURSE I DO, BUT IT'S ALL MY FAULT THAT THIS HAPPENED ...
AND I MIGHT END UP DOING SOMETHING LIKE THIS TO YOU AGAIN.
BUT...

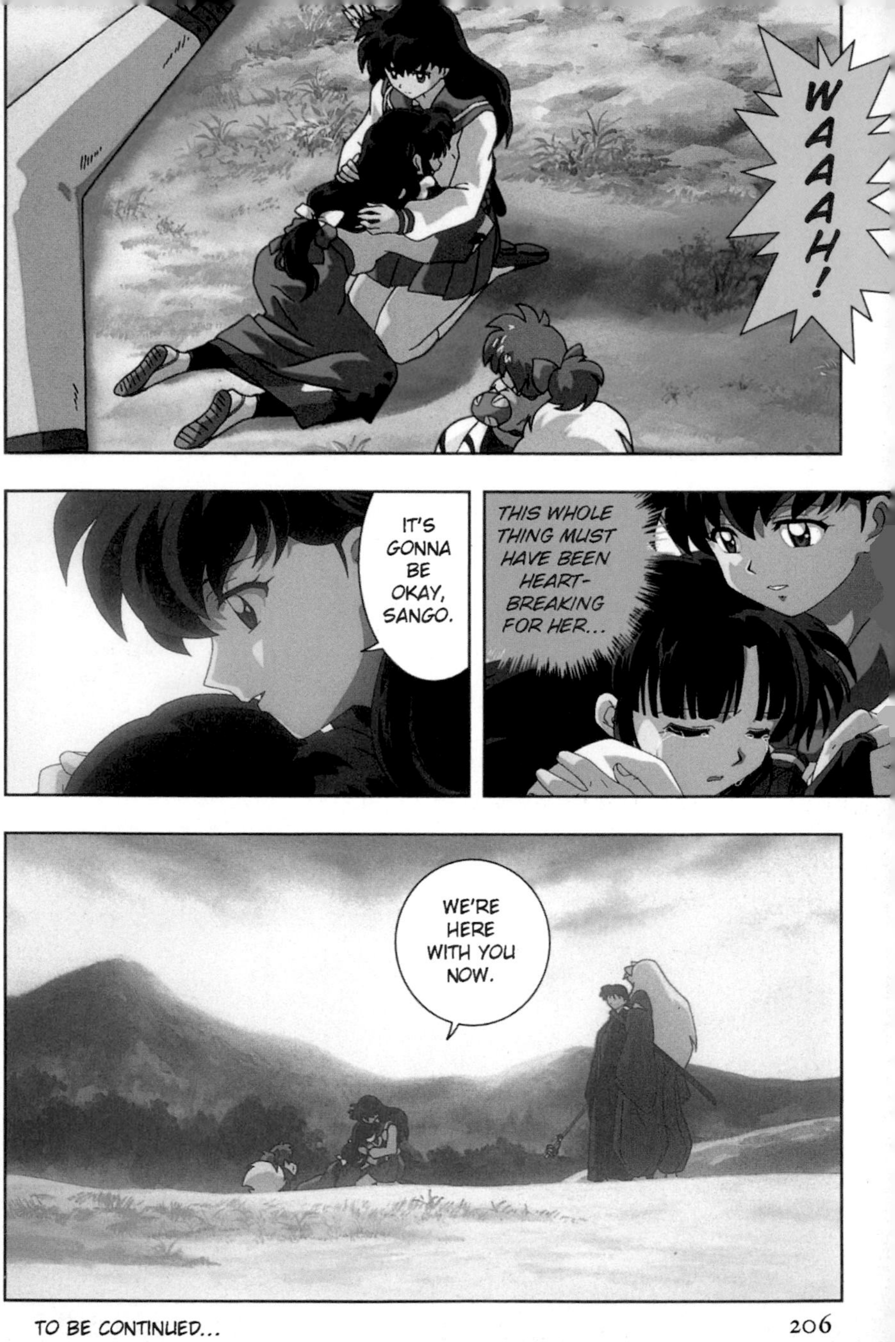
WAAAH!
THIS WHOLE THING MUST HAVE BEEN HEART-BREAKING FOR HER...
IT'S GONNA BE OKAY, SANGO.
WE'RE HERE WITH YOU NOW.

TO BE CONTINUED...

Glossary of Sound Effects

Each entry includes: the location, indicated by page number and panel number (so 3.1 means page 3, panel number 1); the phonetic romanization of the original Japanese; and our English "translation" — we offer as close an English equivalent as we can.

17.2   FX: Pashi (Miroku closes the wind tunnel)
20.3   FX: Gu... (Miroku flexes his hand)

21.3   FX: Gohhh... (whoosh of wind tunnel)

23.4   FX: Toh (Hachi lands)
23.5   FX: Pon
       (Hachi pops, shrinks back to normal size)

29.1   FX: Zaaaa... (water falling)

30.3   FX: Pyon (Myoga hops)

32.5   FX: Shuuu...
       (something emerging from bottle)

33.4   FX: Shuuu...
       (vapor comes out of Mushin's mouth)

34.1   FX: Zawa... (insects buzzing)
34.4   FX: Chari (Inuyasha draws sword)
34.5   FX: Zuba (Inuyasha strikes with sword)

35.1   FX: Bu—n... (vibration of insect wings)
35.2   FX: Bun (Sango throws boomerang)
35.3   FX: Zuba (boomerang shaves off bug's wings)
35.4   FX: Fura...
       (bug totters off without full wings)

36.1   FX: Goh (whoosh)
36.3   FX: Zuba (Miroku's pillow sliced in two)

37.3   FX: Yoro (Miroku unsteady on his feet)
37.5   FX: Ba (strike)

Chapter 28:
Miroku Falls into a Dangerous Trap!

6.4   FX: Pata pata (fanning flames for smoke)

7.3   FX: Gaya gaya (noises of villagers)
7.4   FX: Su... (princess abruptly moves)

8.3   FX: Ka (shining)
8.5   FX: Bun (Sango's boomerang flies)

9.1   FX: Doga (boomerang lands on demon)
9.2   FX: Shuuu... (demon shrinks to mouse size)

12.4   FX: Hishi (woman slinks over to Miroku)

13.3   FX: Meki meki... (transformation sound)

14.1   FX: Don (Miroku pushes the princess away)
14.2   FX: Ga (smack)
14.3   FX: Ta (jumping back)
14.4   FX: Doga (pincers strikes the ground)
14.5   FX: Zuru... (princess's face falls away)

15.2   FX: Zuga
       (pincer strikes ground close to Miroku)
15.3   FX: Ta (Miroku jumps)

16.1   FX: Ba (Miroku jumps)
16.2   FX: Toh (Miroku lands)
16.4   FX: Gohhh... (whoosh of wind tunnel)
16.5   FX: Kira (something sparkling)

17.1   FX: Zaku (sparkly thing enters wind tunnel,
       tearing the sides of Miroku's scar)

38.1 FX: Bun (slash)
38.2 FX: Gata (Miroku falls)
38.4 FX: Gin (blade clangs on staff)
38.5 FX: Shuuuu…
(vapor emanates from Mushin's mouth)

39.2 FX: Pon (Hachi uses his magic)

40.1 FX: Ta ta ta… (running)
40.3 FX: Gohhh… (whoosh)
40.5 FX: Ba (Miroku pushes Hachi)

41.3 FX: Ta (Hachi scampers off)

42.4 FX: Buuu…n… (buzzing of insects)

43.1 FX: Buuu…n… (buzzing of insects)
43.5 FX: Dohn (Hachi crashes)

44.2 FX: Zuba (slash)
44.3 FX: Buuun… (buzzing)
44.4 FX: Buuun… (buzzing)

46.3 FX: Gohhh… (whooshing)
46.4 FX: Goh (whooshing)

47.2 FX: Gohhh (whoosh of demons)
47.3 FX: Zuba (slash)
47.4 FX: Zan (swipe)

48.1 FX: Suu… (demons approach)
48.2 FX: Fu… (demons swoop down on Miroku)
48.4 FX: Ba (demons attack)
48.5 FX: Gohh (whoosh)

49.1 FX: Zuba (slice)
49.5 FX: Doh (Shippo lands on Inuyasha's head)

52.1 FX: Jara
(sutra beads wrap around the Tetsusaiga)
52.2 FX: Bachi (crackling of sword against beads)
52.3 FX: Shuuu… (magic beads sound)
52.5 FX: Jara…
(sutra beads wrap around Inuyasha)

52.6 FX: Bachi bachi (sutra beads start to squeeze)
52.6 FX: Gasha (Inuyasha drops the Tetsusaiga)

53.1 FX: Goh (whoosh of demons)
53.2 FX: Ba (slash)
53.3 FX: Zuba (claw slash)
53.4 FX: Kaaa… (shining, glowing)
53.5 FX: Bachi (beads squeeze)

54.1 FX: Shuuuu… (demon worms snaking about)

55.2 FX: Da (Kagome begins to crawl
out of the trench)

56.2 FX: Giri (Kagome nocks arrow)
56.3 FX: Hyu (arrow flies)
56.4 FX: Ta (charmer jumps)

57.4 FX: Zawa zawa (buzz of demon worms)

58.3 FX: Ga (Inuyasha grabs Mushin by the throat)

59.2 FX: Ba (beads let off painful
electric-looking current)
59.3 FX: Bachi (crackle)
59.4 FX: Doh (Inuyasha drops to his knees)

60.1 FX: Gohhh…
(roar of demons as they approach)
60.2 FX: Chya (Miroku takes off beads)
60.5 FX: Gohhh… (demons whoosh up)

61.2 FX: Ba (Miroku tears away beads)
61.3 FX: Goh (whoosh)
61.4 FX: Gohhh… (whoosh)
61.5 FX: Gohhh… (whoosh)

62.4 FX: Ba (Inuyasha busts out of sutra beads)
62.5 FX: Bachi (Inuyasha punches Mushin)

63.1 FX: Gohhh… (whoosh of wind tunnel)
63.2 FX: Pishi (wind tunnel splits a little wider)
63.3 FX: Zuru (Miroku flies off in wind)
63.5 FX: Ga (Inuyasha grabs wrist)

98.5 FX: Dosa (maimed villager falls down dead)

101.1 FX: Hyu (projectile comes flying)
101.2 FX: Ka (glow from inside house)
101.3 FX: Dohn (boom)

103.4 FX: Da (Inuyasha dashes off)

104.1 FX: Ba (Inuyasha leaps)
104.2 FX: Zuba (slash)
104.3 FX: Dohn (house starts to collapse)
104.4 FX: Dohn (house finishes collapsing)
104.4 FX: Ba (Kohaku leaps away from collapsing house)

105.1 FX: Bun (Kohaku throws blade)
105.2 FX: Gin (Inuyasha deflects blade with Tetsusaiga)
105.3 FX: Shururuu... (chain returns to Kohaku)
105.4 FX: Pashi (Kohaku catches sickle)

110.1 FX: Tu (Kohaku runs away)
110.2 FX: Da (Inuyasha takes off after Kohaku)
110.3 FX: Gu (Inuyasha steps on trap, triggers it)
110.4 FX: Dohn (boom)

111.1 FX: Goh (whoosh of blast)
111.4 FX: Gohh (little Kirara becomes big Kirara)
111.5 FX: Ba (Sango takes off with Kirara)

112.1 FX: Ta ta ta... (Kohaku running)
112.3 FX: Kira (jewel shard sparkling)
112.4 FX: Su... (Kohaku pushes through barrier)

113.1 FX: Ba (Kirara leaps)
113.2 FX: Goh (Sango and Kirara pass through barrier)
113.3 FX: Za (Inuyasha stops short at barrier)

116.1 FX: Goh (Sango and Kirara pass through barrier)
116.2 FX: Toh (Sango alights)
116.5 FX: Su... (Kohaku removes mask)

64.2 FX: Goh (whoosh of demons)
64.3 FX: Chari (Inuyasha grabs sword)
64.4 FX: Kaa (Tetsusaiga transforms)

65.2 FX: Ka (shine as demons disintegrate)

66.1 FX: Gohhhhhh... (whoosh)

67.1 FX: Ta (demon worm charmer flees)
67.2 FX: Bun (Sango throws boomerang)
67.3 FX: Zuba (boomerang slices charmer in two)
67.4 FX: Pashi (bottle falls into Shippo's paws)
67.5 FX: Shuuu... (demon worms emerge and return to bottle)

68.4 FX: Gara (door slides open)

72.1 FX: Sawa (groping)
72.2 FX: Pako (slap)

Chapter 29:
Sango's Suffering and Kohaku's Life

77.2 FX: Gara (door slides open)

80.2 FX: Buuu...n... (fluttering buzzy sound)

82.2 FX: Bun (Inuyasha slashes with sword)

83.2 FX: Bun (slash)

87.1 FX: Pasha (Sango enters water)
87.3 FX: Zaru... (Kagome notices Sango's scar)

92.3 FX: Su... (Sango picks up rock)

93.1 FX: Bun (Sango throws rock)
93.2 FX: Go (monkey takes off running)
93.6 FX: Doga baki (smacks on Inuyasha and Miroku)

95.1 FX: Kyu... (Sango dries off)

98.3 FX: Fura (unsteadiness on feet)

152.1 FX: Jara (chain wraps around Tetsusaiga)
152.3 FX: Gin (clang of metal on metal)
152.4 FX: Ga (sickle strikes Tetsusaiga)
152.5 FX: Bun (Kohaku leaps back)

153.2 FX: Dohh (Kohaku slammed into ground)
153.6 FX: Doh (Inuyasha cuts off sword thrust)

154.2 FX: Baki (punch)
154.3 FX: Zuzaza… (Kohaku slides across ground from force of punch)

156.1 FX: Su… (Kohaku picks up his weapon)
156.2 FX: Bun (Kohaku strikes)
156.3 FX: Zaku (Kohaku hits himself in back)
156.4 FX: Kaa (jewel shard shines)

157.3 FX: Gu (Kohaku pinches at jewel shard)
157.4 FX: Ga (Sango prepares to throw boomerang)
157.5 FX: Bun (boomerang flies)

158.1 FX: Shururu
ru… (boomerang flies)
158.2 FX: Giin (boomerang deflects sword)
158.3 FX: Doh (sword lands in dirt)
158.6 FX: Ta (demons advance)

159.1 FX: Gohhh… (whoosh)

160.1 FX: Ga (Sango grips sword)
160.2 FX: Ta (Kirara running)
160.3 FX: Za (Sango jumps)

161.4 FX: Poh… (glowing orbs grow)
161.5 FX: Kaa (shining)

163.1 FX: Da (running)
163.3 FX: Ta ta ta… (Inuyasha scampers off)

164.1 FX: Gohhh… (Sango whooshes off)
164.4 FX: Gohhh… (whoosh)

165.1 FX: Toh (Sango lands on castle)

118.1 FX: Su… (Naraku appears)

121.3 FX: Ba (Sango prepares to throw boomerang)
121.4 FX: Shu (scythe comes flying)
121.5 FX: Gin (clang)

122.1 FX: Za (Kohaku catches scythe)
122.4 FX: Da (Sango runs toward Naraku)
122.5 FX: Goh (whoosh of gas)

123.1 FX: Gohhh… (whoosh as Naraku disappears)

131.1 FX: Su… (Sango quickly turns away)

133.3 FX: Su (Miroku "getting lost")

134.2 FX: Bun (Kohaku takes practice swing)
134.3 FX: Kin (Kohaku slices bowl)
134.4 FX: Jara (sound of chain)

135.1 FX: Zaku (chains tangle in Kohaku's hands)
135.2 FX: Doh (blade thunks into the ground)

137.4 FX: Basa basa (bird flaps wings)

Chapter 30:
Tetsusaiga Is Stolen! Showdown at Naraku's Castle!

142.4 FX: Pachi Pachi (fire crackles)

148.1 FX: Zawa (figures approach)
148.3 FX: Poh… (shapes grow)

149.1 FX: Da (running)
149.4 FX: Jara (Miroku loosens sutra beads)

150.5 FX: Su (demons rush off)

151.1 FX: Guohh…
151.2 FX: Da (Inuyasha lunges)
151.3 FX: Zuba (Tetsusaiga strike)
151.4 FX: Shururuuru… (Kohaku's projectile)

166.3 FX: Bun (boomerang flies through the air)
166.4 FX: Doga (boomerang hits dirt)

171.3 FX: Ba (Sango launches herself at Naraku)
171.4 FX: Bun (strike)
171.5 FX: Jaki (clang of metal)
171.6 FX: Pashi (sword grasped)

172.1 FX: Gin (clang)
172.2 FX: Zuba (slash)
172.3 FX: Ba (Sango heaves boomerang)
172.5 FX: Toh (Naraku lands)

174.1 FX. Bu (Sango lunges at Naraku)
174.2 FX: Giin (clang)
174.4 FX: Baki (breaking)
174.5 FX: Zuba (Sango falls)

175.1 FX: Doh (Sango lands)
175.3 FX: Guoh (Naraku appears)
175.4 FX: Ga (Kirara bites Naraku)
175.5 FX: Shuuuu...
(poison gas leaks out of Naraku)

176.2 FX: Shuuuu...
(Kirara shrinks back to kitty size)

177.1 FX: Shuru...
(Sango's binding unravels from wrist)
177.2 FX: Shururu
(binding winds itself around Sango)
177.3 FX: Goh (whoosh)
177.4 FX: Shuuuu... (poison gas)
177.5 FX: Doh... (whoosh)

178.4 FX: Su... (Kohaku shuffles forward)

179.2 FX: Su... (Kohaku lifts sickle)

181.2 FX: Zuba (slash)
181.3 FX: Doh (Sango collapses)

182.1 FX: Poh... (boomerang frees itself from roof)
182.2 FX: Fuwa... (boomerang flies)

182.3 FX: Doga (boomerang hits the ground)

183.3 FX: Chari (clink of chain)

184.3 FX: Fura... (Sango unsteady on her feet)

185.2 FX: Dosa (Sango collapses)

186.3 FX: Za (Kohaku goes down on knees)

190.3 FX: Shuuuu... (dust blows up)

191.1 FX: Gohhhhh... (whoosh of poison vapor)

192.1 FX: Shuru...
(Sango unwraps Kohaku's mask)
192.2 FX: Su...
(Sango extends mask toward Kohaku)
192.5 FX: Kira (jewel sparkles)

193. 4 FX: Gyun (arrow shot)

194.1 FX: Dohn (boom)
194.2-3 FX: Gohhhhhhh...
(whoosh as Naraku is pierced)

195.3 FX: Shu (arrow flies)

196.1-2 FX: Gohhhh... (whoosh)

197.1 FX: Goh (whoosh)

198.1 FX: Gohhh (whoosh as Kohaku rises)
198.2 FX: Suu... (Kohaku rises to float away)

199.1 FX: Gohhh (whoosh)
199.2-3 FX: Za za za za (castle starts to dissolve)
199.4 FX: Gohhhh...
(wInd whooshes, bearing castle away)

INUYASHA™

Rated #1 on Cartoon Network's Adult Swim!

In its original, unedited form!

maison ikkoku™

The beloved romantic comedy of errors—a fan favorite!

RANMA ½™

The zany, wacky study of martial arts at its best!

LOVE MANGA?   LET US KNOW!

☐ Please do NOT send me information about VIZ Media products, news and events, special offers, or other information.

☐ Please do NOT send me information from VIZ Media's trusted business partners.

Name: _____

Address: _____

City: _____ **State:** _____ **Zip:** _____

E-mail: _____

☐ Male   ☐ Female   **Date of Birth** (mm/dd/yyyy): ___ / ___ / ___   (Under 13? Parental consent required)

What race/ethnicity do you consider yourself? (check all that apply)

☐ White/Caucasian ☐ Black/African American ☐ Hispanic/Latino

☐ Asian/Pacific Islander ☐ Native American/Alaskan Native ☐ Other· _____

What VIZ title(s) did you purchase? (indicate title(s) purchased) _____

_____

What other VIZ titles do you own? _____

_____

Reason for purchase: (check all that apply)

☐ Special offer ☐ Favorite title / author / artist / genre

☐ Gift ☐ Recommendation ☐ Collection

☐ Read excerpt in VIZ manga sampler ☐ Other _____

Where did you make your purchase? (please check one)

☐ Comic store ☐ Bookstore ☐ Grocery Store

☐ Convention ☐ Newsstand ☐ Video Game Store

☐ Online (site:_____) ☐ Other _____

How many manga titles have you purchased in the last year? How many were VIZ titles?
(please check one from each column)

MANGA

- ☐ None
- ☐ 1 – 4
- ☐ 5 – 10
- ☐ 11+

How much influence do special promotions and gifts-with-purchase have on the titles you buy?
(please circle, with 5 being great influence and 1 being none)

1 2 3 4 5

Do you purchase every volume of your favorite series?

☐ Yes! Gotta have 'em as my own ☐ No. Please explain: ______________________

What kind of manga storylines do you most enjoy? **(check all that apply)**

☐ Action / Adventure	☐ Science Fiction	☐ Horror
☐ Comedy	☐ Romance (shojo)	☐ Fantasy (shojo)
☐ Fighting	☐ Sports	☐ Historical
☐ Artistic / Alternative	☐ Other ______________________	

If you watch the anime or play a video or TCG game from a series, how likely are you to buy the manga? **(please circle, with 5 being very likely and 1 being unlikely)**

1 2 3 4 5

If unlikely, please explain: ______________________

Who are your favorite authors / artists? ______________________

____

What titles would like you translated and sold in English? ______________________

____

THANK YOU! Please send the completed form to:

VIZ media™

NJW Research
42 Catharine Street
Poughkeepsie, NY 12601

Your privacy is very important to us. All information provided will be used for internal purposes only and will not be sold or otherwise divulged.